WITHDRAWN FROM
TSC LIBRARY
TALLAHASSEE
LIBRARY
COMMUNITY COLLEGE

D1608724

Hecho en Tejas

Southwestern Writers Collection Series

Connie Todd, Series Editor

Steven L. Davis, Volume Editor

This series originates from the Southwestern Writers Collection, an archive and literary center established at Texas State University-San Marcos to celebrate the region's writers and literary heritage.

hecho en tejas

an anthology of texas-mexican literature

edited by

dagoberto gilb

UNIVERSITY OF NEW MEXICO PRESS
ALBUQUERQUE

PUBLISHED IN COOPERATION WITH THE
SOUTHWESTERN WRITERS COLLECTION,
TEXAS STATE UNIVERSITY

The photos of Gregorio Barrios Sr.
by permission of Gregg Barrios.

Printed in the United States of America
11 10 09 08 07 06 1 2 3 4 5 6

LIBRARY OF CONGRESS CATALOGING-IN-PUBLICATION DATA

Hecho en tejas : an anthology of Texas Mexican
literature / edited by Dagoberto Gilb.
p. cm.
Text mostly in English with Spanish translation.
ISBN-13: 978-0-8263-4125-9 (cloth : alk. paper)
ISBN-10: 0-8263-4125-X (cloth : alk. paper)
1. American literature—Mexican American authors.
2. Mexican Americans—Texas—Literary collections.
3. American literature—21st century.
I. Gilb, Dagoberto
PS508.M4G55 2007
810.8'086872—dc22
2006028611

COMPOSITION AND DESIGN: *Mina Yamashita*

Contents

part three ▣ photographs from the 1930s

part four ▣ the 1940s

part five ▣ the 1950s

part six ▣ the 1960s

part seven @ the 1970s

part eight ◙ the 1980s

part nine ◙ the 1990s

part ten ▣ the 2000s

Acknowledgments

Conceived a long ten years ago by Steve Davis when he curated then Southwest Texas State University's Southwestern Writers Collection exhibit, "Flores del Nopal," *Hecho en Tejas* would have never been undertaken without not only his encouragement but his alter-worldly work ethic—and even more so managerial competence, which we all realize I do not have. I could not have done any of this without him. And certainly nothing could have been done without the SWWC's director, Connie Todd, who, tireless and patient, kept up her enthusiasm throughout. Editorship is not only the gathering and assembling of material—Steve and Connie were, unquestionably, the producers of this anthology, continually restoking funds of energy and support. Add a fourth indispensable party, who should be titled its associate editor, by the name of Ricardo Angel Gilb, a brilliant—even if a little too indie—undergraduate at Stanford University, who did so much of the physical tramping around in that wonderful library there in Palo Alto and in the cyberspace that I get disoriented in. Finally, there is Elizabeth Hadas, she of immutable, unwavering energy without which . . . well, I can't say this anthology would be seen without her.

I sincerely thank the enormous financial support of the Southwestern Writers Collection. *Hecho en Tejas* is part of their book series, and I pray they feel they have invested their money wisely. Also a huge thank you to the Katherine Anne Porter Literary Center, and Tom Grimes, for generously backing a figure I floated on a whim but the substance of which I became dependent on. Yet another thank you to the Texas Commission for the Arts and to Texas State University. And then one abrazo fuerte más for Sandra Cisneros.

Particular thanks go out to Arturo Madrid at Trinity University and Roberto Trujillo at the Stanford Library. And to Mary Garcia and Bob "Pomerroyo" Pomeroy and, of course, my other brave and good son, Antonio Gilb—they each smoothed roads. More thanks to Terry Allen, Gregg Barrios, Cesar A. Martínez, Sam Coronado, Rose Reyes, Erasmo Guerra, Ramiro Burr, and for last-minute emergencies, Sylvia Véliz, Adriana Castillo, and Isela García.

I couldn't have lived this in Austin without the care from these unique friendships: Armando Villareal, Bill Timberman, John Ledesma, Claude Fiddler, Cristal Garcia, Joshunda Sanders, and Rachel Eliza Griffiths.

Introduction

A young man I will call Michael comes up to me. He wants to talk to me because he was in a class that read a short story he'd submitted which wasn't received very well because it wasn't very good. It was a ghost story. The setting was an old wooden house. He'd created a faceless and colorless cast of characters—two parents, an older boy, and two younger children who all spoke a bland, perfunctory English. The old wooden house was in San Antonio, and he knew it really well. And those characters who lived there were like him, like his family.

In his mid-twenties, Michael lives in San Antonio and was born and raised on the westside—that proverbial poorest and toughest and oldest part of town that all cities have. He is already a father and is raising a daughter by himself. He says he has always wanted to be a writer, but he doesn't want his work to be Latino Hispanic Chicano Whatever. He remembers when he read a particular poet in high school, a San Antonio activista, and he thought, well, this wasn't what he was or how he lived. For instance, he didn't even have an exotic name. His is Michael, not Miguel. His Spanish is lousy, if lousy could mean so bad he'd never seriously use what little he might know because he'd fear he'd get most of it wrong. His parents speak English, he says, and only one grandparent really can't.

What does Michael look like? Este guy es muy moreno, he is very dark. His last name isn't exactly a bland, everyman Smith or Jones either, not a Gonzalez, Hernandez, Rodriguez. It's a name like Zamarripa—no vague descent mystery attached to it. As to ghost stories, I point out to him that they are often set in New England, or Old England, and that's usually because that's where the writer's from. Usually, I explain, writers write about where they are from. And so if he's from San Antonio, and if the story is supposed to be set in San Antonio, and he's Mexican (for those not, that's the internal vernacular for it), wouldn't it be a good idea, even a lot easier . . . but he's American, he insists. He watches American TV. He doesn't like soccer, and down there, where he's never been, they like soccer, and he likes football. He doesn't know how to be exotic. But, I tell him, he's from the westside. He looks at me like I'm making it complicated. So, I say again, don't you see how that isn't Montana or New York, it isn't San Francisco or Dallas, Marseilles or Pamplona? His life isn't exotic, he insists. So I ask him what kind of work he does. He's a manager at a Pizza Hut. And his crew? Well, they're all from, uh, San Antonio. I'm laughing now because what he doesn't want to say is they are all brown people there too. He thinks that isn't exotic! He doesn't think he has a *unique* story to tell. That in the historic city of the Alamo, where the Republic of Texas began and the end of Mexico's national sovereignty ended—this very dirt—he who looks not like anyone on the winner's side of that war, he an adult, responsible man who's earning just above minimum wage as a manager at an "Italian" chain pizza joint with minimum-wage employees who have the same story and descent as him, he wants to tell a ghost story about *Americans* who are . . . like *him*.

But consider the core of what Michael believes: that to reflect on his own life, the people he was born from and with and around, that bringing in his immediate landscape, his historical and family heritage, he'd be making exotic talk. That's how far away he is from himself and understanding how and why he became a manager at Pizza Hut. It's almost as though he were a Chinese child adopted by a middle-class American family who never detected what others saw, or heard what they said about him. That consciousness, political or personal, awareness of history and place would *estrange* him, transform him into someone who wasn't Miguel enough, or too Miguel, or what is that, where does that come from? Or is it simply that he doesn't know, he has never once thought about it before, or has never been told? Then what is this orphan's deprivation?

Where *does* that come from? Why would he defend a ghost story that isn't about Mexican Americans who live in San Antonio in an old wooden house on the poor side of town? Would he be content to raise his daughter on a literature, like his ghost story, that would never be about where she lived, the land and culture she came from, the American stories of her face, her blood? Wouldn't she be a little proud if her own father had published this American story she read? If he had a book of them? And if este loco from el hueso wrote ghost stories, any stories, set there and they were read by people in New England and Old England too?

There is a haunting in Texas, and it is the ghost: a bisabuela gone prematurely, whose son was married to someone's mother, whose abuelito's daughter was married to a tía who was this other's nieto. Hard to know which, how, when, why. But: a mournful voice in a song. Shy eyes in a painting. Joy from an avocado green bedroom and baby blue dining room. Respect wrapped in a black shawl, patience scratched into a wooden toy trinket, love in a piñata or paper flower, work in polished boots and huge buckles, saddles or beaded car-seat covers, hats of hard plastic or straw. Strength in simple mashed frijoles seasoned with oregano, ajo y cebolla, in a hot flour tortilla puffing up on a cast-iron comal. In the pico of fresh serrano chile spooned into a taco and gordita, from a shiver of sweet from a leche quemada candy, in the sigh that comes from the first sip of orchata or agua de jamaica. Though its descendants do survive in the poor neighborhoods of Texas (also known on a larger scale as the cities of El Paso or San

Antonio, as the regions known as the Rio Grande Valley or South Texas), there is too much that feels deprecated, neglected, or ignored by the more financially boastful, self-contained Anglo Texas culture, as though the flesh-and-blood cultural legacy of this Mexican ghost could be dismissed or replaced as though so much of it were like housing projects, transitional or residual, an era that was, not is—or transformed into a market niche, pitched as an advertising campaign, a decorating style or motif.

It's the ghost who hoists up Mexican flags in the Rio Grande Valley. People don't always understand that when they come down here. The voice I hear is Jaime Chahin's, the Dean of the School of Applied Arts at Texas State University. He worked the fields with his family when he was very young, and when he talks of the North, to the east it's Minnesota and to the west it's Washington. When he talks about Idaho, what he can't help talking about most is el cinturon del diablo, "the devil's belt," which, he says, could hold a hundred pounds of potatoes on either side. He is driving me and two dons of Chicano Literature, Arturo Madrid and Rolando Hinojosa, and we are on the road to pay respects to the memory of Tomás Rivera, traveling to his birthplace and grave in Crystal City. The ghost is in every conversation and every silence, even when we've pulled up to a country restaurant with little more than a few tables and chairs and its 8x10 black-and-white publicity photo of the singer Rosita Fernandez that's been on the wall . . . a long time. Even when we talk about breakfast tacos and a particular meat inside, how in El Paso it's called machacha and here it's machacado, or how in Los Angeles or Mexico City, what would be chilaquiles there might be called migas here. When we leave, full, the conversation is of the land and people who are still here or gone or passed on, the children of and their children, about each change and what doesn't seem to ever change, and it is because of the ghost. The ghost both sanctifies and celebrates the gossip about him or her, some whose deeds have gone beyond or some whose legends are local, even ordinary—like a certain Vidal who sold whiskey and was found dead in a motel from an enfarto because he was with a twenty-two-year-old woman, his corpse gotten out of there by the sheriff fast so his good wife would never know. About a George who flipped out one day and shot cows with an M-16. Or . . . but I have looked out the window over there. Two mesquite trees, dark as shadows, on top of a brown grass lomita, no prickly pear near, no other brush, like it's a prop only missing a horse. It's a Texas photo that only someone from Texas would recognize.

Many say that what would be called "el movimiento" began in Crystal City when, in 1963, a group of five Texas Mexicans, empowered by union organization at the Del Monte canning plant, ran for city council and won in a city, like the entire region and state, where government was run by an Anglo minority. And it was Crystal City again in 1969, when high school students walked out and boycotted to demand more than only one Mexican American cheerleader, and bilingual and bicultural education, and simply more institutional respect of the brown people who lived their lives there now and historically. The success of this fight led by José Angel Gutiérrez launched the first Chicano political party, La Raza Unida, which eventually won electoral control of both the city council and school board.

It is all this that the drive takes us toward, except I am distracted, my eyes looking out the car window but seeing somewhere else. Crystal City has, strangely, my own life in it too. For instance, sure, yes, it is that spinach is my favorite vegetable, and Cristal is the "Spinach Capital of the World," and the city's center even honors Popeye with a statue there, and so I think not only of health but strength (and also I studied philosophy, and Descartes, and we the initiated know the unavoidable depth of Popeye's wisdom: I yam what I yam). But watch—once I had a girlfriend I met at UC Santa Barbara, where we both went to college. She was from Eagle Pass. And because we were young, not much sure of anything, she took a long bus ride home to Texas and soon took a job at Crystal City High. I went to El Paso, driving her car across three deserts to eventually bring it to her, blowing out its head gasket, fixing it, and thereby having maybe $30 left, so that I began living in the cheapest hotels, and finally a YMCA for longer than I want to say. She visited me in El Paso once on a weekend and after that she told me she was pregnant. I would marry her and we would be happy for so many years, love so much the sons we raised together. On that same weekend she brought me a book, *Estampas del valle y otras obras* by Rolando Hinojosa-S. It could be she had borrowed the book without checking it out, because it was stamped "Crystal City High School Lib." Probably another good explanation. *Estampas* wasn't only important to me because she gave it to me as a gift, was what she thought I should and would like to read about a region of Texas I only knew through her, but because I was ravenous about books then, and I was only then beginning my want to write, and I wasn't sure of so much about what it was I was doing, what writing was, and, like Michael, I was messed up about who I was, where I came from and belonged. I'd already devoured French and German literature, any dime-store or otherwise paperback Western novel with American Indians as lead characters, especially half-breeds. I read Beat and Grove Press literature, Octavio Paz and Juan Rulfo and the Latin American boom writers. I loved James Baldwin and Langston Hughes, but Richard Wright, he was God. Chicano literature had just begun, and I knew it only through the plays of Luís Valdez, his Teatro Campesino, and the pachangas at Casa de la Raza in Santa Barbara. Those were days when to me Chicano meant someone who was involved with the United Farm Workers and Cesar Chávez, and I had come from the city, from Los Angeles, where adults I knew drove beer and delivery trucks, were butchers, office and shipping and sales clerks, plumbers, repairmen, secretaries, assemblers, mechanics, and taxi drivers. I myself had worked so many jobs already—industrial ones, in factories, both union and not—from early in high school on. Unlike all my big city friends, I liked to eat tomatoes and spinach, but I didn't really have a clue about what it meant to work in the fields, and so that was yet another reason I felt separate from el movimiento that surrounded me, the one who was reading books about philosophy and religion. If Valdez was creating a Califas of archetypes (and sometimes stereotypes), of hip zoot suiters and lowriders, pachucos y las rucas, characters I enjoyed but didn't feel were like me and my both more conflicted and ordinary American experience, what I found in Hinojosa's work bled a vein: He was writing about the common people who were cops or menial bank workers, employed at drugstores or who sold cars, went to little league baseball games and told stories of a living Mexico and the smallest cositas of a local community, like death and birth, who married who inside the community and out, much of it related as gossip and through simple conversation in dialogue. It was, in other words, what I recognized, and so, like much else that suddenly changed in my life from that point on, I began to understand the world I was in too, where I was not only as a workingman, but as a writer I wanted to be.

The writer I am now who is still on such a wondrous, surprising journey—mysterious both in psychic and real space—today I am driving in a car, three decades later, with that book's very Rolando Hinojosa, who I now think of as a friend even, and we are on the road to visit the grave of one of the other legends of Chicano literature, Tomás Rivera.

Which is to say, there is such a tombstone now of our first Chicano generation of writers, and it is, justly, in Crystal City, Texas, in the Benito Juárez Cemetery, where, sure, a few wooden crosses have fallen, but where many stand tagged with tattered blue ribbons or torn miniature American flags, but where everywhere are cement Virgins, vases awaiting or full of fresh pink roses, petals of paper flowers that are purple and red. Names—Rosalva, Estanislado, Euluteria, or Mariana, Ignacio, Juan, Pedro, Beatriz. Rivera's gravestone is pink granite, probably the same quarry rock that is the Texas Capitol, *RIVERA* engraved above the inscriptions, *Florencio M*, Nov. 7, 1903 to Dec. 5, 1959, his father, and then his, *Dr. Tomas H,* Dec. 22, 1935 to May 16, 1984.

There is no ghost in that Crystal City cemetery. That is no haunting we feel. Only pride. Only respect. Look at the impossibly long distance Tomás Rivera traveled before he came to rest in the town where he was born: From a family who migrated from their native home, yearly, to pick crops from the fertile American plains to the north, the poorest of the working poor, he became the writer we know, a teacher, and a university president. A great American story. A great Texas story. A great Mexican American story. It may take a ride to a cemetery once in a while to remember, a ritual of respect for an important loss to hush that ghost. It may take a song. It may take a painting. A poem. A fiction. Or maybe a book with them all.

There is so much misunderstanding about who we are here, where we are from. The extreme Republican right sees us as complicit conspirators with undocumented immigrants who take jobs away from Americans, and as part of the subsequent criminal activity, which begins with an "illegal" border crossing to find work (forget acknowledging the desperation and danger of that), then generates criminal children who overuse the American system of education and health care. The same people and their children, coincidentally, who—much less raging rhetoric on this!—are so valuable for a low-wage, poverty-income workforce which also becomes a rich reservoir for military recruitment, the same people who, despite supporting the American flag by wearing an American uniform, can be accused of disloyalty for equally supporting family with a Mexican flag as well—as if dos patrias is unique only to the people of the border, as if Americans who are Irish and Italian and Jewish, for example, don't exist. But even on the tanned Democratic left there seems to be little more than phrase-book insight gotten out of dealing with the maid, nanny, or gardener. After President George W. Bush's last State of the Union address, the Democratic Party offered its formal reply through one of its Easterners, but also asked Antonio Villaraigosa, the rising star mayor of Los Angeles, to represent the West. His reply was in Spanish. That the Democratic Party put him in a position to speak Spanish to a national audience perpetuates an irritating misconception that Mexican Americans are still and forever immigrants, that our English language skills, like our relationship to this country, are for most weak and secondary. The truth is that Latino voters are either bilingual, as the mayor is, or are monolingual English speakers, while those who struggle with their *inglés* see him as a son or brother speaking it as well as they aspire to themselves, and are proud, thrilled, because he is an American, because he is a Mexican American.

Texas was the frontline of the historic battle that separated Mexico and the Texas Republic, what became the United States, and the attitude which came of that fight was represented by the treatment of its new Mexican American citizens by a special law enforcement agency known as the Rangers (documented most beautifully by Américo Paredes in his classic *With a Pistol in His Hand*). If that violence is the past, then the attitudes that remain are patronizing at best. Even in Texas, Mexican Americans are still considered more a foreign, ethnic minority, one faraway even when its neighborhood might be less than two blocks north or south. If it's poor, as it usually is, what poverty causes is considered innate, a character trait, never socially caused. The kindest attitude portrays the culture as an homage in a children's museum, or as in a folklorico dance show, and the prevailing images, framed and shelved in the state's unconscious, are of men in sombreros and serapes walking burros, women patting tortillas or stuffing tamales in color-frilled white housedresses, while the stories of Mexican adventures are of border whorehouses and tequila drunks—not meant as harmful, only fascinating and wild.

And so it has been with matters intellectual and artistic in Texas. That is to say, if it's good at all, Mexican American work can be charming but not serious, not important, certainly not as important. When it comes to literature, the situation has been much worse than for visual art or music. Until very recently, at best, there was no book, no writer, of Mexican descent who was worthy of being taught in a university course on American or Texas literature. Outside those academic rooms, the situation in Texas has been epitomized by *Texas Monthly*, the magazine of Texas, whose stories are never about a Mexican American cultural life that is equal to what gets attention in malls in Dallas or Houston or Austin, which doesn't do stories that aren't seen as oh-so-exotic or oh-so-cute, that are definitely not intended for a Mexican American readership. We are, like Mexicans on the other side, part of the colorful border palate in their land, even part of Texas history, just not deeply enmeshed in the ruling or money class.

Yeah, I know, I've been muy pesado for a while here in this, right? By heavy I mean . . . like how about un poco bit of fun, eh dude compa guy chief vato? Ay ay, I'm tired of me too, you know? It's hard being an all-important editor, let me tell you. I never been that before either, I admit it. And maybe it's been going to my head, or leaking the light air out my brains because I been squishing so long my, uh . . . ya sabes.

Entonces, let me go forward, let's move on. And you know what, that's exactly what I mean too! Let's move on! I want *Hecho en Tejas* to be a celebration, a literary pachanga with cold beer, frijoles, and, for the few non-Vegan Tejanos who are left, a couple of cow's heads whose smoked meat we fold into a couple of corn tortillas—or hot dogs on white bread buns si quieres, whatever! It is why I invited a few of our singers and songwriters to join in on this anthology because they have acordeones and bajo sextos and, unlike me, good voices and can probably dance good too. I invited some artists to spray paint on the walls and wink at your hot tía or primo (you know, *that* one). I broke out the photo album so that we could sit there and remember the old days when it wasn't work but fishing, or when it was Holy Communion or that crazy wedding and don't you wish you still had that carro, güey?

Much as I want *Hecho en Tejas* to be a book that lands in as many high schools and colleges as it can—and should!—or touches as many Michaels and Jennifers, Miguels and Raquels as possible, I also want it to reach everyday readers of all kinds who love Texas. I want it to be a book that so many can learn from, both the young who don't know and the old who do but want it remembered, both those inside the culture and outside. I want it to be a book everyone wants *out*, not in the bookcase, but right there on the coffee table, bumping against the TV. *Look at this*! Go on, put your coke on it. Drip some chile or Louisiana on page 73 while you're reading. No, that ain't what it's for, but you got napkins and you can use them. That's what they're for. This book is for you to have on your lap.

What I have tried to do is make *Hecho en Tejas* a strong, good read. Not simply as an anthology, a collection of different writers and styles, but as a book with chapters, so that all the voices might form one story, from one family's history. That is, from the front pages to the back, for those who already know a little or a lot about this Texas literature, the book will make them even more proud of the talent, culture, and story, while for those who will find most or all of the material new, yes, they may find a particular poet or writer they especially love, but even without knowing about any single one, what will not be forgotten will be the large of the community as the book puzzles forward, each piece connecting land to history, sorrow to joy, to what is Mexican to what is American, what is assimilated, what cannot be.

I have tried to be comprehensive about our literary history, and in that, *Hecho en Tejas* is a historic publication, collecting all the published Tejano figures that can be in one volume. That it begins with Alvar Nuñez Cabeza de Vaca, the Spaniard abandoned on Galveston Island in the early days of the Conquest, the first to live what would become the first mix of Spanish and indigenous people, should indicate the scope of the book. As expansive as the book is though, only two poems of every poet appear, and I have tried to keep both the nonfiction and fiction sections comparably economical and taut. I want to emphasize that the length or quantity of the selection and the importance of any author is *not* proportional. Nor did I choose pieces that might be what is most well known of any author's work. My goal has been to tell the larger story not only of Raza in Texas, but also the literary evolution that has taken place as it grows from account to letter to corrido to poem to story. The process of selection has been relatively simple—someone who published at least one book outside the neighborhood, or who has publications that are the equivalent of that. These are artists whose writing has risk and ambition attached, or whose credentials come with affirmation through time or celebrity.

What emerges as the pages accumulate is a story of the Texas Mexican first as a Mexican, then as a Texan, again as Mexican, into the in-your-face flowering of the Chicano period, on to the seeding of it which is now, where identity might be more confused or unimportant—or, as it is in music, from alternative to Tejana to mainstream—and where politics, like the adoption of labels (old-school "Chicano," Nixon-era "Hispanic," and progressive "Latino") might be less important to some than self-promotional, more Republican-like marketing concerns, while to others issues still are the burning cause, particularly as we move into what appears to be, as of this writing, a new era of civil rights.

A few years ago, I was asked by the Southwestern Writers Collection, the special collections area of the library at Texas State University in San Marcos, if I would be willing to edit an anthology, with its support, of Texas Mexican Literature. Much as I loved the idea of the book, I was not too enthusiastic about being an anthology editor. But I reconsidered. It's that I like to work, and I'm not against it being hard work. I only hate lousy jobs. This project, I knew, would feel good, and do good. Much like framing a house, you get to know every room, all the easy or odd cuts, where the nails poofed in like from an air gun, where I had to contort my muscles to toenail that one in. You see which rooms go together easy, which seem to take too much time and material and oh well. And like any construction job, there were exhausting overtime days that were too hot—OT days always are, I'm telling you—or which, as it's going, and you see the progress, that once you're in the shade chugging cold water, maybe even a cold one instead, it really feels good . It's been that kind of work, and, relieved that it's done, I'm so glad I got to do it. And—this is how it is when you build something—I am proud to look at it, as impressed that it exists as I am that I was there on the job right where it went up.

The publication of *Hecho en Tejas* is hereby a formal announcement: *We have been here, we are still here.* I want this book to overwhelm the ignorance—and I emphasize the "ignore" root of that word as much as its dumb or mean or nasty connotation—about Raza here in Texas, the people who settled and were settled and still remain in Texas, who will soon be the largest population group in the state, not to mention the region beyond.

Onward y adelante!

part one

before the 1930s

Alvár Núñez Cabeza de Vaca

(Galveston)

from *Chronicle of the Narváez Expedition*

How the Following Day They Brought Other Sick People

Early the next day many Indians came and brought five people who were paralyzed and very ill and who had come for Castillo to cure them. Each patient offered him his bow and arrows, which Castillo accepted, and by sunset he had made the sign of the cross over each of the sick people, commending them to God, our Lord. We all prayed to him as well as we could to restore them to health and he, seeing there was no other way of getting those people to help us so that we might be saved from our miserable existence, had mercy on us. In the morning they all woke up well and hearty and went away in such good health that it was as if they never had had any ailment at all. This created great admiration among them and moved us to thank our Lord and to greater faith in his goodness and the hope that he would save us, guiding us to where we could serve him. For myself I may say that I always had full faith in his mercy and that he would liberate me from captivity and I always told my companions so.

When the Indians had gone with their now healthy Indians, we moved on to others called Cultalchulches and Maliacones, who speak a different language and who were eating prickly pears as well. With them were still others, called Coayos and Susolas, and in another area were the Atayos, who were at war with the Susolas and exchanged arrow shots with them every day.

Álvar Núñez Cabeza de Vaca was a Texan before Texas. Born into nobility, he came to North America as part of a Spanish expedition that would occupy the continent. Poor planning eventually put Cabeza de Vaca, with about eighty survivors of the original expedition, well off course, in rafts fleeing from the natives of Florida. They landed in Galveston in 1528, and by 1532 only four people remained alive, including an African slave. They traveled across Texas and eventually met with another group of Spaniards in 1536, near what is now Sinaloa. The next year Cabeza de Vaca published an account of his journey, urging better treatment of the Indians. He was accused of corruption, and after a pardon, served as a judge until his death.

In this whole country, nothing was spoken of but the wonderful mysteries that God, our Lord, performed through us. They came from far and wide to be cured, and after having been with us two days, some of the Susolas begged Castillo to go and attend to a man who had been wounded, as well as to others that were sick and among whom, they said, was one who was on the verge of death. Castillo was very fearful, especially in frightening and dangerous cases, always afraid that his sins might interfere and prevent the cures from being effective. Therefore the Indians told me to go and perform the cure. They liked me. They remembered that I had cured them while they were out gathering walnuts, for which they had given us walnuts and hides, which had taken place at the time I was on my way to join the Christians. So I had to go, and Dorantes and Estevanico went with me.

When I got close to their huts I saw that the sick man we had been called to cure was dead, for there were many people around him weeping and his lodge was torn down, which is a sign that the owner has died. I found the Indian with his eyes rolled back, without pulse and with all the marks of death, at least it seemed so to me, and Dorantes said the same thing. I removed the mat with which he was covered, and as best I could I prayed to our Lord to restore him to health as well as any others in need. After I had made the sign of the cross and breathed on him many times, they brought his bow and presented it to me, as well as a basket of ground prickly pears, and then they took me to many others who were suffering from sleeping sickness. They gave me two more baskets of prickly pears, which I left for the Indians that had come with us. Then we returned to our living quarters.

Our Indians, to whom I had given the prickly pears, remained. At night they returned, saying that the dead man whom I attended to in their presence had resuscitated, risen from his bed, walked about, eaten, and talked to them, and that everyone I had treated was well and in very good spirits. This caused great surprise and awe, and all over the land nothing else was spoken of. Everyone who heard about it came to us so that we might cure them and bless their children. When the Cultalchulches, who were in the company of our Indians, had to return to their country, before parting they offered us all the prickly pears they had for their journey, not keeping a single one. They gave us flint stones as long as one and a half palms, which are greatly prized among them and with which they cut. They begged us to remember them and pray to God to keep them healthy always, which we promised to do. Then they left, the happiest people on earth, having given us the very best of what they owned.

We remained with the Avavares for eight months, according to our reckoning of the moons. During that time people came to us from far and wide and said that we were truly the children of the sun. Until then Dorantes and the Negro had not cured anyone, but we found ourselves so pressed by the Indians coming from all sides that all of us had to become medicine men. I was the most daring and reckless of all in undertaking cures. We never treated anyone that did not afterward say he was well, and they had such confidence in our skill that they believed that none of them would die as long as we were among them.

These Indians and the ones we left behind told us a very strange tale. From their account it may have occurred fifteen or sixteen years ago. They said that at that time there wandered about the country a man whom they called "Bad Thing," who was short and bearded. Although they could never see his features clearly, whenever he would approach their dwellings their hair would stand on end and they would begin to tremble. In the doorway of the lodge a firebrand would then appear. The man would come in and take hold of anyone he chose. With a sharp knife made of flint, as broad as a hand and two palms in length, he would then make a cut in that person's flank, thrust his hand through the gash, and take out the person's entrails. Then he would cut off a piece one palm long, which he would throw into the fire. Afterward he would make three cuts in one of the person's arms, the second one at a place where people are usually bled, and twist the arm, but would reset it soon afterward. Then he would place his hands on the wounds, which, they told us, would close up at once. Many times he appeared among them while they were dancing, sometimes in the dress of a woman and other times as a man, and whenever he took a notion to do it he would seize a hut or lodge, take it up into the air, and come down with it again with a great crash. They also told us how, many a time, they set food before him, but he would never partake of it. When they asked him where he came from and where he had his home, he pointed to a rent in the earth and said his house was down below.

We laughed a great deal at those stories and made fun of them. Seeing our disbelief they brought us many of those he had taken, they said, and we saw the scars from his slashes in the places they had said. We told them he was a demon and explained as best we could that if they would believe in God, our Lord, and be Christians like ourselves, they would not have to fear that man, nor would he come and do these things to them, and they might be sure that as long as we were in this country he would not dare to appear again. This pleased them greatly and they lost much of their apprehension.

The same Indians told us they had seen the Asturian and Figueroa with other Indians from further along the coast whom we had named the People of the Figs. None of them know how to reckon the seasons by either sun or moon, nor do they count by months and years; they judge the seasons by the ripening of fruit, by the time that fish die, and by the appearance of the stars, and in all of this they are very clever and expert. While with them we were always well treated, although our food was never too plentiful, and we had to carry our own water and wood. Their dwellings and their food are like those of the others we had known, but they are much more prone to hunger, having neither corn nor acorns or walnuts. We always went naked like them and at night covered ourselves with deerskins.

During six of the eight months we were with them we suffered greatly from hunger, because they do not have fish either. At the end of that time the prickly pears began to ripen. Without their noticing it the Negro and I left and went to other Indians further ahead, called Maliacones, at a distance of one day's travel. Three days after we arrived I sent him back to get Castillo and Dorantes, and after they rejoined me we all departed in company of the Indians, who went to eat a small fruit of a certain type of tree, on which they subsist for ten or twelve days, until the prickly pears are fully ripe. There they joined other Indians called Arbadaos, whom we found to be so sick, emaciated, and bloated that we were greatly astonished. The Indians with whom we had come went back on the same trail, and we told them that we wished to remain with the others, which made them sad. So we remained with the others in a field near their dwellings.

When the Indians saw us, they gathered together and, after having talked among themselves, each one took the one of us he had claimed by the hand and led us to their homes. While we were with them we suffered more from hunger than we had with any of the others. In the course of a whole day we did not eat more than two handfuls of the fruit, which was green and contained so much milky juice that it burned our mouths. Since water was very scarce, whoever ate them became very thirsty. Finally we grew so hungry that we purchased two dogs in exchange for nets and other things and a hide that I used to cover myself.

I have said already that we went naked in that land, and not being accustomed to it, we shed our skin twice a year, like snakes. Exposure to the sun and air covered our chests and backs with great sores that made it very painful to carry big and heavy loads, the ropes of which cut into the flesh on our arms.

The country is so rough and overgrown that often after we had gathered firewood in the forest and dragged it out, we would bleed freely from the thorns and spines that cut and slashed us wherever they touched us. Sometimes it happened that I was unable to carry or drag out the firewood after I had gathered it with great loss of blood. In all that trouble my only relief or consolation was to remember the passion of our Savior, Jesus Christ, and the blood he shed for me, and to consider how much greater his sufferings had been from those thorns than I from the ones I was then enduring.

I made a contract with the Indians to make combs, arrows, bows, and nets for them. We also made the matting from which their lodges are constructed and which they greatly need, for, although they know how to make it, they do not like to do any work, in order to be able to go in search of food. Whenever they work they suffer greatly from hunger.

At other times, they would make me scrape skins and tan them, and the greatest luxury I enjoyed was on the day they would give me a skin to scrape, because I scraped it very deeply in order to eat the parings, which would last me two or three days. It also happened that, while we were with these Indians and those mentioned before, we would eat a piece of meat they gave us raw, because if we broiled it the first Indian who came along would snatch it away and eat it. It seemed useless to take any pains, in view of what we might expect, nor did we care to go to any trouble in order to have it broiled and might just as well eat it raw. Such was the life we led there, and we had to earn even that scant sustenance by bartering the objects we made with our own hands.

THE REPUBLIC OF TEXAS had only one Mexican in its Senate and this was Juan Seguín, who had fought for Texas' independence from Mexico and had accepted the surrender of San Antonio in 1836. Seguin served as Chairman of Military Affairs for Texas, then served as mayor of San Antonio, the city where he was born. He became entangled in the racial hostilities of Texas, however, when Mexican leaders claimed he was a still a loyal Mexican subject. He was forced out by suspicious whites in Texas, and when he fled for his safety to Mexico, he was forced into military service and fought with the army of Mexico in the Mexican-American War. He died in Nuevo Laredo.

Juan Seguín (San Antonio)

Letter in his defense

1838. In March, on obtaining a leave of absence for three months, to go to New Orleans, I turned over the command of San Antonio to Colonel Karnes. On my return, I was apprized that my fellow-citizens had done me the honor to elect me as Senator to Congress. During my term, I was appointed as Chairman of the Committee on Military Affairs. At the expiration of my term as Senator, I was elected Mayor of the City of San Antonio.

Here I must digress from my narrative, to call attention to the situation of my family in those times that tried the stoutest hearts.

No sooner was General Cos informed that I had taken an active part in the revolution, than he removed my father from the office of Postmaster, which he had filled for several years. He forced him to leave San Antonio at once, and he had consequently to walk the thirty-three miles which separated him from his rancho, where my family was living. Such was the hurry with which he was compelled to depart, that he was obliged to leave his family, who remained exposed to our fire during the whole siege.

When we received intelligence from our spies on the Rio Grande, that Santa Anna was preparing to invade Texas, my father, with his, my own, and several other families, removed toward the centre of the country.

My family took with them above three thousand head of sheep. They had reached Gonzales when

Santa Anna took possession of San Antonio, and as soon as some other families joined them, they proceeded towards the Colorado, via Columbus. On their arrival at San Felipe de Austin, the citizens of that place, terror struck at the sight of the hurried flight of such a number of families, endeavored to take the advance. The confusion and delay caused on the road by that immense straggling column of fugitives were such, that when my family were beginning to cross the Colorado with their cattle, the enemy was at their heels. General Ramirez y Lesma did not fail to take hold of that rich booty, and the shepherds only escaped by swimming over the river. The loss to three of the families was very severe, nay, irretrievable. They did not stop on their flight, until they reached the town of San Augustine, east of Nacogdoches. When the families received the welcome tidings of the victory of San Jacinto, they went to Nacogdoches. There, all the members of my family, without excepting a single person, were attacked by fever. Thus, prostrated on their couches, deprived of all resources, they had to struggle in the midst of their sufferings, to assist one another. Want of money compelled them to part, little by little, with their valuables and articles of clothing. A son, an uncle, and several more remote relatives of mine fell victims to the disease. Seeing that the fever did not abate, the families determined upon moving towards the interior.

The train presented a spectacle which beggars description. Old men and children were lying in the wagons, and for several days, Captain Menchaca, who was the only person able to stand up, had to drive the whole train, as well as attend to the sick.

The families reached San Antonio at last. There was not one of them who had not to lament the loss of a relative, and to crown their misfortunes, they found their houses in ruins, their fields laid waste, and their cattle destroyed or dispersed.

I, myself, found my ranch despoiled; what little was spared by the retreating enemy, had been wasted by our own army; ruin and misery met me on my return to my unpretending home.

But let me draw a veil over those past and sorrowful days, and resume my narrative.

The tokens of esteem, and evidences of trust and confidence, repeatedly bestowed upon me by the Supreme Magistrate, General Rusk, and other dignitaries of the Republic, could not fail to arouse against me much invidious and malignant feeling. The jealousy evinced against me by several officers of the companies recently arrived at San Antonio, from the United States, soon spread amongst the American straggling adventurers, who were already beginning to work their dark intrigues against the native families, whose only crime was, that they owned large tracts of land and desirable property.

John W. Smith, a bitter enemy of several of the richest families of San Antonio, by whom he had been covered with favors, joined the conspiracy which was organized to ruin me.

I will also point out the origin of another enmity which, on several occasions, endangered my life. In those evil days, San Antonio was swarming with adventurers from every quarter of the globe. Many a noble heart grasped the sword in the defence of the liberty of Texas, cheerfully pouring out their blood for our cause, and to them everlasting public gratitude is due; but there were also many bad men, fugitives from their country, who found in this land an open field for their criminal designs.

San Antonio claimed then, as it claims now, to be the first city of Texas; it was also the receptacle of the scum of society. My political and social situation brought me into continual contact with that class of people. At every hour of the day and night, my countrymen ran to me for protection against the assaults or exactions of those adventurers. Some times, by persuasion, I prevailed on them to desist; some times, also, force had to be resorted to. How could I have done otherwise? Were not the victims my own countrymen, friends and associates? Could I leave them defenceless, exposed to the assaults of foreigners, who, on the pretext that they were Mexicans, treated them worse than brutes. Sound reason and the dictates of humanity would have precluded a different conduct on my part.

Juan Nepamuceno Cortina

(Brownsville)

Proclamation

County of Cameron
Camp in the Rancho del Carmen
November 23, 1859

Compatriots:

A sentiment of profound indignation, the love esteem which I profess for you, the desire which you for that tranquility and those guarantees which are denied you, thus violating the most sacred laws, is that h [*sic*] moves me to address you these words, hoping that may prove some consolation in the midst of your adversity heretofore has borne the appearance of predestination.

The history of great human actions teaches us that in certain instances the principal motive which gives them impulse is the natural right to resist and conquer our enemies a firm spirit and lively will; to persist in and to reach the consummation of this object, opening a path through the obstacles which step by step are encountered, however imposing or terrible they may be.

In the series of such actions, events present themselves which public opinion, influenced by popular sentiment, calls for deliberation upon their effects, to form an exact and just conception of the interests which they promote; and this same public opinion should be considered as the best judge, which, with coolness and impartiality, does not fail to recognize some principle as the cause for the existence

JUAN CORTINA was a wealthy rancher in South Texas in 1859 when he lead a group of his ranch's vaqueros into Brownsville and proclaimed the Republic of the Rio Grande, raising the Mexican flag and screaming "Death to the Gringos!" He and his men continued the battle to regain lost land and cattle until 1875, when the U.S. Army was sent in to suppress his rebellion. Considered a John Brown figure, Benito Juárez, the President of Mexico, appointed him a general of the Mexican army and called him a champion of his race.

of open force and immutable firmness, which impart the noble desire of cooperating with true philanthropy to remedy the state of despair of him who, in his turn, becomes the victim of ambition, satisfied at the cost of justice.

There are, doubtless, persons so overcome by strange prejudices, men without confidence or courage to face danger in an undertaking in sisterhood with the love of liberty, who, examining, the merit of acts by a false light, and preferring that of the same opinion contrary to their own, prepare no other reward than that pronounced for the "bandit," for him who, with complete abnegation of self, dedicates himself to constant labor for the happiness of those who, suffering under the weight of misfortunes, eat their bread, mingled with tears on the earth which they rated.

If, my dear compatriots, I am honored with that name, I am ready for combat. The Mexicans who inhabit this wide region, some because they were born therein, others because since the treaty of Guadalupe Hidalgo, they have been attracted to its soil by the soft influence of wise laws and the advantages of a free government, paying little attention to the reasoning of politics, are honorably and exclusively dedicated to the exercise of industry, guided by that instinct which leads the good man to comprehend, as non-contradictory truth, that only in the reign of peace can he enjoy, without inquietude, the fruit of his labor. These under an unjust imputation of selfishness and churlishness which do not exist, are not devoid of those sincere and expressive evidences of such friendliness and tenderness as should gain for them that confidence with which they have inspired those who have met them in social intercourse. This genial affability seems as the foundation of that proverbial prudence which, as an oracle, is consulted in all their actions and undertakings. Their humility, simplicity, and docility, directed with dignity, it may be that with excess of goodness, can, if it be desired, lead them beyond the common class of men, but causes them to excel in an irresistible inclination towards ideas of equality, a proof of their simple manners, so well adapted to that which is styled the classic land of liberty. A man, a family, and a people, possessed of qualities so eminent, with their heart in their band and purity on their lips, encounter every day renewed reasons to know that they are surrounded by malicious and crafty monsters, who rob them in the tranquil interior of home, or with open hatred and pursuit; it necessarily follows, however great may be their pain, if not abased by humiliation and ignominy, their groans suffocated and hushed by a pain which renders them insensible, they become resigned to suffering before an abyss of misfortunes.

Mexicans! When the State of Texas began to receive the new organization which its sovereignty required as an integrant part of the Union, flocks of vampires, in the guise of men, came and scattered themselves in the settlements, without any capital except the corrupt heart and the most perverse intentions. Some, brimful of laws, pledged to us their protection against the attacks of the rest; others assembled in shadowy councils, attempted and excited the robbery and burning of the houses of our relatives on the other side of the river Bravo; while others, to the abusing of our unlimited confidence, when we entrusted them with our titles, which secured the future of our families, refused to return them under false and frivolous pretexts; all, in short, with a smile on their faces, giving the lie to that which their black entrails were meditating. Many of you have been robbed of your property, incarcerated, chased, murdered, and hunted like wild beasts, because your labor was fruitful, and because your industry excited the vile avarice that led them. A voice infernal said, from the bottom of their soul, "kill them; the greater will be our gain!" Ah! This does not finish the sketch of your situation. It would appear that justice had fled from this world, leaving you to the caprice of your oppressors, who become each day more furious towards you; that, through witnesses and false charges, although the grounds may be insufficient, you may be interred in the penitentiaries, if you are not previously deprived of life by some keeper who covers himself from responsibility by the pretence of your flight. There are to be found criminals covered with frightful crimes, but they appear to have impunity until opportunity furnish them a victim; to these monsters indulgence is shown, because they are not of out race, which is unworthy, as they say, to belong to the human species. But this race, which the Anglo-American, so ostentatious of its own qualities, tries so much to blacken, depreciate, and load with insults, in a spirit of blindness, which goes to the full extent of such things so common on this frontier, does not fear, placed even in the midst of its very faults, those subtle inquisitions which are so frequently made as to its manners, habits, and sentiments; nor that its deeds should be put to the test of examination in the land of reason, of justice, and of honor. This race has never humbled itself before the conqueror, though the reverse has happened, and can be established; for he is not humbled who uses among his fellowmen those courtesies which humanity prescribes; charity being the root whence springs the rule of his actions. But this race, which you see filled with gentleness and inward sweetness, gives now the cry of alarm throughout the entire extent of the land that it occupies, against all the artifice interposed by those who have become chargeable with their division and discord. This race, adorned with the most lovely disposition towards all that is good and useful in the line of progress, omits no act of diligence which might correct its many imperfections, and lift its grand edifice among the ruins of the past, respecting the ancient traditions and the maxims bequeathed by their ancestors, without being dazzled by brilliant and false appearances, nor crawling to that exaggeration of institution which, like a sublime statue, is offered for their worship and adoration.

Mexicans! Is there no remedy for you? Inviolable laws, yet useless, serve, it is true, certain judges and hypocritical authorities, cemented in evil and injustice, to do whatever suits them, and to satisfy their vile avarice at the cost of your patience and suffering; rising in their frenzy, even to the taking of life, through the treacherous hands of their bailiffs. The wicked way in which many of you have been oftentimes involved in persecution, accompanied by circumstances making it the more bitter, is now well known; these crimes being hid from society under the shadow of a horrid night; those implacable people, with the haughty spirit which suggests impunity for a life of criminality, have pronounced, doubt ye not, your sentence, which is, with accustomed insensibility, as you have seen, on the point of execution.

Mexicans! My part is taken; the voice of revelation whispers to me that to me is entrusted the work of breaking the chains of your slavery, and that the Lord will enable me, with powerful arm, to fight against our enemies, in compliance with the requirements of that Sovereign Majesty, who, from this day forward, will hold us under His protection. On my part, I am ready to offer myself as a sacrifice for your happiness; and counting upon the means necessary for the discharge of my ministry, you may count upon my cooperation, should no cowardly attempt put an end to my days. This undertaking will be sustained on the following bases:

First. A society is organized in the State of Texas, which devotes itself sleeplessly until the work is crowned with success, to the improvement of the unhappy conditions of those Mexicans resident therein; exterminating their tyrants, to which end those which compose it ate ready to shed their blood and suffer the death of martyrs.

Second. As this society contains within itself the elements necessary to accomplish the great end of its labors, the veil of impenetrable secrecy covers "The Great Book" in which the articles of its constitution are written while so delicate are the difficulties which must be overcome that no honorable man can have cause for alarm, if imperious exigencies require them to act without reserve.

Third. The Mexicans of Texas repose their lot under the good sentiments of the governor elect of the State, General Houston, and trust that upon his elevation to power he will begin with care to give us legal protection within the limits of his powers.

Mexicans! Peace be with you! Good inhabitants of the State of Texas, look on them as brothers, and keep in mind that which the Holy Spirit saith: "Thou shalt not be the friend of the passionate man; nor join thyself to the madman, lest thou learn his mode of work and scandalize thy soul."

"El corrido de Texas" (The Corrido of Texas)

Parte I
Mi chinita me decía
—Ya me voy para esa agencia,
pá pasearme por el norte
y pá hacerle su asistencia.—

—De la parte donde estés
me escribes no seas ingrato,
y en contestación te mando
de recuerdos mi retrato.—

Adiós estado de Texas
con toda tu plantación,
Me retiro de tus tierras
por no piscar algodón.

Esos trenes de T.P.
que cruzan por la Louisiana,
Se llevan los mexicanos
para el estado de Indiana.

El día veintidós de abril
a las dos de la mañana,
Salimos en renganche
al estado de Louisiana.

Parte II
Adiós estado de Texas
con toda tu plantación,
Me despido de tus tierras
por no pizcar algodón. >>

Part I
Mi chinita told me,
"I'm going to that agency
so that I can travel north
and take care of you."

"Wherever you are
write to me, don't be ungrateful,
and in reply I'll send you
my picture as a remembrance."

Good-bye state of Texas
with all your fields,
I leave your land
so I won't have to pick cotton.

Those trains of the Texas and Pacific Railroad
which cross Louisiana,
They take the Mexicans
to the state of Indiana.

The twenty-second of April
at two o'clock in the morning,
We left in a work gang
to the state of Louisiana.

Part II
Good-bye state of Texas
with all your fields,
I leave your land
so I won't have to pick cotton. >>

Adiós Fort Worth y Dallas,
Poblaciones en un lado
Nos veremos cuando vuelva
de por Indiana y Chicago.

El renganchista nos dice
que no llevemos mujer,
Para no pasar trabajos
y poder pronto volver.

Adiós estado de Texas,
con toda tú plantación,
Me retiro de tus tierras
por no pizcar algodón.

Esos trenes del T.P.
que cruzan por la Louisiana,
Se llevan los mexicanos
para el estado de Indiana.

Good-bye Fort Worth and Dallas,
Towns that are side-by-side,
I'll see you when I get back
from Indiana and Chicago.

The recruiter tells us
not to take women
So we won't have any trouble
and return soon.

Good-bye state of Texas
with all your fields,
I leave your land
so I won't have to pick cotton.

Those trains of the Texas and Pacific
which crosses Louisiana,
They take the Mexicans
to the state of Indiana.

"El Huérfano" (The Orphan) (San Antonio)

Parte I
Estos versos me confundió
que es muy cierto y muy notable,
Es gran desdicha en el mundo
no tener uno a sus padres.

Como la pluma en el aire
anda el hijo ya perdido,
El huérfano y desvalido
pierde el honor y el decoro.

Estas lágrimas que lloro
me recuerdan de mi madre,
Que en cada paso que doy
hoy que reflejo ya es tarde.

Malos ratos y sonrojos
mi madre por mí lloraba,
Con lágrimas en sus ojos
muchos consejos me daba.

Recuerdo que me decía
cuando me salía a pasear,
—No te vayas a tardar,
no acortes la vida mía.—

Se ha de llegar el día
que te acuerdes de tu madre,
Y tu pecho se taladre
de dolor y sentimiento. >>

Part I
These verses confuse me
because it is very true and very notable,
It is a great misfortune in this world
if you don't have your parents.

Like a feather in the air
goes the son, already lost,
Orphan and helpless
he loses honor and decorum.

The tears that I shed
remind me of my mother,
With each step I take
I reflect it is already too late.

In bad times and in worse
my mother cried for me,
With tears in her eyes
she gave me much advice.

I remember her telling me
when I went out,
"Don't stay out too long,
don't shorten my life."

The day will come
when you'll remember your mother,
Your heart will ache
of pain and sentiment. >>

No te cubras de contento,
Dios mío, tú bien lo sabes,
Causa mucho sentimiento
no tener uno a sus padres.

Don't be so content,
my God, you know well,
It causes much grief
when you don't have your parents.

Varias veces de soldado,
otras veces en prisiones,
Mi madre ya tribulada
me llenaba de oraciones.

Sometimes as a soldier,
other times in prison,
My mother already troubled
filled me with prayers.

Para el huérfano no hay sol,
no hay frío tampoco nieve,
De tu pérdida y tu honor
todos se muestran tiranos.

For the orphan there is no sunshine,
there is no cold or snow.
Once he loses his honor
everyone treats him like dirt.

Tios, parientes, hermanos,
lo avergüenzan en la calle,
Dice aprietando sus manos
—Ay, si viviera mi madre.—

Uncles, relatives, brothers,
shame him in the streets,
(He) says, wringing his hands,
"Oh, if only my mother lived."

Parte II
Las madres en este mundo
es faro de la existencia,
Del hijo que con paciencia
le ama con amor profundo.

Part II
The mothers in this world
are the lanterns for existence,
And the son with patience
is loved with profound love.

Los hijos que estén presentes
pongan bastante atención,
En estos tristes lamentos
que dirijo en la ocasión.

Those of you here present
pay close attention,
In this sad lament
I address you on this occasion.

Mi madre era mi consuelo,
era toda mi alegría,
Era mi encanto y ml anhelo,
—¿Adónde estás madre mia?—

My mother was my consolation,
she was my complete happiness,
my charm and my longing,
"Where are you my mother?"

Cuando mi madre vivía
me daba muchos consejos,
Con cariño me decía
—¡No me hagas tantos desprecios!—

—Ay, madre, madre querida
tu hijo llora amargo llanto,
Te fuiste y me dejaste
en tan amargo quebranto.—

Cuando uno tiene a sus padres
goza de dicha y placer,
Mientras que cuando ellos faltan
todo es puro padecer.

O Dios mío, no hallo qué hacer,
Mi madre me ha abandonado
y huérfano me ha dejado
en el mundo a padecer.

A llorar mi soledad
junto de su sepultura,
O Dios ten do mi piedad,
Mira mi triste amargura.

Aquella hermosa criatura
no se borra de mi mente,
Madre mía aquí estoy presente
llorando en tu sepultura.

En fin, madre de mi vida,
ruégale al creador por mí,
Para que en la eterna gloria
me lleve cerca de tí.

When my mother lived
she gave me lots of advice,
With affection she told me
"Don't be so disrespectful!

Ay, mother, my beloved mother,
your son cries bitterly.
You went and left me
in such bitter grief.

Some have their parents
and enjoy happiness and are pleased,
But when they are missing
all is pure suffering.

Oh, my God, I don't know what to do.
My mother has abandoned me.
I have been left an orphan,
left to suffer in this world.

To cry my loneliness
by her sepulchre,
Oh God, pity me,
look at my sad bitterness.

That beautiful child
I will always remember,
Mother I am here
crying at your tomb.

Finally, mother of my life,
pray to the Creator for me,
so that in eternal glory
I will be close to thee.

"La Elena" (El Paso)

Parte I
Estas son las mañanitas,
que yo los voy a cantar,
que dan razón de mi Elena
que la vengo a saludar.

—Abreme la puerta, Elena,
sin ninguna desconfianza,
yo soy Fernando el francés
que vengo desde la Francia.—

—¿Quién es ese caballero
que mi puerta manda abrir?
Mis puertas se hallan cerradas,
¡muchacha encienda el candíl!—

Al abrir la media puerta,
se les apagó el candíl,
se tomaron de la mano,
se fueron para el jardín.

En una cama de flores
se acostaron a dormir.
Como a las once de la noche,
Elena empezó decir:

—¿Qué tienes Fernando mío
que no te acercas aquí
Tendrás amores en Francia
A que los quieres más que a mí?

Part I
These are the verses
that I am going to sing,
they are about my Elena
who I am going to see.

"Open the door for me, Elena,
without any concern,
I am Don Fernando, the Frenchman,
who has just come from France."

"Who is this gentleman
who bids me open my door?
My doors are closed so
light up a candle, young lady."

In opening the door
the candle went out,
They took each other's hand,
and went out into the garden.

On a bed of flowers
they lay down to sleep,
around eleven o'clock at night
Elena spoke up:

"What's the matter, my Fernando,
why won't you come closer,
you must have lovers in France
whom you love more than me?"

—No tengo amores en Francia,
ni los quiero más que a ti
lo que siento es tu marido
que vaya a andar por aquí.—

No temas a mi marido,
que lejos tierras fue a andar,—
se tomaron de la mano,
se fueron a transitar.

Andando en Plan de Barrancas,
sin saber como ni cuando,
cuando encontró don Benito
a Elena con don Fernando.

Vuela, vuela palomita,
párate en aquel ciprés,
anda a ver cómo le fue
a don Fernando el francés.

Parte II
Metió mano a su pistola
y a su rifle diez y séis,
para darle de balazos
a don Fernando el francés.

—No me tiro don Benito,
por la gloria que usted goza.
Son falsos que me levantan,
yo no concozco a su esposa.

—No lo tiro don Fernando,
y dirá que soy tirano,
¿Cómo si no conoce
allí no la traes de la mano?— >>

"I don't have any lovers in France
and there is no one I love more than you.
I am just nervous that your husband
might just be coming by here."

"Don't worry about my husband
he is off traveling far away."
They took each other's hands
and continued on.

While riding in Plan de Barrancas
without knowing exactly how,
Don Benito came upon
Elena and Don Fernando.

Fly, fly little dove,
alight over on that cypress tree.
Go and see what happened
to Don Fernando, the Frenchman.

Part II
He reached for his pistol,
and his sixteen caliber rifle,
ready to shoot
Don Fernando the Frenchman.

"Don't shoot me Don Benito,
for the love of God.
It is false what you are thinking,
I don't know your wife."

"I won't shoot you Don Fernando,
so don't call me a tyrant.
How is it that you don't know her
if you are standing there holding her hand?" >>

—Perdóname esposo mío,
por la grande sensatura,
pues ya no lo hagas por mí,
hazlo per esta criatura.—

—De mí no alcanzas perdón,
de mí no alcanzas ni gloria.
De mí lo único que alcanzas,
tres tiros de mi pistola.—

La pobrecita de Elena,
con qué lástima murió,
con tres tiros de pistola
que su marido le dío.

—Toma, que lleva esa criatura,
y llévasela a mis padres.
Si te preguntan por mí,
tú les digas que no sabes.

—Tú les dirás que no sabes,
yo quedaré por aquí,
y las mujeres casadas
que agarren ejemplo en mí.—

Vuela, vuela palomita,
dale vuelo a tu volido,
anda a ver cómo le fue
a Elena con su marido.

Vuela, vuela palomita,
párate en aquella higuera,
anda a ver cómo le fue
a Elena por traicionera.

"Forgive me my husband,
for my lacking good judgment.
If not for my sake,
then for this child."

"You won't get any forgiveness from me
you won't get anything of the kind.
The only thing you'll get from me are
three shots from my pistol."

Poor Elena,
the agony with which she died.
With three shots from the pistol
which came from her husband.

"Come, take this child
and take her to my parents,
If they ask about me
tell them that you know nothing.

"Tell them you know nothing
and I will remain here,
So that married women
will take an example from me.

Fly, fly little dove,
Go make your rounds,
Go and see how it went
for Elena and her husband

Fly, fly little dove,
Alight in that fig tree,
Go and see how it went
for Elena who cheated on her husband.

"Jesús Cadena" (Chavela) (San Antonio)

Parte I
Señores, voy a cantar
de versos una veintena,
Para recordar de un hombre
llamado Jesús Cadena.

Jesús le dice a José,
—Vamos al baile a La Parra,
a cantar una canción
al compás de una guitarra.—

Salieron de San Antonio
llegaron a San Andrés,
Se tomaron unos tragos
y volvieron otra vez.

Llegaron a San Andrés
y se fueron acercando.
A ese baile de La Parra
que se estaba principiando.

Por toda esta calle arriba
corre una piedra linterna,
Y esta noche voy al baile
a bailar con mi Chavela.

Jesús le dice a José,
—Pues hombre yo aquí me quedo,
Son las doce de la noche
y la verdad yo tengo miedo.— >>

Part I
Gentlemen, I will sing for you
twenty verses,
To recall a man
named Jesús Cadena.

Jesús says to José,
"Let's go to the dance at La Parra
to sing a song
accompanied by a guitar."

They left San Antonio
and arrived in San Andres,
They had a few drinks
and returned again.

They arrived in San Andres
and they got closer,
To that dance at La Parra,
which was just beginning.

Along this uphill road
runs a firefly stone,
Tonight I am going to the dance,
to dance with my Chavela.

Jesús says to José,
"Well, man, I'm staying here
it's twelve o'clock,
and truthfully, I'm scared." >>

Decía doña Manuelita
—Comadre, no andes bailando,
Por aquí paso Jesús
dice que te anda tanteando.—

Doña Manuelita said,
"Intimate friend, don't run around dancing,
Jesús is around
and he says he's spying on you."

Y le contestó Chavela
con una fuerte risada.
—No tenagas miedo comadre
que al cabo no me hace nada.—

Chavela answered
with a strong laugh,
"Don't be afraid my intimate friend,
he won't harm me."

Un baile se celebraba
de mucho pompa y corrido,
Chavela andaba en los brazos
de un hombre desconocido.

A dance was celebrated
with much pomp and festivity,
Chavela was in the arms
of a stranger.

Cuando Jesús llegó al baile
a Chavela se dirigió,
Como era la más bonita
Chavela lo *desaigró*.

When Jesús got to the dance
he went straight to Chavela,
Since she was the prettiest one,
she neglected him.

Yo *desaigrado* no quedo
porque ni nunca he quedado,
Pues que pensaría Chavela,
¿que yo soy un desdichado?

I am not disgraced,
nor have I ever been
Well, what would Chavela think,
that I am a miserable one?

Parte II
Jesús le dice a Chavela,
—Tú no vayas a bailar.
Si sigues en tus caprichos,
te puedes perjudicar.—

Part II
Jesús says to Chavela
"You'd better not dance,
If you continue with your flirting,
you can get yourself in trouble."

Cuando anunciaron la pieza
Chavela ya estaba en ansia,
Como a nadie le temía
todo lo tiraba en chanza.

When they announced the next piece
Chavela was most anxious,
Since she feared no one
and tossed everything to chance.

Jesús sacó su pistola
para darse de balazos,
Chavela le respondió
—Véngase prieto a mis brazos.—

Y le contestó Jesús,
—Quítate de aquí, Chavela,
No creas que tú estás tratando
con un muchacho de escuela.—

Chavela lo agarró el brazo
metiéndole para adentro,
Brindándole una cerveza
para borrarle el intento.

Jesús sacó su pistola
tres tiros le disparó,
Dos se fueron por el viento
y uno fue el que le pegó.

Decía la güera Chavela
cuando estaba malherida,
—Esto de querer a dos
comadre cuesta la vida.—

Decía la güera Chavela,
cuando estaba agonizando,
—Mucho cuidado muchachas
con andarlos mancornando.—

Un balazo lo tenía
al lado del corazón,
Y entre todas sus amigas
la llevaron al panteón. »

Jesús took out his pistol
prepared for a shootout,
Chavela answered him,
"Come to my arms you swarthy one."

Jesús replied,
"Get out of here, Chavela,
Don't think that you're dealing
with a schoolboy."

Chavela grabbed his arm
and took him inside,
Toasting him with a beer
to erase his intentions.

Jesús took out his pistol
and fired three shots,
Two went into the air
And one hit her.

Said the fair Chavela,
when she was badly wounded,
"This business of loving two,
my intimate, can cost your life."

Said the fair Chavela,
when she was in agony,
"Be very careful,
girls, when you two-time them."

One bullet she had
at the side of her heart,
And by all her friends
she was carried to the graveyard. »

Ya con ésta me despido
abrochándome una espuela,
ya les canté los versitos
de la traidora Chavela.

Ranchito de San José,
estado de Nuevo León,
Murió La güera Chavela,
por jugar una traición.

Now with this I take my leave
fastening my spur,
I've already sung to you the little verses
of the fickle Chavela.

Little ranch of San José,
state of Nuevo Leon,
The fair Chavela is dead
for playing a deception

"El Contrabando del Paso" (The Contraband of El Paso) (El Paso)

Parte I
En el día siete de agosto,
estábamos desperados,
que nos sacaran de El Paso
para Kiansis mancornados.

Yo dirijo mi mirada
por todita la estación,
a mi madre idolatrada
que me dé su bendición.

Nos sacaron de la corte
a las ocho de la noche,
nos llevaron para el depot
nos montaron en un coche.

Ni mi madre me esperaba,
ni siquiera mi mujer,
adiós todos mis amigos,
¿Cuándo los volveré a ver?

Allí viene silbando el tren
ya no tardará en llegar,
les dije a mis compañeros
que no fueran a llorar. >>

Part I
On the seventh day of August,
we were feeling desperate,
They took us from El Paso
towards Kansas, chained together.

I direct my glances
all around the station,
Looking for my beloved mother
that she may give me her blessing.

They took us from the courthouse
[jail] at eight o'clock at night,
They took us to the depot
and put us on a coach.

But my mother was not there
waiting, not even my wife,
Good-bye to all of my friends,
When will I see you again?

There comes the train whistling
it will arrive shortly,
I said to my companions
not to cry. >>

Ya voy a tomar el tren
me encomiendo a un Santo Fuerte,
ya no vuelvo al contrabando
porque tengo mala suerte.

Ya comienza a andar el tren,
ya repica la campana,
le pregunto a Mister Hill
que si vamos a Louisiana?

Mister Hill con su risita
me contesta:—No señor,
pasaremos de Louisiana
derechito a Leavenworth.—

Corre, corre, maquinita,
suéltale todo el vapor,
anda deja a los convictos
hasta el plan de Leavenworth.

Yo les digo a mis amigos
que salgan a *exprimentar*,
que le entren al contrabando
a ver donde van a dar.

Parte II

Les encargo a mis paisanos
que brincan el charco y cerco,
no se crean de los amigos
que son cabezas de puerco.

Que por cumplir la palabra
amigos de realidad,
cuando uno se halla en la corte
se olvidan de la amistad.

Now I am going to take the train
I commend myself to the Strong Saint,
I shall never go back to smuggling
because I have bad luck.

Now the train begins to move,
and the bell is ringing,
I ask Mister Hill
if we are going to Louisiana.

Mister Hill, with his little smile
replies, "No sir,
we go through Louisiana
straight to Leavenworth."

Run, run little locomotive,
with a full head of steam,
And let the convicts run
until we reach Leavenworth.

I say to my friends
that want to experiment,
That they get involved in contraband
and see where it gets them.

Part II

I recommend to my countrymen
that when crossing the river and the fence
Do not trust your friends
who are self-serving hypocrites.

I lived up to the word
truly we were friends,
But when you land in jail
the friendship is forgotten.

Yo les digo con razón
porque algunos compañeros,
en la calle son amigos
porque son convenencieros.

I say with good reason
because some of my companions,
On the streets they are your friends
because it suits their interests.

Pero de esto no hay cuidado
ya lo que pasó voló,
algún día se han de encontrar
donde me encontraba yo.

But let us forget the past
that which happened is behind us,
One day they will find themselves
in the same position I am in now.

Es bonito el contrabando
se gana mucho dinero,
pero lo que más me puede
condenar un prisionero.

Contraband is very nice
one can make a lot of money,
But what happens is
a prisoner is condemned.

Vísperas de San Lorenzo
como a las once del día,
visitamos los umbrales
de la penitenciaría.

Vespers of Saint Lawrence
at about eleven o'clock in the morning,
We stepped on the threshold
of the penitentiary.

Unos vienen con un año,
otros con un año y un día,
otros con dieciocho meses,
a la penitenciaria.

Some come with one year,
others with a year and a day,
others with eighteen months,
to the penitentiary.

El que hizo estas mañanitas
le han de otorgar el perdón,
si no están bien corregidos
pues ésa fue su opinión.

The person who wrote these verses
they should grant him a pardon,
If they are not incorrigibles,
well, they have their opinion.

Ahí te mando mamacita
un suspiro y un abrazo,
aquí dan fin las mañanas
del Contrabando de El Paso.

My little mother I am sending you
a sigh and an embrace,
Here we finish with the verses
of the Contraband of El Paso.

"Contrabandistas Tequileros" (Tequila Smugglers) (Del Rio)

Parte I	**Part I**
En mil *nuevecientos* treinta, señores pon atención, En la cárcel de Del Río fue trovada esta canción.	In 1930, gentlemen, your attention please, In the jail of Del Rio this song was made into poetry.
De la cárcel de Del Río ni me quisiera acordar, Que el diecisiete de marzo nos iban a sentenciar.	I would just as soon not remember the jail of Del Rio Where on the 17th of March they were going to sentence us.
Nos sacaron de la cárcel derecho a la Calle Real, Y nos dice el Colorado ya los voy a retratar.	They took us out of the jail straight to the Calle Real And the Colorado told us that he was going to take our pictures.
Luego que nos retrataron a la cárcel nos llevaron, Sin saber nuestra sentencia porque no nos la explicaron.	After they had taken our pictures they took us to the jail, And we didn't know our sentence because they didn't explain it to us.
Bonita cárcel en Del Río pero a mí no me consuela, Porque dan puros frijoles y on platito de avena.	A pretty jail in Del Rio, but it doesn't console me Because they just give us beans and a little plate of oatmeal.
Bonita cárcel en Del Río pero aún no se puede creer, Son contados los amigos que te quieren ir a ver.	A pretty jail in Del Rio, but it's still unbelievable, You can count the friends that want to go see you.

Yo les digo a mis amigos
cuando vayan a pasar,
Fíjense en los denunciantes,
no los vayan a entregar.

Yo les digo a mis amigos
cuando estén al otro lado,
Fíjense en las veredas
per donde va el Colorado.

Quizá ya en el Naqueví
aprehende a un compañero,
Que vendió a un denunciante
el día treinta de enero

Fíjate bien denunciante
porque lo estoy diciendo,
Que por amor al dinero
nos *estuvistes* vendiendo.

Pero de eso no hay cuidado,
ni tampoco hay que pensar,
Vamos a tomar cerveza
y en seguida a vacilar.

Parte II

Pero de eso no hay cuidado,
ya lo que pasó voló,
Por causa de un denunciante,
preso aquí me encuentro yo.

Yo anduve en muchas parrandas
con amigos en buen carros,
Y hoy me llevan prisionero
ni quien me traiga un cigarro. »

I tell my friends
when they are going to cross [the river],
Watch out for the informers,
that they don't turn you in.

I tell my friends
when they're on the other side,
Be careful on the trails
where the Colorado passes.

Perhaps in Naqueví
they have already caught a comrade
Who sold liquor to an informer
on the 30th day of January.

Watch it, informer,
because I am telling it,
That for love of money
you were selling us.

But of that there is no danger
neither must one think,
We're going to drink some beer
and later mess around.

Part II

But of that there is no danger,
what has happened is over,
Because of an informer
I find myself a prisoner here.

I went on many sprees
with friends in good cars
And today they take me prisoner
with no one to bring me a cigarette. »

Ya no llores mamacita,
te llevo en mi corazón,
Por entrarle al contrabando
me lleva la prohibición.

Don't cry, little mother,
I carry you in my heart,
For bringing in contraband,
Prohibition agents have taken me.

Entiéndanlo amigos míos
y pongan mocha atención,
Por andar vendiendo el trago
nos llevan a Leavenworth.

Understand it my friends
and take much care,
For going around selling drink,
they're taking us to Leavenworth.

La máquina del S.P.
corte con mucha violencia,
Y se lleva los convictos
derecho a la penitencia.

The Southern Pacific engine
runs with much violence,
And it takes the convicts
straight to the penitentiary.

Estos versos son compuestos
por toditos en reunión,
Unos por el contrabando
y otros por la inmigración.

These verses are made by everyone
in a get-together,
Some because of contraband
and others because of immigration.

Adiós mi madre querida,
solo tú lloras mis penas,
Ya nos llevan prisioneros
mancornados con cadena.

Good-bye my dear mother,
only you cry for my sorrows,
They are taking us prisoners
joined together with a chain.

Adiós mi madre querida,
me voy a la penitencia,
Cuando salga nos veremos,
si el Señor me da licencia.

Good-bye my dear mother,
I'm going to the penitentiary,
When I get out,
we'll see each other God willing.

Adiós cárcel de Del Río,
adiós torres y campanas,
Adiós todos mis amigos,
adiós lindas mexicanas.

Good-bye Del Río jail,
good-bye towers and bells,
Good-bye all my friends,
good-bye beautiful Mexican girls.

Los que viven en Del Río
gozan de tranquilidad,
Porque ellos toman tequila
con mucha facilidad.

Ya con ésta me despido,
porque siento mucho frío,
Aquí se acaba cantando,
del contrabando Del Río.

Those who live in Del Rio
enjoy tranquility,
Because they drink
tequila with great ease.

Now with the time I say good-bye
because I'm feeling very cold,
And here we finish singing
of the Contraband of Del Rio.

"Ballad of Gregorio Cortéz" (Rio Grande Valley)

Parte I
En el condado del Carmen
miren lo que ha sucedido,
Murió el *sherife* mayor
quedando Román herido.

Otro día por la mañana
cuando la gente llegó,
Unos a los otros dicen
no saben quien lo mató.

Se anduvieron informando
como tres horas después,
Supieron que el malhechor
era Gregorio Cortéz.

Insortaron a Cortéz
por toditito el estado
Vivo o muerto que se aprehenda
porque a varios ha matado.

Decía Gregorio Cortéz
con su pistola en la mano,
—No siento haberlo matado
al que siento es a mi hermano.—

Part I
In the country of the Carmen
look what has happened
The sheriff died leaving
Román wounded.

The following morning
when the people arrived
Some said to the others
they don't know who killed him.

They were investigating
and about three hours later
They found out that the wrongdoer
was Gregorio Cortéz.

Cortéz was wanted
throughout the state
Alive or dead may he be apprehended
for he has killed several.

Said Gregorio Cortéz
with his pistol in his hand,
"I'm not sorry for having killed him,
It's for my brother that I feel sorry."

Decía Gregorio Cortéz
con su alma muy encendida,
—No siento haberlo matado
la defensa es permitida.—

Venían los americanos
que por el viento volaban,
porque se iban a ganar
tres mil pesos que les daban.

Siguió con rumbo a Gonzáles,
varios *sherifes* lo vieron,
no lo quisieron seguir
porque le tuvieron miedo.

Venían los perros *jaunes*
venían sobre la huella
Pero alcanzar a Cortéz
era alcanzar a una estrella.

Decía a Gregorio Cortéz
—Pa' qué se valen de planes,
si no pueden agarrarme
ni con esos perros *jaunes*.— »

Said Gregorio Cortéz
with his soul aflame
"I'm not sorry for having killed him,
self defense is permitted."

The Americans came
they flew like the wind,
Because they were going to win
the three thousand pesos reward.

They continued toward Gonzáles
several sheriffs saw him
They did not want to continue
because they were afraid of him.

Came the hound dogs
they came on his trail
But to reach Cortéz
was to reach a star.

Gregorio Cortéz said
"What's the use of plans
If you can't catch me
Even with those hound dogs." »

Parte II
Decían los americanos
—Si lo vemos que le haremos
si le entramos por derecho
muy poquitos volveremos.—

En el redondel del rancho
lo alcanzaron a rodear,
Poquitos más de trescientos
y allí les brincó el corral.

Allá por el Encinal
a según por lo que dicen
Se agarraron a balazos
y les mató otro *sherife*.

Decía Gregorio Cortéz
con su pistola en la mano,
—No corran rinches cobardes
con un solo mexicano.—

Giró con rumbo a Laredo
sin ninguna timidez,
—¡Síganme rinches cobardes,
yo soy Gregorio Cortéz!—

Part II
The Americans said,
"If we see him what shall we do to him;
If we face him head on
very few will return."

In the ranch corral
they managed to surround him.
A little more than 300 men
and there he gave them the slip.

There around Encinal
from all that they say
They had a shoot-out
and he killed another sheriff.

Gregorio Cortéz said,
with his pistol in his hand,
"Don't run, you cowardly Rangers
from one lone Mexican."

He turned toward Laredo
without a single fear,
"Follow me, you cowardly Rangers,
I am Gregorio Cortéz."

Gregorio le dice a Juan
en el rancho del Ciprés,
—Platícame qué hay de nuevo,
yo soy Gregorio Cortéz.—

Gregorio le dice a Juan,
—Muy pronto lo vas a ver,
anda háblale a los *sherifes*
que me vengan a aprehender.—

Cuando llegan los *sherifes*
Gregorio se presentó,
—Por la buena si me llevan
porque de otro modo no.—

Ya agarraron a Cortéz
ya terminó la cuestión,
la pobre de su familia
la lleva en el corazón.

Ya con esto me despido
con la sombra de un Ciprés,
aquí se acaba cantando
la tragedia de Cortéz.

Gregorio says to Juan
at the ranch of the Cypress,
"Tell me what's new
I am Gregorio Cortéz."

Gregorio says to Juan,
"Very soon you will see,
go and talk to the sheriffs
that they should come and arrest me."

When the sheriffs arrive
Gregorio presented himself,
"You'll take me if I wish it,
because there is no other way."

Now they caught Cortéz,
now the case is closed;
His poor family
he carries in his heart.

Now with this I take my leave
in the shade of a cypress,
Here we finish singing
the tragedy of Cortéz.

"Capitán Charles Stevens" (Rio Grande Valley)

Parte I

Oigan señores los que les voy a cantar,
estos sucesos yo los canto y no lo olviden,
Pues ya murió el jefe prohibicionista
y que en vida se nombraba Charles Stevens.

Este quu tiene de "águila los ojos"
y que dio medida en dondequiera,
Es el retrato mismo los despojos
de él que en vida le nombraban "la pantera."

Él no por eso perderá su alma,
no maldijo jamás su ingrata suerte,
Como hombre soportó con toda calma
en el horrido campo de la muerte.

Más debido al valor que éste tenía,
Charles Stevens el jefe que yo nombro,
Cuando buscaba la cerveza hacía
que todo el mundo le tuviera asombro.

Cayó herido y entonces con denuedo,
siguió Murphy con igual valor,
Pelió intrépido y sin miedo,
sostuvo aquella lucha con honor.

Al lado siempre de su fiel amigo,
él mismo lo llevó hasta el hospital,
Debatió para hacer que otro enemigo
moviera el auto en el Camino Real.

Un mexicano, luego sin más cosa
lo meten en un lío porque oyó
como muere de pronto en Santa Rosa,
En silencio el secreto se incognó. »

Part I

Listen, men, to what I am about to sing,
these events, I sing about and don't forget them,
Because the head prohibitionist is dead
and who in life was named Charles Stevens.

He who has "eagle eyes"
and who lived up to his name everywhere,
It's the same picture as the despoilers,
He who in life was known as "the panther."

Not for that will he lose his soul,
nor will he ever curse his ungrateful luck,
Like a man he withstood all calmly
in the horrible camp of death.

Owing to the courage that he had,
Charles Stevens, the man to whom I am referring,
When looking for beer, he astonished
everyone in the whole world.

He fell injured and then with boldness,
followed Murphy with equal courage.
Who fought gallantly and without fear,
continuing that struggle with honor.

At his side, always his faithful friend,
he took him to the hospital.
He fought to make the enemy
move the car out of the way.

A Mexican, then, without further ado
got into a fix because he heard
how suddenly he dies in Santa Rosa.
In silence the secret was kept safe. >>

Parte II

Ahora en confusión queda pendiente
la esposa de Guajardo en el condado,
Si es que compruebe así ser inocente,
o la encuentra culpable el gran jurado.

Oír esta tragedia y triste historia,
por Dios que esto huele ya muy mal,
Si la falta de un padre es tan notoria
la de una madre en prisión no tiene igual.

Lo de siempre sucedió, lector querido,
los hechos a la historia ya pasaron,
Solo un pobre mexicano se ha perdido
y los otros matadores se han pelado.

La muerte del valiente Charles Stevens
ha venido a descubrir que en San Antonio,
No son los *bootleggers* los que solo viven,
son de otra parte los que crían el demonio.

Y seguirá la ley haciendo esfuerzos
para evitar las bebidas embriagantes,
Y yo continuaré cantando versos
aunque parezca mal a los pedantes.

Aunque se quiebren todas las botellas
por agentes de la ley que a todos pasos,
Relucirán las ilusiones bellas
a través de los vidrios y los vasos.

No olviden, por lo tanto estos alardes,
no hay a quién no le duela su pellejo.
Los mismos son valientes que cobardes
y tal como el refrán lo dice un viejo.

Part II

And now in confusion what is pending,
Guajardo's wife in the county jail,
Was waiting to see if proven innocent
or if the grand jury will find her guilty.

Listen to this tragedy and sad story,
for God's sake, this smells bad,
If the lack of a father is so notorious,
that of a mother in prison has no equal.

The usual thing happened, dear reader,
these deeds have now become history.
Only one poor Mexican has been lost
while the other killers have gotten away.

The death of the brave Charles Stevens
has made it known that in San Antonio,
It's not just the bootleggers who live there,
These trouble makers come from another place.

The law will continue to make efforts
to prohibit intoxicating drinks,
And I will continue singing verses,
even though the pedants don't like it.

Even if all the bottles are broken
by the agents of the law, in any case,
All the beautiful illusions will shine
through the glassware and the glass.

Meanwhile, don't forget this display,
there is no one whose own skin won't hurt.
The same who are brave are cowards
just as it's said by this old man.

part two

the 1930s

Lydia Mendoza (Houston)

"La Pollita" (The Hen)

Yo tengo, yo tengo para hacer crías
una po, una pollita en mi casa
cantando, cantando no más lo pasa
y no po, y no pone todavía.

Dicen que le hace, pero no le hace
tan chiquitita quiere casarse
dicen que le hace, le hace, le hace
ay ay ay. . . . . . pero no le hace.

Un día, un día se me escapó
sin que na, sin que nadie lo supiera
y llegó, y llegó con sus pollitos
siendo una, siendo una polla soltera.

Otro día, otro día me la encontré
arriba, arriba de una tinaca
abajó, abajó estaban los huevos
y arriba, y arriba estaba la paja.

I have a hen, I have a hen in my house
that is for raising chicks,
but she spends all of her time singing,
and has yet to lay an egg.

They say that she cares, but she doesn't,
so young, and she wants to marry,
they say that she cares, she cares, she cares,
ay ay ay. . . . . but she doesn't.

One day, one day she escaped from me,
without anyone, without anyone noticing,
and she returned, and she returned with her chicks
even though she was an unmarried hen.

Another day, another day I found her
on top of, on top of a water trough,
underneath, underneath were the eggs
and on top, on top was the straw.

BORN IN HOUSTON and touring with her family, Lydia Mendoza, the "lark of the border," was the first important Tejano vocalist. In 1999, she received a National Medal of the Arts in recognition of her lifetime achievement.

FERMINA GUERRA was born on Buena Vista Ranch, near Laredo. She earned both a bachelor's and a master's degree from the University of Texas. Her academic work and her books focused on the folklore of her native region, including traditional medicinal practices, music, and stories about animals. She taught at Texas A&M University in Kingsville, as well as acting as both a teacher and administrator of several elementary schools.

Fermina Guerra (Laredo)

from "Rancho Buena Vista: Its Ways of Life and Traditions"

High Water

Ever-present in the minds of ranch people is the question of water. The foremost topic of conversation among them is the condition of the range, the prospect of rain, the water of the tanks. This part of the country has never found good well water to pump up with windmills, and tanks are depended on for stock water.

In the old days there were no tanks. The cattle watered at the two or three creeks in the country. In time of drouth [*sic*] they were driven the eighteen miles to the Nueces River. There was never trouble over water rights. Through the years these ranchmen kept the peace among themselves; the struggle with Nature occupied their chief energies. The first fence went up in 1891. Don Florencio's son, Donato, used to go out of his way before and after school to watch the fence-building operations being carried on by the Callaghan Ranch hands, who were erecting a fence between Buena Vista Ranch and theirs.

Three times in the history of Buena Vista Ranch La Becerra Creek has been half a mile wide—in 1878, 1903, and 1937. Of course, the oldest flood is the most romantic. Don Justo and his wife were still living then, old and set in their ways. Their ranch house was of mesquite poles and adobe, thatched with grass and set on the very banks of La Becerra Creek.

One day it started to rain; torrents poured down. As the creek began to rise and there was no abatement of the downpour, the other members of the family grew frightened. Not Don Justo. He had seen rain before; nothing ever came of it. But the rain poured all night and a second day; the creek continued to rise.

Now it was up to the corral, adjoining the house. No matter; it would go down presently. A second night, and a third day, the rain continued pouring. At dusk on the third day, the water began to enter the house. A young matron, wife of Don Carmen, holding her child in her arms, told her husband to take her to higher ground. She feared remaining in the house another night with that constantly rising water. Gladly enough, be complied. Before leaving, he begged his aged father and mother to accompany him, but they laughed. "You will get all wet for nothing," they said. "We have a roof over our heads. What if there is a little water in the house?"

But the young mother set out for the hill to the east. Before she reached it, she was obliged to swim to save herself and child, her husband aiding her. The rain was still pouring so hard that they got lost in the brush, but they went on eastward.

Eventually they found themselves on a well-known hill. Don Florencio's ranch was just a mile to the northwest. The mother asked her husband to go down there and ask for some dry clothing for the baby as the night was cold and it was still raining hard. Willingly enough, Don Carmen set out.

On reaching the house, he told Don Florencio what had happened at the upper ranch. Hurriedly the latter saddled his best horse and set out to see what he could do to persuade his parents to leave their house and take to the hills. The water was not so high at Buena Vista, though it was at the door of the main house.

About daybreak, he reached the shore opposite his parents' ranch. There was a raging torrent between him and them. From afar off, barely to be seen among the tree tops, he could discern the roof of the house and two people perched on it. He could hardly hear their feeble cries, so great was the distance.

Like most ranchmen of his time, Don Florencio could not swim. He depended upon his horse to carry him across streams. This task his present mount refused to perform. Time after time he forced the animal into the water, only to have it turn back. At length, he returned to his own ranch for a fresh mount. This horse, too, refused to venture out into the flood. So Florencio was forced to flounder at the edge of the current and watch those faraway forms, fearing to see them disappear from sight. But, towards evening, the waters began to recede, and the next day he was able to go out and rescue the exhausted old people from their predicament.

The flood of 1903 was unusual in that no rain accompanied it. One hot, sunny morning Don Florencio noticed what appeared to be a cloud of mist rising rapidly from the bushes south of the house along the creek. It was coming fast, with a rushing sound. Suddenly, he realized that a wall of water, far wider than the creek banks, was bearing down upon him. One of his laborers was down the creek bed driving some goats to higher ground. Racing his horse, he hurried to get within calling distance of the man, Carlos. The laborer saw Don Florencio and heard his call, but, not realizing that the danger was so close, went leisurely on with his work. Suddenly the turbulent water was upon him, and he was borne along with it as it swirled among the bushes. Fortunately, after his first fright, he was able to collect his wits sufficiently to grasp at an overhanging limb and so save his life.

The flood of 1937 was more prosaic; the creek itself did no particular damage, but the water destroyed all but three tanks in a radius of twenty miles and left the range worse off than before the rain.

Such is the life of the ranchmen of Southwest Texas; drouth and flood; too much water or not enough; then, now, and always.

La Cautiva

Three miles south of Buena Vista Ranch was the ranch of Antonia Hinojosa, la cautiva. She was a romantic figure in the region, a former captive of the Indians. As a young woman she had lived in the Mexican state of Chihuahua. She had married young and had an infant son.

One day she went down to a creek near her hut to wash clothes and took her infant along. While she was there, a band of roving Indians from across the border came upon her and her child. They captured her, and, cutting the ears off her son, left him lying on the creek bank. She never saw him again.

For a number of years she lived among the Indians, at length becoming the wife of one of them. By him she had a daughter, Lola. But she longed to escape. In a battle between tribes she was taken by the enemy and separated from her daughter. The Indian man grieved for her and told Lola the Spanish name of her mother and urged her to seek her if anything ever happened to him. Then it happened that Lola's Indian father was killed in a personal fight with another brave. In some way Lola escaped or got cut off from the Indians and grew up among white people. She never ceased searching for her mother, but it was many years before she found her.

Meanwhile, the mother, Antonia Hinojosa, had been released by the Indians because the United States government made them give up all their captives. She came to La Becerra Creek and took up a homestead. She lived alone and often had not even a laborer to help her.

She made bags out of cowhides to carry away the earth she painstakingly dug out of the burrow pit of her tank; that little tank is still to be seen on her ranch.

Her ranch house was of stone, brought from the bed of La Becerra Creek. The stones are now part of a modern house on the neighboring ranch of Cesario Benavidez.

Once, during the Indian raids, she closed up her horses in her corral and herself mounted guard upon them day and night. When the Indians arrived, she stood her ground and talked them out of countenance so that they left her unmolested.

Through a long life she had many trials and adventures. But she prospered. One of her laborers was the ill-fated victim of Justo Manta, the 'bad-man' of the region. At length, when she was a feeble old woman, her daughter learned of her whereabouts. Lola was about sixty years old at the time and lived in Austin. She came alone to her mother's ranch. The old woman was not proud to acknowledge her half-Indian daughter, but she felt a tenderness toward her and thus they lived together for a few years.

The daughter decided to return to Austin, but she left word with friends and neighbors that they should advise her immediately if Antonia fell ill. Several years passed before the call came. Upon receiving word of her illness, Lola set out from Austin post haste. But Antonia, being 105 years old, did not live till her daughter arrived. Lola heard of her mother's death when she reached a ranch about five miles away.

The shock was too great for the aged traveler; she was unable to continue her journey. Soon she herself died, and the two are buried side by side on the ranch of 'La Cautiva.'

The Trasquilas

In the early days of Buena Vista Ranch there were few cattle. All of the ranchmen kept herds of sheep guarded by *pastores*. The grass was lush, the range was unfenced and there was a good market for the wool. Shearing was done twice a year, in April and in September. Itinerant sheep-shearers came to each ranch in turn, bringing their own entourage, including a sturdy woman cook, whom they always called "Madre."

It was amusing to hear them at meal time calling out, "Madre"-this, and "Madre"-that, to the bustling woman who attended to their wants.

The ranchmen marveled at their skill and at their attention to their work. There was no siesta in the heat of the day; there was no stop for *merienda* in the afternoon. Furthermore, their dexterity with the flying shears was a thing to watch with awe. A good workman would shear a hundred sheep a day. When twenty such men were at work in the sheep-shearing sheds, the bleating of the sheep, the snipping of the shears, the joking voices of the workers, and the warning cry of "Golpe," as a sheared sheep was released to go bounding out of the shed, blended to make an uproar foreign to the usual somnolent scene. This cry of "Golpe" was a signal given by a shearer when he finished shearing a sheep and let it loose. It was a warning to the other shearers to be ready to dodge, for the sheep would make its way blindly into the pen and might stumble into anything in its path.

Besides the shearers, there were men to carry the wool and men to pack it. This packing was done with the help of a tall wooden rack on which jute sacks were stretched. One man filled the sack; another tramped the wool into it with his feet so that each sack might hold as much as possible.

When the shearing and packing were done, Don Florencio and his sons loaded the wool into ox carts and made their trip to Laredo, where wholesale wool dealers bought his wool.

Here he bought provisions. Early in his married life he established here, too, a town house. At first he built a tiny place of mesquite poles, thatched with straw; later, he built a stone house; then, one of lumber, big and rambling. Now, this, too, has been replaced by a twelve-room brick dwelling, modern in every detail.

Here at Laredo his ten children were born; here, and at the ranch, he and his wife spent their busy days. But the ranch held the center of their affections. He asked his children to bury him there.

A stone's throw behind the ranch house one may see his grave.

"Don Pedrito Jaramillo"

El día cuatro de julio,
presente lo tengo yo,
que Pedrito Jaramilio
ese día se retiró.

Adiós, hermano Pedrito,
échanos tu bendición
a todos estos hermanos
que estamos en la reunión.

Adiós, hermano Pedrito,
de la ciencia espiritual,
aquí nos quedamos tristes,
sabe Dios si volverás.

No se te olvide, Pedrito,
déjanos recomendado
a todos estos hermanos
que se encuentran a tu lado.

Cuando viene amaneciendo
el corazón nos avisa
del hermanito que era,
el que ya se retiraba.

No nos dejes, hermanito,
no nos dejes padecer,
ponnos en el corazón
lo que debemos de hacer.

A las tres de la mañana,
quedándome yo dormido,
oí una voz que decía:
—Adiós, hermanos queridos.—

Pues ya te vas, hermanito,
a los aires extranjeros,
ya te vas a retirar
a los reinos de los cielos.

On the fourth day of July, I remember it well,
Pedrito Jaramillo on that day went away.

Farewell, brother Pedrito, give your blessing
to all these brothers and sisters who are at the meeting.

Farewell, brother Pedrito of the spiritual science;
saddened we remain; God knows if you will return.

Don't you forget, Pedrito, be sure to commend us
to all those brothers and sisters who are by your side. »

When the day begins to dawn, our hearts remind us
of the dear brother we had and who has now gone.

Do not leave us, dear brother, do not leave us to suffer;
show us in our hearts the things that we have to do.

At three o'clock in the morning, I happened to fall asleep,
and I heard a voice that said, "Farewell, beloved brothers and sisters."

Now you leave us, dear brother, for other climes;
now you are going away to the Kingdom of Heaven.

Josefina Niggli (San Antonio)

"False Blue" and "Discontent"

FALSE BLUE

At one time, señor, I was very rich.
I was possessed of a wife,
A rooster,
And twelve hens.
But now, señor, I own nothing but the
rooster.

I had a friend who was true to me
Until he met my wife.
Louisa was beautiful
Only in the eyes of men.
Her skin was a magnolia blossom
Dipped in Spanish wine;
Her hair was a cloud of night
Unbound by stars;
Her lips were a maid's kiss,
And her nose a slim, straight line.
But her eyes, señor,
Were bluer than Lake Chalco at mid-day;
Bluer than the sky against the soft, pink
evening sun.
Bluer than blue:
Her eyes.

But my friend came and saw my wife.
Saw also my twelve hens.
So, in the night,
He stole them away,
Leaving nothing but a black band on the
rooster
To show he was in mourning.

WHILE JUST A FEW YEARS OLD, Josefina Niggli moved from Nuevo León, Monterrey, where she was born, to San Antonio. She spent her childhood moving back and forth between the two cities and attended Incarnate Word College, where her first poems were written, earning her bachelor's degree. She went on to a master's degree for the University of North Carolina as a playwright. Niggli then returned to Mexico to work in theater at the Universidad Autónoma de Mexico. A collection of Niggli's plays was published in 1945, and she later studied drama in Ireland. Niggli also wrote three novels, including her most famous, *Mexican Village* in 1945, and served as president of the Business and Professional Women's Club in Sylva, North Carolina. She passed away in 1983.

Discontent

Place—*An Inn.*

Characters—*Three old men seated before the fire.*

The First Old Man

I dreamed one day
Of becoming a *gendarme**
Or a soldier,
From the hills beyond Mexico City.
General Lozano used to tell me
Stories of men who died
In the flame of their patriotism.
I wanted to be one of these . . . .
But I married Sara.
Now I sit in front of my door
And watch the goats
Turn into pink pearls beneath the sun.

The Second Old Man

As for me,
I felt the call of the sea.
The *señor* at the *Casa Grande*†
Would talk by the hour
Of lands that were drops of green ink
Upon the golden breast of the ocean.
I could feel in my fingers
Bright gems to grace dull hair.
Beneath my hands
The bronze shoulder of a girl
More beautiful than death.
But the *Señor* sent me to the Gulf
And I became sea-sick.

---

*Gĕndär´mĕ—Policeman.

†Cäsa´Grändĕ—Large house.

Rosita Fernandez (San Antonio)

"Mi fracaso" (My Ruin)

Cuando nada pedí al amor,
llegaste tú,
y el miedo de volver a sufrir
no me hacía querer.
Pudo más el dulzor de tu voz,
me venció el calor de tu ser.

Tú, también, me lograste engañar,
Lastimar y sangrar mi herido corazón,
y aunque sé que hoy vuelvo a padecer,
no te culpo si ya sé que mi fracaso
es siempre querer.

When I had nothing to ask of love,
you arrived,
and the fear of suffering again,
made me hesitant.
But the sweetness of your voice
and the warmth of your soul changed my mind.

But you too were unfaithful,
and made my heart bleed,
and although I know I will once again
waste away, I don't blame you, I now
know that to love will always be my ruin.

Rosita Fernandez was born in Monterrey and began singing boleras and rancheras in San Antonio with her uncles and became famous as the star of the Fiesta Noche del Rio in San Antonio.

"La tísica" (The Consumptive Girl)

¡Qué negra está la noche!
¡Cuántas estrellas!
Abre la ventana, madre,
yo quiero verlas.—
—No, hija de mi vida,
tú estás enferma
y el sereno de la noche
matarte pueda.—

—Al toque de la una,
madre, yo muero,
y debajo de mi cama
aúlla el perro.—
—No, hija de mi vida,
no digas eso,
tú estás muy mejorada,
ven, dame un beso.—

—Si viene Jorge a verme
no dejen que entre
porque él a mí me ha dicho
que no me quiere,
porque él a mí me ha dicho,
'Quiero a Dolores'
y sólo a mí me basta
que tú me llores.

—Yo de mortaja quiero
mi ropa blanca,
la ropa que tenía
para mis bodas,
que vengan mis amigas,
me traigan flores,
que vengan todititas,
menos Dolores.—

"How dark is the night!
How many stars!
Open the window, mother,
I want to see them."
"No, my darling daughter,
you are ill,
and the night dew
might kill you."

"When the clock sounds one,
mother, I will die,
and the dog is howling
under my bed."
"No, my darling daughter,
do not say that;
you are much better now;
come, give me a kiss."

"If Jorge comes to see me,
do not let him come in,
for he has said to me
that he does not love me,
for he has said to me,
'I love Dolores,'
and I do not need anyone
to weep for me but you.

"I want my white clothes
to be my winding sheet,
the clothes that I had
for my wedding;
let my girl friends come,
let them bring me flowers;
let them all come,
except Dolores."

"Dime sí, sí, sí" (Tell Me Yes, Yes, Yes)

Acabo de llegar de la majada,
de cueros traigo lleno un carretón,
se los traigo a regalar a mi Librada,
la dueña de mi corazón.

Dime sí, sí, sí, dime no, no, no,
aguardiente traía pero ya se me acabó;
dime sí, sí, sí, dime no, no, no,
aguardiente traía pero ya se me acabó.

I have just arrived from the sheep pens,
I am bringing in a wagon full of hides;
I have brought them as a gift to my Librada,
the mistress of my heart.
Tell me yes, yes, yes; tell me no, no, no;
I brought some spirits with me, but now they are all gone.

part three

photographs from the 1930s

Gregorio Barrios Sr. (1908–1962) was born in Monterrey, Nuevo León, México. He was a traveling photographer as a teenager. He left Mexico for the United States during the Cristero uprising in the late 1920 and immigrated to the United States. He worked as a local studio photographer in San Antonio and was a member of the Texas Professional Photographers Association since 1934. He later moved to Victoria where he raised a family as the owner of his own photography studio.

OF THE STATES

VENUS
FAMILY DAY
WED THUR
RECUERDOS DE LO VALLE
DUEL IN THE JUNGLE

GOLIAD LUMBER CO.

DRINK
Coca-Cola
Sun Spot

part four

the 1940s

Chelo Silva (Brownsville)

"Mal Camino" (The Wrong Path)

Ya te vas por mal camino, corazón
a cumplir con tu destino es la razón,
y aunque mucho voy a extrañarte
nada más te digo adíos.

Si la vida tus ensueños marchitó
y nos separa a los dos,
en mis ansias de adorarte
me conformo con mirarte
y nomás te digo adíos.

You are down the wrong path, my love
to realize your destiny, or so you say,
and although I will miss you
all I can say is good-bye.

If life has withered your dreams
and separated us from each other,
despite my need to adore you
I'll content myself just to look at you
and only tell you good-bye.

CHELO SILVA STARTED SINGING at the Continental Club in Brownsville, where she was born. After her recording debut, she became the most famous Tejana vocalist of the century.

Servando Cárdenas was born south of the Rio Bravo, in Linares, Nuevo Leon. He came to Texas at age seventeen, and quickly began publishing the very first literary journals for Mexican Americans, *Alma Azul* and *Cumbres*. He worked for a Spanish language weekly, *La Libertad*, and continued starting publications for many years as owner of a print shop in San Diego. He wrote and published over three hundred poems. Cardenas also served in the army in World War II, and died in San Diego.

Servando Cárdenas (San Diego)

"A Washington" and "Los Pachucos"

A Washington

Salud a la memoria del hombre entre los grandes
El más esclarecido varón de Norteamérica,
Cuya voz libertaria se oyera hasta los Andes,
Retando virilmente de Aibión la faz colérica.

Feliz la tierra sea, que vio nacer al hombre
De voluntad de hierro de espíritu dinámico,
Que más tarde le diera independencia y nombre,
Curando sus heridas con bienestar balsámico.

Es Washington el hombre más grande de la historia.
Que tienen los vecinos del norte, cual simbólico
Timbre de su orgullo, quien hizo que en la gloria
Su País viviera baja un cielo vitriólico.

Salud a la memoria de quien cual sus soldados
Arrostró los peligros en los combates hórridos;
Por eso fueron ellos sus más fieles aliados,
Y nunca el enemigo logró verlos impróvidos.

Fue Washington el hombre que en realidad hermosa,
Hiciera un pueblo libre de su ilusión quimérica.
Formó de la súbdita de Albión, la poderosa,
La grande y respetada Nación de Norteamérica.

—*Febrero*, 1933

Los Pachucos

Melena que va huyendo al peluquero,
un sombrero grandote en la cabeza,
una pluma muy larga en el sombrero
y saco hasta la corva, de una pieza.

Van en turno después los pantalones:
tienen en la cintura pliegues miles,
de cadera a chamorro dos balones
y en la parte de abajo dos fusiles.

Dos pulgadas de suela en los zapatos;
en sus modos y en todo son iguales,
en su trato común se hablan de "batos"
y cuando hay más confianza de "carnales."

Para amar ellos buscan su "pachuca,"
y aunque se llame Paz, Juana a Josefa
ellos les llaman vulgarmente "ruca,"
al padre "Jefe" y a la madre "Jefa."

Decir "voy a dormir, luego te veo"
ninguna ciencia en el lenguaje entraña;
ellos dicen: "Por hay te barvoleo,
voy a tirar una poca de pestaña."

Si de una dulce música al abrigo,
en la noche a bailar fueron un rato,
otro día le dicen al amigo:
"¡Que si tiré chancla anoche, bato!"

Y si van a pedir una peseta,
a cualquiera se la piden con soltura
diciéndole en mitad de la banqueta:
"¡Órale, cáigase con una sura!"

Un diálogo escuché cierta mañana
mientras café en un restaurant tomaba,
de un pachuquito que perdió una hermana,
y un amigo que el pésame le daba:

"¡Hey, carnal!, ¿cierto que torció su sista?"
"Simón, cuai"—le contesta el infelice.
El otro, con su cara que contrista:
"Lo acompaño en sus centímetros"—le dice.

Si hay alguno que no les da buen trato,
y se muestra orgulloso y estirado,
fastidiados le dicen: "Chale, bato,
diatiro se me muestra muy cerrado." >>

Después de andar dos de ellos a la greña,
oí de uno la excusa interesante:
"Cuando él sacó su 'escupe' rajé leña,
pues yo olvidé mi 'fila' allá en el 'chante.'"

Por otro pachuquito después supe
lo que tan sólo en su lenguaje encaja,
que en su modo de hablar llaman "escupe"
a la pistola y "fila" a la navaja.

"Estaba en el mono con la rucaila
muy Agustín Lara y muy cerrado,
cuando llega el gabacho y me la baila
y me dejó solano y apañado."

Quiere decir que estaba muy a gusto
con la dama en el cine, cuando un gringo
llega y se la quita y le da un susto;
esto puede pasar cualquier domingo.

Lo del día, lector, no tiene caso,
lo metí para hacer el consonante,
que yo en poesía por salir del paso
meto ripio tras ripio y adelante.

Es necesario ya, lector ameno,
a este retrato dar toques finales,
que en razón de conciencia ya está buena
dejar en santa paz a los "carnales."

Ruben Ramos (Austin)

"El Gato Negro"

A mí me llamen El Gato Negro, todas las leyes me buscan ya
soy peligroso según lo dicen un desalmado y un criminal

Desde muy chico me eché a los vecios, todo lo malo conozco yo
conozco a todos los traficantes, y criminales de la nación

Desde las sierras allá en Chihuahua, con carga Blanca viajaba yo
y entre las barbas de los Sheriffes cruzaba Aduanas de Emigración

Cargas enteras de Yerbabuena, llevé a Chicago y a Nueva York
y varias veces por mala suerte, caí en las celdas de la prisión

Allá en Laredo, en una emboscada, con los Sheriffes me la riflé
me fuí por Alice tirando al Norte, ni de la muerte yo me acordé

Por San Antonio, pasé de noche, llegando a Houston no sé por qué
los Patrulleros tenían aviso, y del Corral me les escape

Temible Carcel de Kansas City, famosa carcel de San Quintín
de San Antonio su Carcel Nueva, del quinto piso me les salí

El Gato Negro no se despide, desaparece de la Región
cuando me miran todo de negro, y ojos borrados ese soy yo

Born into a family of migrant workers and musicians, Ruben Ramos, "El Gato Negro," began his musical career at an early age in his uncle's orquesta and, later, playing with his brothers in a band out of Austin, the Mexican Revolution.

They call me El Gato Negro, all the laws are already looking for me
I am dangerous, so they say, ruthless and a criminal

From a young age, I threw myself to vices, all the bad things I know
I know all the dealers and criminals of the nation

From the mountains of Chihuahua, loaded with a white load, I traveled
and under the sheriff's beard I crossed Immigration Customs

Full loads of good weed I carried it to Chicago and New York
and several times, because of bad luck, I fell in the cells of a prison

Over in Laredo, in an ambush, with the Sheriff I took the risk
I went through Alice going north, not even death agreed with me

Through San Antonio, I passed at night, arriving in Houston I don't know why
the patrolmen were alerted, and from Corral I escaped

Fearsome jail of Kansas City, famous jail of San Quintin
from San Antonio's new jail, from the fifth floor I escaped

El Gato Negro doesn't say farewell, he disappears from the region
when you see me all in black and gray eyes, that's me

"Mucho me gusta mi novia" (Much Do I Like My Sweetheart)

Y mucho me gusta mi novia,
me gusta nomás porque me habla inglés;
anoche le preguntaba
que si me amaba
y me dice:—*Yes.*—

Oh, my little darling,
please dime que sí,
mamacita linda,
she belong to me.

And much do I like my sweetheart,
I like her especially because she talks English to me;
last night I asked her if she loved me,
and she says to me, "*Yes.*"

Oh, my little darling,
please say "yes" to me,
darling little mamma,
she belong to me.

Felix Longoria (Three Rivers)

Correspondence

Corpus Christi, Tex., Jan. 10, 1949
Hon. Lyndon Johnson
U.S. Senate
Washington, D.C.

The American GI Forum, an independent veterans organization, requests your departments immediate investigation and correction of the un-American action of the Rice Funeral Home, Three Rivers, Texas, in denying the use of its facilities for the reinterment of Felix Longoria, soldier killed in Luzon, Philippine Islands and now being returned for burial in Three Rivers, based solely on his Mexican ancestry.

In direct conversation, the funeral home manager, T. W. Kennedy, stated that he would not arrange for funeral services and use of his facilities because, he said, "Other white people object to use of the funeral home by people of Mexican origin." In our estimation, this action is in direct contradiction of those same principles for which this American soldier made the supreme sacrifice in giving his life for his country and for the same people who now deny him the last funeral rites deserving of any American hero regardless of his origin.

The Rice home is the only funeral home in Three Rivers. This is a typical example of discriminatory

FELIX LONGORIA was a truck driver and father of a young daughter, living in the town of Three Rivers. He was drafted into World War II and killed in action in the Philippines. In 1948, three years after his death, the only funeral parlor in the town refused to allow a wake and funeral to be held. This prompted the GI Forum, an organization created to help Mexican American veterans, to intervene. They were unsuccessful initially, but through their efforts Lyndon Johnson, the Texas senator, arranged a burial for Longoria in Arlington National Cemetery, making Longoria a hero to those who fought to end discrimination in Texas.

Corpus Christi, Tex., Jan. 10 1949

Hon. Lyndon Johnson
U.S. Senate
Washington, D. C.

The American GI Forum, an independent veterans organization, requests your departments immediate investigation and correction of the un-American action of the Rice Funeral Home, Three Rivers, Texas, in denying the use of its facilities for the reinterment of Felix Longoria, soldier killed in Luzon, Philippine Islands and now being returned for burial in Three Rivers, based solely on his Mexican ancestry.

In direct conversation, the funeral home manager, T. W. Kennedy, stated that he would not arrange for funeral services and use of his facilities because, he said, "Other white people object to use of the funeral home by people of Mexican origin". In our estimation, this action is in direct contradiction of those same principles for which this American soldier made the supreme sacrifice in giving his life for his country and for the same people who now deny him the last funeral rites deserving of any American hero regardless of his origin.

The Rice home is the only funeral home in Three Rivers. This is a typical example of discriminatory practices which occur intermittently in this State despite our efforts to prevent them. We believe action from your office will do much toward elimination of similar shameful occurence in the future.

(Signed) Dr. Hector P. Garcia, pres
American GI Forum

practices which occur intermittently in this State despite our efforts to prevent them. We believe action from your office will do much toward elimination of similar shameful occurence in the future.

(signed) Dr. Hector P. Garcia, pres
American GI Forum

Western Union
Jan. 11, 1949
DA494 WM09
W.SND165 LONG GOVT PD=SN Washington DN 11 537P=
Dr. Hector P. Garcia, President=
American GI Forum=Corpus Christi, Tex=

Retel. I deeply regret to learn that the prejudice of some individuals extends even beyond this life. I have no authority over civilian funeral homes, nor does the federal government. However, I have today made arrangements to have Felix Longoria buried with full military honors in Arlington National Cemetery here at Washington where the honored dead on our nations wars rest. Or, if his family prefers to have his body interred nearer his home he can be reburied at Fort Sam Houston National Military Cemetery at San Antonio. There will be no cost. If his widow desires to have him reburied in either cemetery, she should send me a collect telegram before his body is unloaded from an army transport at San Francisco, January 13 this injustice and prejudice is deplorable. I am happy to have a part in seeing that this Texas hero is laid to rest with the honor and dignity his service deserves=

Lyndon B. Johnson USS=

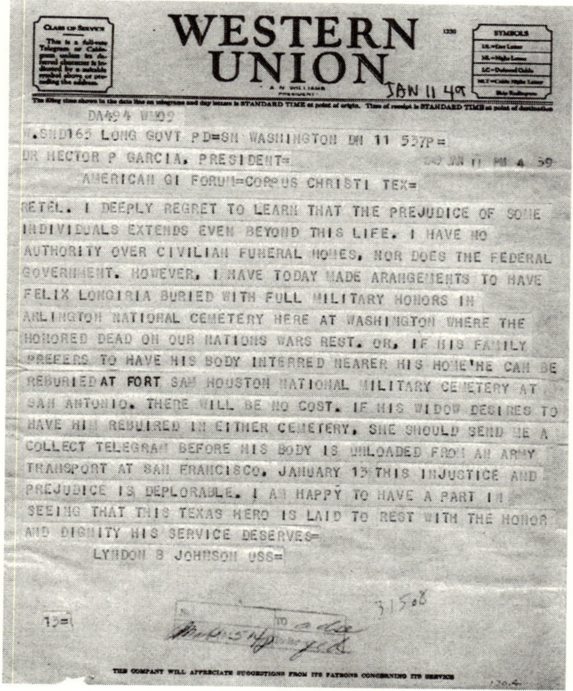
WESTERN UNION
JAN 11 49

DA494 WM09
W.SND165 LONG GOVT PD=SN WASHINGTON DN 11 537P=
DR HECTOR P GARCIA, PRESIDENT=
AMERICAN GI FORUM=CORPUS CHRISTI TEX=

RETEL. I DEEPLY REGRET TO LEARN THAT THE PREJUDICE OF SOME INDIVIDUALS EXTENDS EVEN BEYOND THIS LIFE. I HAVE NO AUTHORITY OVER CIVILIAN FUNERAL HOMES, NOR DOES THE FEDERAL GOVERNMENT. HOWEVER, I HAVE TODAY MADE ARANGEMENTS TO HAVE FELIX LONGIRIA BURIED WITH FULL MILITARY HONORS IN ARLINGTON NATIONAL CEMETERY HERE AT WASHINGTON WHERE THE HONORED DEAD ON OUR NATIONS WARS REST. OR, IF HIS FAMILY PREFERS TO HAVE HIS BODY INTERRED NEARER HIS HOME HE CAN BE REBURIED AT FORT SAM HOUSTON NATIONAL MILITARY CEMETERY AT SAN ANTONIO. THERE WILL BE NO COST. IF HIS WIDOW DESIRES TO HAVE HIM REBUIRED IN EITHER CEMETERY, SHE SHOULD SEND ME A COLLECT TELEGRAM BEFORE HIS BODY IS UNLOADED FROM AN ARMY TRANSPORT AT SAN FRANCISCO, JANUARY 13 THIS INJUSTICE AND PREJUDICE IS DEPLORABLE. I AM HAPPY TO HAVE A PART IN SEEING THAT THIS TEXAS HERO IS LAID TO REST WITH THE HONOR AND DIGNITY HIS SERVICE DESERVES=

LYNDON B JOHNSON USS=

31508

2

STATEMENT Feb 9: 1949

On January 7, 1949 I went to Three Rivers, Texas, my former home-town to make arrangements for my husband's (late Felix Longoria) funeral. I went to the Rice Funeral Home, only funeral home in Three Rivers, Texas owned by Mr. T.W. Kennedy to have the funeral arrangements made. He agreed to handle the arrangements, but when I told him I wanted his body kept at the Chapel, he said, "Well, Mrs. Longoria, I have lots of Latin friends but I can't let his body rest at this Chapel, because the whites won't like it". After he told me that, and not expecting it, I agreed to have the body taken to my house there at Three Rivers, until reburial.

I returned to Corpus Christi to consult with my family about the incident. One of my sisters immediately got in contact with the "American GI Forum", a Veterans Organization of which Dr. Hector P. Garcia is president and I authorized Dr. Garcia to try to get the use of the Chapel for my husband's services. I told Dr. Garcia that unless he could get the Chapel, we would bury him instead at Corpus Christi. Dr. Garcia then called Mr. Kennedy and was told by Mr. Kennedy that "they had never let the Latin Americans use the Chapel and were not starting now, even if he was a soldier killed in action". Dr. Garcia also called the Caller-Times, a local newspaper and a Caller-Times reporter, Mr. George Groph, who then called Mr. Kennedy and was told the same thing.

Mrs Beatrice Longoria

Mrs. Beatrice Longoria

130.22

130 22

Statement

Feb. 9, 1949

On January 7, 1949, I went to Three Rivers, Texas, my former home-town to make arrangements for my husband's (late Felix Longoria) funeral. I went to the Rice Funeral Home, only funeral home in Three Rivers, Texas owned by Mr. T. W. Kennedy to have the funeral arrangements made. He agreed to handle the arrangements, but when I told him I wanted his body kept at the Chapel, he said, "Well, Mrs. Longoria, I have lots of Latin friends but I can't let his body rest at this Chapel, because the *whites* won't like it." After he told me that, and not expecting it, I agreed to have the body taken to my house there at Three Rivers, until reburial.

I returned to Corpus Christi to consult with my family about the incident. One of my sisters immediately got in contact with the "American GI Forum," a Veterans Organization of which Dr. Hector P. Garcia is president and I authorized Dr. Garcia to try to get the use of the Chapel for my husband's services. I told Dr. Garcia that unless he could get the Chapel, we would bury him instead at Corpus Christi. Dr. Garcia then called Mr. Kennedy and was told by Mr. Kennedy that "they had never let the Latin Americans use the Chapel and were not starting now, even if he was a soldier killed in action." Dr. Garcia also called the Caller-Times, a local newspaper and a Caller-Times reporter, Mr. George Groph, who then called Mr. Kennedy and was told the same thing.

(signed) Mrs. Beatrice Longoria

Santiago Jiménez Sr. (San Antonio)

"Ay Te Dejo en San Antonio" (I'm Leaving You in San Antonio)

Ya no quiero que me beses ni besarte
ni mirarte ni siquiera oír tu voz,
porque supe que tenías otro amante,
y en Laredo ya tenías otros dos.

Te gusta mucho el baile,
y bailas al compás.
Te vas hasta Laredo y
quieres más y más.

Soy ranchero, jugador y navegante,
ya me voy para nunca más volver.
Me dejastes sin dinero y sin rolante,
por el mundo te me echastes a correr.

Ya me voy, ay te dejo en San Antonio,
Tu mañita no te la puedo quitar.
Hay momentos que pareces el demonio
cuando mueves la cintura pa' bailar.

Santiago Jiménez Sr. was born into a musical family in San Antonio and became known as an accordion player and then more well known for his *tololoche* (contrabass) playing, which became part of the sound of *conjunto* developing in that decade.

I don't even want to kiss you or for you to kiss me,
or to look at you or even hear your voice,
because I found out that you have another lover,
and in Laredo you already had two others.

You like to dance very much,
and you dance right to the beat.
You'll go all the way to Laredo and
still want more and more.

I'm a rancher, a gambler and a rambler,
and now I'm leaving and never coming back.
You left me without money and without a car,
you've taken to running 'round the world on me.

Now I'm going, I'm leaving you here in San Antonio.
I can't take away your cheating ways.
There are times you look just like the Devil
when you move your little waist to dance.

part five

the 1950s

Jovita González (Corpus Christi)

"The Devil on the Border"

Si se descuidan
    las jóvenes bellas
El diablo verde
    cargará con ellas.
	If the fair maidens
	    are not careful
	The green devil will
	    carry them away.

This is what children are told down at the border when they do not mind their elders about staying indoors during the noon day heat. The Evil One no doubt feels at home during the terrific heat of the noon day hour as he wanders among the ranches of the Rio Grande country. And it is because of this heat no doubt that Satan's visitations to the border country are not uncommon.

I have been told of three such visitations. The first one is a housewife's tale, the place, time and names of the characters being unknown. The second visitation happened recently at a cave near Devil's River in the vicinity of Del Rio and was told to me by a University of Texas student whose father witnessed the incident. The third is an old border legend, very popular because in it the Evil One gets fooled by a *vaquero*.

(1)

On an out of the way ranch lived a *vaquero*, poor in the world's goods but blessed with many children. However he did not consider the children a blessing but rather as a curse. When the last one came he was very much vexed and decided to do away with it. The idea of shedding his own baby's blood was repugnant

JOVITA GONZÁLEZ was born in Roma, Texas. She received her B.A. from Our Lady of the Lake College and her M.A. from the University of Texas. After graduation she studied, under the guidance of J. Frank Dobie, the folklore of her native region, and became president of the Texas Folklore Society. Her focus on her culture led to her involvement with LULAC, of which she also became president. She continued her studies in folklore while teaching high school, helping create informative works about Chicanos for high school students. She died in 1983.

to him. After much thinking he thought of an excellent plan. He placed the child in a box far from the house and sat there day and night to keep his wife from feeding the infant. The baby cried until it got so weak that no sound came from its mouth. All the while the mother, frantic with grief, begged her husband to save the child. But he would not yield. Then, wild in her despair, she cursed him and ended by saying "May the Devil get you."

About midnight of that same day the whole ranch was enveloped in a terrific whirlwind, the smell of sulphur was suffocating, and a dust of ashes choked the people. Above the roaring of the wind a piercing cry of death was heard. No one dared to go to the place where the man and the baby had been, for all remembered the wife's curse.

With the coming of daylight, the people's fears were dispersed and they approached the place. The baby was dead. A white dove, probably its spirit, hovered over the little corpse. As for the man, all that remained of him was a heap of greenish yellow sulphur.

(2)

Now we shall hear in the words of the University student concerning the second apparition as her father saw it.

"The story I am about to tell will not be believed by many, but it really happened down the Devil's River, where the Evil One had been locked up in a cave. It was told to me by my father, a God-fearing, truth-loving man.

"One evening as he was sitting on the porch of our house, smoking his after-dinner cigarette, a stranger called on him. He was a handsome man who looked more like a Spaniard than a Mexican. He showed letters of introduction from friends. Being a very hospitable man, my father gave him lodging for as long as he wished to make our home his home.

"He was a cattle buyer. He said he had come to Del Rio to buy stock, and my father introduced him to the ranchmen of the vicinity. There was something strange and mysterious about him, something that made you shrink when you approached him. As long as he stayed in our house he was never known to invoke the name of God or the saints, but as a host it was not my father's duty to question him about his religious convictions.

"One morning, as usual, he rode away to the neighboring cattle ranches. At night he did not return. Two days passed and still he did not come back. Since every one knew he had several thousand pesos, his disappearance was arousing great curiosity, and since he had been our guest, my father, fearing to arouse suspicion, organized a searching party.

"As he knows every crag, thicket and cave in the Devil's River Country, he led the party. So engrossed was he in his reflections that he did not realize how far ahead of the others he was. So he stopped on the bank of the river to wait. Suddenly he heard groans coming from the direction of the opposite bank. He swam across and the moans sounded much nearer. Apparently someone was in great pain, for the groans were heart-rending and chilled his blood. He walked along the bank until he came upon a cave formed by the river. The moans were right at his back, and then he realized that someone was in the cave.

"Crouching on all fours, he entered and what he saw was enough to make any stout man tremble. A man was buried up to his neck in the sand. His face was gashed and scratched horribly. One of his eyes was black and so swollen that it was closed. His hair was standing on end. His beard was clotted with blood. The raw nose bone protruded above torn skin. It was the stranger. As soon as he saw my father, he cried out in a piercing voice:

"'Don't come near me. The devil is here. Don't you see him there at the corner of the cave?'

"My father moved nearer.

"'Go back, I tell you. Do you want him to get you as he got me? See how he leers and jeers at me.' And saying this, the unfortunate stranger tried to bury his head in the sand.

"My father, who had often heard of how the devil had attacked other people, was chilled with horror at what he heard. But he had a Rosary in his pocket and, taking it out, made the sign of the Cross and commanded the evil spirit to depart. He must have left, for the stranger gave a sigh of relief, saying:

"'He has gone. Get me a drink of water.'

"My father left to go get the water. When he returned, the Evil Spirit was there again, for the man was shaking and trembling like one possessed crying out, 'He is there again. Take out your cross.'

"The sign of the cross was made again and the man was again at peace.

"He was taken out of the cave and placed on the bank of the river. While my father went to fetch a burro on which to carry him home the man sat by the edge of the river holding the Rosary in his hand.

"Soon the searching party returned and as the man was lifted from the ground to the burro, the Rosary fell from his hands. Something like a whirlwind enveloped the group, and to their consternation both the burro and rider were carried up in the air. The man screamed, the burro brayed, and the people, realizing the significance of the whole thing, said a prayer. A sound like the bellow of a bull was heard up in the air and beast and man fell to the ground.

"For weeks the patient suffered. His physical injuries and the psychological effects of the devil's visitation had made a wreck of him. When he recovered, a priest was called. The priest heard his confession and gave him absolution. Then the man told my father what had happened. The morning he left home as he came near Devil's River he was taken up into the air by what he thought was a whirlwind. However he noticed he was holding on to something slippery, long, and slimy. As he looked up he saw the awful face of the devil. He tried to turn loose but the cloven hoofs of the Evil One beat him on the face and his hands were stuck to the tail. Satan took him over the whole town of Del Rio and the cemetery and finally dropped him in the cave. The Evil One then tortured him with his presence and because of that he had buried himself in the sand.

"The stranger stayed until he regained his health and finally disappeared without explanation. Whether he went home or was carried away by the devil is a thing that has puzzled those who knew him."

(3)

It was an abnormally hot day in Hell. The big devils and the small devils were all busy feeding the fires, making final preparations to give a warm reception to a barber, a student, and a banker who had announced their arrival. A timid knock sounded on the door, and Satan, who was sitting on a throne of flames, sent one of his henchmen to see who the arrivals might be. In walked four men. One, razor in hand, gave away his profession; the second held on to a wallet like Judas Iscariot to his; the third exhibited a notebook devoid of notes. The three were abnormally terrified. The fourth did not appear a bit impressed by the fiery reception awarded them, but with the coolness and nonchalance of one accustomed to such things glanced about with look of curiosity. He was an athletic sort of a man, wore a five gallon hat, *chivarras* and spurs, and played with a lariat he held in his hands. He seemed to be as much at home as the others were terrified. Before he was assigned any particular work, he walked to where a devil was shoveling coals, and, taking the shovel from his hands, began to work. Satan was so much impressed that he paid no attention to the others but went to where the stranger was. He did not like this man's attitude at all. He liked to watch the agony on the face of the condemned, but here was this man as cool as a September morn. He went through the flames, over the flames, into the flames and did not mind the heat at all. This was more than his Satanic Majesty could endure. Approaching the man, he commanded him to stop and listen to what he had to say. But the man would not stop and kept on working.

"O, well," said Satan, "if that's the way you feel keep it up, but I really would like to know something about you and were you come from."

"If that's the case," the stranger replied, "then I feel I must satisfy your curiosity. I am

Pedro de Urdemañas by name. I have lived through the ages deceiving people, living at the expense of women who are foolish enough to fall in love with me. Now as a beggar, now as a blind man I have earned my living. As a gypsy and a horse trader in Spain, then as a soldier of fortune in the new world I have managed to live without working. I have lived through the equatorial heat of South America, through the cold of the Andes and the desert heat of the Southwest. I am immune to the heat and the cold, and really bask in the warmth of this place."

The Devil was more impressed than ever and wanted to know more of this strange personage.

"Where was your home before you came here?" he continued

"Oh, in the most wonderful land of all. I am sure you would love it. Have you ever been in Texas?"

The devil shook his head.

"Well, that's where I come from. It is a marvelous country."

"Indeed?" said the Evil One, "and what is it like?"

Pedro described the land in such glowing terms that the Devil was getting interested in reality. "And what's more," continued Pedro, "there is plenty of work for you down there."

At this Satan cocked his ears, for if there was one thing he liked better than anything else it was to get more workers for his shops.

"But, listen," he confided, "you say there are many cows there. Well, you see I have never seen one and would not know what to do were I to see one."

"You have nothing to fear about that. There is a marked similarity between you and a cow. Both have horns and a tail. I am sure you and the cows will become very good friends."

After this comparison, Satan was more anxious than ever to go to this strange land where cows lived.

So early the next day before the Hell fires were started, he set out earth-bound. Since his most productive work had been done in the cities and he knew nothing about ranch life, Satan left for Texas gaily appareled in the latest New York style. He knew how to dress, and as he strolled through the earth seeking for Texas, he left many broken hearts in his path.

Finally, on an August day he set foot on a little prairie surrounded by thorny brush, near the lower Rio Grande. It was a hot day indeed. The sand that flew in whirlwinds was hotter than the flames of the infernal region. It burned the Devil's face and scorched his throat. His tongue was swollen; his temples throbbed with the force of a hammer beat. As he staggered panting under the noonday heat, he saw something that gladdened his eyes. A muddy stream glided its way lazily across a sandy bed. His eyes caught sight of a small plant bearing red berries, and his heart gladdened at the sight of it. It was too good to be true. Here was what he wished for the most—water and fresh berries to eat. He picked a handful of the ripest and freshest, and with the greediness of the starved put them all into his mouth. With a cry like the bellow of a bull he ducked his head in the stream. He was burning up. The fire that he was used to was nothing compared to the fire from the chile peppers that now devoured him.

But he went on, more determined than ever to know all about the land that he had come to see. That afternoon he saw something that, had he not been a devil, would have reminded him of heaven. The ripest of purple figs were growing on a plant that was not a fig tree.

"Here," though Satan, "is something I can eat without any fear. I remember seeing figs like these in the Garden of Eden." Hungrily he reached for one, but at the first bite he threw it away with a cry of pain. His mouth and tongue were full of thorns. With an oath and a groan he turned from the prickly pear and continued his journey.

Late that same day, just before sunset, he heard the barking of dogs. He continued in the direction from whence the sound came, and soon he came to a ranch house. A group of men, dressed like Pedro de Urdemañas—that new arrival in Hell who had sent him to Texas—ran here and there on horses gesticulating. The sight of them rather cheered Satan up.

And then he saw what Pedro told him he resembled—a cow. Here was a blow indeed. Could he, the king of Hell, look like one of those insipid creatures, devoid of all character and expression? Ah, he would get even with Pedro on his return and send him to the seventh hell, where the greatest sinners were and the fire burned the hottest. His reflections were interrupted by something that filled him with wonder. One of the mounted men threw a cow down by merely touching its tail.[†] "How marvelous!" thought Satan. "I'll learn the trick so I can have fun with the other devils when I go back home."

He approached one of the *vaqueros* and in the suavest of tones said, "My friend, will you tell me what you did to make the lady cow fall?"

The cowboy looked at the city man in surprise, and with a wink at those around him replied, "Sure, just squeeze its tail."

Satan approached the nearest cow—an old gentle milk cow—gingerly, and squeezed its tail with all his might.

[†]The art of throwing a cow by tailing it used to be extensively practiced on Texas ranches. It is known as *colear*.

Now, as all of you know, no decent cow would allow any one, even though it be the king of Devils, to take such familiarity with her. She ceased chewing her cud, and, gathering all her strength in her hind legs, shot out a kick that sent Satan whirling through the air.

Very much upset and chagrined, he got up. But what hurt more were the yells of derision that greeted him. Without even looking back, he ran hell-bound, and did not stop until he got home. The first thing he did on his arrival was to expel Pedro from the infernal region. He would have nothing to do with one who had been the cause of his humiliation. And since then Satan has never been in Texas, and Pedro de Urdemañas still wanders though the Texas ranches always in the shape of some fun-loving *vaquero*.

"Los mexicanos que hablan inglés" (The Mexicans Who Speak English)

En Texas es terrible
por la revoltura que hay,
no hay quién diga "hasta mañana,"
nomás puro *goodbye.*

Y *jau-dididú mai fren,*
en ayl sí yu tumora,
para decir "diez reales"
dicen *dola yene cuora.*

Yo enamoré una tejana,
y de esas de sombrilla,
le dije:—¿Te vas conmigo?—
y me dijo:—¡*Luque jía*!—

Enamoré otra catrina,
de esas de garsolé,
le dije:—¿Te vas conmigo?—
y me dijo:—¿*Huachu sei*?—

Luego me fui pa'l dipo
a hablar con doña Inés,
yo le hablaba en castellano
y me contestó en inglés.

Todos queremos hablar
la lengua americana,
sin poder comprender
la nuestra castellana.

Y en Texas es terrible
por la revoltura que hay,
no hay quién diga "hasta mañana,"
nomás puro *goodbye.*

In Texas it is terrible
how things are all mixed up;
no one says "*hasta mañana*,"
it's nothing but "*goodbye*."

And "*howdy-dee-do, my friend,*
and I'll see you tomorrow";
when they want to say "*diez reales*"
they say "*dollar and a quarter*."

I made love to a Texas-Mexican girl,
one of those with a parasol;
I said to her, "Will you go along with me?"
and she told me, "*Looky heah!*"

I made love to another fashionable lady,
one of those with a *garsolé*;
I said to her, "Will you go along with me?"
and she told me, "*What you say?*"

Then I went to the depot
to talk to Doña Inés;
I talked to her in Spanish,
and she answered me in English.

All of us want to speak
the American language,
without understanding
our own Spanish tongue.

In Texas it is terrible
how things are all mixed up;
no one says "*hasta mañana*,"
it's nothing but "*goodbye*."

Américo Paredes made his impact through his original scholarship and is considered the father of Chicano Studies. His academic career did not begin immediately: born in Brownsville in 1915, he did not attend college until after working as a journalist in the 1930s and spending some time in the Army. In 1951 he graduated summa cum laude from the University of Texas. He earned his Ph.D. studying the life of Gregorio Cortez, which became his first book, *With His Pistol in His Hand*. The book assured Paredes of success as a scholar, and both its biting wit and well-researched attack on the prevailing, overly heroic myth of the Texas Ranger won him a wide readership. He taught Anthropology and English for many years at the University of Texas and continued his work after retirement, publishing books on Texas folklore and the novel *George Washington Gomez*.

Américo Paredes (Brownsville)

from *With His Pistol in His Hand*

Nuevo Santander

The Lower Rio Grande Border is the area lying along the river, from its mouth to the two Laredos. A map, especially one made some thirty or forty years ago, would show a clustering of towns and villages along both river banks, with lonely gaps to the north and to the south. This was the heart of the old Spanish province of Nuevo Santander, colonized in 1749 by José de Escandón.

In the days before upriver irrigation projects, the Lower Rio Grande was a green, fertile belt, bounded on the north and south by arid plains, situated along a river which, like the Nile, irrigated and fertilized the lands close to its banks and periodically filled countless little lakes, known as resacas and esteros. Isolated by natural barriers, the country was still unexplored long after the initial wave of Spanish conquest had spent itself and Spain was struggling with the problems created by her earlier successes. Spanish colonization had gone as far north as New Mexico on the west, and to the east it had jumped overseas to Texas. The Lower Rio Grande, known as the Seno Mexicano (the Mexican Hollow or Recess), was a refuge for rebellious Indians from the Spanish presidios, who preferred outlawry to life under Spanish rule. Thus, at its earliest period in history the Lower Rio Grande was inhabited by outlaws, whose principal offense was an independent spirit.

Toward the middle of the eighteenth century

Spanish officialdom decided that better communications were needed between Texas and Mexico City, routes which would cross the Seno Mexicano. José de Escandón was ordered to colonize the Lower Rio Grande. Four months after his appointment, Escandón was already on his way with parties of exploration.

Escandón was a wise and far-sighted administrator, and his methods were different from those of most Spanish colonizers. The *presidio*, symbol of military authority over settlers and Indians alike, was not part of his plans. The soldiers assigned to each settlement of Nuevo Santander were settlers too, and their captain was the colony's most prominent citizen.

The colonists came from the settled Spanish families of surrounding regions and were induced to settle on the Rio Grande by promises of free land and other government concessions. One of these concessions was freedom from interference by officialdom in the faraway centers of population. The colony of Nuevo Santander was settled much like the lands occupied by westward-pushing American pioneers, by men and their families who came overland, with their household goods and their herds.

The Indians seem to have given little trouble. They were neither exterminated in the English manner, nor enslaved according to the usual Spanish way. They lived in the same small towns as the Spanish settlers, under much the same conditions, and were given a measure of self-government.

By 1775, a bare six years after the founding of Nuevo Santander, there were only 146 soldiers still on duty among 8,993 settlers. There were 3,413 Indians in the towns, not counting those that still remained in a wild state.[1] In succeeding generations the Indians, who began as vaqueros and sheepherders for the colonists, were absorbed into the blood and the culture of the Spanish settlers. Also absorbed into the basically Spanish culture were many non-Spanish Europeans, so that on the Border one finds men who prefer Spanish to English, who sometimes talk scornfully about the "Gringos," and who bear English, Scottish, Irish, or other non-Spanish names.

By 1755 towns had been founded near the present site of Laredo—the only north-bank settlement of the time—and at Guerrero, Mier, Camargo, and Reynosa on the south bank. The colonists were pushing into the Nueces-Rio Grande area in search of pasturage for their rapidly increasing herds. Don Blas María Falcón, the founder of Camargo, established a ranch called La Petronila at the mouth of the Nueces at about this time.

By 1835 there were three million head of livestock in the Rio Grande-Nueces area, according to the assessments of the towns along the Rio Grande.[2] Matamoros, founded near the river mouth in 1765 by people from Reynosa, had grown into the metropolis of the colony with 15,000 inhabitants. The other riverbank towns, though not so large, were correspondingly prosperous. The old province of Nuevo Santander was about to emerge from almost a century of isolation and growth, when war in Texas opened the period of border strife.

The Rio Grande people

Most of the Border people did not live in the towns. The typical community was the ranch or the ranching village. Here lived small, tightly knit groups whose basic social structure was the family or the clan. The early settlements had begun as great ranches, but succeeding generations multiplied the number of owners of each of the original land grants. The earliest practice was to divide the grant among the original owner's children. Later many descendants simply held the land in common, grouping their houses in small villages around what had been the ancestral home. In time almost everyone in any given area came to be related to everyone else.

The cohesiveness of the Border communities owed a great deal to geography. Nuevo Santander was settled comparatively late because of its isolated location. In 1846 it took Taylor a month to move his troops the 160 miles from Corpus Christi to Brownsville. In 1900 communications had improved but little, and it was not until 1904 that a railroad connected Brownsville with trans-Nueces areas, while a paved highway did not join Matamoros with the interior of Mexico until the 1940's.

The brush around Brownsville in the 1870's was so heavy that herds of stolen beef or horses could be hidden a few miles from town in perfect secrecy.[3] Even in the late 1920's the thick chaparral isolated many parts of the Border. Ranches and farms that are now within sight of each other across a flat, dusty cotton land were remote in those days of winding trails through the brush. The nearest neighbors were across the river, and most north-bank communities were in fact extensions of those on the south bank.

The simple pastoral life led by most Border people fostered a natural equality among men. Much has been written about the democratizing influence of a horse culture. More important was the fact that on the Border the landowner lived and worked upon his land. There was almost no gap between the owner and his cowhand, who often was related to him anyway. The simplicity of the life led by both employer and employee also helped make them feel that they were not different kinds of men, even if one was richer than the other.

Border economy was largely self-sufficient. Corn, beans, melons, and vegetables were planted on the fertile, easily irrigated lands at the river's edge. Sheep and goats were also raised in quantity. For these more menial, pedestrian tasks the peon was employed in earlier days. The peon was usually a *fuereño,* an "outsider" from central Mexico, but on the Border he was not a serf. Peón in Nuevo Santander had preserved much of its old meaning of "man on foot." The gap between the peon and the vaquero was not extreme, though the man on horseback had a job with more prestige, one which was considered to involve more danger and more skill.

The peon, however, could and did rise in the social scale. People along the Border who like to remember genealogies and study family trees can tell of instances in which a man came to the Border as a peon (today he would be called a *bracero*) and ended his life as a vaquero, while his son began life as a vaquero and ended it as a small landowner, and the grandson married into the old family that had employed his grandfather—the whole process taking place before the Madero Revolution. In few parts of Greater Mexico before 1910 could people of all degrees—including landowners—have circulated and obviously enjoyed the story of Juan, the peon who knew his right, and who not only outwitted his landowning employer but gave him a good beating besides, so that the landowner afterward would never hire a peon who "walked like Juan."

This is not to say that there was democracy on the Border as Americans recognize it or that the average Borderer had been influenced by eighteenth-century ideas about the rights of man. Social conduct was regulated and formal, and men lived under a patriarchal system that made them conscious of degree. The original settlements had been made on a patriarchal basis, with the "captain" of each community playing the part of father to his people. . . .

The patriarchal system not only made the Border community more cohesive, by emphasizing its clanlike characteristics, but it also minimized outside interference, because it allowed the community to govern itself to a great extent. If officials saw fit to appoint an *encargado* to represent the state, they usually chose the patriarch, merely giving official recognition to a choice already made by custom.

Thus the Rio Grande people lived in tight little groups—usually straddling the river—surrounded by an alien world. From the north came the *gringo*, which term meant "foreigner." From the south came the *fuereño*, or outsider, as the Mexican of the interior was called. Nuevo Santander had been settled as a way station to Texas, but there was no heavy traffic over these routes, except during wartime. Even in the larger towns the inhabitants ignored strangers for the most part, while the people of the remoter communities were oblivious of them altogether. The era of border conflict was to bring greater numbers of outsiders to the Border, but most Borderers treated them either as transients or as social excrescences. During the American Civil War and the Mexican Empire, Matamoros became a cosmopolitan city without affecting appreciably the life of the villages and ranches around it. On the north bank it took several generations for the new English-speaking owners of the country to make an impression on the old mores. The Border Mexican simply ignored strangers, except when disturbed by violence or some other transgression of what he believed was "the right." In the wildest years of the Border, the swirl of events and the coming and going of strange faces was but froth on the surface of life.

In such closely knit groups most tasks and amusements were engaged in communally. Roundups and brandings were community projects, undertaken according to the advice of the old men. When the river was in flood, the patriarchal council decided whether the levees should be opened to irrigate the fields or whether they should be reinforced to keep the water out, and the work of levee-building or irrigation was carried out by the community as a whole. Planting and harvesting were individual for the most part, but the exchange of the best fruits of the harvest (though all raised the same things) was a usual practice. In the 1920's, when I used to spend my summers in one of the south-bank ranch communities, the communal provision of fresh beef was still a standard practice. Each family slaughtered in turn and distributed the meat among the rest, ensuring a supply of fresh beef every week.

Amusements were also communal, though the statement in no way should suggest the "dancing, singing throng" creating as a group. Group singing, in fact, was rare. The community got together, usually at the patriarch's house, to enjoy the performance of individuals, though sometimes all the individuals in a group might participate in turn.

The dance played but little part in Border folkways, though in the twentieth century the Mexicanized polka has become something very close to a native folk form. Native folk dances were not produced, nor were they imported from fringe areas like southern Tamaulipas, where the *huapango* was danced. Polkas, mazurkas, waltzes, lancers, *contra-danzas*, and other forms then in vogue were preferred. Many Border families had prejudices against dancing. It brought the sexes too close together and gave rise to quarrels and bloody fights among the men. There were community dances at public spots and some private dances in the homes, usually to celebrate weddings, but the dance on the Border was a modem importation, reflecting European vogues.

Horse racing was, of course, a favorite sport among the men. In the home, amusements usually took the form of singing, the presentation of religious plays at Christmas, tableaux, and the like. This material came from oral tradition. Literacy among the old Border families was relatively high, but the reading habit of the Protestant Anglo-Saxon, fostered on a veneration of the written words in the Bible, was foreign to the Borderer. His religion was oral and traditional.

On most occasions the common amusement was singing to the accompaniment of the guitar: in the informal community gatherings, where the song alternated with the tale; at weddings, which had their own special songs, the *golondrinas*; at Christmastime, with its *pastorelas* and *aguinaldos*; and even at some kinds of funerals, those of infants, at which special songs were sung to the guitar.

The Nuevo Santander people also sang ballads. Some were songs remembered from their Spanish origins, and perhaps an occasional ballad came to them from the older frontier colony of Nuevo Mexico. But chiefly they made their own. They committed their daily affairs and their history to the ballad form: the fights against the Indians, the horse races, and the domestic triumphs and tragedies—and later the border conflicts and the civil wars. The ballads, and the tradition of ballad-making as well, were handed down from father to son, and thus the people of the Lower Rio Grande developed a truly native balladry.

It was the Treaty of Guadalupe that added the final element to Rio Grande society, a border. The river, which had been a focal point, became a dividing line. Men were expected to consider their relatives and closest neighbors, the people just across the river, as foreigners in a foreign land. A restless and acquisitive people, exercising the rights of conquest, disturbed the old ways.

Out of the conflict that arose on the new border came men like Gregorio Cortez. Legends were told about these men, and ballads were sung in their memory. And this state of affairs persisted for one hundred years after Santa Anna stormed the Alamo.

Mier, the Alamo, and Goliad

In the conflict along the Rio Grande, the English-speaking Texan (whom we shall call the Anglo-Texan for short) disappoints us in a folkloristic sense. He produces no border balladry. His contribution to the literature of border conflict is a set of attitudes and beliefs about the Mexican which form a legend of their own and are the complement to the *corrido*, the Border-Mexican ballad of border conflict. The Anglo-Texan legend may be summarized under half a dozen points.

1. The Mexican is cruel by nature. The Texan must in self-defense treat the Mexican cruelly, since that is the only treatment the Mexican understands.

2. The Mexican is cowardly and treacherous, and no match for the Texan. He can get the better of the Texan only by stabbing him in the back or by ganging up on him with a crowd of accomplices.

3. Thievery is second nature in the Mexican, especially horse and cattle rustling, and on the whole he is about as degenerate a specimen of humanity as may be found anywhere.

4. The degeneracy of the Mexican is due to his mixed blood, though the elements in the mixture were inferior to begin with. He is descended from the Spaniard, a second-rate type of European, and from the equally substandard Indian of Mexico, who must not be confused with the noble savages of North America.

5. The Mexican has always recognized the Texan as his superior and thinks of him as belonging to a race separate from other Americans.

6. The Texan has no equal anywhere, but within Texas itself there developed a special breed of men, the Texas Rangers, in whom the Texan's qualities reached their culmination.

This legend is not found in the cowboy ballads, the play-party songs, or the folk tales of the people of Texas. Orally one finds it in the anecdote and in some sentimental verse of nonfolk origin. It is in print—in newspapers, magazines, and books—that it has been circulated most. In books it has had its greatest influence and its longest life. The earliest were the war propaganda works of the 1830's and 1840's about Mexican "atrocities" in Texas, a principal aim of which was to overcome Northern antipathy toward the approaching war with Mexico.[4] After 1848, the same attitudes were perpetuated in the works, many of them autobiographical, about the adventurers and other men of action who took part in the border conflict on the American side. A good and an early example is the following passage from *Sketches of the Campaign in Northern Mexico*, by an officer of Ohio volunteers.

> The inhabitants of the valley of the Rio Grande are chiefly occupied in raising stock. . . . But a pastoral life, generally so propitious to purity of morals and strength of constitution, does not appear to have produced its usually happy effect upon that people . . . vile rancheros; the majority of whom are so vicious and degraded that one can hardly believe that the light of Christianity has ever dawned upon them.[5]

In more recent years it has often been the writer of history textbooks and the author of scholarly works who have lent their prestige to the legend. This is what the most distinguished historian Texas has produced had to say about the Mexican in 1935.

> Without disparagement, it may be said that there is a cruel streak in the Mexican nature, or so the history of Texas would lead one to believe. This cruelty may be a heritage from the Spanish of the Inquisition; it may, and doubtless should, be attributed partly to the Indian blood. . . . The Mexican warrior . . . was, on the whole, inferior to the Comanche and wholly unequal to the Texan. The whine of the leaden slugs stirred in him an irresistible impulse to travel with rather than against the music. He won more victories over the Texans by parley than by force of arms. For making promises—and for breaking them—he had no peer.[6]

Professor Webb does not mean to be disparaging. One wonders what his opinion might have been when he was in a less scholarly mood and not looking at the Mexican from the objective point of view of the historian. In another distinguished work, *The Great Plains*, Dr. Webb develops similar aspects of the legend. The Spanish "failure" on the Great Plains is blamed partly on the Spanish character. More damaging still was miscegenation with the Mexican Indian, "whose blood, when compared with that of the Plains Indian, was as ditch water."[7] On the other hand, American success on the Great Plains was due to the "pure American stock," the "foreign element" having settled elsewhere.[8]

How can one classify the Texas legend—as fact, as folklore, or as still something else? The records of frontier life after 1848 are full of instances of cruelty and inhumanity. But by far the majority of the acts of cruelty are ascribed by American writers themselves to men of their own race. The victims, on the other hand, were very often Mexicans. There is always the implication that it was "defensive cruelty," or that the Mexicans were being punished for their inhumanity to Texans at the Alamo, Mier, and Coliad.

There probably is not an army (not excepting those of the United States) that has not been accused of "atrocities" during wartime. It is remarkable, then, that those atrocities said to have occurred in connection with the Alamo, Goliad, and the Mier expedition are universally attributed not to the Mexican army as a whole but to their commander, Santa Anna. Even more noteworthy is the fact that Santa Anna's orders were protested by his officers, who incurred the dictator's wrath by pleading for the prisoners in their charge. In at least two other cases (not celebrated in Texas history) Santa Anna's officers were successful in their pleading, and Texan lives were spared. Both Texan and Mexican accounts agree that the executions evoked horror among many Mexicans witnessing them—officers, civilians, and common soldiers.[9]

Had Santa Anna lived in the twentieth century, he would have called the atrocities with which he is charged "war crimes trials." There is a fundamental difference, though, between his executions of Texan prisoners and the hangings of Japanese army officers like General Yamashita at the end of the Pacific War. Santa Anna usually was in a rage when he ordered his victims shot. The Japanese were never hanged without the ceremony of a trial—a refinement, one must conclude, belonging to a more civilized age and a more enlightened people.

Meanwhile, Texas-Mexicans died at the Alamo and fought at San Jacinto on the Texan side. The Rio Grande people, because of their Federalist and autonomist views, were sympathetic to the Texas republic until Texans began to invade their properties south of the Nueces. The truth seems to be that the old war propaganda concerning the Alamo, Goliad, and Mier later provided a convenient justification for outrages committed on the Border by Texans of certain types, so convenient an excuse that it was artificially prolonged for almost a century. And had the Alamo, Goliad, and Mier not existed, they would have been invented, as indeed they seem to have been in part.

The Texan had an undeniable superiority over the Mexican in the matter of weapons. The Texan was armed with the rifle and the revolver. The ranchero fought with the implements of his cowherding trade, the rope and the knife, counting himself lucky if he owned a rusty old musket and a charge of powder. Lead was scarce, old pieces of iron being used for bullets. Possession of even a weapon of this kind was illegal after 1835, when Santa Anna disarmed the militia, leaving the frontier at the mercy of Indians and Texans. Against them the ranchero had to depend on surprise and superior horsemanship. Until the Mexican acquired the revolver and learned how to use it, a revolver-armed Texan could indeed be worth a half-dozen Mexicans; but one may wonder whether cowards will fight under such handicaps as did the Borderers. The Rio Grande people not only defended themselves with inadequate armament; they often made incursions into hostile territory armed with lances, knives, and old swords.[10]

The belief in the Mexican's treachery was related to that of his cowardice. As with the Mexican's supposed cruelty, one finds the belief perpetuated as a justification for outrage. Long after Mexicans acquired the revolver, "peace officers" in the Nueces-Rio Grande territory continued to believe (or pretended to do so) that no Mexican unaided could best a Texan in a fair fight. The killing of innocent Mexicans as "accomplices" became standard procedure—especially with the Texas Rangers—whenever a Border Mexican shot an American. The practice had an important influence on Border balladry and on the lives of men such as Gregorio Cortez.

The picture of the Mexican as an inveterate thief, especially of horses and cattle, is of interest to the psychologist as well as to the folklorist. The cattle industry of the Southwest had its origin in the Nueces—Rio Grande area, with the stock and the ranches of the Rio Grande rancheros. The "cattle barons" built up their fortunes at the expense of the Border Mexican by means which were far from ethical. One notes that the white Southerner took his slave women as concubines and then created an image of the male Negro as a sex fiend. In the same way he appears to have taken the Mexican's property and then made him out a thief.

The story that the Mexican thought of the Texan as a being apart and distinguished him from other Americans belongs with the post cards depicting the United States as an appendage of Texas. To the Border Mexican at least, Texans are indistinguishable from other Americans, and *tejano* is used for the Texas-Mexican, except perhaps among the more sophisticated. The story that the Mexican believes he could lick the United States if it were not for Texas also must be classed as pure fiction. The Border Mexican does distinguish the Ranger from other Americans, but his belief is that if it were not for the

United States Army he would have run the Rangers out of the country a long time ago.

Theories of racial purity have fallen somewhat into disrepute since the end of World War II. So has the romantic idea that Li Po and Einstein were inferior to Genghis Khan and Hitler because the latter two were bloodier and therefore manlier. There is interest from a folkloristic point of view, however, in the glorification of the Plains savage at the expense of the semicivilized, sedentary Indian of Mexico. The noble savage very early crept into American folklore in the form of tales and songs about eloquent Indian chiefs and beautiful Indian princesses. Such stories appear to have had their origin in areas where Indians had completely disappeared.[11] On the frontier the legend seems to have been dichotomized. After the 1870's, when the Indian danger was past, it was possible to idealize the Plains savage. But the "Mexican problem" remained. A distinction was drawn between the noble Plains Indian and the degenerate ancestor of the Mexican.

The legend has taken a firm grip on the American imagination. In the Southwest one finds Americans of Mexican descent attempting to hide their Indian blood by calling themselves Spanish, while Americans of other origins often boast of having Comanche, Cherokee, or other wild Indian blood, all royal of course. The belief also had its practical aspects in reaffirming Mexican racial inferiority. The Comanche did not consider Mexican blood inferior. Mexican captives were often adopted into the tribe, as were captives of other races. But the Comanche had never read the Bible or John Locke. He could rob, kill, or enslave without feeling the need of racial prejudices to justify his actions.

Even a cursory analysis shows the justification value of the Texas legend and gives us a clue to one of the reasons for its survival. Goldfinch puts most Americans coming into the Brownsville-Matamoros area after the Mexican War into two categories: those who had no personal feeling against the Mexicans but who were ruthless in their efforts to acquire a fortune quickly, and those who, inclined to be brutal to everyone, found in the Mexican's defenseless state after the war an easy and safe outlet for their brutality.[12] It was to the interest of these two types that the legend about the Mexican be perpetuated. As long as the majority of the population accepted it as fact, men of this kind could rob, cheat, or kill the Border Mexican without suffering sanctions either from the law or from public opinion. And if the Mexican retaliated, the law stepped in to defend or to avenge his persecutors.

In 1838 Texas "cowboys" were making expeditions down to the Rio Grande to help the Rio Grande people fight Santa Anna. In between alliances they stole their allies' cattle. McArthur states that their stealing was "condemned by some" but that it was "justified by the majority on the ground that the Mexicans belonged to a hostile nation, from whom the Texans had received and were still receiving many injuries; and that they would treat the Texans worse if it were in their power to do so."[13] In the 1850's and 1860's when the filibuster William Walker—a Tennessean—operated in Central America, he did so to the cry of "Remember the Aiamo!"[14] Al Capone in the 1920's, sending his men off to take care of some German shopkeeper who had failed to kick in, might just as well have cried, "Remember Caporetto, boys! Remember the Piave!" But perhaps Scarface Al lacked a sense of history.

This does not explain why the legend finds support among the literate and the educated. The explanation may lie in the paucity of Texas literature until very recent times. Other peoples have been stirred up by skillfully written war propaganda, but after the war they have usually turned to other reading, if they have a rich literature from which to draw. J. Frank Dobie has said that if he "were asked what theme of Texas life has been most movingly and dramatically recorded . . . I should name the experiences of Texans as prisoners to the Mexicans,"[15] If it is true that the best writing done about Texas until recent times was ancient war propaganda directed against the Mexicans, it is not strange that the prejudices of those early days should have been preserved among the literate. The relative lack of perspective and of maturity of mind that Mr. Dobie himself deplored as late as 1952 in writers about the Southwest also played its part.[16]

Is the Texas legend folklore? The elements of folklore are there. One catches glimpses of the "false Scot" and the "cruel Moor," half-hidden among the local color. Behind the superhuman Ranger are Beowulf, Roland, and the Cid, slaying hundreds.[17] The idea that one's own clan or tribe is unique is probably inherent in certain stages of human development. Sometimes the enemy is forced to recognize the excellence of the hero. Achilles' armor and the Cid's corpse win battles; the Spanish hosts admit the valor of Brave Lord Willoughby, the Englishman; and the Rangers recognize the worth of Jacinto Treviño, the Mexican.

The difference, and a fundamental one, between folklore and the Texas legend is that the latter is not usually found in the oral traditions of those groups of Texas people that one might consider folk. It appears in two widely dissimilar places: in the written works of the literary and the educated and orally among a class of rootless adventurers who have used the legend for very practical purposes. One must classify the Texas legend as pseudo folklore. Disguised as fact, it still plays a major role in Texas history. Under the guise of local pride, it appears in its most blatant forms in the "professional" Texan.

Notes

1. William Curry Holden, *Fray Vicente Santa María: Historical Account of the Colony of Nuevo Santander*, Master's thesis, University of Texas, 1924, p. xi.

2. Cecil Bernard Smith, *Diplomatic Relations between the United States and Mexico*, Master's thesis, University of Texas, 1928, p. 5.

3. *Informe de la Comisión Pesquisidora de la Frontera del Norte*, Mexico, 1877, p. 32.

4. See J. Frank Dobie, *The Flavor of Texas*, Dallas, 1936, pp. 125ff., for some of the aims and the effects of this type of work.

5. [Luther Giddings], *Sketches of the Campaign in Northern Mexico*, New York, 1853, p. 54.

6. Walter Prescott Webb, *The Texas Rangers*, Cambridge, 1935, p. 14.

7. Walter Prescott Webb, *The Great Plains*, Boston, 1931, pp. 125–26.

8. *Ibid.*, p. 509.

9. For a Mexican condemnation of the Alamo and Goliad, see Ramón Martínez Caro, *Verdadera idea de la primera campaña en Tejas*, Mexico, 1837, published one year after the events.

10. J. Frank Dobie in *The Mustangs*, New York, 1954, pp. 195 and 261, makes some interesting observations about the Mexican armament of the time.

11. See Austin E. Fife and Francesca Redden, "The Pseudo-Indian Folksongs of the Anglo-American and French-Canadian," *Journal of American Folklore*, Vol. 67, No. 265, pp. 239–51; No. 266, pp. 379–94.

12. Goldfinch, *Juan N. Cortina*, p. 40.

13. Daniel Evander McArthur, *The Cattle Industry of Texas, 1685–1918*, Master's thesis, University of Texas, 1915, p. 50.

14. Dobie, *The Flavor of Texas*, p. 5.

15. *Ibid.*, p. 125.

16. J. Frank Dobie, *Guide to Life and Literature of the Southwest*, Dallas, 1952, pp. 90–91

17. In epic story, however, the enemy is rarely cowardly. Very often it is one of the hero's own side who is the least admirable character—Thersites among the Greeks, the Counts of Carrión among the Castilians, the weeping coward among the Border raiders.

"Desde México he venido" (From Mexico Have I Come)

Desde México he venido
nomás por venir a ver
esa ley americana
que aquí manda la mujer.

En México no se ha visto,
ni en la frontera del Norte,
que intimiden a los hombres
llevándolos a la corte.

Yo soy un triste pelado,
guiado por mi cruel fortuna,
he venido a conocer
los patos en la laguna.

Y ¡ay, ay! qué bonito es Texas
en tiempo que hay elección,
verás los yanquis de puro
y a los de nuestra nación.

En tiempo que hay elección
son puro *aló* y *jai mai fren*,
¡ay, navaja, no te amelles!
ya viene llegando el tren.

Ya pasada la elección
ya no hay *mai fren* ni hay *aló*,
pongan cuidado, señores,
que ese tiempo se acabó.

From Mexico have I come, just to come and see
this American law that says the woman is boss.

This is never seen in interior Mexico, nor on the northern Border,
that men should be intimidated by taking them to court.

I am just a poor bum, guided by my cruel fortune;
I have come to get acquainted with the ducks in the lagoon.
[I've come to meet the cuckolds in their own surroundings.]

Ay, ay! But Texas is a fine place during election time;
you will see the cigar-smoking Yankees and our own people as well.

During election time they are nothing but "*hello*" and "*hi, my friend.*"
Razor, don't lose your edge! The train is just coming in.
[Flattery, do your stuff! Success is in sight.]

But once elections are past, there's no more "*my friend*" or "*hello*";
better look out, gentlemen, for that time is no more.

Rubén Salazar was born in Cuidad Juárez, Chihuahua, but grew up across the Rio Grande in El Paso. He served in the Army during the Korean War, and attended the University of Texas at El Paso upon his return, studying journalism there and working for the *El Paso Herald Post* while still in college. After graduation he moved to California and worked for the *Los Angeles Times*, eventually becoming bureau chief in Mexico City. In 1968 he began covering the Mexican-American community in Los Angeles, the role which put him at an antiwar demonstration in 1970, where he was shot in the head with a teargas canister and killed by a policeman. Though investigators ruled the death a homicide, no one was brought to trial. Since his death, Salazar has become a symbol of both the mistreatment of Mexican Americans by police and of journalistic bravery and skill.

Rubén Salazar (El Paso)

"La Nacha Sells Dirty Dope . . ."

La Nacha Sells Dirty Dope at $5 a "Papel"
Herald-Post Reporter Makes Purchase from Border "Queen"

August 17, 1955

EL PASO, Texas—La Nacha is the Dope Queen of the Border. She is big stuff. But she will sell you one "papel" (paper) of heroin just like any "pusher" on a street corner.

If you aren't too far gone, the dirty-looking stuff in the folded paper is good for two shots. But that's true only for those who are beginning.

A dope addict, whom I will call "Hypo," buys the $10 size. It has more than the two of the $5 papers, Hypo said. One lasts him a day—most days.

He Met the Queen

La Nacha—right name Ignacia Jasso—lives in a good house in a bad neighborhood. She's fat, dark, cynical and around 60. She deals out misery from her comfortable home.

She sells usually what is called a "dirty load," which is one that is not white as heroin should be, but a dirty, dusty color.

Her prices are in American money. She does business with many American addicts. She's as casual about it as if she were selling tortillas.

Hypo took me to La Nacha's home and introduced me to the dope queen.

I visited her twice. The first time Hypo and I bought a $5 paper of heroin. The second time we bought the large economy $10 size.

The papers contained dope all right. I saw Hypo, an El Paso married man of 24 whose 19-year-old wife has a three-month-old baby, inject himself with the "carga" (load).

He's Got to Have It

Hypo, who says he wants to be cured, cannot live without heroin. It costs him about $10 a day—or hours of excruciating pain. Hypo prefers heroin to pain and gets the $10 a day any way he can. He sold all his furniture for heroin. He was evicted from his apartment for not paying rent. He has stolen, borrowed and now has given me his story for $15 which he spent on heroin.

Hypo and I went to visit La Nacha in the afternoon. We parked the car a few blocks from her house. She lives in Bellavista district, which means "Beautiful View." It is far from beautiful. The streets are unpaved and most of the houses are adobe. Naked kids were running about the streets.

We turned on Mercuro alley and walked toward La Nacha's house, which is on the corner of the alley and Violetas (Violets) street. Hers is the only decent-looking house in the neighborhood. It is yellow and has fancy iron grillwork on the windows.

She Has a TV Set

Hypo and I walked through the nicely kept green patio.

Inside, the house has all the conveniences of a modern home: gas, stove, nice living room furniture, TV and a saint's statue on the wall.

I had been to Hypo's El Paso apartment and couldn't help thinking about his bare rooms after he had sold the furniture for heroin. The last time I had been at Hypo's apartment, I had seen the baby on the floor on a blanket and Hypo's wife sitting in a cornet watching the baby. There was a sad, vacant look in her eyes.

Once inside the house, which Hypo knows so well that he doesn't even bother to knock, we met Nacha's daughter. She was sitting on a bed talking to another woman. Hypo told her he was going away and wanted to introduce me so I could buy the stuff myself.

"You'll have to ask Mother," Nacha's daughter said.

Then I was introduced to Nacha's son. He is heavyset, wears a mustache and had on an expensive watch.

I noticed a stool nearby which had white strips of paper neatly arranged on top.

She Looked Him Over

Then La Nacha came in. I remembered Hypo's advice that I should be polite to her. She gave me the once-over, I was introduced. She sat in front of the stool and started working the strips. They were the heroin papers.

Hypo told La Nacha that I was a musician working in a dance hall in El Paso and wanted to start buying "loads."

La Nacha glanced at my arms. Hypo explained that I wasn't a "mainliner." That I just liked to "jornear"—breathe the heroin. A "mainliner" is one who injects himself with a hypodermic needle.

La Nacha said, "All right, any time."

"At night we sell it across the street," La Nacha's daughter said,

Hypo asked La Nacha for "a nickel's worth." She handed me a paper of heroin. (She wanted to know if I would handle the stuff, Hypo told me later.) Hypo gave her $5 and we left.

Quicker and Better

After we bought the load we went to a cheap hotel in Juarez. There I saw Hypo, who is a "mainliner," inject himself with heroin.

"You feel better quicker that way," Hypo said.

"Mainliners" need a cup of water, a syringe with a needle, an eye dropper, a bottle cap and the expensive heroin to make them feel, in Hypo's word, "normal."

"A man who is hooked (that is, one who has the habit bad) never feels normal unless he's had at least two shots a day," Hypo said.

I watched Hypo go through the process of injecting himself with heroin. First he carefully placed half a paper of heroin in the bottle cap with a knife. Then with an eye dropper he placed a few drops of water in the cap. He took a match and placed it underneath the cap while holding it with the other hand. After it was heated Hypo dropped a tiny ball of cotton in the cap. "This is so the hypodermic can suck all the heroin out the cap," Hypo explained. The cotton works like a filter.

Wild Eyes Gleam

Hypo then placed the hypodermic syringe in the cap and the brownish substance could be seen running up into the syringe.

Hypo's wild eyes gleamed with excitement.

Hypo crouched on the floor balanced on the front of his shoes. He injected the heroin in his vein. His vein was swollen from so many punctures.

Almost as soon as the heroin had gone into his vein he started rocking back and forth. I asked him how he felt.

"Muy suave, ese," he said. "Real good."

Before long he passed out. His stomach sounded like a washing machine. He snored loudly and uncomfortably. I tried to wake him. I couldn't. So I went home.

Took an Overdose

Later he explained that he had taken an overdose.

"The load was real clean and I misjudged the amount I should have taken," Hypo said. "I could have died."

The second time I saw Hypo we must have bought a load not as clean or he judged the right amount. For the reaction was much different. Before he injected himself he looked worse than I had ever seen him. His eyes looked like two huge buttons. He complained of pains all over his body. Hypo couldn't even hold a cigarette because of his shaking hands.

We went to La Nacha's and bought some heroin. We only stayed a minute. Hypo needed to be "cured" quick.

After he injected himself this time he actually looked better than before, talked better and acted better. He was only half dead—instead of three quarters.

He stopped shaking. He smoked almost calmly and was talkative. "I've got to quit this habit," he said. "For my little daughter's sake. I love her very much. God, I wish I could stop it."

I, too, hope he can.

Freddy Fender (San Benito)

"Before the Next Teardrop Falls"

If he brings you happiness,
Then I wish you all the best.
It's your happiness that matters
Most of all.

But if he ever breaks your heart,
If the teardrops ever start,
I'll be there
Before the next teardrop falls.

Si te quiere de verdad,
Y te da felicidad,
Te deseo lo mas bueno pa' los dos.
Pero si te hace llorar,
A mí me puedes hablar.
Y estaré contigo cuando triste estas.

I'll be there
Anytime you need me
By your side
To dry away
Any teardrops that you cry.

And if he ever leaves you blue,
Just remember—I love you.
And I'll be there
Before the next teardrop falls.

I'll be there
Before the next teardrop falls.

Born Baldemar Huerta in San Benito, Freddy Fender became known as the "Mexican Elvis" for being the first to combine Tejano music with the sound of rock and roll.

Flaco Jiménez (San Antonio)

"Mi Borrachera" (My Drunkenness)

Me emborracho porque traigo un sentimiento
Porque traigo muchas ganas de tomar
Me emborracho porque así es como me siento
Mas dichoso sin afanes ni pesar.

Desde luego que perdí mi prenda amada
Hay derecho no hay derecho de tomar
Para mí que es necesaria la tomada
Con pretexto o sin pretexto me da igual.

Yo soy libre como el ave como el viento
Yo no debo mas que a Dios este existir.
Me emborracho porque traigo un sentimiento
Vaciladas que son parte del vivir.

El rasgueo de una lira maltratada
Lo que alegra la cantina donde voy
Ya mi mente de recuerdos va borrada
Para hacerme lo borracho que yo soy.

Sí señores ésta es mi borrachera
Como todas por la causa de un querer
Ya sean buenas resbalosas o embusteras
Por una hembra estoy dispuesto a padecer.

I get drunk because I have a feeling
Because I have a great desire to drink
I get drunk because that's the way I feel
More joyful without worries or sorrow.

Of course I lost the one I love
There is a right, there is no right to drink
To me I think drinking is necessary
with a reason or without one to me it's the same.

I'm free like the bird or the wind
I don't owe anything except my existence to God.
I get drunk because I have a feeling
Another foolishness which is part of life.

The strumming of a beat up lira
That's what brings joy to the bar where I go
My mind is already erased of all memories
That makes me the drunk that I am.

Yes sirs, this is my drunkenness
Like all, because of a love
Be they good, slutty or liars
For a female I'm willing to suffer.

FLACO JIMÉNEZ is one of the foremost *conjunto* musicians of his generation, achieving a great level of popularity by combining the *conjunto* sound with other popular forms of music, he is successful outside of Texas, playing to audiences as far away as Europe.

"El crudo" (The Man with the Hangover)

Al pie de un verde nopal
yo me acosté,
at ruido de unas guitarras
yo me dormí,
al grito de unos borrachos
yo desperté,
¡qué crudo estoy!
quiero curame y no hay con qué.

Pero ¡ay, Dios mío!
quítame esta cruda,
porque esta cruda
me va a matar.
La Virgen de Guadalupe me ha de salvar,
¡qué crudo estoy!
la cantinera no quiere fiar.

I lay down at the foot of a green cactus;
I fell asleep to the sound of some guitars;
I woke up to the yelling of some drunks.
What a hangover!
I'd like to cure it, but I lack the wherewithal.

But, oh my Lord! Take this hangover away,
for this hangover is going to kill me.
The Virgin of Guadalupe will surely save me.
What a hangover!
The barmaid will not trust me [for the price of a drink].

part six

the 1960s

Daniel Garza (Hillsboro)

"Saturday Belongs to the Palomía"

Every year, in the month of September, the cotton pickers come up from the Valley, and the braceros come from Mexico itself. They come to the town in Texas where I live, all of them, the whole *palomía*. "Palomía" is what we say: it is slang among my people, and I do not know how to translate it exactly. It means . . . the cotton pickers when they come. You call the whole bunch of them the *palomía*, but one by one they are cotton pickers, *pizcadores*.

Not many of them have traveled so far north before, and for the ones who have not it is a great experience. And it is an opportunity to know other kinds of people, for the young ones. For the older ones it is only a chance to make some money picking cotton. Some years the cotton around my town is not so good, and then the *pizcadores* have to go farther north, and we see them less.

But when they come, they come in full force to my little town that is full of gringos. Only a few of us live there who speak Spanish among ourselves, and whose parents maybe came up like the *pizcadores* a long time ago. It is not like the border country where there are many of both kinds of people; it is gringo country mostly, and most of the time we and the gringos live there together without worrying much about such matters.

In September and October in my town, Saturdays belong to the *pizcadores*. During the week they are in the fields moving up and down the long cotton rows with big sacks and sweating frightfully, but making

Born close to Hillsboro, Daniel Garza studied at Texas Christian University and served as an officer in the U.S. Army. Under the tutelage of Texas writer John Graves, in 1962 his story "Saturday Belongs to Palomía" was published in *Harper's* where it also received its Southwest Literature Award. No book by him was ever published.

centavitos to spend on Saturday at the movie, or on clothes, or on food. The gringos come to town during the week to buy their merchandise and groceries, but finally Saturday arrives, and the *pizcadores* climb aboard their trucks on the cotton farms, and the trucks all come to town. It is the day of the *palomía*, and most of the gringos stay home.

"*Ay, qué gringos*!" the *pizcadores* say. "What a people to hide themselves like that. But such is life . . ."

For Saturday the *pizcadores* dress themselves in a special and classy style. The girls comb their black hair, put on new bright dresses and low-heeled shoes, and the color they wear on their lips is, the way we say it, enough. The boys dress up in black pants and shoes with taps on the heels and toes. They open their shirts two or three buttons to show their chests and their Saint Christophers; then at the last they put a great deal of grease on their long hair and comb it with care. The old men, the *viejos*, shave and put on clean plain clothes, and the old women put on a tunic and comb their hair and make sure the little ones are clean, and all of them come to town.

They come early, and they arrive with a frightful hunger. The town, being small, has only a few restaurants. The *pizcadores*—the young ones and the ones who have not been up from Mexico before—go into one of the restaurants, and the owner looks at them.

One who speaks a little English says they want some *desayuno*, some breakfast.

He looks at them still. He says: "Sorry. We don't serve Meskins."

Maybe then one of the *pachuco* types with the long hair and the Saint Christopher says something ugly to him in Spanish, maybe not. Anyhow, the others do not, but leave sadly, and outside the old men who did not go in nod among themselves, because they knew already. Then maybe, standing on the sidewalk, they see a gringo go into the restaurant. He needs a shave and is dirty and smells of sweat, and before the door closes they hear the owner say: "What say, Blacky? What'll it be this morning?"

The little ones who have understood nothing begin to holler about the way their stomachs feel, and the *papás* go to the market to buy some food there.

I am in the grocery store, me and a few gringos and many of the *palomía*. I have come to buy flour for my mother. I pass a *pizcador*, a father who is busy keeping his little ones from knocking cans down out of the big piles, and he smiles to me and says: "*¿Qué tal, amigo*?"

"*Pues, así no más*," I answer.

He looks at me again. He asks in a quick voice, "You are a Chicano?"

"*Sí.*"

"How is it that you have missed the sun in your face, *muchacho*?" he says. "A big hat, maybe?"

"No, señor," I answer. "I live here."

"You have luck."

And I think to myself, yes, I have luck; it is good to live in one place. And all of a sudden the *pizcador* and I have less to say to each other, and he says adiós and gathers up his flow of little ones and goes out to the square where the boys and girls of the *palomía* are walking together.

On the square too there is usually a little lady selling hot tamales. She is dressed simply, and her white hair is in a bun, and she has a table with a big can of tamales on it which the *palomía* buy while they are still hot from the stove at the little lady's home.

"*Mamacita, mamacita*," the little ones shout at their mothers. "Doña Petra is here. Will you buy me some tamalitos?"

Doña Petra lives there in the town, and the mothers in the palomía are her friends because of her delicious tamales and because they go to her house to talk of the cotton picking, of children, and maybe of the fact that in the north of Texas it takes somebody like Doña Petra to find good *masa* for tamales and tortillas. Away from home as the *pizcadores* are, it is good to find persons of the race in a gringo town.

On the street walk three *pachucos*, seventeen or eighteen years old. They talk *pachuco* talk. One says: "Listen, *chabos*, let's go to the good movie."

"O.K.," another one answers. "Let's go flutter the good eyelids."

They go inside a movie house. Inside, on a Saturday, there are no gringos, only the *palomía*. The *pachucos* find three girls, and sit down with them. The movie is in English, and they do not understand much of it, but they laugh with the girls and make the *viegos* angry, and anyhow the cartoon—the mono, they call it—is funny by itself, without the need for English.

Other *pachucos* walk in gangs through the streets of the town, looking for something to do. One of them looks into the window of Mr. Jones' barber shop and tells the others that he thinks he will get a haircut. They laugh, because haircuts are something that *pachucos* do not get, but one of them dares him. "It will be like the restaurant," he says. "Gringo scissors do not cut Chicano hair."

So he has to go in, and Mr. Jones looks at him as the restaurant man looked at the others in the morning. But he is a nicer man, and what he says is that he has to go to lunch when he has finished with the customers who are waiting. "There is a Mexican barber across the square," he says. "On Walnut Street. You go there."

The *pachuco* tells him a very ugly thing to do and then combs his long hair in the mirror and then goes outside again, and on the sidewalk he and his friends say bad things about Mr. Jones for a while until they get tired of it, and move on. The gringo customers in the barber shop rattle the magazines they are holding in their laps, and one of them says a thing about cotton pickers, and later in the day it is something that the town talks about, gringos and *pizcadores* and those of my people who live there, all of them. I hear about it, but forget, because September in my town is full of such things, and in the afternoon I go to the barber shop for a haircut the way I do on Saturdays all year long.

Mr. Jones is embarrassed when he sees me. "You hear about that?" he says. "That kid this morning?"

I remember then, and I say yes, I heard.

"I'm sorry, Johnny," he says. "Doggone it. You know I'm not . . ."

"I know," I say.

"The trouble is, if they start coming, they start bringing the whole damn family, and then your regular customers get mad," he says.

"I know," I say, and I do. There is no use in saying that I don't, because I live in the town for the other ten or eleven months of the year when the *palomía* is not here but in Mexico and the Valley. I know the gringos of the town and what they are like, and they are many different ways. So I tell Mr. Jones that I know what he means.

"Get in the chair," he says. "You want it short or medium this time?"

And I think about the *pizcador* in the grocery store and what he said about my having luck, and I think again it is good to live in one place and not to have to travel in trucks to where the cotton is.

At about six in the afternoon all the families begin to congregate at what they call the *campo*. *Campo* means camp or country, but this *campo* is an area with a big tin shed that the State Unemployment Commission puts up where the farmers who have cotton to be picked can come and find the *pizcadores* who have not yet found a place to work. But on Saturday nights in September the *campo* does not have anything to do with work. The families come, bringing tacos to eat and maybe a little beer if they have it. After it is dark, two or three of the men bring out guitars, and some others have concertinas. They play the fast, twisty *mariachi* music of the places they come from, and someone always sings. The songs are about women and love and sometimes about a town that the song says is a fine town, even if there is no work there for *pizcadores*. All the young people begin to dance, and the old people sit around making certain that the *pachucos* do not get off into the dark with their daughters. They talk, and they eat, and they drink a little beer, and then at twelve o'clock it is all over.

The end of Saturday has come. The old men gather up their sons and daughters, and the mothers carry the sleeping little ones like small sacks of cotton to the trucks, and the whole *palomía* returns to the country to work for another week, and to earn more *centavitos* with which, the Saturday that comes after the week, to go to the movies, and buy groceries, and pay for tamalitos of Doña Petra and maybe a little beer for the dance at the *campo*. And the mothers will visit with Doña Petra, and the *pachucos* will walk the streets, and the other things will happen, all through September and October, each Saturday the same, until finally, early in November, the cotton harvest is over, and the *pizcadores* go back to their homes in the Valley or in Mexico.

The streets of my town are empty then, on Saturdays. It does not have many people, most of the year. On Saturday mornings you see a few gringo children waiting for the movie to open, and not much else. The streets are empty, and the gringos sit in the restaurant and the barber shop and talk about the money they made or lost on the cotton crop that fall.

John Francisco Rechy was born in El Paso and attended college there, at what was then called Texas Western University. After serving in the Army, he went on to New York. His first novel *City of Night* grew out of his experiences there, including time spent as a male prostitute, and also contained descriptions of his experiences in California and his hometown of El Paso. *City of Night* was an international bestseller and earned Rechy his reputation as both an important writer and sexual outlaw. He was the recipient of the first PEN-USA West's Lifetime Achievement Award in 1997, and now teaches at the University of Southern California.

John Rechy (El Paso)

"El Paso del Norte"

This is about El Paso (and Juarez: the Southwest), which so long was just a hometown to me and which now is different from any other section in America.

El Paso and Juarez are in the middle of the Texas, New Mexico, and Mexico white, white desert surrounded by that range of mountains jutting unevenly along the border. At sundown the fat sun squats on the horizon like a Mexican lady grandly on her front porch. Appropriately.

Because only geographically the Rio Grande, which in the Southwest is a river only part of the time and usually just a strait of sand along the banks of which sick spiders weave their webs, divides the United States from Mexico. Only geographically. The Mexican people of El Paso, more than half the population—and practically all of Smeltertown, Canutillo, Ysleta—are all and always and completely Mexican, and will be. They speak only Spanish to each other and when they say the Capital they mean Mexico DF.

Oh, but, once it was not so. When the War came, Christ, the Mexicans were American as hell. The young men went to war wearing everything that was authorized, sometimes even more. Huge stars appeared on the southside tenement and government-project windows. OUR SON IS SERVING AMERICA. My mother wore my brother's Purple Heart to Mass and held it up when the Priest gave his blessing.

Outside El Paso City, giant machines dig into the mountains for ores (Smeltertown), and beyond that (where I used to climb poetic as hell) is a tall beautiful mountain.

The Mountain of Cristo Rey.

Huge processions go up this holy mountain. The people of El Paso, Ysleta, Canutillo, of Smeltertown and of Juarez march up climbing for hours, chanting prayers. The procession starts downtown in El Paso, outside the churches, and the groups join each other in the streets, kneeling at intervals on inspiration, carrying placards of the Virgin, Saints in colors. Small bands jazz solemnly, crying dissonant sounds. The shawled ladies of the Order of Saint Something grip rosaries and mumble and feel—as rightly so as anyone in the world—Holy. The priests in bright drag lead them up. They carry sadfaced saints. The small bands stay behind at the foot of the mountain, the musicians wiping the sweat off their dark faces, and drinking cool limonada and mingling with the sellers of coca-cola, religious medals. The procession winds up the mountain slowly past the crude weatherbeaten stations of the cross along the path. And at the top, finally—where they say Mass, the people kneeling on the rocks in the blazing white sun—is The Statue.

It is a primitive Christ.

Fifty-feet tall. And it looks like a Mexican peasant. Mr. Soler made it. I think he was a kind of semi-atheist who didnt believe in God but believed in the Virgin Mary.

But the poor Mexican Christ, what it has to look down on—the line of desperate ants, as the Magazine (I think it was *Time*, or if it wasnt they would have) called it, of mustached, strawhatted men, braceros invading America.

Because the Rio Grande, no matter what you think, is usually dry, as I said, just sand and scrawny spiders and fingery indentations where water should be or was. Sometimes it is very full, though, and beautiful, and then the Rio Grande is like a dirty young black animal full of life rushing along the sand, swallowing the bushy dry banks. And I would walk along its bank, to the mountains. But usually it is so dry that the wetbacks can enter Sacred Country by merely walking across the River.

On their way to Georgia?

Well, I've heard that from I dont know how many people. They say, for some strange reason, that Georgia is a kind of heaven where all good spiks go—some crossing into the country illegally, others standing at the Santa Fe Bridge lined up all rags and cloth bags and wooden and cardboard boxes and holy amulets, whiskers, waiting to be inspected by the Customs-gods. The Magazine also said, well, wasn't it natural, those wetbacks wanting to come into America?—Christ, they heard about sweet-tasting toothpaste. It really said that. And if sweet-tasting American toothpaste aint enough to make a man face the Border Patrol (as Bad as L.A. fuzz) and the excellent labor conditions in progressive Georgia, well, man, what is? The Magazine said it was sad, all those displaced wetbacks, but all that happened though was that they were sent back, but they tried to come across again and again and again.

(I remember a dead bracero near the bank of the Rio Grande, face down drowned in the shallow water, the water around him red, red, red. Officially he had drowned and was found, of course, by the Border Patrol. And his wife will go on thinking forever he made it with a beautiful blonde Georgia woman—loaded with toothpaste—and so, therefore, never came back to her and the even-dozen kids.)

Which brings me to this—

The hatred in much of Texas for Mexicans. It's fierce. (They used to yell, Mexicangreaser, Mexicangreaser, when I went to Lamar Grammar School, and I thought, well, yes, my mother did do an awful lot of frying but we never put any grease on our hair, and so it bothered me—if God was Mexican, as my mother said, why did He allow this?) Many of them really hate us pathologically, like they hate the Negroes, say, in Arkansas. Here, it's the bragging, blustering bony-framed Texan rangers/farmers/ranchers with the Cadillacs and the attitude of Me-and-god on My ranch. It has nothing to do with the Alamo any more. It's just the full-scale really huge (consistent with everything Big in Texas—and Alaska wont change anything) Texan inferiority complex. Dig: the Texas rancher strutting across San Jacinto Plaza, all bones and legs, getting kicks from sitting, later, booted-feet propped getting a shine from the barefoot spik kid, tipping him 50 cents—not just sitting like you and I would get a shine but sitting Grandly, and strutting across the Border owning the streets, I hope he gets rolled. They dont really dislike Mexicans in Texas if theyre maids and laborers.

So the Mexicans live concentrated on the Southside of El Paso largely, crowded into tenements, with the walls outside plastered with old Vote-for signs from years back and advertisements of Mexican movies at the Colon—the torn clothes just laundered waving on rickety balconies along Paisano Drive held up God knows how. Or if not, in the Government projects, which are clean tenements—a section for the Mexicans, a section for the Negroes. Politely. Row after row of identical box houses speckled with dozens and dozens of children.

So this, the Southside, is of course the area of the Mean gangs. The ones on the other side are not as dangerous, of course, because they are mostly Blond and mostly normal Anglo-American kiddies growing up naturally and what can you expect? Like the ones from Kern Place—all pretty clean houses at the foot of Mount Franklin—and if those kiddies carry switchblade knives, at least they keep them clean, and when they wear boots, they are Cowboy Boots.

The southside gangs—that's a different thing. Theyre black-haired. And tense. Mean and bad, with Conflict seething. El Paso's southside (the Second Ward) gave birth to the internationally famous Pachucos. (Paso—Pacho.) They used to call them boogies, marijuanos, the zoot-suits—and the baggy pants with the pegged ankles were boogiepants, and, man, those tigers walked cool, long graceful bad strides, rhythmic as hell, hands deep into pockets, shoulders hunched. Much heart. They really did wear and still sometimes do those hats that Al Capp draws—and the chains, too, from the belt to the pocket in a long loop.

And sitting talking Mexican jive, *mano*, under the El Paso streetlamps along Hill and Magoffin and Seventh, around Bowie High School and next to the Palace Theater digging Presley and Chuck Berry and Fats Domino, outside the dingy 40-watt-bulb-lighted Southside grocery stores, avoiding *la jura*, the neo-Pachucos with dreamy junk eyes and their chicks in tight skirts and giant pompadours and revealing 1940-style sweaters hang in the steamy El Paso nights, hunched, mean and bad, plotting protest, unconscious of, though they carry it, the burden of the world, and additionally, the burden of Big Texas.

Well, look. In East Texas. In Balmorhea, say. In Balmorhea, with its giant outdoor swimming pool (where that summer the two blond tigers and I went swimming, climbed over the wall and into the rancid-looking night water) there were signs in the two-bit restaurant, in Balmorhea-town then, that said WE DO NOT SERVE MEXICANS, NIGGERS OR DOGS. That night we went to the hick movie, and the man taking the tickets said, You boys be sure and sit on the right side, the left is for spiks. So I said I was on the wrong side and walked out. Later at Kit's aunt's ranch, the aunt waited until the Mexican servant walked out and then said, miserabıy, Ah jaist caint even eat when they are around. And because earlier had made me feel suddenly a Crusader and it was easy now, I walked out of the diningroom and said well then I shouldnt be here to louse up your dinner, lady.

And you never know it—to look at that magnificent Texas sky.

And something quite something else . . .

Once upon a time in El Paso there was a band of fairies—yes, really, in El Paso, Texas—and this city became a crossroads between the hot Eastcoast and the cool Westcoast (fuzz-wise, vice-wise) or the hot Westcoast and the cool Eastcoast, depending on where oh where the birls had got Caught Jay-Walking. And soon San Jacinto Plaza, (or Alligator Plaza—sleepy crocodiles in a round pond, so tired and sleepy they dont even wake up when little kids grab them by their tails and flip them into the water) was a fairy paradise, rebel. The birls would camp there in that little park—the queens with pinched-in waists, lisps, painted eyes, digging the soldiers from Fort Bliss, proclaiming Too Much. Alas, they went the way of all fairies. The Inevitable Clean-Up came, and the fuzz swooped on them jealously and to jail they went, all fluttering eyelashes justifying gay mother love.

Now it is not the same passing through the park not seeing the queens, not hearing their delighted squeals of approbation floating into the clean summer Texas air. Not the same at all.

At Christmas is when Mexican El Paso is magnificent. I dont mean the jazz at San Jacinto Plaza (trees and lights and Christmas carols and Santa Claus). I mean the Southside Christmas. A lot of them—most of them, in fact—put up trees, of course, but many of them put up nacimientos. My father used to start putting ours up almost a month before Christmas when we lived on Wyoming Street. It's a large boxlike thing—ours was, anyway—about six-feet wide, six-feet tall, eight-feet deep, like a room minus the front wall (the minus faces the windows, which are cleaned to sparkle), and inside is a Christmas scene. Ours had the manger and the Virgin of course and St Joseph, and angels hanging from strings floating on angelhair clouds. To the sides of the manger were modern-looking California miniature houses, with real lights in them—some had swimming pools. And stone mountains. On one was the Devil, red, with a wired neck so that the slightest movement made it twitch, drinking out of a bottle. Christ was coming, and naturally the Devil would be feeling low. My father painted an elaborate Texas-like sky behind the manger, with clouds, giant moon, the works—lights all over, and he enclosed the boxlike nacimiento with Christmas-tree branches, and then, one year, he had a real lake—that is, real water which we changed daily. The wisemen on their way. Christmas lights, bulbs, on top. He moved the wise men each night, closer to the manger. The Christchild wasnt there yet—He wasnt born. Then on Christmas Eve everyone came over. My mother led the rosary. We all knelt. Someone had been chosen to be the padrino—the godfather—of the Christchild to be born that night. He carried the Child in his hands, everyone kissed it ("adored" it), and then finally He was put into the manger, in the hay. We prayed some more. *Dios te salve, Maria, llena eres de Gracia.* . . . At the stroke of midnight, the Child was born. Then there was a party—tamales, buñuelos, liquor.

Most Mexicans are Catholic, of course. My friend Sherman is an intelligent Catholic from Evanston and he said it was bad when Catholics substitute, like the Mexican people he loves so much (Sherman in Chihuahua City that time trying so hard to look like a Mexican peasant, with Indian sandals and muslin shirt—him, six-feet-two and Scandinavian curly blond!—and people staring at him thinking he came probably from the American moon), the image of the Virgin for that of Christ. He loves the Virgin himself, a lot, but still he says Christianity should mean Christ. (He says he would rather see the Mexicans worship the Sun, incidentally, like their Indian ancestors, than become protestants, because for a while the Baptists especially had a full-scale campaign going, and pretty soon, on the doors of the broken-down southside houses they tried to invade with irresistible chocolate American candy and bright colors for the shoeless children living in cardboard houses along the Border appeared signs THIS IS A CHRISTIAN HOME PROTESTANT PROPAGANDA WILL NOT BE ALLOWED.)

But that's not what I started to say, which was this—

The Patron of Mexico is the Virgin of Guadalupe. The story says She appeared to Juan Diego, one day, and in order to make the incredulous know that he had indeed seen Her, She stamped Herself on his shawl, and that is the one you see in Mexican churches, all stars and blue robe. Oh, how tenderly they believe in the Virgin of Guadalupe (even the Priests!), and how they love Her, the Mother of all Mexico.

How they Respect mothers because of it. Mothers are a Grand Mexican thing. They belong sacredly in Mexico and the Mexican Southwest.

Dig: a serious Mexican movie. The favorite theme. The son goes away. The little Old Mexican Mother stands at the dingy door with her black shawl sheltering her from the drizzling rain. Christ. The son goes away, and forgets about her. He becomes a Great Matador, lured by women like Maria Bonita before the President's wife—and this is only gossip—chased her out. Wow! The Little Mother in the Black Shawl wanders over Mexico, working for harsh people—like sewing in a factory where, she's so old, poor thing, she cant keep up with the heftier ladies. She comes at last into a very rich home in Mexico City. Of course. It is her son's home. But he doesnt recognize her, and she decides not to tell him who she is so he wont be ashamed of her. She'll just be satisfied to be near him. He is gruft. "Old woman, look how much dust has accumulated on this my favorite table." "Yes, sir." She wipes it. He is cruel, yells at her despite the pitiful black shawl. She takes it, and this is true. Mexican mothers and wives do take It—not Americans, and this is what grips a Mexican audience. Loyalty. One day the Big Corrida comes on. The wife is digging it on television (she cant bear to go it live). The matador is gored. The shawled Mother screams, MI HIJO!!!! The wife knows now, and being Mexican herself and on the way to becoming a Mexican Mother, she hugs the Old Lady. They run out, get a cab, go to the bullring. There he is. Unconscious. Dying. The beautifully dressed wife pulls the shawl off the little old Mother and proclaims to the dying matador, "Die if God wills it—but not without knowing that—This—Is—Your—Mother!!!!" Everyone is crying, the unnatural son repents (as he must), and all three live happily ever after.

This is real. Mexicans really love Mothers. Americans dont. I dont have a single American acquaintance whose mother faints everytime he comes home and again when he leaves. Mine does. The Mexican mother-love has nothing to do with sex, either. You can imagine an American wanting to make it with his mother. She is slick. She looks almost as young and bad as he does. But can you imagine making it with your mother if she wears a Black Shawl, and, even if she doesnt, if she acts all the time like she is wearing One?

How does it follow, then, that a little Mexican kid (as I will tell you later) can say to an ugly big Texan tourist, HEY MEESTER YOU WANT MY MOTHER SHE IS CHERRY? I'll explain it by describing something else. Someone related to me lived with a woman for 25 years. Suddenly they decided to make it permanent. Get married. After 25 years, remember. Not silently, you believe it. They had a real Mexican bash, with caterers and mariachies, and the bride's 26-year-old daughter (from another engagement) crying all over the place—and the bride dressed in WHITE, and the Priest that married them and had been invited over saying well, God was certainly smiling in pleasure to see His laws being obeyed.

There's a Mexican Saint you make bets with. San Calletano, patron of gamblers . . .

Mexican religion is a very real thing, not lukewarm at all, nor forbidding and awesome. Mexican Catholics (and this, again, includes the Priests) believe in a God with two hands, two feet, eyes—the works. The Devil has horns, a tail, and he is most certainly red. Each church in the Mexican sections of the Southwest, and all of them in Juarez have Real patron saints, who guard them. On their days, they have kermesses—this is like a fair. On the really big days (for example, in May, the month of the Virgin Mary), the Indians (who are Catholics although their religion is still magnificently pagan, having room in it for Mayan, Aztec, other legends—witchcraft—right along with the story of Jesus). come into the City. The matachines (they used to scare me, like the beggars I will tell you about later) are Indians, dressed in all kinds of feathers, painted all over, making dance marathons, dancing for hours. Some Indians—I think the Tarahumaras—run all the way from somewhere like Chihuahua City to Juarez, offering I suppose that amount of exerted energy to the Virgin. In religious frenzy, they burn an effigy of Satan—a kind of man-shaped catherine wheel. They light him up and the bastard burns shooting fire straight from hell. The people yell up a storm, and the Politicians and Gangsters shoot real bullets into the air in this tribute to the Virgin Mary.

Juarez!

Time and time they try to clean it up. But Juarez is Dirty. And will be dirty long after we are gone.

The same close acquaintance I mentioned before is a gangster in Juarez. They really have bigtimers there, like they used to have in Chicago. You can always tell them by the way they wear Western-type gabardine clothes *a-la-mejicana*, and hand-tailored boots (NOT square cowboy-type), and always, always, but ALWAYS, sun-glasses, especially blue ones. My relation in question belongs to a very respected Mexican class—the gamblers, the gangsters, the pimps, the politicians.

At night, Juarez is all lights and neon signs. Clip-joints. Cab-drivers pouncing on tourists. This is your chance to find out If It Is True What They Say About Oriental Girls (i.e., does their Snatch slant?). Find out, they say, from Chinese Movie Stars. Get dirty postcards made to order. Peepshows. Men, women, dogs—sometimes a horse. And the little urchin barefoot Mexican boys saying, HEY MEESTER and they really do say meester YOU WANT MY MOTHER SHE IS CHERRY. Bars and cabarets. Exotic entertainment. The Chinese Palace. The Stork. The 1–2–3. Girls, girls, girls. The thickly painted prostitutes stand in a line openly soliciting at bars—big fat red lips, narrow-waved long hair falling over great big dangling earrings.

At the Taxco they had this magnificent woman who looked like Mopsy of the cartoon. A genius. To wit: She dyed her hair *bright green*. And her costume was a large green powder-puff, same shade, right on her snatch. That started one of the many clean-ups. So she had to get decent. She added two tiny green powderpuffs, the color of her dyed hair, to her nipples. . . .

In the early clear-blue Texas-Mexico mornings, the whores, the pimps, the politicians, the gangsters, the gamblers—that is, the upper classes—are all asleep, the rich ones in their grand mosaic houses (sometimes the roof leaks, but, oh, rebel, the luxury of them pads!). And then another group of people takes over the City—the vendors and the invalids and the beggars.

Youve never seen anything like it—never so many people lacking legs, eyes, hands—the legless rushing around in their homemade wagons on skate wheels, with padded cloth knuckles rolling themselves along. At almost every corner, outside the market, along the park in front of the Church of Guadalupe, you see the gaunt women sitting draped in black shawls. You cant tell if there is anything wrong with their eyes or if they are just rolling them in a kind of poverty-frenzy. They used to frighten the hell out of me, they reminded me of Death when I used to think of Death as ugly. Around these women there are two or three or more kids, all filthy, mud caking on their legs, and inevitably a baby suckling their withered breasts, where Im sure nothing is coming. *Madre de Misericordia*, they chant, *virjen sagrada de los dolores, una caridad*. And kids without legs, hobbling along on tree branches. And so much damned ugly poverty.

The market is all sounds and colors—and of course odors and smoke. All along the streets. *Aqui, marchante*, says a seller luring the buyer from a competitor. Prices fall fantastically, and a kind of haywire auction in which the buyer has no part goes on fiercely. Stands of cheap jewelry like broken kaleidoscopes, medallions of Christ and the Virgin, Indian masks, limeade and orchata (drunk by everyone out of the same two glasses), leather whips, hasaderos (like cheese), tacos in railroadcar-like restaurants outside, tortillas pounded by the squatting women. And flies all around, always, lord, yes, always flies—especially around the red watermelon slices or pineapple slices where the little girl stands absently with a stick with thin strips of paper tied to it to shoo the flies unsuccessfully to the next stand and fans herself instead. And Mexican toys (always with strings to be pulled and someone kicks someone, or a chicken bites a woman, or a rock falls on an Indian). Paper flowers—different colors, from one stalk, covered with wax to make them look velvety—skirts with gaudy pictures of the Virgin of Guadalupe, of Catholic churches in the City. Boots (purple, yellow, green)—and everyone calling at the same time. Hot "rubies" for a dollar—"emeralds," "diamonds" for pennies. And the flies buzzing.

Outside, in the streets, especially outside the market the kids in empty parking lots offer to watch tourists' and American shoppers' cars while theyre gone—or offer to carry groceries to the streetcar (sometimes running away with them to hungry brothers and sisters—I hope), or offer to show you the City, or take you to a whorehouse.

I forget exactly on what day it is—the 16th of September or the 5th of May—both are important dates in Mexican history, like the 4th of July—the population, of the Mexican cities, gathers outside the City Hall, the Courthouse, etc., waiting for the President, the Governor, or the Mayor, depending, to give *El Grito*—The Yell. At midnight, it comes. VIVA MEXICO! And they echo, QUE VIVA!!!!

And cockfights!

And witches—lots of them.

They hold a position in the Mexican Southwest almost as respected as that of the priests. There's a kind of hierarchy among them, headed by Don Ben (the Pope of El Paso's witches). A problem too big for an ordinary witch is referred finally to Don Ben, a root-twisted old, old man. (He wont die—he'll shrink.) I remember when I was a kid, an *espiritu maligno* kept bugging us, misplacing my father's glasses. We ended up going to Don Ben. He fell into a dramatic trance, and when he woke, he said, *My tata Dios* (daddy God) is so busy right now He suggests we call Him later. We called later, and *tata Dios* said to leave the *espiritu* alone and it would go away.

My second-aunt ("she of the blue hair and the deer eyes—ahhh!"—Don Ben's description of her) has had a picture of her husband, inverted in a glass of strange liquid, behind her bedroom door, for years. About 40 years ago he left her—and this will bring him back some day.

And why should devout Mexican Catholics (as they are) consult witches (as they do)? For the same reason that a man with a sick ear goes to an ear specialist. . . .

And bullfights.

But they dont get the best bullfighters at the Juarez arena, although sometimes they do. The real sight—when the bullfight aint good—are the Americans in huge Mexican hats being so Mexican, and the inevitable cluster of Mexicans around them, the fawning ones glorifying the grand American—these are the sick ones—and then the opportunists, hoping the money will rub off and willing to see to it that it does.

At dawn, on a lady's birthday—even now and in El Paso—five or six men gather outside her window, singing and playing their guitars. The sun is about to come out. They sing softly,

Estas son las mañanitas
Que cantaba el Rey David.
A las muchachas bonitas
Se las cantaba él así. . . .

Now the lady comes coyly to the window, standing there until they have finished the soft dawn singing. Now all the neighbors' windows are up and everyone is listening. (No one thinks of calling the police.) Then the lady invites the serenaders inside, and they all have early-morning coffee, *pan de dulce, menudo.* Then the sun is up in the sky.

The Southwest sky. Beautiful and horrifying. And therefore Wonderful.

Because in all the blunder and bluster of Texas about the wrong things, one thing is really so. The sky.

When it is beautiful it is depthless blue. The sky in other places is like an inverted cup, this shade of blue or gray or black or another shade, with limits, like a painted room. Not in the Southwest. The sky is really millions and millions of miles deep of blue—and in summer, clear magic electric blue.

(How many stars are there in the sky? was our favorite six-year-old children riddle. The answer: *cincuenta.* Which means fifty, but also: countless. And it's true, so true.)

Before the summer storms, the clouds mass and roll twisting in the sky clashing fiercely, sweeping grandly across the sky. Then giant mushrooms explode. The sky groans, opens, it pours rain.

But before the windstorms, everything is calm, and then a strange ominous mass of gray gathers in the horizon. Then swiftly, in a moment it seems, blowing with the wind, the steel clouds cover the sky, and youre locked down here, so lonesome suddenly youre cold. The wind comes. The tumbleweeds rush with it.

And always there's the fearful wailing.

AMADO MURO has the strange distinction of not becoming a Chicano until late in his life. "Amado Muro" was born Chester Seltzer in Cleveland, Ohio. He studied journalism at the University of Virginia and creative writing at Kenyon College. His career in journalism was interrupted when he was put in prison for his antiwar stance during World War II. After his release, Seltzer moved to El Paso, marrying Amada Muro and borrowing her name, with slight alteration, as his pseudonym. He published short stories set in the Mexican-American community, and articles concerning hobos while he was employed as a journalist. The background of Amado Muro was not discovered until after his death.

Amado Muro/Chester Seltzer

(El Paso)

"Cecilia Rosas"

When I was in the ninth grade at Bowie High School in El Paso, I got a job hanging up women's coats at La Feria Department Store on Saturdays. It wasn't the kind of a job that had much appeal for a Mexican boy or for boys of any other nationality either. But the work wasn't hard, only boring. Wearing a smock, I stood around the Ladies' Wear Department all day long waiting for women customers to finish trying on coats so I could hang them up.

Having to wear a smock was worse than the work itself. It was an agonizing ordeal. To me it was a loathsome stigma of unmanly toil that made an already degrading job even more so. The work itself I looked on as onerous and effeminate for a boy from a family of miners, shepherds, and ditchdiggers. But working in Ladies' Wear had two compensations: earning three dollars every Saturday was one; being close to the Señorita Cecilia Rosas was the other.

This alluring young woman, the most beautiful I had ever seen, more than made up for my mollycoddle labor and the smock that symbolized it. My chances of looking at her were almost limitless. And like a good Mexican, I made the most of them. But I was only too painfully aware that I wasn't the only one who thought this saleslady gorgeous.

La Feria had water fountains on every one of its eight floors. But men liked best the one on the floor where Miss Rosas worked. So they made special trips to Ladies' Wear all day long to drink water and look at her.

Since I was only fourteen and in love for the first time, I looked at her more chastely than most. The way her romantic lashes fringed her obsidian eyes was especially enthralling to me. Then, too, I never tired of admiring her shining raven hair, her Cupid's-bow lips, the warmth of her gleaming white smile. Her rich olive skin was almost as dark as mine. Sometimes she wore a San Juan rose in her hair. When she did, she looked so very lovely I forgot all about what La Feria was paying me to do and stood gaping at her instead. My admiration was decorous but complete. I admired her hourglass figure as well as her wonderfully radiant face.

Other men admired her too. They inspected her from the water fountain. Some stared at her boldly, watching her trimly rhythmic hips sway. Others, less frank and open, gazed furtively at her swelling bosom or her shapely calves. Their effrontery made me indignant. I, too, looked at these details of Miss Rosas. But I prided myself on doing so more romantically, far more poetically than they did, with much more love than desire.

Then, too, Miss Rosas was the friendliest as well as the most beautiful saleslady in Ladies' Wear. But the other salesladies, Mexican girls all, didn't like her. She was so nice to them all they were hard put to justify their dislike. They couldn't very well admit they disliked her because she was pretty. So they all said she was haughty and imperious. Their claim was partly true. Her beauty was Miss Rosas' only obvious vanity. But she had still another. She prided herself on being more American than Mexican because she was born in El Paso. And she did her best to act, dress, and talk the way Americans do. She hated to speak Spanish, disliked her Mexican name. She called herself Cecile Roses instead of Cecilia Rosas. This made the other salesladies smile derisively. They called her La Americana or the Gringa from Xochimilco every time they mentioned her name.

Looking at this beautiful girl was more important than money to me. It was my greatest compensation for doing work that I hated. She was so lovely that a glance at her sweetly expressive face was enough to make me forget my shame at wearing a smock and my dislike for my job with its eternal waiting around.

Miss Rosas was an exemplary saleslady. She could be frivolous, serious or demure, primly efficient too, molding herself to each customer's personality. Her voice matched her exotically mysterious eyes. It was the richest, the softest I had ever heard. Her husky whisper, gentle as a rain breeze, was like a tender caress. Hearing it made me want to dream and I did. Romantic thoughts burgeoned up in my mind like rosy billows of hope scented with Miss Rosas' perfume. These thoughts made me so languid at my work that the floor manager, Joe Apple, warned me to show some enthusiasm for it or else suffer the consequences.

But my dreams sapped my will to struggle, making me oblivious to admonitions. I had neither the desire nor the energy to respond to Joe Apple's warnings. Looking at Miss Rosas used up so much of my energy that I had little left for my work. Miss Rosas was twenty, much too old for me, everyone said. But what everyone said didn't matter. So I soldiered on the job and watched her, entranced by her beauty, her grace. While I watched I dreamed of being a hero. It hurt me to have her see me doing menial work. But there was no escape from it. I needed the job to stay in school. So more and more I took refuge in dreams.

When I had watched her as much, if not more, than I could safely do without attracting the attention of other alert Mexican salesladies, I slipped out of Ladies' Wear and walked up the stairs to the top floor. There I sat on a window ledge smoking Faro cigarettes, looking down at the city's canyons, and best of all, thinking about Miss Rosas and myself.

They say Chihuahua Mexicans are good at dreaming because the mountains are so gigantic and the horizons so vast in Mexico's biggest state that men don't think pygmy thoughts there. I was no exception. Lolling on the ledge, I became what I wanted to be. And what I wanted to be was a handsome American Miss Rosas could love and marry. The dreams I dreamed were imaginative masterpieces, or so I thought. They transcended the insipid realities of a casual relationship, making it vibrantly thrilling and infinitely more romantic. They transformed me from a colorless Mexican boy who put women's coats away into the debonair American, handsome, dashing and worldly, that I longed to be for her sake. For the first time in my life I reveled in the magic of fantasy. It brought happiness. Reality didn't.

But my window ledge reveries left me bewildered and shaken. They had a narcotic quality. The more thrillingly romantic fantasies I created, the more I needed to create. It got so I couldn't get enough dreaming time in Ladies' Wear. My kind of dreaming demanded disciplined concentration. And there was just too much hubbub, too much gossiping, too many coats to be put away there.

So I spent less time in Ladies' Wear. My flights to the window ledge became more recklessly frequent. Sometimes I got tired sitting there. When I did, I took the freight elevator down to the street floor and brazenly walked out of the store without so much as punching a time clock. Walking the streets quickened my imagination, gave form and color to my thoughts. It made my brain glow with impossible hopes that seemed incredibly easy to realize. So absorbed was I in thoughts of Miss Rosas and myself that I bumped into Americans, apologizing mechanically in Spanish instead of English, and wandered down South El Paso Street like a somnambulist, without really seeing its street vendors, cafes and arcades, tattoo shops, and shooting galleries at all.

But if there was confusion in these walks there was some serenity too. Something good did come from the dreams that prompted them. I found I could tramp the streets with a newly won tranquility, no longer troubled by, or even aware of, girls in tight skirts, overflowing blouses, and drop-stitch stockings. My love for Miss Rosas was my shield against the furtive thoughts and indiscriminate desires that had made me so uneasy for a year or more before I met her.

Then, too, because of her, I no longer looked at the pictures of voluptuous women in the *Vea* and *Vodevil* magazines at Zamora's newsstand. The piquant thoughts Mexicans call *malos deseos* were gone from my mind. I no longer thought about women as I did before I fell in love with Miss Rosas. Instead, I thought about a woman, only one. This clear-cut objective and the serenity that went with it made me understand something of one of the nicest things about love.

I treasured the walks, the window-ledge sittings, and the dreams that I had then. I clung to them just as long as I could. Drab realities closed in on me chokingly just as soon as I gave them up. My future was a time clock with an American Mister telling me what to do and this I knew only too well. A career as an ice-dock laborer stretched ahead of me. Better said, it dangled over me like a Veracruz machete. My uncle Rodolfo Avitia, a straw boss on the ice docks, was already training me for it. Every night he took me to the mile-long docks overhanging the Southern Pacific freight yards. There he handed me tongs and made me practice tripping three-hundred-pound ice blocks so I could learn how to unload an entire boxcar of ice blocks myself.

Thinking of this bleak future drove me back into my fantasies, made me want to prolong them forever. My imagination was taxed to the breaking point by the heavy strain I put on it.

I thought about every word Miss Rosas had ever said to me, making myself believe she looked at me with unmistakable tenderness when she said them. When she said: "Amado, please hang up this fur coat," I found special meaning in her tone. It was as though she had said: "Amadito, I love you."

When she gave these orders, I pushed into action like a man blazing with a desire to perform epically heroic feats. At such times I felt capable of putting away not one but a thousand fur coats, and would have done so joyously.

Sometimes on the street I caught myself murmuring: "Cecilia, *linda amorcita,* I love you." When these surges swept over me, I walked down empty streets so I could whisper: "Cecilia, *te quiero con toda mi alma*" as much as I wanted to and mumble everything else that I felt. And so I emptied my heart on the streets and window ledge while women's coats piled up in Ladies' Wear.

But my absences didn't go unnoticed. Once an executive-looking man, portly, gray, and efficiently brusque, confronted me while I sat on the window ledge with a Faro cigarette pasted to my lips, a cloud of tobacco smoke hanging over my head, and many perfumed dreams inside it. He had a no-nonsense approach that jibed with his austere mien. He asked me what my name was, jotted down my work number, and went off to make a report on what he called "sordid malingering."

Other reports followed this. Gruff warnings, stern admonitions, and blustery tirades developed from them. They came from both major and minor executives. These I was already inured to. They didn't matter anyway. My condition was far too advanced, already much too complex to be cleared up by mere lectures, fatherly or otherwise. All the threats and rebukes in the world couldn't have made me give up my window-ledge reveries or kept me from roaming city streets with Cecilia Rosas' name on my lips like a prayer.

The reports merely made me more cunning, more doggedly determined to city-slick La Feria out of work hours I owed it. The net result was that I timed my absences more precisely and contrived better lies to explain them. Sometimes I went to the men's room and looked at myself in the mirror for as long as ten minutes at a time. Such self-studies filled me with gloom. The mirror reflected an ordinary Mexican face, more homely than comely. Only my hair gave me hope. It was thick and wavy, deserving a better face to go with it. So I did the best I could with what I had, and combed it over my temples in ringlets just like the poets back in my hometown of Parral, Chihuahua, used to do.

My inefficiency, my dreams, my general lassitude could have gone on indefinitely, it seemed. My life at the store wavered between bright hope and leaden despair, unrelieved by Miss Rosas' acceptance or rejection of me. Then one day something happened that almost made my overstrained heart stop beating.

It happened on the day Miss Rosas stood behind me while I put a fur coat away. Her heady perfume, the fragrance of her warm healthy body, made me feel faint. She was so close to me I thought about putting my hands around her lissome waist and hugging her as hard as I could. But thoughts of subsequent disgrace deterred me, so instead of hugging her I smiled wanly and asked her in Spanish how she was feeling.

"Amado, speak English," she told me. "And pronounce the words slowly and carefully so you won't sound like a country Mexican."

Then she looked at me in a way that made me the happiest employee who ever punched La Feria's time clock.

"Amadito," she whispered the way I had always dreamed she would.

"Yes, Señorita Cecilia," I said expectantly.

Her smile was warmly intimate. "Amadito, when are you going to take me to the movies?" she asked.

Other salesladies watched us, all smiling. They made me so nervous I couldn't answer.

"Amadito, you haven't answered me," Miss Rosas said teasingly. "Either you're bashful as a village sweetheart or else you don't like me at all."

In voluble Spanish, I quickly assured her the latter wasn't the case. I was just getting ready to say "Señorita Cecilia, I more than like you, I love you" when she frowned and told me to speak English. So I slowed down and tried to smooth out my ruffled thoughts.

"Señorita Cecilia," I said. "I'd love to take you to the movies any time."

Miss Rosas smiled and patted my cheek. "Will you buy me candy and popcorn?" she said.

I nodded, putting my hand against the imprint her warm palm had left on my face.

"And hold my hand?"

I said "yes" so enthusiastically it made her laugh. Other salesladies laughed too. Dazed and numb with happiness, I watched Miss Rosas walk away. How proud and confident she was, how wholesomely clean and feminine. Other salesladies were looking at me and laughing.

Miss Sandoval came over to me. "*Ay papacito,*" she said. "With women you're the divine tortilla."

Miss de la Rosa came over too. "When you take the Americana to the movies, remember not to speak Christian," she said. "And be sure you wear the pants that don't have any patches on them."

What they said made me blush and wonder how they knew what we had been talking about. Miss Arroyo came over to join them. So did Miss Torres.

"Amado, remember women are weak and men aren't made of sweet bread," Miss Arroyo said.

This embarrassed me but it wasn't altogether unpleasant. Miss Sandoval winked at Miss de la Rosa, then looked back at me.

"Don't go too fast with the Americana, Amado," she said. "Remember the procession is long and the candles are small."

They laughed and slapped me on the back. They all wanted to know when I was going to take Miss Rosas to the movies. "She didn't say," I blurted out without thinking.

This brought another burst of laughter. It drove me back up to the window ledge where I got out my package of Faros and thought about the wonderful thing that had happened. But I was too nervous to stay there. So I went to the men's room and looked at myself in the mirror again, wondering why Miss Rosas liked me so well. The mirror made it brutally clear that my looks hadn't influenced her. So it must have been something else, perhaps character. But that didn't seem likely either. Joe Apple had told me I didn't have much of that. And other store officials had bulwarked his opinion. Still, I had seen homely men walking the streets of El Paso's Little Chihuahua quarter with beautiful Mexican women and no one could explain that either. Anyway it was time for another walk. So I took one.

This time I trudged through Little Chihuahua, where both Miss Rosas and I lived. Little Chihuahua looked different to me that day. It was a broken-down Mexican quarter honeycombed with tenements, Mom and Pop groceries, herb shops, cafes, and spindly salt-cedar trees; with howling children running its streets and old Mexican revolutionaries sunning themselves on its curbs like iguanas. But on that clear frosty day it was the world's most romantic place because Cecilia Rosas lived there.

While walking, I reasoned that Miss Rosas might want to go dancing after the movies. So I went to Professor Toribio Ortega's dance studio and made arrangements to take my first lesson. Some neighborhood boys saw me when I came out. They bawled "*Mariquita*" and made flutteringly effeminate motions, all vulgar if not obscene. It didn't matter. On my lunch hour I went back and took my first lesson anyway. Professor Ortega danced with me. Softened by weeks of dreaming, I went limp in his arms imagining he was Miss Rosas.

The rest of the day was the same as many others before it. As usual I spent most of it stealing glances at Miss Rosas and slipping up to the window ledge. She looked busy, efficient, not like a woman in love. Her many other admirers trooped to the water fountain to look at the way her black silk dress fitted her curves. Their profane admiration made me scowl even more than I usually did at such times.

When the day's work was done, I plodded home from the store just as dreamily as I had gone to it. Since I had no one else to confide in, I invited my oldest sister, Dulce Nombre de María, to go to the movies with me. They were showing Jorge Negrete and María Felix in *El Rapto* at the Colon Theater. It was a romantic movie, just the kind I wanted to see.

After it was over, I bought Dulce Nombre *churros* and hot *champurrado* at the Golden Taco Cafe. And I told my sister all about what had happened to me. She looked at me thoughtfully, then combed my hair back with her fingertips as though trying to soothe me. "Manito," she said, softly. "I wouldn't . . ." Then she looked away and shrugged her shoulders.

On Monday I borrowed three dollars from my Uncle Rodolfo without telling him what it was for. Miss Rosas hadn't told me what night she wanted me to take her to the movies. But the way she had looked at me made me think that almost any night would do. So I decided on Friday. Waiting for it to come was hard. But I had to keep my mind occupied. So I went to Zamora's news stand to get the Alma Nortena songbook. Pouring through it for the most romantic song I could find, I decided on *La Cecilia*.

All week long I practiced singing it on my way to school and in the shower after basketball practice with the Little Chihuahua Tigers at the Sagrado Corazón gym. But, except for singing this song, I tried not to speak Spanish at all. At home I made my mother mad by saying in English, "Please pass the sugar."

My mother looked at me as though she couldn't believe what she had heard. Since my Uncle Rodolfo couldn't say anything more than "hello" and "goodbye" in English, he couldn't tell what I had said. So my sister Consuelo did.

"May the Dark Virgin with the benign look make this boy well enough to speak Christian again," my mother whispered.

This I refused to do. I went on speaking English even though my mother and uncle didn't understand it. This shocked my sisters as well. When they asked me to explain my behavior, I parroted Miss Rosas, saying, "We're living in the United States now."

My rebellion against being a Mexican created an uproar. Such conduct was unorthodox, if not scandalous, in a neighborhood where names like Burgiaga, Rodriguez, and Castillo predominated. But it wasn't only the Spanish language that I lashed out against.

"Mother, why do we always have to eat *sopa, frijoles, refritos, mondongo,* and *pozole?*" I complained. "Can't we ever eat roast beef or ham and eggs like Americans do?"

My mother didn't speak to me for two days after that. My Uncle Rodolfo grimaced and mumbled something about renegade Mexicans who want to eat ham and eggs even though the Montes Packing Company turned out the best *chorizo* this side of Toluca. My sister Consuelo giggled and called me a Rio Grande Irishman, an American Mister, a gringo, and a *bolillo.* Dulce Nombre looked at me worriedly.

Life at home was almost intolerable. Cruel jokes and mocking laughter made it so. I moped around looking sad as a day without bread. My sister Consuelo suggested I go to the courthouse and change my name to Beloved Wall which is English for Amado Muro. My mother didn't agree. "If *Nuestro Señor* had meant for Amadito to be an American he would have given him a name like Smeeth or Jonesy," she said. My family was unsympathetic. With a family like mine, how could I ever hope to become an American and win Miss Rosas?

Friday came at last. I put on my only suit, slicked my hair down with liquid vaseline, and doused myself with Dulce Nombre's perfume.

"Amado's going to serenade that pretty girl everyone calls La Americana," my sister Consuelo told my mother and uncle when I sat down to eat. "Then he's going to take her to the movies.

This made my uncle laugh and my mother scowl.

"*Qué pantalones tiene* (what nerve that boy's got)," my uncle said, "to serenade a twenty-year-old woman."

"La Americana," my mother said derisively. "That one's Mexican as pulque cured with celery."

They made me so nervous I forgot to take off my cap when I sat down to eat.

"Amado, take off your cap," my mother said. "You're not in La Lagunilla Market."

My uncle frowned. "All this boy thinks about is kissing girls," he said gruffly.

"But my boy's never kissed one," my mother said proudly.

My sister Consuelo laughed. "That's because they won't let him," she said.

This wasn't true. But I couldn't say so in front of my mother. I had already kissed Emalina Uribe from Porfirio Díaz Street not once but twice. Both times I'd kissed her in a darkened doorway less than a block from her home. But the kisses were over so soon we hardly had time to enjoy them. This was because Ema was afraid of her big brother, the husky one nicknamed Toro, would see us. But if we'd had more time it would have been better, I knew.

Along about six o'clock the three musicians who called themselves the Mariachis of Tecalitlán came by and whistled for me, just as they had said they would. They never looked better than they did on that night. They had on black and silver charro uniforms and big, black, Zapata sombreros.

My mother shook her head when she saw them. "Son, who ever heard of serenading a girl at six o'clock in the evening," she said. "When your father had the mariachis sing for me it was always two o'clock in the morning—the only proper time for a six-song *gallo.*"

But I got out my Ramirez guitar anyway. I put on my cap and rushed out to give the mariachis the money without even kissing my mother's hand or waiting for her to bless me. Then we headed for Miss Rosas' home. Some boys and girls I knew were out in the street. This made me uncomfortable. They looked at me wonderingly as I led the mariachi band to Miss Rosas' home.

A block away from Miss Rosas' home I could see her father, a grizzled veteran who fought for Pancho Villa, sitting on the curb reading the Juarez newspaper, *El Fronterizo.*

The sight of him made me slow down for a moment. But I got back in stride when I saw Miss Rosas herself.

She smiled and waved at me. "Hello, Amadito," she said.

"Hello, Señorita Cecilia," I said.

She looked at the mariachis, then back to me.

"Ay, Amado, you're going to serenade your girl," she said. I didn't reply right away. Then when I was getting ready to say "Señorita Cecilia, I came to serenade you," I saw the American man sitting in the sports roadster at the curb.

Miss Rosas turned to him. "I'll be right there, Johnny," she said.

She patted my cheek. "I've got to run now, Amado," she said. "Have a real nice time, darling."

I looked at her silken legs as she got into the car. Everything had happened so fast I was dazed. Broken dreams made my head spin. The contrast between myself and the poised American in the sports roadster was so cruel it made me wince.

She was happy with him. That was obvious. She was smiling and laughing, looking forward to a good time. Why had she asked me to take her to the movies if she already had a boyfriend? Then I remembered how the other salesladies had laughed, how I had wondered why they were laughing when they couldn't even hear what we were saying. And I realized it had all been a joke, everyone had known it but me. Neither Miss Rosas nor the other salesladies had ever dreamed I would think she was serious about wanting me to take her to the movies.

The American and Miss Rosas drove off. Gloomy thoughts oppressed me. They made me want to cry. To get rid of them I thought of going to one of the "bad death" cantinas in Juárez where tequila starts fights and knives finish them—to one of the cantinas where the panders, whom Mexicans call *burros,* stand outside shouting "It's just like Paris, only not so many people" was where I wanted to go. There I could forget her in Jalisco-state style with mariachis, tequila, and night-life women. Then I remembered I was so young that night-life women would shun me and *cantineros* wouldn't serve me tequila.

So I thought some more. Emalina Uribe was the only other alternative. If we went over to Porfirio Díaz Street and serenaded her I could go back to being a Mexican again. She was just as Mexican as I was, Mexican as *chicharrones.* I thought about smiling, freckle-faced Ema.

Ema wasn't like the Americana at all. She wore wash dresses that fitted loosely and even ate the *melcocha* candies Mexicans liked so well on the street. On Sundays she wore a Zamora shawl to church and her mother wouldn't let her use lipstick or let her put on high heels.

But with a brother like Toro who didn't like me anyway, such a serenade might be more dangerous than romantic. Besides that, my faith in my looks, my character, or whatever it was that made women fall in love with men, was so undermined I could already picture her getting into a car with a handsome American just like Miss Rosas had done.

The Mariachis of Tecalitlan were getting impatient. They had been paid to sing six songs and they wanted to sing them. But they were all sympathetic. None of them laughed at me.

"Amado, don't look sad as I did the day I learned I'd never be a millionaire," the mariachi captain said, putting his arm around me. "If not that girl, then another."

But without Miss Rosas there was no one we could sing *La Cecilia* to. The street seemed bleak and empty now that she was gone. And I didn't want to serenade Ema Uribe even though she hadn't been faithless as Miss Rosas had been. It was true she hadn't been faithless, but only lack of opportunity would keep her from getting into a car with an American, I reasoned cynically.

Just about then Miss Rosas' father looked up from his newspaper. He asked the mariachis if they knew how to sing Cananea Jail. They told him they did. Then they looked at me. I thought it over for a moment. Then I nodded and started strumming the bass strings of my guitar. What had happened made it only too plain I could never trust Miss Rosas again. So we serenaded her father instead.

Sunny Ozuna (San Antonio)

"Talk To Me, Talk To Me"

Talk to me, talk to me
I love the things you say
Talk to me, talk to me
In your own sweet gentle way

Let me hear, tell me dear
Tell me you love me so
Talk to me, talk to me
Tell me what I want to know

The many ways, you speak of love
I've heard before
But it sounds so good, everytime
Please say the part I love, just once more
Darling, I'm so glad you're mine

Talk to me, talk to me
Hold me close, whisper low
Talk to me, baby can't you see?
Darling, I love you so

The many ways you speak of love
I've heard before
But it sounds so good, everytime
Please say the part I love, just once more
Darling, I'm so glad you're mine.

Talk to me, talk to me
Hold me close, whisper low
Talk to me, baby, can't you see?
Darling, I love you so.

Sunny Ozuna and the Sunglows were formed at Burbank Vocational School in San Antonio. His still popular "Talk to Me" hit number eleven on the pop charts and twelve on R&B charts in 1963.

Ricardo Sánchez (El Paso)

"Soledad was a girl's name" and "Homing"

Soledad was a girl's name

June 10, 1963, Soledad

Soledad was a girl's name
years ago
at jefferson high,
and she was soft and brown
and beautiful,
i used to watch her,
and think her name
was ironic
and poetic,
for she was Soledad Guerra,
solitude and war,
and she used to always smile
con ternura morena
como su piel,
and now in this soledad
that i am leaving soon,
this callous nation
of bars and cement and barbarity,
it seems strange
that a name can call out to me
and mesmerize me
yet repel me,
one a girl, now a woman,
and the other
a jagged prison world
where hate
is a common expletive,
seems everyone hates,
seems everyone is a convict,
even the guards and counselors
do time here,
everyday trudging into
this abysmal human warehouse.

Ricardo Sánchez's unique path to becoming a well-known poet began in a neighborhood of El Paso called El Barrio del Diablo. Sanchez dropped out of high school and joined the Army, then did years in prison before beginning to write poetry. His first book of poems, *Canto y Grito Mi Liberación*, was published in 1971 by Mictla, which he had helped start, was reprinted by a New York publisher. With the attention it received and help from the Ford Foundation, Sanchez, who had never finished high school, was able to enter a Ph.D. program at the Union Graduate School in Cincinnati, working in American Studies and cultural linguistic theory. A proud member of the Brown Beret and fearless political dissident, he guest lectured at universities throughout the country, from El Paso to Alaska, before ending up a tenured professor at Washington State University. Sanchez learned that he had cancer while he was there and died at age fifty-four in El Paso.

am leaving
and it hurts,
funny that it hurts,
i see the faces of my friends,
we joke about my getting out,
                    and they ask pleading things,
                    "DO IT ONE TIME FOR ME, ESE!"
just one time, carnal,
nomás una vez,
hell, bato, i'll go all over
and do it a million times
recalling all the sadness
that hides
within this place;
i'll do it a jillion times
for me, for you, for all of us,
and maybe the next soledad i see
is a morenita from el chuco
i had been too timid
to ask out . . . it's strange
that i recall her,
but then la pinta
makes you think/regret.
but huáchenle, batos,
when i'm doing it for us
i'll probably burst out laughing,
not at you or me or even at some ruca,
but at all the pendejadas,
at all the crazy lies
that say that we are savage;
i'll laugh at mean ass convicts
who terrify the world
yet love to eat ice cream,
i'll laugh at convicts scurrying
from cell block to the canteen
with books of scripted money
to purchase cokes and cookies
and candy bars as well;
i'll laugh at contradictions
and yet within i'll hurt
remembering xmas packages
and letters full of pain;
recalling those sad moments
when night became the coverlet
and darkness filtered songs,
when all alone i'd die
realizing just how sordid
a prison life can be . . .

yes, i'll laugh, carnales,
just like we all want to laugh,
not to mock us nor to spite you,
just to say i understand,

pero eso sí, compiras,'
no quiero regresar.

March 10, 1971
otra vez el penco al
estable, back to the calles
y locuras that
hide smirkingly within
e.p.t. twilights,
dreaming míctla dreams

Homing

homing, ese, amidst
old/known faces,
with familia embraces
and love/kisses
flooding each moment
of re-encounter,
la jefita hovering
over her returned children,
carnalas, sobrinos/sobrinas,
suegros, todo el tribu
estrechando bienllegadas;

cruising over to pete duarte's,
chacha marín rapping on the way,
passing familiar sights,
seeing el índio on the streets
walking toward his sense of nirvana,
el hippie flirting with life,
melo curbing on the edge
of his botella,
nina, rosie, rojas, géra,
lupe, lalo, and new faces
within chuco movimiento,
y el borracho
tirando tórica bruta—es algo
rete sabroso being back,
rapping with gardéa, siqueiros,
tony parra, pat,
and host of raza
about building up
míctla publications
to thus change
the horrid imagery
that has ever haunted us;

homing, batos, homing
into the nether world
of causa y sangre y corazón,
and even the caustic words
of lozito (el parole officer)
cannot mar
the happiness
of being back
in this city of callejas y rincones,
of pobreza y raza y duelos . . .

homing once again
as i cruise my renault r-10
over the crumbling ruins
of el Diablo, that land of DDT batos
who used to slice up life and hope
with filero and herre,
            shooting up carga/chiva/dreams
into blueridged veins
            hiding beneath la grasa of brown flesh,
finding sanctuary
within the torpor,
                        but life is hell
                        within poverty & self-hate,

homing as i see skeletal remains
of that home that saw me grow
at 3920 Oak, later avenida de las américas,
and now just a dead hulk
where only voices of the past
can find refuge
            if you listen closely—and carnal,
i think even la llorona
used to live in el diablo
            over by the algodonales del ayer,
            there by the river as it cuts/flows
through sand and cactus, >>

when we used to slip over or under the fence
surrounding Isla de Córdova, that chunk of land
            that méxico used to own, now traded in
as part of the chamizal pact,
and at those ranchitos
where we would trip out on mota/yesca/grifa
and dance
all night
to música rete chicana/mexicana y bien rascuache,
or when even younger
we used to slip through the fence
and rip off watermelons, cantaloupes, and chavalas
and the old rancheritos
would threaten us with rusty/dysfunctional shotguns
spraying birdshot
overhead, and we would laugh
with childhood's mirth,
in that barrio del eastside
where i learned
to rub up against willing girls
who wanted to rub up against us
and Doña Chuyita
would run after us,
throwing bricks/rocks—anything she could—
at us and dare us to stop, and we never did,
just shouted at her, and later she would
grab me with her brown/wrinkled tarahumara hands
and between the dark stained bits of teeth
within her 108 year old mouth admonish me
that if she were a few years younger, why,
hell, bato, she would marry me and make
a man out of me, then she would laugh
and tell me to scoot home,
and i would, looking back
at that old/furrowed woman,
índia-patarajada from the mountains
of chihuahua

who still chopped wood and ran
through the alleys of my barrio,
barefooted with a red kerchief
tied around her left ankle,
                for strength in running she would say,
and galavanted about,
Doña Jesusita, Chuyita: Doña Chúris,
and we loved her
in our pranksterway,
especially when she would sit us down
and regale us with stories
of life in those mountains
when there existed no cars,
just burros and tired people
who knew how to dance and sing
and live off the land,
her face was rivuletted
with time and her eyes
were hawklike and strong,
the folds of skin
on her arms
were skeins of brown earth;
                once she caught me smoking,
                i was fifteen or so, and she
                asked me if my father, Don Pedrito
                approved and I said maybe, puede que sí,
                and i offered her a cigarette,
                she smiled and said that i could not buy
                her silence, that here before the sky
                i would have to know
                that her bosom was not a warehouse
                where secrets could be stored,
but then seeing my youthful fears
                she told me not to worry
                for things done in the open are not secrets. >>

that barrio
now dead and full of shards,
I found a rusty empty can of Mitchell's Beer,
a relic of those times
almost twenty years before
when Mitchell's had reigned
and all the barrio had drunk it,
I found it beside the crumbling wall
of that home my father had painstakingly built
when I had been a four year old toddler,
back then when we had lived
in a one room home
that grew into other rooms
with timely expansions by my father;
i saw remains
of cinderblock fences
where my brothers, Sefy and Pete,
would strum guitars and sing,
and they would tell me
to go inside that it was late,
and in my eight year old world
they seemed big,
for a five and six year span
can mean a totally different world,
and years later
would I come home on leave
to bury them
and cry softly
for the remembrances
culling loneliness in mind/soul;

home again to el paso,
but no longer to my barrio,
but to alien worlds
which had been home for rivals
when I had been tush-hogging
with the X-9 batos,

riding herd on other barrios,
no longer
encaged within the mind searing stench
of Disneyland or the coliseum at rodeo time,
no, seeing
through tears of recollection
a barrio dead, gone into time's shards
with juareños searching through the rubble
for still useful things,
                                        bricks, boards, iron grill work,
any goddamn thing that can be marketed
in los serajeros in south juárez,
            at that enclave of junk yards,
and seeing them take
that still remaining doorframe
from what used to be the doorway to our kitchen
cut my soul
and severed forever
my linkage to my barrio,
and I felt bloody anger
coursing through my mind;

turned, scowling,
to see a superfreeway
being built
to make it easier for tourists
to make it to juárez bistros and whorehouses,
realized
that barrios must make way for progress,
and as i left,
to file another parole report,
heard soft voices of the past . . .

José Angel Gutierrez is one of the most important figures in the political struggles of Chicanos for several decades. He grew up in Crystal City and went to college at Texas A & M in Kingsville. While in college in the 1960s, Gutierrez began his involvement in politics, starting several organizations devoted to getting more Chicanos to vote and participate in the political process. Most notably he started La Raza Unida Party, which aimed to get Chicanos more power in his hometown of Crystal City, but which expanded across the Southwest. His efforts led to many threats from the police and others, but Gutierrez continued both his activism and his studies. His first self-published book, *A Gringo Manual On How to Control Mexicans,* is a classic in political effrontery. He earned a Ph.D. from the University of Texas and a J.D. from Bates College of Law in Houston and has held several elected offices. He is a practicing attorney and teaches at the University of Texas at Arlington.

José Angel Gutiérrez (Crystal City)

from *The Making of a Chcano Militant*

The Beginning of Chicanismo

During these years of the 1950s, my generation began calling themselves Chicanos, as we didn't like the term Latin American. Hardly anybody, except the braceros, called themselves Mexican. The Mexicans called us *Pochos,* meaning Mexicans who are trying to be Anglos and not succeeding very well. Success at being a Pocho meant you spoke good English, without a trace of an accent, and dressed like a gringo, with loafers or Hush Puppies, button-down collars, Levi's jeans, and no hats, much less a cowboy hat. You denied being Mexican as best you could and tried to hang around with Anglos. If you could cover up your Mexicanness, then you were called *agavachado.*

For the Anglos we also had various names, such as gringo, *gavacho, bolillo, blanco, pan blanco, huero, americano,* and *norte americano.* There are many explanations for the meaning of these names. Gringo, some say, comes from the lyrics of a song that the invading U.S. Army often sang in the campaign against Mexico in 1846: "*Green grows* the laurel. . . ." The French-style bread, which is white on the inside, is called a *bolillo.* Napoleon III's invasion of Mexico and subsequent occupation for a limited time had introduced French bread into the Mexican cuisine. *Blanco* and *pan blanco* refer to the color white and to white bread. These names refer not only to the whiteness of the Anglos' skin but also to what was perceived as their sour body smell; white bread has that color, and a sour smell from the yeast and pre-servatives. *Huero* is used for any light-skinned person, Anglo, Mexican, or of any nationality, and means, simply, "light skinned." The words *americano* and *norte americano* are used as both literal and exclusive descriptors of Anglos. Sometimes, Mexicans and Mexican Americans will also call themselves *americanos* because these lands, the North and South continents are both "American." People recognize the political and social reality, however. The Anglos have monopolized the term "American" or *americano* for their exclusive, but erroneous, use. *Norte americano* is used to further drive home the point that the user is describing or referring to a gringo. *Gavacho* is a term that escapes me—its origins are sketchy, the term meaning "from the Pyrénées," or "French-like"—but I have heard it used all my life. I know it is not derogatory, as when Chicanos use the word "gringo," which usually refers to a racist Anglo who has an anti-Mexican attitude, is open about his prejudice, has airs of racial superiority, and acts out those feelings, beliefs, attitudes, and opinions against Mexican people.

The name calling helped keep the groups apart. It defined who "us" and "them" were. Chicanos occupied, often side by side, the same general physical space as that of Anglos. We definitely were not, however, a part of their reality. We existed, but did not matter to them. I learned very early that there are several reasons for this. Anglos historically have learned how to dominate Mexicans without a large police force; psychological violence, fear, physical harm, and economic reprisals were their methods. The police and Texas Rangers were effectively employed against us from 1826 to the present time. In addition, economic dependence on whites has been the formal arrangement. With our lands stolen and now in their hands, the whites have the ability to profit from our land, our labor, our consumption of goods, our tax payments, and our presence as "illegals." *We* have to work for *them*, by and large, and we work for them on their own terms. Any attempt to organize or rebel has historically met with immediate retaliation. By making some of us "illegal," they pit us against each other, and all of them against all of us, legal or otherwise. The tag of "illegal" also lowers the wage-earning capacity to whatever the worker must accept, not what the economic system will bear. The Anglo legal system was and remains oppressive. It was used, along with the armed thugs, the Texas Rangers, the INS border patrol, and local police not only to legally steal our lands but also—and more importantly—to keep them. Laws were passed aimed directly at subordinating us. Any of the history books mentioned earlier, including Alfredo Mirande's *Gringo Justice* (1987), detail this process. As the "underclass" of that era, we did not count or matter. We existed to serve exclusively the interests of the Anglos.

The Segregation of Chicanos in Cristal

At the public schools, we still are segregated. The grammar school I attended in the 1950s was predominantly Anglo, and the DeZavala school was predominantly Mexican, as was *el campo,* near the airport. Today, the migrant program, bilingual education, compensatory (remedial) education, special education, and many vocational classrooms are filled with only children of Mexican ancestry. Those of us who did ultimately enter a "white" school, such as the grammar school in "Cristal," were further segregated within the school building by "grade." There was a fifth year grade-one class, a fifth year grade-two class, and a fifth year grade-three class; the "one" was all Anglo, the "two" mostly Mexican students with a few Anglos, and the "three" was all Mexican. This practice continued into the junior high grades, and in another modified fashion, into high school.

At the end of the school day, as at the end of the work day, the Anglos went to their side of town and the Mexicans retreated to their side of town, primarily across the railroad tracks. The Anglos stayed among themselves; their white world was exclusive. We were not invited to their social functions. In fact, it was illegal for a Mexican to join the Crystal City Country Club, to swim at the city pool on the Anglo swim days, to be buried in the Anglo cemetery, to join the service clubs like the Lions Club or Chamber of Commerce, or to join an Anglo Boy Scout troop. The only time some Anglos and Mexicans came together was at the Catholic church. Even there, the priest had a separate service for Anglos billed as the "English language" mass, even though in those years all mass services were said in Latin. The other religious rituals were also segregated; protestant Mexicans such as the Methodists, the Pentecostal groups (*los alleluias* we called them, because they yelled and screamed during their services), and the Baptists had their own churches, for Anglos only. Later came the Mormons and the Jehovah's Witnesses, and they sought out Mexicans for conversion. The Mormons never built a church, they just came to do missionary work among the Chicano "natives." The Jehovah's Witnesses built churches for Mexicans and most of us hate them because they tell our people not to vote, not to get involved in civic affairs or protest bad conditions because the end of the world is near. The Jehovah's Witnesses don't have any time to spare in getting ready for Armageddon. The Chicano members of these other churches did not practice their faith with Anglos in their buildings, either. Apartheid of Mexican people by Anglos in South Texas extended beyond the political, economic, and social realm into religious practice.

The Three Destinies of Chicanos

My world was comprised of three spheres: the parental Mexican world, the Anglo school world, and my Chicano peer world. I've often thought of writing a book about my three destinies and, perhaps I will, after this book. As a child, it was not difficult to move between these worlds. This is so because children are largely ignored, have no civil rights to assert, and are not usually subjected to direct attack for being Mexican, though their parents are. Also, as a child, I had not yet learned of the prejudice against Mexicans that the Anglo world held. I was naive and uninformed about history, economics, politics, and culture. I once wrote a poem entitled "22 Miles," which I began with "at 22 miles, I could see my first 8 weren't," meaning that I didn't realize much about me, about being a Mexican, about Anglos, and, like most children, about my environment and life in general until the age of eight.

As I got older, I found it increasingly more difficult to move with ease in and out of my three spheres. The classroom curriculum, particularly with regard to the history and contribution of Mexican people, did not jibe with my home version; I found with more frequency it becoming necessary to choose between historical versions. Daily, I faced obstacles because I was Mexican or Chicano and had to make choices having to do with my culture: do I eat in the school cafeteria with most of the Anglos and hardly any of the Mexican kids? (The Mexican kids had no money and there was no school lunch program, then.) Even if I take a lunch to school to be with my Chicano kind, will it be a sandwich of white bread or tortilla tacos? Which kind of tortillas—corn or white flour, real Mexican or Chicano tortillas? Do I sit or play with Chicanos or Anglos? Do I talk with the pretty *gringita* girl or the pretty Chicana? If I ask gringo kids to play after school, will it be at my house or theirs? And will they say, "I'm sorry! Noooooo! You are Mexican!"? Should I continue to pronounce "ch" words with a Chicano accent, like "sh," after the teacher corrects me in front of everybody for saying things like "shurch," "shicken" and "share" for church, chicken and chair? Should I say "Meese" when I can say "Miss," in order to sound like the other Chicanos? Am I related to George Washington, the father of my country and Davy Crockett, the hero of the Alamo? Am I to be as proud of my biological father, Angel Gutierréz Crespo, the medical doctor for the Mexican people of Cristal, esteemed by many of them as their "hero" for saving a life? Is Santa Ana a traitor for fighting to keep Texas a part of Mexico and trading his life for that land, unlike Lorenzo de Zavala, who conspired to take Texas and destroy the government of Mexico? Which of these two men is a *vendido* (sellout)? Why should I be taught to feel shame for the fact that the Mexicans won at the Alamo? Besides, none of the gringos in the Alamo were from Texas or legal residents. They were all illegal aliens who had crossed into Mexican Texas from Kentucky, Tennessee, and other places.

It is always easier to retreat within a familiar world. As Chicanos we are constantly choosing one from among the three options. There is no pervasive Chicano culture for us yet, but we are working on it. Ilan Stavans attempts to describe the assimilation process for all Latinos in the United States in *The Hispanic Condition* (1995). He confuses the condition of Chicanos, a people who have always been here, with those recent immigrants from Central and South America, including himself. In many respects, these Latinos are not unlike the European immigrants that came, in yesteryear, voluntarily to assimilate into the "Anglo" culture of the United States. Some persons of Mexican ancestry totally deceive themselves while attempting to deceive others, by claiming to be "American," just like an Anglo. Invariably this is the subject, over drinks at cocktail parties and in arguments between Chicano militants and members of the right-wing, hawkish American G.I. Forum. Persons of Mexican ancestry can claim to be "Hispanic" today, when they opt for being more Spanish than Mexican. This Hispanic identity is not Mexican, to be sure, and is also geographically and historically impossible for those of us with a Mexican ancestry in the Southwest that spans generations.

The Cure-All "I'm Sorry!"

When we state our names in Spanish, invariably some Anglo will tell us, "I am sorry, but I don't speak Spanish." They feign embarrassment when told that we are not speaking Spanish, simply telling them our names! Anglos also love to use the "I'm sorry" as an all-purpose excuse. Sometimes they add "I'm *soooo* sorry!" on a second try to cool down the situation, in case we didn't get their intonation and emphasis right the first time. Regardless of how severe the personal transgression is, they always think that an "I'm sorry" will soothe it away. Chicanos hear countless "I'm sorry's" in a lifetime and we don't believe any of them to be genuine. An "I'm sorry" said *en español* from one Spanish speaking person to another certainly is not going to soothe the hurt; after a serious personal transgression that a Chicano commits against another Chicano, the wrong-doer best get ready, make a stand, and fight like an angry devil, for all hell will usually break loose shortly from the offended party.

The new Hispanic identity as a generic term for la raza (the race), all Spanish-speaking peoples, was born with the 1980 census, and the term was kept in use for the subsequent 1990 census. In the previous four enumerations, from 1940 to 1970, the U.S. Bureau of the Census had been unable to fix a label on this diverse and complex ethnic group. In Spanish, each subgroup of la raza has no problem with the question "What are you?" The group members of each subgroup will answer with a nationality, such as "*Soy Panameño!*" "*Soy Cubano!*" "*Soy Mexicano!*" and the like. In response to the same question in English, we trip mentally over the acceptable term for the ethnic group: "I'm Chicano! I'm an American! I'm a Puerto Rican! I'm a Cuban American!" According to the Census, however, we are not in charge of our self-description. We have lost our primordial right of agency, to represent ourselves to the world with an identity of our choice.

There are Spanish-speaking children today who have, in their lifetime, not heard of a descriptive ethnic group label other than Hispanic. The Census Bureau and the mainstream media are busy instilling in all that the proper term for Spanish-speaking people and their progeny, even if the latter be English-speaking monolingual, is Hispanic. In order to reject the Hispanic label on a census form, an employment application, a questionnaire, or other similar survey instrument, a Chicano must skip "Hispanic," mark "Other," and then fill in the blank with "Chicano" or another word choice. Reluctantly, however, most Chicanos mark "Hispanic" because it is currently so imposing and all-pervasive.

We are also confronted with a forced choice of race in the Census designations. Prior to 1940 we were racially unclassified. We were neither "Mongoloid" (Red Indian or Yellow Asian), "Caucasoid" (White Anglo), or "Negroid" (Negro, then Black, now African American); we were classified as "Other Race." Then, the League of United Latin American Citizens, LULAC, a civil rights organization of middle-class Mexican Americans formed in the 1920s, begin to press for the racial designation of persons of Mexican ancestry to be white, and prevailed. After the 1940 census, Mexican Americans have been racially classified as Caucasian, or white. Beginning with the 1980 census, and the switch to the label Hispanic, the Census Bureau now requests of Hispanics only to pick a racial designation among four choices: White; Black; American Indian, Eskimo, and Aleut; or, Asian and Pacific Islander. This is a neat trick on us. We are now further divided among ourselves and from others on the issue of race; the concept of la raza is no longer a common denominator of culture, as it once was.

Estéban "Steve" Jordan (San Antonio)

"El corrido de Jhonny el Pachuco"

(The Corrido of Jhonny the Pachuco)

"Este es el corrido de un pachucón
de por allá de Robstown, Tejas:
se creía muy slika y le dieron chicharrón.
Ahora verás:"

Voy a cantarles un corrido de muy al alba
Lo que ha pasado en la Main de Robstown;
Este es la historia de un pachuco muy rocote
Era muy loco, traficante y coredor.

Juan se llambaba pero le decían "el Jhonny."
Muy taraliol, muy engreído en el amor.
A las pachucas más greñudas se llevaba,
Allá en McAllen no dejaba ni una flor.

Un día domingo que andaba muy taralaílo.
A la cantina le corrieron a chismear:
—Cuídiate Jhonny, que por allí te andan güachando.
Son muchos cholos, no te van a pilorear. »

Known as the "Jimi Hendrix of the accordion" and inducted into the Conjunto Hall of Fame, "Steve" Jordan, from San Antonio, is most recognized for pushing the accordion to its limit, playing everything from traditional *conjunto* to rock, jazz, and zydeco.

"This is the story of a badass pachuco from Robstown, Texas;
he thought he was pretty slick
but he ended up getting burned.
Here's how it happened."

I'm going to sing you a great corrido
About what happened on Main Street in Robstown;
This is the story of one badass pachuco,
who was a drug trafficer and a real wild guy.

His name was Juan but everyone called him "Jhonny,"
He drank a lot and loved to chase women;
He hung out with the seediest pachuca girls,
And in McAllen he didn't leave a single flower untouched.

One Sunday when he was pretty drunk,
They came to the bar and told him:
"Look out Jhonny, they're watching you,
Don't let those cholos come and get you." >>

No tuvo tiempo de montar en su carrucha.
Y de rembaisa se le echaron de a montón.
—Ando muy alto-les gritaba-y no me agüito,
Cuando un pilero travesó su corazón.

Y las cantinas de la Main están cerradas.
Todos los cholos se dedican a rezar.
Y por las calles las cholitas van pasando
A ver al Jhonny que lo van a embalsamar.

Allá en un chante ya muy triste llora un chavo.
Y las pachucas ni se acuerdan por su Juan,
Y entra su jefa y lo consuela con cariño,
Porque al "Jhonito" no le queda ni un carnal.

Aquí termino de contarles esta historia
De un pachucote muy engreído en el amor.
Que se creyó de las pachucas más greñudas,
Por eso mismo lo mandaron al panteón.

He didn't have time to get into his car.
They all came rushing at him:
"I'm pretty drunk," he shouted,
"And I'll stay and fight,"
When the bullet pierced his heart.

Now all the bars on Main Street are closed.
And the cholos are all off praying,
And the chola girls are all passing by
To see the remains of Jhonny who they are taking to embalm.

And in a house a boy is crying,
The pachucas don't even remember him.
His mother comes in to quiet him,
Because little Jhonny doesn't even have a brother.

And this is the end of the story,
The story of this badass pachuco
Who hung out with the seediest pachuca girls.
And because of it they've sent him to his grave.

Abelardo "Lalo" Delgado (El Paso)

"Stupid America" and "The Chicano Manifesto"

Stupid America

with a big knife
on his steady hand
he doesn't want to knife you
he wants to sit on a bench
and carve christ figures
but you won't let him.
stupid america, hear that chicano
shouting curses on the street
he is a poet
without paper and pencil
and since he cannot write
he will explode.
stupid america, remember that chicanito
flunking math and english
he is the picasso
of your western states
but he will die
with one thousand masterpieces
hanging only from his mind.

Abelardo Delgado was born in Chihuahua and came to El Paso at age twelve. After high school he worked in construction and at a community center in El Paso for several years. Once he graduated from the University of Texas at El Paso, he worked with César Chávez's farmworker movement, and later became executive director of the Colorado Migrant Council. During this time he began publishing his poems, including his most famous "Stupid America" in 1969, and reading his works every chance he had, whether to an audience of thousands or at a wedding. Delgado was one of the first products of the Chicano political movements of the 1960s and 1970s, and his poems are often explicit reflections of that history, told from what Delgado called his "poetic perspective." At the time of his death he was living in Denver, Colorado.

The Chicano Manifesto

this is in keeping with my own physical condition
for i am tired—too tired perhaps for this rendition. . . .
but la raza is also tired
and la raza cannot wait
until i rest
she wants her rest also
but there is much catching up to do.
anglos have asked (i think sincerely)
what it is that you chicanos want?
those with power to be,
influencing our lives, have asked. . . .
is it understanding?
is it that you want us to tolerate you?
is it admittance?
and when i heard those questions
like remote control my chicano anger took over
and i answered the arrogant questioning . . .
no . . . we do not want any of that
or the question "what do you want" either
you see, you can afford to sit in libraries
and visit mexico and in a way
learn to understand us much better than we do ourselves
but understanding a thing
and comprehending are two different matters. . . .
tolerate is a word we use
in reference to borrachos,
we do not wish you strain
yourselves with toleration
of our, supposedly, intolerable ways
and . . . yes . . . question of admittance
is a fine one for it puts you inside and us outside
asking like cats and dogs in the rain to be let in.
the nature of your questions
assumes you have something to offer.
but there is one thing i wish
you would do for us, >>

in all your dealings with us,
in all your institutions
that affect our lives
deal with us as you openly claim you can,
justly. . . . with love. . . . with dignity.
correct your own abuses on la raza
for your own sake and not for ours
so you can have some peace of mind.
for. . . . you see. . . . we only lack a piece of bread
which comes cheaper according to your own value system
let me tell you what we want,
not from you but from ourselves and for ourselves. . . .
we want to let america know that she
belongs to us as much as we belong in turn to her
by now we have learned to talk
and want to be on good speaking terms
with all that is america.
from government we want to become
visible and not merely legislated
and supervised but included
in the design of laws and their implementation.
from education we want the most that it can offer,
a history that tells it like it is,
principals, teachers, counselors, college professors. . . .
scholarships, curriculum, testing
and all this from chicanos a la chicana
and this we are not asking por favor
but merely as an overdue payment
and we might even forget the previous score.
from the church we very piously ask
less sermon and more delivery
more priests to preach Christ's merciful justice,
less alms and tokens in the name of charity
and more pinpointment of the screwing going on.
from los chicanos del barrio y de los campos
we also have some strong demands
(among ourselves there is much more confianza)

we want you to plot a clean escape but very soon,
lose your habit of speaking in low voices
and of walking with cabezas agachadas,
we are poor only in the material
for your heritage is very rich.
from chicanos with a little
bit of wealth and power les
pedmios una mano
but to give los olvidados
not a damn thing. . . . they are asking
for your hand. . . . but only in amistad
as brothers that you, even if you don't want to, are.
and finally to the draft board
we have a few words to share with you
no la jodan. . . . metan gabachos tambien
our manifesto i know is general
but we saved the specific for the end
for the chicano migrant is about
to become like your american buffalo. . . . extinct. . . .
those who claim that was a crime with animals
are now in good position to prevent one with humans
or will the migrant honor come as always. . . . post humous

part seven

the 1970s

Roy Benavidez (Cuero)

from *The Three Wars of Roy Benavidez*

Time weighs heavy on your hands when you're confined to the hospital—especially when you're confined to that narrow bunk-sized bed that seems to harden with each passing day. What do you do when you've counted all the ceiling tiles, told your jokes until everyone is tired of listening to them, and threatened to throw up if the guy in the next bunk begins telling stories about his girl back home?

Hospital time, for me at least, was tedium time. I counted the hours, then the minutes each day as I waited for it to be time to roll out of that hospital bed and try to get those feet and legs moving again. Hospital time was also a time to think, to remember those events and those people who had influenced your life, for good or bad. In my mind, I returned to Germany.

I remembered the evening Frank Torres and I stepped out of the KBS Bar onto the West Berlin street. It was a beautiful night and we were feeling no pain. Somewhere along the way we had lost Ralph Gonzalez; we were too loaded to remember where. We had just returned to 6th Infantry Regiment headquarters from a week of exercises in the West German countryside, and we were tired and thirsty.

An overnight pass was going a long way toward taking care of the thirst. Tomorrow was Sunday—then we would rest. We were young. It was 1958, I was 24, and I was going back to the States in less than a week to see Lala. Wedding bells were in my future for sure.

Outside the bar at the curb, two men—Americans—were arguing in loud voices. From the

Roy Benavidez was born in Cuero the son of a sharecropper. He dropped out in the seventh grade and was forever tortured by taunts that he was a "dumb Mexican." He joined the Special Forces of the U.S. Army and was sent to Vietnam. On May 2, 1968, Sergeant Benavidez rushed into a helicopter with a three-man crew to rescue a patrol of trapped men. When the helicopter crashed, he pulled the wounded from the wreckage, kept fighting, was shot several times. Clubbed and stabbed by a North Vietnamese soldier, Benavidez killed him as he carried one of his men to safety. Benavidez was thought to be dead and was even zipped into a body bag. Thirteen years after the incident, he was awarded the Congressional Medal of Honor for his valor. "I'm proud to be an American," he is quoted as saying as he died in a San Antonio hospital.

looks of it, they were servicemen. At the time, there were two ways to appear in public in Berlin—either in uniform or in civilian dress that included a coat and tie. We were emissaries of our government and were expected to dress as such. And behave as such. That's why the two men caught our attention.

Their clothing and haircuts marked them as U.S. servicemen. It was their behavior that was questionable. One was drunk out of his mind; the other was trying to persuade him to get into the taxi waiting beside them. The drunk was having none of it, cursing his companion in a loud voice for pulling him away from his fräulein in the bar.

The light fell on their faces as they swayed in an alcoholic rhumba, and I recognized them both as first lieutenants in our outfit. I walked over to see if I could help.

"Sit, can I give you a hand?" I asked the relatively sober one.

"Corporal," replied the lieutenant, apparently recognizing me despite my civilian dress. "Maybe you can give me some help with my buddy here."

"What the hell are you doing here, Corporal?" slurred the drunk, fixing me with what he thought was a withering stare. Instead, he looked cross-eyed.

"Nothing much, sir. Can I help you there?" I turned to see if Torres was nearby to assist, but he was standing well away from us. He was having none of it; Frank hated gringos anyway.

I turned back just as the lieutenant started swinging. "Get away from me!" he spluttered. "Take your hands offa me. Ain't no goddamn enlisted man gonna touch me," he screamed, getting louder and more violent. I grabbed one arm and held on, while his friend reached for the other. The incident was getting out of hand and we were drawing a crowd.

"Cold cock him, Benavidez!" Torres shouted from behind me. And without thinking, I did it, catching him with a solid right to the jaw.

He went down without a word, slumping into the back seat of the cab. I stared at him with my mouth open. I had just slugged an officer. The intoxicated man's fellow officer looked at me, the shock on both our faces blending nicely under the glare of the street lamp.

"Sir . . ." I said, not sure what to say, but knowing that there was nothing but trouble ahead.

"Come on, Ben, let's get out of here." It was Torres pulling on my sleeve.

Without another word to me, the lieutenant jumped into the taxi on top of his unconscious buddy and slammed the door as the cab pulled out into the traffic.

Torres was still pulling on my arm, eager to get away as quickly as possible. "Goddamn, Ben, you didn't have to hit him."

"What do you mean?" I said, stumbling after him. "You told me to hit him."

"Wait a minute, you're not going to blame me for you slugging an officer." We had stopped beneath a streetlight and were about to get into it not twenty feet from where I had just assaulted an officer. Reason returned to us before it went any farther, and we headed back to our unit. The fun had suddenly gone out of the evening.

I couldn't sleep that night. I just knew the shit was going to hit the fan when Monday came.

You've really done it this time, Benavidez, I thought. You've been getting into trouble ever since you got into this army. Now, it's going to be jail. They'll probably throw in a dishonorable discharge too.

Lying on my bed in the barracks, staring up into the night, I could see Uncle Nick the day I told him I was going into the army—going to be a soldier.

"You'll never make it, Roy," he snorted. "You're hardheaded and can't control your mouth. You won't even make it through boot camp."

But there had been no turning back. After two years of National Guard duty, including eight weeks at radio maintenance school at Fort Knox, Kentucky, I was convinced that army life was for me. At the school, I had seen up close men who carried themselves with pride and self respect—paratroopers. I wanted to be one of them more than anything I had wanted in my life.

Twenty years old, my mind was made up. Anyway, what was there for me if I spent the rest of my life in El Campo? Just another poor Mexican in a small Texas town full of them.

"Him? That's old Roy. He's the Mexican who works down at the Firestone place. Yeah, you can probably get him to clean up the brush on your place. Just give him a few bucks."

Unh-uh! No way was I going to settle for that. But it was close. I did pretty poorly on the tests the army insisted I take before they waived the results and took me anyway. They needed men who wanted to be there.

Lying there in that silent German night, I tossed and turned, forced to view each of the indictments of my past as each and every one flickered across the inside of my eyelids like old newsreels.

There I was—fighting in the Golden Gloves tournament in Fort Worth. At least, I'd managed to channel my combative instincts along more respectable lines. The school bully was now a boxer—an eleven-year-old fighter who had taken on everything in his class around El Campo.

But in that cow-town arena a white boy beat me to a pulp. It was no contest. Afterward, in the locker room, my brother, Roger, raged at the humiliation that

I . . . he . . . hell, the whole Hispanic race had suffered at the hands of a gringo kid.

After basking in the glow of victory at ringside, my opponent walked into the room—alone. Without a word to me, Roger jumped the youngster and began working him over. The boy was tired, but I think he could still have given Roger all he wanted. My split lip was stark evidence of his ability. Without thinking, I had jumped into the fight. Roger and I dragged the boy, kicking and screaming, into one of the toilet stalls at the end of the room. We plunged his head into the evil-smelling bowl; I reached for the handle and flushed it.

Then we panicked. Almost dressed, I snatched the rest of my clothes, and we ran. It was the end of my boxing career. And so much for good sportsmanship.

My first week in boot camp. I got into a fight with a cook. Standing at a sink, washing vegetables, I didn't hear my name called over the sound of the running water.

"Hey you! I'm talking to you!"

A hand on my shoulder spun me around. Without thinking, I slammed my fist into the man's chest and sent him flying onto the hot stove behind him. He wasn't badly hurt, but with less than a week in the service, I found myself in hot water. It was not a good beginning.

In the pre-dawn darkness as the hands on my wristwatch toiled toward Sunday morning. I heard myself as I stood up in the middle of more than one crowded bar: "Anybody here think they can whip the ass of a good Indian?" There always seemed to be someone who thought they could.

"Booze, bad habits, and bad company are going to get you in trouble, Roy." That old saw of my Uncle Nick's played itself over in my mind as I lay there. It came back to me with the punch of a proclamation from God himself.

With the insight from a heavy dose of fear and remorse, I could see clearly how my behavior over the past three years had propelled me to this crisis in my life. I wouldn't even be in Germany if it hadn't been for my mouth.

In 1956, following my first tour overseas in South Korea, I returned to Fort Chaffee, Arkansas. I was due a thirty-day leave before reassignment. But before I left for home, I treated myself to a night on the town.

Before the evening was over, I found myself loaded in some little out-of-the-way honky-tonk mouthing off to some guy dressed in civvies. Considering the trouble the event caused me, I wish I could remember more of it. I do recall squaring off against the man but no blows were exchanged. The blow came the next day when I learned that I'd picked on a master sergeant in personnel.

By the end of the day, I had orders in my hand to go to Germany. Goodbye, thirty-day leave. All it took for an assignment to be speeded up or delayed was for someone—

a personnel sergeant?—to practice a little sleight of hand and switch paper from one pile to another.

I found myself in Augsburg in the Federal Republic of Germany with the 11th Airborne Division. All things considered, I was delighted. To be airborne had been my goal since joining the army. Now, although I was still a long way from being a paratrooper, I at least felt a bit nearer to my dream. The 11th even had a jump school; with a little luck, I might find myself enrolled as a student.

"Booze, bad habits, and bad company are going to get you in trouble, Roy."

How true. Only a week in Germany and Uncle Nick's warning proved to be just as valid.

Along with two airborne buddies, Ernie Trujillo and Frank Montoya, I made a stop at the Hillbilly Bar there in Augsburg.

"If you're ever going to be a trooper, Roy, you've got to learn that you don't take no shit off of nobody," Montoya had announced as we made ourselves comfortable at a table. The juke box was belting out "Fräulein," Bobby Helms' latest hit.

Trujillo pointed to a table of four enlisted men next to us, none of them wearing airborne wings. "Take those legs over there . . ." he said. A "leg" is any nonairborne-qualified soldier.

"Nobody in airborne buys the first drink when there's a leg around to do it for him," Montoya interrupted.

I was a "leg" myself, but hell, with my buddies I felt airborne.

I took the hint and when the waitress came over, I ordered: "*Drei brau, bitte,* and give the bill to those damn legs over there."

The "legs" in question ignored me—with the exception of one. "Hey," the biggest member of the group said, turning to look at me, "I ain't buyin' your damn beer." He continued to glare, the cross-eyed stare of a pissed drunk, for a moment longer before turning back to his buddies.

Our beer arrived, and the girl stood nervously waiting for someone to pay her. She looked first at me and then to the next table.

"Fräulein, I said the legs'll pay."

Almost before I got the words out, he stood over me. He was spoiling for a fight. I recognized a kindred soul.

"You little son-of-a-bitch, I said I ain't buyin' no goddamn beer for you!"

I stood up too. He was big . . . six feet three if he was an inch. I was looking him square in the chest. Speaking of short, the situation had all the makings of a brief encounter.

I was overmatched, so I did the only reasonable thing: I kicked him as hard as

I could in the balls. I had left sportsmanship gurgling down that toilet in Fort Worth.

He bent double, smooth like a well-oiled jackknife, an anguished gasp escaping his lips. Taking him by the shoulders, I spun him around, planted the sole of my boot on his butt and sent him crashing back into the table with his buddies who had not moved.

"Drink up fast," I said, turning back to Trujillo and Montoya. "If we're still here when he gets up, he's gonna kill us." We were out in less than a minute.

I was on the carpet within twenty-four hours. I had put the man in the hospital. There was already enough bad blood between the airborne and regular troops before I had gotten involved, Sergeant Villareal told me as I stood before him in his office. There had even been a number of fights between them.

"If you stay here, Benavidez, somebody may try to even things up with you," he said. Colonel Cassidy had ordered a halt to fighting among U.S. servicemen, Villareal went on. They had been making progress keeping a lid on things. I was not a good influence, he said, and shipped me off to Berlin. Since I learned later that the Colonel had considered a court martial, I got off easy. But there went my chance at jump school. The airborne would have to wait.

And in the time I had been in Berlin, the only trouble I had been in was one or two missed bedchecks. Now, with less than a week to go until I headed for home, I was finally in real hot water, if someone reported what went on outside that bar.

Sunday morning finally arrived. I had spent part of the night praying that nothing would come of last evening's encounter. I decided to follow up my prayers with some action. After dressing, I went to the chapel for early Mass and a last-minute confession, for good measure.

The priest, concealed by the privacy of the confessional, did not seem as disturbed as I was by my recent transgression. Perhaps he was expecting the revelation of a rape or murder when I admitted at the outset that I had committed a terrible sin. Hitting an officer didn't measure up.

"I'm sure it's not as serious as you think, my son," he counseled, his voice quiet and reassuring. "Certainly it was only an accident."

"Accident! Like hell it was, Father," I blurted out. "I slugged the guy."

He still wasn't convinced of the seriousness of the situation. I had figured the whole deal was worth at least two rosaries, but he sent me away with a penance of only six "Our Fathers" and three "Hail Marys."

"Benavidez! Corporal Benavidez!"

It was the platoon sergeant. Monday morning was finally here, and it looked like it was going to live up to my expectations.

"Report to the first sergeant."

As I walked down the hall to his office, my last hope vanished. The previous evening outside the NCO club, I had passed the lieutenant I had popped Saturday night. I had given him the snappiest salute possible; he returned it casually without a hint in his expression that I was more than just any other soldier. Perhaps there was a chance this whole mess would pass without my seeing the inside of the stockade.

The futility of that thought struck home when I entered the orderly room and the first sergeant speared me with an icy stare. He looked like he couldn't believe what he was seeing.

First Sergeant Charlie Turner was an old World War II and Korean veteran. They called him the "Tiger," and at that moment, I felt like I was being stalked.

"You really done it this time, Benavidez," he said. "Come on, the company commander wants to see you."

As I followed him out, I whispered an aside to the company clerk seated at a nearby desk: "Why's he want to see me?'

"Don't talk to me, Benavidez," he muttered without even looking up. I shrugged and went on through the door. It was a dumb question anyhow.

Walking down that corridor to the CO's office, I knew how a condemned man felt on the last mile. I wished the priest was with me. Let him tell the company commander that it was "not as serious as you think, my son."

I stood at attention before my commanding officer. "Corporal Benavidez reporting as ordered, sir." I was scared stiff.

"Stand at ease, Corporal."

He sat at his desk and looked me over for a few seconds. It seemed like hours. I wondered if the first sergeant, standing at my side, could bear my heart pounding.

"I hear you had some fun Saturday night," he finally said, leaning forward.

I wasn't sure how to respond to that. What did he mean? "Yes, sir," I replied in as near a noncommittal voice as I could muster.

"Well, for a man going home in a few days, you sure don't look too happy."

"To tell the truth, Captain, I don't feel too good right now."

"Look, Corporal," he said, dropping the slightly mocking tone, "I'm aware there was some trouble Saturday night between you and someone else. I understand the situation, and I want to be fair."

"Yes, sir," I answered again, swallowing bard. I didn't look at him. Instead, I focused my eyes on the wall behind him—on a plaque hung there.

"You've been a pretty good soldier while here," he went on. "No trouble to really speak of." Not until now. I was making up for lack of quantity with a double dose of quality. I wished I were somewhere else. The words on that plaque. I had read them before someplace.

"Like I said, I want to be fair. So, I'm going to ask you a question, and I want a 'yes' or a 'no' from you. Understand?"

I pulled my attention back from the inscribed tablet behind the captain's desk. Fear can do strange things to a man. Rather than concentrate on a hopeless situation, my mind had actually wandered, seeking a safer place to light.

Now, I realized what he was saying. He's giving me a way out, I thought. At least, he seemed to be. I tried to gather my thoughts. If I read him right, he was willing to accept whatever answer I gave him.

"Did you strike an officer Saturday night, Corporal Benavidez?"

Well, there it was. My gaze shifted back to the wall behind his desk. Suddenly, I recognized the inscription there. The captain was a West Point graduate; the polished face of the plaque was stamped with the academy seal and tile West Point code of honor. The words were there before me: "Duty, Honor, Country. I do not lie, cheat, or steal, or tolerate those who do."

The captain was waiting for my answer, at my side, the first sergeant stood, a frown beginning to crease his forehead.

It just kind of welled up inside me. I had wanted to be a soldier, a good soldier, the best soldier I could be. At least that's what I had been telling myself. But my actions said otherwise. Maybe it was time I took a stand.

God knows, I was no West Point graduate—just a semiliterate Mexican kid from South Texas who never even made it to high school. But if I really wanted my career in the service to ever amount to anything, those words needed to mean just as much to me as to the man sitting in front of me—even if believing in them meant the end of my career and maybe loss of my freedom.

The captain leaned forward, his hands clasped before him on the desktop.

"Well, Corporal, did you or didn't you?" He spoke as if he couldn't understand the reason for my hesitation.

"Yes, sir." It was not much more than a whisper. I couldn't believe I was saying it. My guts balled up into a knot, and I thought I was going to be sick. Four days before I was to go home and I had just bought a ticket to the stockade and possibly a dishonorable discharge.

I heard the first sergeant's breath hiss through his clenched teeth; the sudden intake of air was the closest he would allow himself to a gasp of astonishment at my words.

"What did you say, soldier?" The captain wasn't sure of his ears either.

"Yes, sir, Captain. I hit that officer the other night."

"Jesus Christ," muttered the sergeant at my side, unable to restrain himself any longer. I think he would have hit me if the captain hadn't been staring at both of us.

"Wait outside, Corporal Benavidez," the captain said, placing both hands palms down on the desk and pushing back. His words cracked with authority.

I was alone outside the CO's office in the hall for only a few minutes before the first sergeant joined me. He proceeded to chew me out, questioning every part of my character, parentage, and intelligence . . . especially my intelligence.

"You're a damn fool, Benavidez. I don't understand you. You could have walked right out of here without a problem. He gave you a chance."

"I know, First Sergeant." I didn't understand me either. But it didn't make any difference; it was too late to change my mind. It was going to be a long time before I saw Lala now.

I thought for a second I could hear the captain on the phone in his office. He was probably calling the MPs. Finally, the door opened and the captain looked out into the corridor.

"First Sergeant," he called, ignoring me. "The PFC can go now." He disappeared and the door closed.

I looked at the first sergeant; he stared back at me, shock on both of our faces. PFC. Private First Class. That was all, I thought. He'd busted me from corporal to PFC for knocking an officer cold. Relief flooded through me.

"You're a lucky Mexican, Benavidez, damn lucky," snorted the first sergeant. "Now, get out of here."

Unfortunately, my day with the captain was not over. I fell under his gaze once more. Standing outside the company office that afternoon, I was looking over the bulletin board when Torres rounded the corner and walked by. He'd heard of my morning encounter with the CO.

"Hey, I see you got KP from the captain, Ben," he called out in passing. I still felt resentment toward Frank: if he had given me a hand with that drunk in the first place, all this might have been prevented.

But then maybe it wouldn't have made any difference. I seemed to have the knack for saying and doing the wrong thing at the wrong time without anybody's help. I proceeded to demonstrate it as I called out to his retreating back: "I don't have KP; I'm going home." And louder as he moved on down the corridor, "So, you can just kiss my ass!"

I didn't hear the door to the orderly room open behind me. "What did you say, Private?" I turned. It was the captain. Without thinking—a Benavidez trait—I answered the question. "Sir, I said you can just kiss my ass."

"You want to come in here, Benavidez?"

Oh my God, not again, I thought. I was back in trouble again. This was turning into a nightmare.

I followed him through the company office into his private one. Coming or going, he had the choice of using the door into the main office or the private entrance into the hall where I had sweated it out only that morning. If he'd come out the private door, he probably wouldn't have even noticed me standing there at the bulletin board. What luck.

The first sergeant was standing in the outer office when the two of us paraded through. His eyes widened in disbelief.

In the captain's office I tried to explain that it had not been him I was speaking to. I started to tell him that I wouldn't tell an officer to kiss my ass. Right, no more than I would strike one. I changed my mind.

"I didn't see anyone else, Private," he replied. "It was just you and me in that hallway."

"Aw . . . please, sir."

He began to laugh, and it dawned on me that things were not as bad as my paranoid mind thought them to be. He just couldn't pass up the opportunity to put me back on the hot-seat for a few minutes. I wasn't sure I appreciated the captain's sense of humor.

I was only partly right about his motives for calling me in. After his laughter subsided, he revealed his curiosity. Why, he wondered, had I answered as I did and what was so fascinating about that plaque on the wall?

I did my best to explain my feelings to him. I had screwed up more than my share since joining the army. I didn't want to be a troublemaker. Maybe it finally occurred to me standing there before him that there had to be a point beyond which I was unwilling to go if I was to have a chance to be the soldier I had dreamed of becoming. Lying to my commanding officer was that point.

"I guess reading the words on that plaque brought it home, sir," I continued. "I may not be West Point material, but that's the kind of soldier I want to be."

He looked at me thoughtfully for a few moments and then, standing, offered me his hand. "Well, Benavidez, if you intend to make the army your career, and I hope you do, follow the lead of those words in that code and you'll make a good soldier."

I walked out of his office, and in a week I was back in the U.S.

Tomás Rivera (Crystal City)

"The Night Before Christmas"

Christmas Eve was approaching and the barrage of commercials, music and Christmas cheer over the radio and the blare of announcements over the loud speakers on top of the stationwagon advertising movies at the Teatro Ideal resounded and seemed to draw it closer. It was three days before Christmas when Doña Maria decided to buy something for her children. This was the first time she would buy them toys. Every year she intended to do it but she always ended up facing up to the fact that, no, they couldn't afford it. She knew that her husband would be bringing each of the children candies and nuts anyway and, so she would rationalize that they didn't need to get them anything else. Nevertheless, every Christmas the children asked for toys. She always appeased them with the same promise. She would tell them to wait until the sixth of January, the day of the Magi, and by the time that day arrived the children had already forgotten all about it. But now she was noticing that each year the children seemed less and less taken with Don Chon's visit on Christmas Eve when he came bearing a sack of oranges and nuts.

"But why doesn't Santa Claus bring us anything?"

"What do you mean? What about the oranges and nuts he brings you?"

"No, that's Don Chon."

"No, I'm talking about what you always find under the sewing machine."

Tomás Rivera was born in Crystal City, and throughout his childhood he accompanied his family in the fields as a migrant worker. He attended Southwest Texas State College, then went on to the University of Oklahoma for an M.A. in Spanish and a Ph.D. in Romance languages and literature in 1969. Two years later his most famous work, *. . . Y no se la tragó la tierra/ . . . And the Earth Did Not Devour Him,* based on his experiences as a migrant worker, was published as the first in a series of publications by the Chicano activist publisher Quinto Sol out of Berkeley, California. A professor, he also worked in education administration, becoming the chancellor of the University of California at Riverside and helping to found the National Council of Chicanos in Higher Education.

"What, Dad's the one who brings that, don't think we don't know that. Aren't we good like the other kids?"

"Of course, you're good children. Why don't you wait until the day of the Reyes Magos. That's when toys and gifts really arrive. In Mexico, it's not Santa Claus who brings gifts, but the Three Wisemen. And they don't come until the sixth of January. That's the real date."

"Yeah, but they always forget. They've never brought us anything, not on Christmas Eve, not on the day of the Three Kings."

"Well, maybe this time they will."

"Yeah, well, I sure hope so."

That was why she made up her mind to buy them something. But they didn't have the money to spend on toys. Her husband worked almost eighteen hours a day washing dishes and cooking at a restaurant. He didn't have time to go downtown and buy toys. Besides, they had to save money every week to pay for the trip up north. Now they even charged for children too, even if they rode standing up the whole way to Iowa. So it cost them a lot to make the trip. In any case, that night when her husband arrived, tired from work, she talked to him about getting something for the children.

"Look, viejo, the children want something for Christmas."

"What about the oranges and nuts I bring them."

"Well, they want toys. They're not content anymore with just fruits and nuts. They're a little older now and more aware of things."

"They don't need anything."

"Now, you can't tell me you didn't have toys when you were a kid."

"I used to *make* my own toys, out of clay . . . little horses and little soldiers . . ."

"Yes, but it's different here. They see so many things . . . come on, let's go get them something . . . I'll go to Kress myself."

"You?"

"Yes, me."

"Aren't you afraid to go downtown? You remember that time in Wilmar, out in Minnesota, how you got lost downtown. Are you sure you're not afraid?"

"Yes, yes, I remember, but I'll just have to get my courage up. I've thought about it all day long and I've set my mind to it. I'm sure I won't get lost here. Look, I go out to the street. From here you can see the ice house. It's only four blocks away, so Doña Regina tells me. When I get to the ice house I turn to the right and go two blocks and there's downtown. Kress is right there. Then, I come out of Kress, walk back towards the ice house and turn back on this street, and here I am."

"I guess it really won't be difficult. Yeah. Fine. I'll leave you some money on top of the table when I go to work in the morning. But be careful, vieja, there's a lot of people downtown these days."

The fact was that Doña Maria very rarely left the house. The only time she did was when she visited her father and her sister who lived on the next block. And she only went to church whenever someone died and, occasionally, when there was a wedding. But she went with her husband, so she never took notice of where she was going. And her husband always brought her everything. He was the one who bought the groceries and clothing. In reality she was unfamiliar with downtown even though it was only six blocks away. The cemetery was on the other side of downtown and the church was also in that direction. The only time that they passed through downtown was whenever they were on their way to San Antonio or whenever they were returning from up north. And this would usually be during the wee hours of the morning or at night. But that day she was determined and she started making preparations.

The next day she got up early as usual, and after seeing her husband and children off, she took the money from the table and began getting ready to go downtown. This didn't take her long.

"My God, I don't know why I'm so fearful. Why, downtown is only six blocks from here. I just go straight and then after I cross the tracks turn right. Then go two blocks and there's Kress. On the way back, I walk two blocks back and then I turn to the left and keep walking until I'm home again. God willing, there won't be any dogs on the way. And I just pray that the train doesn't come while I'm crossing the tracks and catches me right in the middle . . . I just hope there's no dogs . . . I hope there's no train coming down the tracks."

She walked the distance from the house to the railroad tracks rapidly. She walked down the middle of the street all the way. She was afraid to walk on the sidewalk. She feared she might get bitten by a dog or that someone might grab her. In actuality there was only one dog along the entire stretch and most of the people didn't even notice her walking toward downtown. She nevertheless kept walking down the middle of the street and, luckily, not a single car passed by, otherwise she would not have known what to do. Upon arriving at the crossing she was suddenly struck by intense fear. She could hear the sound of moving trains and their whistles blowing and this was unnerving her. She was too scared to cross. Each time she mustered enough courage to cross she heard the whistle of the train and, frightened, she retreated and ended up at the same place. Finally, overcoming her fear, she shut her eyes and crossed the tracks. Once she got past the tracks, her fear began to subside. She got to the corner and turned to the right.

The sidewalks were crowded with people and her ears started to fill up with a ringing sound, the kind that, once it started, it wouldn't stop. She didn't recognize any of the people around her. She wanted to turn back but she was caught in the flow of the crowd which shoved her onward toward downtown and the sound kept ringing louder and louder in her ears. She became frightened and more and more she was finding herself unable to remember why she was there amidst the crowd of people. She stopped in an alley way between two stores to regain her composure a bit. She stood there for a while watching the passing crowd.

> "My God, what is happening to me? I'm starting to feel the same way I did in Wilmar. I hope I don't get worse. Let me see . . . the ice house is in that direction—no it's that way. No, my God, what's happening to me? Let me see . . . I came from over there to here. So it's in that direction. I should have just stayed home. Uh, can you tell me where Kress is, please? . . . Thank you."

She walked to where they had pointed and entered the store. The noise and pushing of the crowd was worse inside. Her anxiety soared. All she wanted was to leave the store but she couldn't find the doors anywhere, only stacks and stacks of merchandise and people crowded against one another. She even started hearing voices coming from the merchandise. For a while she stood, gazing blankly at what was in front of her. She couldn't even remember the names of the things. Some people stared at her for a few seconds, others just pushed her aside. She remained in this state for a while, then she started walking again. She finally made out some toys and put them in her bag. Then she saw a wallet and also put that in her bag. Suddenly she no longer heard the noise of the crowd. She only saw the people moving about—their legs, their arms, their mouths, their eyes. She finally asked where the door, the exit was. They told her and she started in that direction. She pressed through the crowd, pushing her way until she pushed open the door and exited.

She had been standing on the sidewalk for only a few seconds, trying to figure out where she was, when she felt someone grab her roughly by the arm. She was grabbed so tightly that she gave out a cry.

> "Here she is . . . these damn people, always stealing something, stealing. I've been watching you all along. Let's have that bag."

"But . . ."

Then she heard nothing for a long time. All she saw was the pavement moving swiftly toward her face and a small pebble that bounced into her eye and was hurting a lot. She felt someone pulling her arms and when they turned her, face up, all she saw were faces far away. Then she saw a security guard with a gun in his holster and she was terrified. In that instant she thought about her children and her eyes filled with tears. She started crying. Then she lost consciousness of what was happening around her, only feeling herself drifting in a sea of people, their arms brushing against her like waves.

"It's a good thing my compadre happened to be there. He's the one who ran to the restaurant to tell me. How do you feel?"

"I think I must be insane, viejo."

"That's why I asked you if you weren't afraid you might get sick like in Wilmar."

"What will become of my children with a mother who's insane? A crazy woman who can't even talk, can't even go downtown."

"Anyway, I went and got the notary public. He's the one who went with me to the jail. He explained everything to the official. That you got dizzy and that you get nervous attacks whenever you're in a crowd of people."

"And if they send me to the insane asylum? I don't want to leave my children. Please, viejo, don't let them take me, don't let them. I shouldn't have gone downtown."

"Just stay here inside the house and don't leave the yard. There's no need for it anyway. I'll bring you everything you need. Look, don't cry anymore, don't cry. No, go ahead and cry, it'll make you feel better. I'm gonna talk to the kids and tell them to stop bothering you about Santa Claus. I'm gonna tell them there's no Santa Claus, that way they won't trouble you with that anymore.

"No, viejo, don't be mean. Tell them that if he doesn't bring them anything on Christmas Eve, it's because the Reyes Magos will be bringing them something."

"But . . . well, all right, whatever you say. I suppose it's always best to have hope."

The children, who were hiding behind the door, heard everything, but they didn't quite understand it all. They awaited the day of the Reyes Magos as they did every year. When that day came and went with no arrival of gifts, they didn't ask for explanations.

Tino Villanueva (San Marcos)

"Scene from the Movie *GIANT*" and "I Too Have Walked My Barrio Streets"

Scene from the Movie *GIANT*

What I have from 1956 is one instant at the Holiday
Theater, where a small dimension of a film, as in
A dream, became the feature of the whole. It
Comes toward the end . . . the café scene, which
Reels off a slow spread of light, a stark desire

To see itself once more, though there is, at times,
No joy in old time movies. It begins with the
Jingling of bells and the plainer truth of it:
That the front door to a roadside café opens and
Shuts as the Benedicts (Rock Hudson and Elizabeth

Tino Villanueva grew up in San Marcos embarrassed about being a migrant worker. Like many, Villanueva did not go straight to college but spent time working and was drafted into the Army, serving in Panama where he began to take an interest in the culture of the Americas. When he returned to San Marcos, he took a B.A. from Southwest Texas State University, went to the State University of New York for an M.A., and Boston College for his Ph.D. Winner of an American Book Award, considered by many to be the finest Chicano poet, he began writing at Southwest Texas State University and published his first book, *Hay Otra Voz Poems*, in 1972. He teaches at Boston University.

Taylor), their daughter Luz, and daughter-in-law
Juana and grandson Jordy, pass through it not
Unobserved. Nothing sweeps up into an actual act
Of kindness into the eyes of Sarge, who owns this
Joint and has it out for dark-eyed Juana, weary

Of too much longing that comes with rejection.
Juana, from barely inside the door, and Sarge,
Stout and unpleased from behind his counter, clash
Eye-to-eye, as time stands like heat. Silence is
Everywhere, acquiring the name of hatred and Juana

Cannot bear the dread—the dark-jowl gaze of Sarge
Against her skin. Suddenly: bells go off again.
By the quiet effort of walking, three Mexican-
Types step in, whom Sarge refuses to serve . . .
Those gestures of his, those looks that could kill

A heart you carry in memory for years. A scene from
The past has caught me in the act of living: even
To myself I cannot say except with worried phrases
Upon a paper, how I withstood arrogance in a gruff
Voice coming with the deep-dyed colors of the screen;

How in the beginning I experienced almost nothing to
Say and now wonder if I can ever live enough to tell
The after-tale. I remember this and I remember myself
Locked into a back-row seat—I am a thin, flickering,
Helpless light, local-looking, unthought of at fourteen.

I Too Have Walked My Barrio Streets

Andando por San Antonio arriba
vi la quietud de la pobreza:
rechinaban los goznes quebrados,
las puertas cansadas querían
ir a sollozar o a dormir.
⁂
Se preparaba para el fuego
la madera de la pobreza.

"Arrabales (Canción Triste)"
—Pablo Neruda

I too have walked my barrio streets,
seen life not worth the lingering grief.

(As a child and migrant,
I've picked clean straight rows of cotton
when the Summers were afire.
And driven by hunger, I've come face to face
with the uprooted fury of the West Texas wind.
I've slept on floors of Winter's many corners,
on linoleum-covered dirtfloors
of the hard-sprawled Panhandle.
I've taken refuge under cowsheds
when all of driving Winter rained down a sea
of stiff mud.)

I too have walked my barrio streets,
smelled patio flowers burning in the stabbing sun,
and those in grandma's flower-pots are weary flowers
that do not wilt, instead, they're crushed
by bitter dust from streets forgotten,
a corrosive dust set loose
by the official attitude of Health Department trucks:
I've tasted that official dust from which
official voices have appeared to thunder:

Yore outhouse's gotta go. It's unsanitary, and b'sides,
The City of San Marcos is askin' all of y'all with
out houses ta git inside plumbin.' After all, y'all've
had a drainage system come through heah for the last
three years. Ya got one month ta do it in. OK, amigo?

(I've printed my name at different schools
for indifferent teachers
who've snickered at my native surname,
who've turned me in "for speaking Spanish on
    the premises"
long before Jamestown,
and so I've brightly scrawled transcending obscenities
in adolescent rage.)

I too have walked my barrio streets,
gone among old scars and young wounds
who, gathering at the edge of town, on nearby corners,
mend their broken history with their timely tales.

(I've been quizzed on Texas history—
history contrived in dark corridors
by darker still textbook committees.
I've read those tinged white pages where the ink
went casting obscurantism across the page:
the shadows had long dried into a fierce solid state.
And Bigfoot Wallace had always been my teacher's hero,
and what's worse, I believed it,
oh, how we all believed it.)

I too have walked my barrio streets,
seen over-worked and hollow-eyed men
in the unemployment line, their wrinkled bodies worked-over
like the sharecropped furrows they once grew
under day-long mules steady as the plowing sun. >>

(With many others,
I've thrust a picket sign into the chanting Boston air:
Work's too hard,
pay's too low,
Farah pants have got to go!
I've struck down
what Farah slacks
were hanging on the racks, and down the street,
what sold-out lettuce came to the sell-out counters
of the East:
¡Obreros unidos,
jamás serán vencidos!)

I too have walked my barrio streets,
heard those congenial strangers
who put up their finest drawl in yearly, murdered Spanish!

Voutin poar mey. Yeu soay eil meijoar keindideitou
para seyerveerleis.

But somewhere in the bred fever of the barrio,
Carmelita López, in a sad dress, clutches the warmth
of her raggedy doll;
Carmelita cries out for milk, and so drowns out
the paid political pronouncement.
Carmelita, with the languid frame,
shrivels in November's fever, and her laid-off *papi*
can only wish to fix the roof that sprung a leak
a year or two ago.

Pablo, I too have walked my barrio streets.
And this I say: that in our barrio,
where a whole country is a parody of itself,
there's still plenty of wood to burn,
and that the winds of the people
are keeping all flames aglow,
until the mighty hand that holds dominion over
    Man is bent back at the finger joints;
until the swivel chairs of official leather
    are rooted out from thickly-soiled, pile carpets;
until all pain is driven out at last from the naked barrio.

Walking around.
So many times we've walked along
interminable streets, Pablo.
Yet one loud question keeps pounding in my ear:

> A poet's devotion, can't it reach beyond mere walking,
> beyond found words
> when the people are stirring into the glowing wind?

Little Joe (Temple)

"A la guerra ya me llevan" (They're Taking Me to War)

A la guerra ya me llevan, madrecita
Me agarraron en la revelia de ayer
Hay te quedas sin tu hijito muy solita
Sabrá dios si nos volveremos a ver

Hay le entregas este sobre retornado
A mi novia que no sabe en donde estoy
Y le dices que me llevan de soldado
Y a otras tierras muy lejanas yo me voy

Ya no lloras madrecita por mi suerte
Que soy hombre y mi destino fue pelear
Y si acaso en el combate hallo la muerte
Yo no quisiera que tu vayas a llorar

En mi pecho siempre llevo la medalla
Que mi madre me la dio con tanta fe
Y si acaso no me alcanza la metralla
A tus brazos madrecita volvere

Aquí dejo a mis pobres padrecitos
Que desde niño batallaron con apá
Cuando miran ya volar los aeroplanos
Que me llevan derechito a Kuwait

They're taking me to war, sweet mother
They're taking me against my will
You have to stay without your very lonely son
God will know if we'll see each other again

Give this addressed envelope to my girlfriend
Who does not know where I am
Tell her that they are taking me as a soldier
And to other lands far away I am going

Don't cry sweet mother for my luck
For I'm a man and my destiny was to fight
And if in combat I find death
I wouldn't want you to cry

On my chest I always carry the medallion
That my mother gave me with so much faith
And if the shrapnel doesn't reach me
To your arms, sweet mother, I'll return

Here I leave my poor parents
As a boy I battled with dad
Now when you look up as the airplanes fly
They are taking me straight to the war

ALONG WITH THE BAND LITTLE JOE Y LA FAMILIA, Temple native Little Joe Hernandez is credited with a new sound, a mix of norteño ballads and polkas with a touch of big-band swing, blues, and country.

Rolando Hinojosa (Mercedes)

"Voces del barrio," "A Sunday in Klail," and "Es el agua"

Voces del barrio

Cuando el sol se baja y los bolillos dejan sus tiendas, el pueblo americano se duerme para no despertar hasta el día siguiente.

Cuando el sol se baja y la gente ha cenado, el pueblo mexicano se aviva y se oyen las voces del barrio: la gente mayor, los jóvenes, los chicos, los perros . . .

Dicen que la Sooner Contracting de Ardmore anda buscando gente . . .

Si no me equivoco, uno de los contratistas es Vîctor Jara, el Pirulí.

¿Con ése? Ni a cruzar la calle, contimás el estado.

Niños, váyanse a jugar a la calle y dejen a los mayores hablar.

¡A la momita, a la momita! Ese poste de telefón es el home-base.

Tules virules, nalgas azules.

Juan Barragán bebe leche y caga pan.

¡No se vale ver, no se vale ver!

Te las hago largas a ti y a Vargas, si no las das, ¿pa qué las cargas? >>

Rolando Hinojosa was born in Mercedes. After serving in the Army during the Korean War, he earned his B.A. from the University of Texas. He taught high school for a few years before going to New Mexico Highlands University for a M.A. and the University of Illinois for a Ph.D. Beginning his career as a professor, he also began publishing fiction. His first book of short stories *Estampas del valle y otras obras* garnered him national attention, and in 1976 won the Premio Casa de las Americas for his novel *Klail City y sus alrededores*. After teaching in Kingsville and the University of Minnesota, Hinojosa became professor at the University of Texas and is admired and much studied for his prolific series of books set around the fictional Rio Grande Valley city of Klail.

Pin marín de don pingüé
Cúcara, mácara, pípere fue

Dos y dos son cuatro; cuatro y dos son seis; seis y dos son ocho: y ocho, diez y seis.

Cuenta la tablita
que ya la conté
Cuéntala de vuelta
que ya me cansé.

¿Y por qué no saliste anoche?

No me dejaron; ya sabes. ¿Te quedaste esperando?

Hasta la una.

Pobrecito.

No te burles.

Si no me burlo, Jehú . . . ándale, vámonos al parque.

¿Y tu hermanito?

Ahí anda, jugando a las escondederas.

Vente.

Cuidado que nos ven agarrados de la mano.

Ah, raza . . .

¿De veras te quedaste esperando?

Hasta la una . . .

¿Y qué le dijo la enfermera, doña Faustina?

Pues casi nada, quiere que le saquemos las anginas al niño.

¿Y eso pa qué?

Dice que sin anginas no le darán tantos catarros.

Esas son cosas de los gringos que no tienen más qué hacer.

Ahora voy yo, ahora voy yo: ¿Quieren tortillas duras?

¡No!

¿Duras?

¡No!

Ah, ¡durazno!

Ahora yo, que va la mía: Lana sube, lana baja.

¡La navaja!

No sé, cuñao, eso de irse con contratista desconocido está arriesgado.

De acuerdo, si hay veces que con los conocidos . . .

Claro . . . Verdá . . . Ya lo creo . . .

¿No me explico, Federico?

¿Me entiendes, Méndez?

No me chingues, Juan Dominguez.

¡Niños, no molesten a los mayores!

Creo que ya es hora de irnos. ¿Dónde estará Adela? Eh, tú, Andrés ¿qué se hizo tu hermana?

La dejé en el parque, amá.

Ve por ella, ándale. Hasta mañana, doña Faustina.

Si Dios es servido, doña Barbarita.

Ahora le toca al barrio dormir. En los barrios se habla de mucho y, como de milagro, siempre se halla de qué hablar noche tras noche.

El barrio puede llamarse el Rebaje, el de las Conchas, el Cantarranas, el Rincón del Diablo, el Pueblo Mexicano—verdaderamente los títulos importan poco.

Lo importante, como siempre, es la gente.

A Sunday in Klail

"Let's go! Let's go! Let's have a little action out here! Let's go! He's blind as a bat! Nobody hurt, nobody hurt! Say hey!"

The one yelling is Arturo Leyva:

Bookkeeper by profession,
Baseball's his obsession.
He had the measles at the age of four,
Cagón's the nickname which at school be bore.

Arturo doesn't understand fully the phrase "nobody hurt" but he repeats it because it's something he's heard since he was a child. This is not to say that Arturo doesn't know English; on the contrary, he defends himself rather well in the language. Nevertheless, the phrase "nobody hurt" is still a mystery to him.

Arturo is at Leones Park watching the 30–30 team from Klail play in a double-header with the Sox from Flora. It's a tough battle; Lázaro "Skinny" Peña hasn't allowed a hit (not even to his mother, should doña Estela get up to bat). The game is getting hot. Baseball is one of the few luxuries Arturo allows himself.

Even the birds know that Arturo is the husband of Yolanda Salazar, the only daughter of don Epigmenio who got a rupture before the Second World War (this rupture is strictly medical; the other, the moral rupture, he's had since he first drew breath). Arturo is allied with his father-in-law against doña Candelaria Munguía de Salazar. Perhaps Arturo doesn't know that Dr. Niccolo Machiavelli existed but he has intuited that in union there is strength.

The alliance is *de rigueur* because doña Candelaria is very despotic. In spite of all that, Arturo goes his own way, without any snags. He hasn't any problems with Yolanda; he knows how to handle her.

Among the people in Leones Park is Manzur Chajín, the confectioner. He is Lebanese, but people call him *el árabe*. Chajín lives in the barrio and is married to a Chicana (Catarina de Leon). By the time they'd been married two months, she knew how to make that round, red candy with peanuts; to be sure, it's not that difficult, but anything is better than nothing at all. Chajín, like most of his countrymen, pronounces p's as if they were b's and when he speaks about don Manuel, he says that he's such a good boliceman that he doesn't need his bistol. Chajín doesn't sell candy at the park; he lets the kids do it because that's what being a boss is all about.

Arturo went to piss and now he's back. In the meantime, Skinny is really making them toe the line: It's the eighth inning and he still hasn't allowed a hit (not even to his mother, doña Estela, etc . . .).

"Say hey, 30–30! Say hey!"

"Arturo."

"Yea?"

"Uh, nothing. Forget it . . ."

Here comes don Manuel Guzmán: he doesn't understand very much about baseball although he realizes not everyone can get seriously involved in that sport. It's very hot (it's August) but don Manuel, as usual, has on a white shirt with sleeve garters and a black tie. And, again as usual, he's wearing his swiss watch with the gold watch chain, items he received as part of an inheritance from don Victor Peláez.

"Arturo!"

"What is it, don Manuel?"

"Yolanda just left. She says to pick her up at your mother-in-law's."

"Yessir, sir."

Arturo Leyva is more at ease. He loves Yolanda, yes, and it would never occur to him to take on a mistress—perish the thought!—but baseball is baseball and—what the hell!—not every day is Sunday. Skinny hasn't allowed a hit and we're in the tenth inning: the problem is the Sox have two black brothers as their battery: Mann Moore, the pitcher, and his brother Clyde, the catcher; and to make things worse, the Klail 30–30 is what is known as "good field, no hit."

Arturo, although he's a bookkeeper, is tough: tonight, after the game, he'll take

Yolanda to the dance on Hidalgo Street and then, later on, to bed, because besides being tough, he's also a "fulfiller."

I believe it's already been said he knows how to handle Yolanda.

Es el agua

My name is Fructuoso Alaniz García, and I was so named for my Saint's Day, the twenty-first day of January; in English, according to my granddaughter Lucía, my name means *bountiful, productive.* Myself, I find it proper that one so named should be chosen to work the land, to know it, and to give it life so that it—the land—return part of that life in grain and cereal, in vegetables and, yes, in fruits of labor and of bounty to that person who prepared the land and watched the crops grow from nothing but a hope and a handful of seeds.

When I work my land, the one I own, I work it the same way I work somebody else's land. It makes no difference; none, really. Land is land, and when all is said and done, or, as we say, when the music is over, one leaves the terrain—*el terreno*—for somebody else to occupy. But, one must leave the land clean, weeded, and ready for that somebody else who comes to it with that hope and that handful of seeds I spoke of.

I'm from here, the Valley; a northbank borderer like my father, like his father, and his, too. A Mexican, of course, but an American by birth, yes. And once, when I was nineteen-years-old, in 1918, I was sent to France, but as you can see, I came back. Two of my cousins, José Antonio and Francisco García, did not. My granddaughter Lucía—and she, too, worked the land until she was seventeen-years-old—my granddaughter says that my cousins are remembered—is that the word?—*remembered*?—anyway, my granddaughter says that they are remembered in Austin, the capital. Yes, they are in a park at the University where the young men play football. She saw the metal plaques in that park, took down the dates and of where and when they died, and yes, they are the same José Antonio and Francisco García, all right. That's something I didn't know about, the memorial plates. Yes, I was in France, and the land there was tired, I remember, but it's come back to feed its people, hasn't it? Ha! One thing about land, Professor, God's not making anymore, it isn't going anywhere, and you got to work it, that's all there is to it.

I've worked the land in Minnesota, Michigan, Ohio, places like that. We used to drive up from the Valley to Texarkana, Texas, across to Arkansas—they had some bad roads there in my day—and on to Poplar Bluff in Missouri. From there we'd go east to the Mississippi River to Cairo, Illinois, and then north to Kankakee; from there, east to again to Reynolds, Indiana—that's on Route 420—and then north to New Buffalo,

Michigan. Well, once in Michigan, we'd pick plums, cherries, grapes; soft fruit. But, if we'd drove on to east Michigan, we'd pick cucumbers in Pinconning or beets and then if we'd go south, to Ohio, we'd pick tomatoes there.

This could be done if we drove, if we had a car of our own. If we went by truck, on a contract, then we'd go where they'd take us. Sometimes we'd meet in Hoopeston, Illinois, and separate from there. Some friends and relatives of ours from the Valley worked for years for one family in Iowa; one family. They owned a nursery, and they needed special people for that; I worked there, too, seven or eight seasons, I guess.

My wife, she made the trips, too; we travelled together for twenty-seven years, and once we worked in Wyoming with some people who came up from Laredo, Texas. My wife died ten years ago . . . our son, Marcos, died two years ago, in a truck-train accident in Monon, Indiana. My granddaughter Lucía was unhurt, and she's a student in Austin, at the University. My son's widow, Estéfana, lives in our house, and she runs it now; my wife and I raised her from childhood, and she's been part of the family since she was a baby. Estéfana is one of the best and one of the fastest lettuce cutters and packers in the Valley—she's as good as some men I know and better than some others. And, she can read and write English, too. Her cousin, Isaura, is a schoolteacher, and in the summertime, Isaura teaches school for free in the school we built out in the field. She buys pencils and writing tablets, and she teaches reading and writing and the numbers to the kids. She does it because she says it is necessary; once in a while, some friends come and help her, but no matter what, Isaura is there everyday. Working . . .

My grandson, Balde, is twenty-three-years old, and he already owns a used-truck; he and a friend of his, a Valley boy named Raúl Santoscoy, is his partner. Balde is a champion hay stacker, yes he is; in competition, too. Raúl drives the truck and the two of them contract for hay hauling in North Texas: Amarillo, Plainview; what we call up 'up north,' *el norte.* Balde is my granddaughter's older brother, and he sends her money to Austin for her schooling. She's an example, he says, and he's proud of his sister; well, so are we, but Balde is also a fine young man who is not afraid of hard work.

We have a saying here in the Rio Grande Valley: *es el agua:* it's the water, the Rio Grande water. It claims you, you understand? It's yours and you belong to it, too. No matter where we work, we always comeback [*sic*]. To the border, to the Valley.

Es el agua, yes.

The Valley is a good place. It's hard, sure—*seguro*—but there's farm work, and one just has to be harder than the work. And the Valley is different, too, and it makes us different, somehow. When we leave it to go to the Yakima Valley or to Oregon for the hops or to Nampa in Idaho, we're home there, too. Why? Well, because the workers there are Valley people, yes. And, and, and the kids who have never been to the Valley say they're from there because that's where their folks are from. *Es el agua;* their parents talk about the Valley, see, and the kids know.

This is changing, of course, but everything changes, it is in the nature of things: I'll show you. When my wife and our friends picked cotton—and this is just an example—we picked in the Valley from June to August, and then the owner plowed the ground in September.

Well, by late August some of us'd go to Central Texas to pick or to West Texas in October and November, to places like Brownfield and Lamesa. Sometimes we'd go to Arkansas or to Missouri for cotton and to Tennessee, but not now and not for some twenty years now; machines do it, but they can't do everything. No, you still need *la mano de obra,* the human hand, the eye to see and to distinguish. Machines don't take pride in what they do, they can't . . . But we did, and do. Yes.

Work is work, and most of it is hard; but that's expected. What's a bother—and shameful, too—is where one has to live in the American Midwest: in our cars or trucks, or on the ground, in a *carpa*—a tent—or in chicken and turkey coops; these are the worst. Yes. Terrible . . . it isn't always like that, no, but even once is enough, believe me. But one endures, one survives, and one even survives and endures *racismo* and *prejuicio*—racism, prejudice—from everybody, even our own. But I can't change it and God won't, as we say . . . *Pero tampoco nos rajamos*—we won't crack, we won't throw up our hands and say: "I give up." No. *No nos rajamos y ya;* we won't give up, and that's it . . . But, after all the work and travel, it's back to the Valley for more work. *Es el agua,* yes.

Ha! Those who claim hard work never killed anybody are fooling themselves and their friends. Hard work is hard, that's why they call it that; it's killing—but there's a certain kind of pride—foolish pride, perhaps-—and understandable, too—but a family is proud of what it does and of what it can *do.* It's like when I was in France sixty-years-ago—one was there—and one *stayed* there until they said, "Let's go. Let's go home." And that is the way it is when we are in Indiana or Iowa or in the Red River Valley of Minnesota, one is there, then someone says, "Let's go home. To Texas. Home. To the Valley."

Es el agua.

Santiago Jiménez Jr. (San Antonio)

"Qué bonito es San Antonio" (How Beautiful San Antonio Is)

Qué bonito es San Antonio
Es la joya del país
Es un pueblo muy hermoso
Tengo orgullo ser de aquí

Mi bonito San Antonio
Nadie lo puede negar
Con sus bonitas mujeres
Para llevar a pasear

Caminando por el parque
Y jardines por el río
Recordando el Álamo
La gente muy unidos

Es un pueblo aluminado
Con el templo del Señor.
Tengo orgullo de tejano
Porque aquí nacido yo

How beautiful San Antonio is
It's the jewel of the country
It's the city most lovely
I am proud of being from here

My beautiful San Antonio
Nobody can deny it
With its beautiful woman
That you can take around anywhere

Walking through the park
And the gardens by the river
Remembering the Alamo
The people very united

It's a city so lit up
With a temple of the Lord
I am proud to be Tejano
Because I was born here

Unlike his older brother Flaco, Santiago Jr. has striven to keep the traditional music of hi s father, Don Santiago Sr., alive with songs in Spanish, dealing with real-life situations of work and love.

El paseo de las flores
Qué bonito carnival
Es el templo de las fiestas
Todos vienen a gozar

El mariachi con sus cantos
Y su grito original
Me recuerdo de mi tiempos
Que pensaba enamorar

Las mujeres son hermosas
Unas vienen y otras van
Ellas te hablan con los ojos
Otras señas te darán

El conjunto y la jamaica
Con el bajo y la acordeón
Péscate una de la mano
Ya bailar alrededor

Ya con ésta me despido
Estos besos les canté
Si no son de San Antonio
Bienvenidos son usted

Mi bonito San Antonio
Nunca de poder olvidar
Mientras Dios me dé licencia
Siempre aquí me he de quedar

The walk around the flowers
How beautiful is carnival
It's the temple of the parties
Everybody comes to enjoy

The mariachi with their songs
And its cry so unique
I remember my own times
That I thought I fell in love

The woman are so beautiful
Some come and some go
They talk to you with their eyes
Other teases they give you

The conjunto and the jamaica
with the bajo and the accordian
stick out one of your hands
and let's dance around

So with this I bid goodbye
These kisses I sing to you
If you aren't from San Antonio
Welcome are you all

My beautiful San Antonio
I can never forget you
As long as God gives me permission
It is here that I will stay.

ESTELLA PORTILLO TRAMBLEY'S career has kept her close to her native El Paso. She attended the University of Texas at El Paso and, after years of teaching high school and working as an administrator, she became resident dramatist at the El Paso Community College, managing production as well as instructing. She also hosted a radio show, and these experiences convinced her to become a writer. She has written plays, short stories, and two novels

Estela Portillo Trambley

(El Paso)

"La Yonfantayn"

Alicia was forty-two and worked hard at keeping her weight down. Not hard enough, really, and this was very frustrating for her—to never quite succeed. She wanted to be pencil thin like a movie star. She would leaf through movie magazines, imagining herself in the place of the immaculately made-up beauties that stared back at her. But in essence she was a realist and was very much aware of the inevitable bodily changes as years passed. She often studied her face and figure in the mirror, not without fears. The fantasy of glamor and beauty was getting harder and harder to maintain. It was no easy task, getting old. Why didn't someone invent some magic pill . . .

Sitting naked, defenseless, in a bathtub brimming with pink bubbles, she slid down into the water to make the usual check. She felt for flabbiness along the thighs, for the suspicious cottage cheese called tired, loose fat on her underarms. Suddenly she felt the sting of soap in her eye. Carefully she cupped water in her hand to rinse it out. Damn it! Part of her eyelashes were floating in the water. It would take close to an hour to paste new ones on again. Probably Delia's fault. Her girl was getting sloppy. Mamie was a new face at the beauty parlor, anxious to please the regular customers. Maybe she would ask for Mamie next time. No dollar tip for Delia after this. The soapy warmth of her body was almost mesmerizing. In her bubbly, pink realm Alicia was immortal, a nymph, sweet smelling, seductive, capable of anything.

Heck! She had to get out of the bath if she had to paste the damned eyelashes on. She stood up, bubbles dripping merrily off her nice, plump body. She had to hurry to be in time for her blind date. She giggled. A blind date! She could hardly believe that she had agreed to a blind date. Agreed? She smiled with great satisfaction and murmured to herself, "You insisted on nothing else, my girl. You wanted him served on a platter and that's the way you're getting him."

Rico was her yard boy, and at Katita's wedding she had seen Rico's uncle, Buti, from afar. Such a ridiculous name for such a gorgeous hunk of man. From that moment on she had been obsessed with the thought of owning him. It was her way, to possess her men. That way she could stay on top—teach them the art of making her happy. "Oh, I have such a capacity for love!" she told herself. Humming a love song, she stepped out of the bathtub and wrapped a towel gracefully around her body, assuming the pose of a queen. A middle-aged queen, the mirror on the bathroom door told her. There are mirrors and there are mirrors, she gloomily observed. She sucked in her stomach, watching her posture. But the extra pounds were still here and there. Time had taken away the solid firmness of youth and replaced it with extra flesh. She turned away from the mirror, summarizing life under her breath. "Shit!"

The next instant she was all smiles again, thinking of the long-waisted bra that would smooth out her midriff and give her an extra curve. Then there was the green chiffon on her bed, the type of dress that Loretta Young would wear. She visualized herself in the green chiffon, floating toward Buti with outstretched hand. There would be the inevitable twinkle of admiration in his eye. In her bedroom she glanced at the clock on her dresser. It was late. With rapid, expert movements, she took out creams, lipstick, eyeshadow, rouge, and brushes from her cosmetic drawer. She wrapped a towel around her head and had just opened the moisture cream when she remembered the eyelashes. Did she really need them? She remembered Lana Turner with her head on Clark Gable's shoulder, her eyelashes sweeping against her cheeks. Max Factor's finest, Alicia was sure of that.

Hell! She rummaged hurriedly around the bottom drawer until she found a plaster container with the words "Max Factor" emblazoned on the cover. Anything Lana did, she could do better. She took out a bottle of glue, then carefully blotted the excess cream from her eyes and began the operation.

"Hey, slow down!" yelled Rico as Buti made a turn on two wheels.

Rico turned around to check the load on the back of the pickup. They were returning from Ratón where at the ranger's station they had gotten permits to pick piñones in the Capitán Mountains. Buti had presented the rangers with a letter from Don Rafael Avina giving him permission to pick piñón nuts from his private lands. Buti had also signed a contract with the Borderfield Company to deliver the piñones at the railroad yards in Ancho, New Mexico, where the nuts would be shipped along with cedar wood to Salt Lake City. His first profitable business venture since he had arrived in the United States. He had a check from Borderfield in his pocket. He was well on his way to becoming what he had always wanted to be—a businessman. From there, a capitalist—why not? Anything was possible in the United States of America. He even had enough piñones left to sell to tienditas around Valverde and a special box of the best piñones for his blind date, the richest woman in Valverde. Things were coming up money every which way. He had had qualms about letting Rico talk him into the blind date until Rico started listing all the property owned by Alicia Flores: two blocks of presidios, ten acres of good river land, an office building. That made him ecstatic. Imagine him dating a pretty widow who owned an office building! There was no question about it—he was about to meet the only woman in the world that he would consider marrying. By all means, she could have him. It was about time he settled down.

All that boozing and all those women were getting to be too much for him. What he needed was the love and affection of one good, wealthy woman. Yes, ever since he had met Don Rafael things had gone for the better. Only six months before he had even considered going on welfare. Poker winnings had not been enough, and his antique shop had not been doing very well. He had resorted to odd jobs around Valverde, a new low for Buti. Then he had met Don Rafael at El Dedo Gordo in Juárez.

At the Fat Finger everybody knew Buti. That's where he did the important things in his life—play poker, start fights, pick up girls, and most important of all, drink until all hours of the morning. It was his home away from home. His feet on native soil and mariachi music floating through his being—that was happiness. One early dawn when only Elate, the bartender, and Buti were left at the Fat Finger—they were killing off a bottle of tequila before starting for home—who stumbles in but this little fat man with a pink head, drunker than a skunk. He fell face down on the floor soon enough. Buti helped him up, dusted him off, and led him to the table where Elote had already passed out.

"You sit right there. I'll get us another bottle." Buti wove his way between tables and made it to the bar. The little man just sat, staring into space until Buti nudged him with a new bottle of tequila.

"Where am I?" the little man asked, clearing his throat.

"In the land of the brave . . ." Buti responded with some pride.

"Where's that?"

"The Fat Finger, of course."

The friendship was cemented over the bottle of tequila. The little man had been a good ear. Focusing on the pink head, with tears in his eyes, Buti had unloaded all his woes on the little fat man. Buti recounted how he had tried so hard to become a capitalist in the land of plenty to no avail. He tried to look the little fat man in the eye, asking, "Are you a capitalist?"

"Yes," assured the little man, with a thick tongue. "I am that."

"See what I mean? Everybody who goes to the United States becomes a capitalist. Now—look at me. Great mind, good body—what's wrong with me?"

"What you need is luck," advised the little man with some wisdom, as he reeled off his chair.

Buti helped him up again and shook his head. "That's easier said than done. I know the principles of good business—contacts, capital, and a shrewd mind. But where in the hell do I get the contacts and the capital?"

"Me," assured the little fat man without hesitation. "Me, Don Rafael Avina will help you. I'm a millionaire."

"That's what they all say." Buti eyed him with some suspicion.

"Don't I look like a millionaire?" demanded the little man, starting to hiccup. The spasmodic closure of the glottis caused his eyes to cross. Buti looked at him, still with some suspicion, but decided that he looked eccentric enough to be a millionaire. "Okay, how're you going to help me?"

"First you must help me," said Don Rafael between hiccups, "find my car."

"Where did you park it?"

"I don't know. You see, I have no sense of direction," confessed Don Rafael, leaning heavily on Buti. "It's a green Cadillac."

That did it. A man who owned a Cadillac did not talk from the wrong side of his mouth. "Can you give me a hint?"

Don Rafael had gone to sleep on his shoulder. Now is the time to be resourceful, Buti told himself. How many green Cadillacs can be parked in a radius of six blocks? Don Rafael could not have wandered off farther than that on his short, little legs. It would be a cinch, once he sobered up Don Rafael enough for him to walk on his own speed.

It took six cups of coffee, but Don Rafael was able to hold on to Buti all the way to Mariscal, where Buti spotted a lone green Cadillac parked in front of Sylvia's place, the best whorehouse in Juárez.

"Hey, Don Rafael." Buti had to shake the little man from his stupor. "Is that the car?"

Don Rafael squinted, leaning forward then back against Buti. "Is it a green Cadillac?"

"A green Cadillac."

"That's my car." Don Rafael began to feel around for the keys. "Can't find my keys." Buti helped him look through all his pockets, but no keys.

"You could have left them in the ignition."

"That would be dumb." Don Rafael kept searching until Buti pushed him toward the car to look. Sure enough, the keys were in the ignition.

"There are your keys and your car." Buti gestured with a flourish.

"Then let's go home."

"Your home?" queried Buti.

"Why not? You can be my guest for as long as you like—if you can stand my sister . . .

"What's wrong with your sister?"

"Everything. Does everything right, prays all the time, and is still a virgin at fifty."

"See what you mean. You could drop me off at my place in Valverde."

They drove off, and it was not until they were crossing the immigration bridge that they heard the police sirens. A police car with a red flashing light cut right across the path of the green Cadillac. In no time, three police officers pulled Buti and Don Rafael roughly out of the car.

"What is the meaning of this?" demanded Don Rafael, sobering up in a hurry.

"You're under arrest," informed a menacing-looking officer.

"What are you talking about?" Buti asked angrily, shaking himself free from another officer's hold.

"You stole that car," accused the first officer.

Don Rafael was indignant. "You're crazy. That's my car!"

"That's the mayor's car. He reported it stolen."

"The mayor's car?" Buti was dumbfounded. He would never believe another little fat man with a pink head again.

"I have a green Cadillac," sputtered Don Rafael. "I demand to see my lawyers."

"Tomorrow you can call your lawyer. Tonight you go to jail," the third officer informed them with great stoicism. All of Don Rafael's screaming did no good. They wouldn't even look at his credentials. So the two had to spend a night in jail. Buti diplomatically offered Don Rafael his coat when he saw the little man shivering with cold, and even let him pillow his pink head on his shoulder to sleep. Buti had decided there was more than one green Cadillac in the world and that Don Rafael threw his weight around enough to be rich. Don Rafael snuggled close to Buti and snored all night.

They were allowed to leave the next morning after Don Rafael made a phone call and three lawyers showed up to threaten the government of Mexico with a lawsuit for false arrest. Outside the jail stood Don Rafael's green Cadillac from heaven knows where.

On the way home, Don Rafael gave Buti a written permit to pick piñones on his property for free, so Buti could count on a clear profit. Don Rafael wrung Buti's hand in goodbye, making him promise he would come up to Ratón to visit him and his sister, which Buti promised to do. Yes, Buti promised himself, he would soon go to Ratón for a social visit to thank Don Rafael for the piñones. He was well on his way to becoming a capitalist.

"Hey, Buti," called out Rico, "you just passed your house."

Buti backed the pickup next to a two-room shack he had built on the edge of his sister's one acre of land. The two-room house sported a red roof and a huge sign over the door that read "Antiques." After the roof and the sign, he had built himself an indoor toilet of which he was very proud. That had been six years before when he had come from Chihuahua to live with his sister and to make a fortune. He had fallen into the antique business by chance. One day he had found an old Victrola in an empty lot. That was the beginning of a huge collection of outlandish discards—old car horns, Kewpie dolls, wagon wheels, a stuffed moose head, an old church altar. At one time he had lugged home a huge, rusty commercial scale he claimed would be a priceless antique someday. The day he brought home the old, broken merry-go-round that boasted one headless horse painted blue, his sister, Trini, had been driven to distraction. She accused him of turning her place into an eyesore and ordered him to get rid of all the junk.

"Junk!" exclaimed Buti with great hurt in his voice. "Why, all these antiques will be worth thousands in a few years."

Rico had to agree with his mother—the place was an eyesore. After parking the pickup, Rico reminded Buti about his date with Alicia that night.

"Put on a clean shirt and shave, okay, Buti?"

"Baboso, who you think you talking to?"

"She's a nice lady, don't blow it," Rico reminded him.

"Sure she is. I'm going to marry her," Buti informed his nephew, who stared at him incredulously.

"She's not the marrying kind, Tío," Rico warned him.

"She's a widow, ain't she? She gave in once."

"That's cause she was sixteen," explained Rico.

"How old was he?" Buti inquired.

"Seventy and very rich."

"Smart girl. Never married again, eh? What for?"

"She's had lovers. Two of them."

"Smart girl. What were they like?"

Rico wrinkled his brow trying to remember. "The first one was her gardener. She took him because she claimed he looked like Humphrey Bogart."

"Humf—what?"

"Don't you ever watch the late late show? He was a movie star."

"What happened to him?"

"Humphrey Bogart? He died."

"No, stupid, the gardener."

"He died too. Fell off the roof fixing the television antenna."

Buti wanted all the facts. "What about the second lover?"

"He had a cleft in his chin like Kirk Douglas," Rico remembered.

"Another movie star? What's this thing with movie stars?"

"That's just the way she is." Rico added reassuringly, "But don't worry, Tío. She says you are the image of Clark Gable."

After the dog races, Buti took Alicia to Serafín's. It had become their favorite hangout. For one thing, the orchestra at Serafín's specialized in cumbias, and Buti was at his best dancing cumbias. No woman could resist him then. He could tell that Alicia was passionately in love with him by the way she clung to him and batted those ridiculous lashes. As he held the sweet-smelling, plump body against him and expertly did a turn on the floor, she hissed in his ear, "Well, are you going to move in?"

"Haven't changed my mind," he informed her in a cool, collected voice.

"Oh, you're infuriating!" She turned away from him, making her way back to the table. He noticed that the sway of her hips was defiant. Tonight could be the night. She plopped down on the table. "I've had it with you, Buti."

"What do you mean?" He tried to look perplexed.

"Stop playing cat and mouse."

"Am I suppose to be the mouse?" His voice was slightly sarcastic. "I've never been a mouse."

"Let's put our cards on the table." Her voice sounded ominous.

"Okay by me."

"Well then, don't give me that jazz about you loving me too much to live with me in sin. Sin, indeed! When I hear about all those girls you run around with . . ."

"Used to run around with," corrected Buti, looking into her eyes seductively. "I only want you. You are the world to me. Oh, how I want to make love to you. It tortures me to think about it. But I must be strong."

"There you go again. Come home with me tonight and you can make love to me all you want to." It was her stubborn voice.

"Don't say those things, my love, I would never sully our love by just jumping into bed with you." Buti was proud of the fake sincerity in his voice. "Our love is sacred. It must be sanctified by marriage."

"Marriage be damned!" Alicia hit her fists on the table. She was really angry now. He could tell. She accused him, "You just want my money."

"You're not the only girl with money. But you are the only woman I could ever love." Buti was beginning to believe it himself.

"You liar! All the girls you've had have been penniless, submissive, ignorant wetbacks from across the river." Her anger was becoming vicious now.

"Wait a minute." Buti was not playing a game anymore. He looked at the woman across the table, knowing that she was a romantic little fool, passionate, sensuous, selfish, stubborn, domineering, and full of fire. That's the kind of woman he would want to spend the rest of his life with. Nevertheless, he took affront. "What am I? I'm penniless—not quite, but almost. You could say I'm a wetback from across the river. And you, in your mindless way, want me to submit. Stop throwing stones. We seem to have the same likes!"

She looked at him with her mouth opened. She had sensed the sincerity in his voice. She could tell this was not a game anymore.

She knew she had been ambushed, but she would not give in.

"If you love me, and I believe you do, you'll come live with me, or—" there was a finality in her voice, "I simply will not see you again."

"I will not be another notch on your belt." There was finality in his voice too.

"Hell!" Alicia slammed the half-empty can of her beer against the porch railing. She hated the smell of honeysuckle, the full moon and the heavy sense of spring. She hated everything tonight. And look at her—this was her sixth can of beer—thousands of calories going straight to her waistline. She hated herself most of all. Buti was through with her. He must be, if what Rico had told her was true. He had come over to help her plant some rosebushes, and she had casually asked him how Buti was doing these days. According to Rico, he spent a lot of time up in Ratón visiting his friend Don Rafael Avina and his unmarried sister.

"Is she rich?" Alicia asked nonchalantly.

"Very rich," Rico answered in innocence, setting the young rosebushes up against the fence.

She didn't ask much more, but knowing Buti, she could put two and two together. He had found himself a greener pasture and a new playmate. He loves me. I know he loves me, but I've lost him forever, she despaired. She couldn't stand it anymore—the moon, the smell of honeysuckle. She went back into the house and turned the late late show on television. She threw a shawl over her shoulders and huddled a corner of the sofa. She sighed deeply, her breasts heaving under her thin negligee.

She recognized the actress on the screen. It was Joan Fontaine with her usual sweet, feminine smile and delicate gestures. She always looked so vulnerable, so helpless. Clark Gable came on the screen. Oh, no—why him? Even his dimples were like Buti's. Damn it all. She wanted to see the movie. They had had some kind of quarrel and Joan Fontaine had come to Clark to ask forgiveness, to say she was wrong. Joan's soft, beautiful eyes seem to say, You can do what you wish with me. You are my master . . . Alicia began to sniffle, then the tears flowed. Especially when she saw big, strong, powerful Clark become a bowl of jelly. All that feminine submissiveness had won out. Joan Fontaine had won the battle without lifting a finger. Hell, I'm no Joan Fontaine, thought Alicia. But Clark was smiling on the screen, and Alicia couldn't stand it any longer. She turned off the set and went out into the night wearing only a negligee, a shawl, and slippers. She didn't care who saw her. She was walking—no, running—toward Buti's shack almost a mile away. The princess was leaving her castle to go to the stable; it was her movie now, her scenario. She was Joan Fontaine running toward the man she loved, Clark Gable. It mustn't be too late. She would throw herself at his feet—offer him all she had. She suddenly realized the night was perfect for all this!

The lights were on. She knocked at the door, one hand against her breast, her eyes wide, beseeching . . . in the manner of Joan Fontaine.

"What the hell . . ." Buti stood in the doorway, half of a hero sandwich in his hand.

"May I come in?" There was a soft dignity in her voice. Buti took a bite of his sandwich and stared at her, speechless. She walked past him into the room, and when she heard the door close, she turned around dramatically with outstretched arms. "Darling . . ."

"You're drunk." Buti guessed.

"I only had five beers," she protested hotly, then caught herself. "No, my love, I'm here for a very good reason . . ." Again, the Fontaine mystique.

Buti took another bite from the sandwich and chewed nervously.

"Don't you understand?" She lifted her chin and smiled sweetly like she had seen Joan Fontaine do it hundreds of times. Buti shook his head unbelievingly. She began to pace the floor gracefully, her voice measured, almost pleading. "I've come to tell you that I was wrong. I want to be forgiven. How could I have doubted you? I'm so ashamed—so ashamed." Words straight from the movie.

Buti finished off the sandwich, then scratched his head. Alicia approached him, her hand posed in the air, then gently falling against his cheek. "Do you understand what I'm saying?"

"Hell no, I think you've gone bananas."

She held back her disappointment with strained courage. "You're not helping much, you know." She bit her lip, thinking that Clark Gable would never have made an unkind judgment like that. She looked into his eyes with a faint, sweetly twisted smile, then leaned her head against his shoulder. She was getting to him.

There was worry in his voice. "Are you feeling okay?"

She began to cry in a very un-Joan Fontaine-like way. "Why can't you be more like him?"

"Like who?"

"Like Clark Gable, you lout!" She almost shouted it, regretfully.

Buti's eyes began to shine. She was beginning to sound like the Alicia he knew and loved. "Why should I be like some dumb old movie star?"

"Don't you see?" She held her breath out of desperation. "It's life . . ."

"The late late show?" He finally caught on—the dame on television.

"You were watching it too!" She accused him, not without surprise.

"Had nothing else to do. They're stupid, you know."

"What!" Her dark eyes blazed with anger.

"Those old gushy movies . . ." He gestured their uselessness.

"That proves to me what a brute you are, you insensitive animal!" She kicked his shin.

"Well, the woman, she was kind of nice."

"Joan Fontaine . . ."

"Yonfantayn?"

"That's her name. You're not going to marry her, are you?" There was real concern in her voice.

"Yonfantayn?" He could not keep up with her madness.

"No—that woman up in Ratón."

"Berta Avina?" The whole scene came into focus. Buti sighed in relief.

"Rico told me she is very rich."

"Very rich."

"Is she slender and frail and soft-spoken like . . ."

"Yonfantayn?" Buti silently congratulated himself on his subtle play.

"Yes . . ."

Buti thought of Berta Avina, her square, skinny body, her tight lipped smile. He lied, "Oh, yes. Berta is the spitting image of Yonfantayn."

"I knew it. I knew it!" Alicia threw herself into his arms. "Please please, marry me. You beast, I love you so."

"Can't marry you tonight, querida. We have better things to do." He pulled her roughly against him, with the Clark Gable smile, and then he kissed her again and again. Still relying on his dimples, he picked her up without too great an effort and headed for the bed. She tried to push him away, protesting coyly, "No, we can't. We mustn't. Not before we are married."

He stopped in his tracks, not believing his ears. This was the woman who had nagged him and begged him to jump into bed with her. Now he couldn't believe his ears.

"Say that again."

"I said, not until we're married."

"Why? That's not my Alicia talking."

"Well, that's what she would say."

"Who would say?"

"Joan Fontaine, silly!"

"Well, I saw a movie myself last night, something about the wind . . ."

"*Gone with the Wind.*"

"Yes, that one with the guy you like, the one that looks like me."

"Clark Gable."

"He says to this beautiful, strong-willed, bossy woman—'Frankly, my dear, I don't give a damn!'"

He winked at her and threw her on the bed.

"Trágico Fin De Alfredo Gómez Carrasco" (The Tragic End of Alfredo Gómez Carrasco)

Paredes de Huntsville, Texas
Donde se sembró el terror
Arrogantes criminales
Desafiaron la prisión

El año setenta y cuatro
Sábado tres se presenta
En Agosto fue el final
De esta tragedia sangrienta

Fue Carrasco, fue Domínguez
Que a las paredes retaron
Dos temibles criminales
Que a la prisión amagaron

Once días con once noches
Desafiaron la prisión
Con diez guardias prisioneros
Guardianes con devoción »

Walls of Huntsville, Texas
Where terror was planted
Arrogant criminals
Defied prison

The year seventy four
Saturday the third it happened
The end of August
Of this bloody tragedy

It was Carrasco, it was Dominguez
That challenged the walls
Two feared criminals
That tricked the prison

Eleven days and eleven nights
They defied the prison
With ten prison guards
Guards with devotion »

Fred Gómez Carrasco was born in San Antonio and chose the gang and criminal life. As leader of a drug cartel that linked San Antonio and Laredo to Monterey and Guadalajara in the 1970s, he became the most wanted and notorious crime figure in Texas. He was killed in Huntsville State Prison in 1974 after conducting, at eleven days, the longest prison-hostage siege of the century. More corridos have been written about him than even Gregorio Cortez.

Fue Carrasco el sublevado
Que prometió asesinar
A todos los prisioneros
Si no obtenía libertad

Ya Carrasco tenía fama
De ser violento y capaz
De cumplir con su promesa
De uno por uno matar

El Jefe de la prisión
Hombre consciente al hablar
Carrasco entrega tus armas
No te vamos a matar

Carrasco le contestó
Yo quiero mi libertad
Yo no sigo prisionero
Y me tendrán que matar

Después de mucho debate
La prisión le concedió
Camión blindado de acero
Lo que Carrasco pidió

Once días con once noches
Tuvieron pa'preparar
Como un caballo de Troya
Un instrumento fatal

Un cajón hecho de tablas
Reforzado con cartón
Y llevarse a cuatro rehenes
Y escapar de la prisión

Carrasco was the rebel
That promised to kill
Every prisoner
If his freedom wasn't granted

Already Carrasco had fame
For being violent and capable
Of carrying out his promise
Of killing each one by one

The prison warden
A man aware as he spoke
Carrasco turn in your weapons
We are not going to kill you

Carrasco answered
I want my freedom
I will not remain a prisoner
And you will have to kill me

After much debate
The prison consented
Steel bulletproof bus
Is what Carrasco demanded

Eleven days and eleven nights
They had to prepare
Like the Trojan Horse
A fatal instrument

A box made of boards
Reinforced with cardboard
And carrying four hostages
to escape from prison

A las nueve de la noche
Con media para las diez
Abajaron cauteloso
Con las diez presas también

Adentro de aquel cajón
Que Carrasco construyó
Iban tres de los convictos
Con cuatro rehenes de honor

Por fuera iban los demás
Como carne de cañón
Pues Carrasco sin conciencia
Lo hacía por su salvación

Abajaron poco a poco
A su esperado final
Cuando el agua les pegó
Carrasco empezó a tirar

El Capitán de los rinches
Fue el primero que cayó
Pero el chaleco de maya
Las balas no traspasó

Siguiendo la balacera
Ni quien lo fuera a pensar
Que al momento de la muerte
Solito se iba a matar

Mató a la primera mujer
Que le enseño compasión
Iba esposada de él
No se atentó el corazón »

At nine that night
With half an hour to ten
They came down cautiously
With the ten prisoners also

Inside that box
That Carrasco built
There were three of the convicts
With four hostages of honor

On the outside were the others
Like canon meat
Carrasco without a conscious
Did it for his own salvation

They came down slowly
To their awaited end
When the water hit them
Carrasco started shooting

The captain of the guards
Was the first to fall
Though through the bulletproof vest
The bullets didn't puncture

The shooting continued
No one ever thought
That at the time of death
He would end up killing himself

He killed the first woman
That showed him compassion
She was handcuffed to him
But it didn't move his heart »

Murió también su maestra
Domínguez la ejecutó
Después como los cobardes
También solo se mató

Cuevas el otro rebelde
A la muerte le temió
Primero hirió al Padrecito
Y luego se desmayó

Cuatro muertos, tres heridos
Es la herencia del que hiere
Que el que vive en la violencia
Entre ella misma se muere

El alma que se suicida
Viola la ley del camino
Es cobarde y tenebroso
No enfrentarse a su destino

Ya murió Alfredo Carrasco
Ni un amigo fue a llorar
Solito bajó a su tumba
Nadie lo fue a acompañar.

His teacher also died
Domínguez executed her
Later like the cowards
He killed himself

Cuevas the other rebel
was afraid of dying
First he wounded the priest
and then he fainted

Four dead, three wounded
Is the legacy for the injured
For he who lives in violence
Dies within that violence

The soul that commits suicide
Violates the law of the way
It's cowardly and sinister
To not face its own destiny

Alfredo Carrasco has died
Not a friend went to mourn him
He descended to his tomb all alone
No one was there to accompany him.

Cecilio García-Camarillo (Laredo)

"Talking to the Rio Grande" and "Space"

from Talking to the Rio Grande

¿Pero cómo jodidos le hago para resolver la situación? Old river, how can I reject with my body la maña of wanting to own her? ¿Cómo puedo dejar de ser lo que soy? How? I'd have to die and be reborn. If I were a rattlesnake and could change skins I'd be renewed. I'd be young with a glistening new skin. I'd drink your waters with a new soul. Maybe then I wouldn't have the need of wanting her by my side. I'd even be able to forgive my father. To be renewed, but first I'd have to die.

I almost died once, remember? Yes, I was in junior high, and my friends from school and I played hookey, and I took them in my old car to the family ranch. Man, aquellos sí eran tiempos locotes. And then I showed them something special, la noria, so deep and mysterious. I remember my cousins Kiko and Pepé digging it years before, and I was always afraid to get close to it. But now my friends were right up to the rim of the well, and they saw some snakes at the bottom. They got all excited and started shooting at them with two .22-caliber rifles. I yelled no, son víboras negras, they're harmless. Están allá abajo porque hay ratas y se las van a comer. But they just kept shooting like maniacs. Then they argued about who was going to go down the ladder to get the snakes so we could take them back to Laredo and scare the shit out of people, but nobody had the guts to volunteer. Then someone said I should go down 'cause after all it was my ranch and I was used to

Writers in the Chicano Movement of the 1960s and 1970s often published their own poetry and started their own periodicals when no one else would speak for Chicanos. Cecilio García-Camarillo, born in Laredo, is a perfect example. After attending the University of Texas, he published his work in chapbooks throughout the 1970s and was editor and publisher of the most important Chicano literary magazine of the period, *Caracol.* An NEA winner, he was host of *Espejos de Aztlán,* a cultural affairs program in Albuquerque, until his death from cancer in 2002.

those kinds of things, and they circled me and called me joto, miedoso, chicken shit and pussy. My heart started jumping all over the place, but I decided to go down anyway. I'd show them que mi verga estaba más gruesa than all of theirs put together.

I started going down and it felt warm, with a tightness then a release, as if the dark and damp well were pulsating. There was a thick old smell all around. I could barely see the bottom, but I knew the snakes were dead, probably killed twenty times over. I went lower, trying to focus on the snakes. The well now felt cool and exhilarating. Suddenly I saw a movement all around me. I couldn't believe that the dark walls were moving all around me. Then I realized there were thousands of crickets living there and the shooting had agitated them. I stood still and looked at them for a moment. They were like a black blanket moving in waves. Then my friends again me rayaron la madre and even threw stones, and I felt so alone and scared. The crickets got more excited when my foot slipped and I almost fell. With one hand I braced myself against the wall of the well, but when I did that the crickets began jumping. I felt their cool and spiny legs all over my body, and then they started chirping, first a few chirping softly, then more. I had my balance now, then by the thousands the crickets were chirping louder and louder all around me. Their song relaxed me, and I did not feel scared of them any more. It seemed as if they were playing their cricket song so that I wouldn't hear my drunk father or my friends yelling obscenities. I didn't care about falling off the ladder or about the snakes. The rhythm of the crickets' song kept coming into me, filling up my mind and every part of my body like a soothing dream. I knew my face was smiling, yes, I was at peace with myself for the first time in my life, and at that moment that's all that mattered in the world. The song of the crickets and I became one.

Space

i feel the gabacho eyes
like blue pus
on my body

the leader
opens his mouth
& the forked-tongue
darts through the fangs
as he whips at me
a cynical laugh

breathing deep
i hold my space
against the invasion

they are trying to make me feel
as small as a pile of shit
they butcher me with laser words
then spit at my soul

but i hold my space
breathing evenly
against the centuries of oppression

y les digo otra vez
in my broken chicano english

que aquí es aztlán
que aquí nacimos
que aquí es nuestra casa
que todavía estamos resistiendo
la conquista europea

they are hating me
with their abusive fears
as i breathe into my space
& hold my space

against the racism
& ignorance
of these brothers

Nepthalí de León (San Antonio)

"Of Bronze the Sacrifice" and "Llevan Flores"

Of Bronze the Sacrifice

Oh! The dead leaves are fallen.

As ill butterflies they crash
Upon the fiery ground.

And a frigid ice wind sweeps
    sweeps from the blue mountain.

Now the sky of silver weeps
    weeps many cold teardrops . . .

        The maiden,
        The jewel,
Flower of the Aztec kingdom
More beautiful than cold moons,
By the night-stars envied . . .
Weeps, weeps in her troubled sleep.
So still is all,
    but in silence weeps in its troubled sleep.

Oh Tenochtitlán!
    Cradle of the Gods
    Cradle of Bronze warriors
    Turn your eyes into silver—
    Turn your heart into stone.

        The maiden
        The jewel,
The virgin bloom of the land,
From the jungles and the plains,

Nepthalí de León was born in Laredo and attended high school while doing migrant work with his family. De León served in the army and studied in several institutions from Texas to Mexico, but has no formal academic training in any of the arts he is recognized for. He was a major contributor of the seventies art and literary celebration known as the Flor y Canto festivals. In addition to his poetry, he has written children's stories for teaching, worked with school systems throughout the Southwest, and helped start Trucha, a small press in Lubbock that publishes emerging Chicano writers. His visual work is also gaining attention, and he remains a full-time poet and painter living in San Antonio.

The virgin of spirit pure,
as clean as the white snow
from Ixtaccihuatl the bloom
faithful and true in love.
The maiden
the sweet sacrificial flower
weeps and sings of her deep pain.

This night, night of Tlaloc
She of the black strands
blacker than the feathers
of the sacred serpent,
She of the tiger looks,
She of the astute limbs
Faster than eagle wings
Quicker than fish fins
—Her blood she must see it run!

Oh Tenochtitlán! Cradle of the Gods,
Cradle of Bronze warriors,
Turn your eyes into silver
Turn your heart into stone!

The maiden
The jewel,
She knows it all,
Her body flies in dark anguish
Gyrating toward the stars,
Like frightened desperate arrows.
arrows of anguish,
arrows of fear,
Falling like a bird,
a ravaged beast,
or the hypnotic song
of fiery Netzahualcóyotl.

The maiden
The jewel,
She knows it all,
Her pure body with no blemish
Her sad and beautiful spirit
Must tonight be broken,
Must tonight be ravaged
As the tiger tears the bodies
When he breaks the eyes
When he steps on spiders.

Oh! She must die
The empire's jewel
For the golden Gods
For the Gods of fire—
Quetzalcóatl, Huitzilipochtli,
Gods of life, Gods of fire.

But now! The child knows,
She must tell us of the fiery story,
She must tell us of her blood and glory
that will give oceans,
that will give life
to the god of suns,
and to the Goddess
Coatlique.

Oh Dance, Autumn-night Dance
Night of the cold teardrops
That fall as the dead leaves fell
When with horror the warrior saw—
his love!
With tears and green screams torn.

II

The sky of silver weeps,
weeps many cold teardrops.

Huitzilipochtli is dead. >>

III

From the land of fires roared Quetzalcóatl,
the God of life, of the fire feathers,
savage the warrior,
of fury,
of fire,
of ice.

Black armies with hatred looked—
The night and its dark forces . . .
—anxiously spied the skies
Searching the God of life
the valiant,
the heroic
Quetzalcóatl Coatlique.

With cries of a tiger he battled—
Oh! Glorious the fight, of fire and blood
Cutting the dark forces—
the night,
the fog,
and the cold.

To far-away corners all shadows ran,
fleeing from the god of war—
the god whose eyes shone
with triumph and fire,
which gave life—
to the wheat,
to the corn,
to the men.

But oh! costly the victory.
Quetzalcóatl Coatlique bleeded in cascades
Of cruel wounds who wailed in red voices,
And it came, oh it came,
the evening gray
and the young warrior
suffered white hair.

And the God Quetzalcóatl dying
gave light to the warrior
the valiant,
the martyr,
Huitzilipochtli.

Oh valiant warrior!
Even though weakened and white in his hair,
With fury he fought the forces of darkness,
Lost was the battle, now all was in vain,
now all was foreseen
the loss and the glory
were already seen.

Huitzilipochtli is dead.

The black wings of the night now fall.
and fall,
Drowning our faithful warrior,
Whose blood flies out in rays
Like many anxious arrows.
Redder than the quetzal feathers
or the altar stone
turns the horizon.

IV

Oh Tenochtitlán!
Cradle of the Gods
Cradle of Bronze warriors
Turn your eyes into silver—
Turn your heart into stone!

And do not weep, bold warrior
Forget your love now sacrificed.
Your eyes are deep caverns
Where never the sun shone.

The maiden,
The jewel,
She must now die—
That with her blood she may give life
to the bold,
to the brave
Quetzalcóatl.

Whose ferocious arms, whose ferocious eyes,
Will roar from the East with new life,
And pushing the shadows that the night nestles
his hands will give light and life
to the wheat,
to the corn,
to the men . . .

Oh! Tenochtitlán!
Cradle of valiant men
Hide your bronze heart
that you carry in your hand,
Never let your furious arms
forget your destiny and glory.

V

Ay! The dead leaves are fallen.

As ill butterflies they crash
Upon the fiery ground.

And a frigid wind sweeps
sweeps from the blue mountain.

And the sky of silver weeps
weeps many a teardrop.

Llevan Flores

Llevan flores en los dientes
tigres y arañas frías.

Muy poca gente llora
(la esquina pide silencio)
y los perros ladran tristes
en el barrio de los pobres.

Esquinas de puños huecos
¡ladran Chicano Power!

En la tumba solitaria
las flores no se marchitan.
El joven de bronce un día
No muerde mosaicos fríos.

Mientras batos y poetas
llenan de dulces frescos
(¡Ay! ¡Son de cariño y odio!)
una piñata vieja—
un bato en las esquinas
halla plomo en sus heridas.

llevan flores en los dientes
tigres y arañas frías.

Roberto Pulido (Edinburg)

"La tumba de Villa" (The Tomb of Pancho Villa)

Cuantos jilgueros y cenzontles veo pasar.
Pero ay! Qué triste cantan estas avecillas!
Van a Chihuahua a llorar sobre Parral.
Donde descansa el General Villa.

Lloran al ver aquella tumba
Donde descansa para siempre el General.
Sin un clavel ni flor alguna,
Solo hojas secas que le ofrece el vendaval.

De sus Dorados, nadie quiere recordar
que Villa duerme bajo el cielo de Chihuahua.
Sólo las aves que gorjean sobre Parral
van a llorar sobre su tumba abandonada.

Sólo uno fue que no ha olvidado,
a su sepulcro su oración fue murmurar,
amigo fiel, cual bien soldado,
grabó en su tumba:
—Estoy presente general.—

Canten jilgueros y cenzontles sin parar
Y que sus trinos se oigan en la serranía.
Mas cuando vuelen bajo el cielo de Parral,
lloren conmigo por aquel Francisco Villa.

Adiós, adiós mis avecillas,
yo también quiero recordarle a mi nación
que allá en Parral descansa Villa
en el regazo del lugar que tanto amó.

CALLED "EL PRIMO" BY HIS FANS, Pulido, from Edinburg, is best known for fusing traditional orchestra brass style with conjunto in his mid-1970s group, Los Classicos.

How many mountain birds and mockingbirds I see go by.
But how sadly these birds do sing.
They go to Chihuahua to cry over Parral
Where General Francisco Villa lies at rest.

They cry on seeing that tomb
where the General rests forever.
Not one carnation nor any other flower,
only dried leaves offered by the strong south wind.

Of his Dorados, none wants to remember
that Villa sleeps under the Chihuahua sky.
only the birds that chirp over Parral
go to cry over his abandoned tomb.

There is one alone who has not forgotten,
who has gone to murmur a prayer over his grave,
a loyal friend, like the faithful soldier he is,
engraved upon Villa's tomb the words:
"I am present and accounted for, my General."

Let the mountain birds and mockingbirds sing, don't stop
so your trills may be heard in the mountains
all the more so when you fly under the skies of Parral,
cry with me for that Francisco Villa.

Goodbye, goodbye my little birds.
I too want to remind my nation
that Villa rests there in Parral,
in the lap of the land he loved so much.

Angela de Hoyos (San Antonio)

"The Feeling is Mutual" and "Go Ahead, Ask Her"

The Feeling is Mutual

Sinner now home
- redeemed at church -
I am back to normal:

I growl at the world
and the world
returns the compliment.

Born in Coahuila, Mexico, Angela de Hoyos moved with her family to San Antonio early in her life. She took classes at several schools around San Antonio and began publishing her poetry in the late 1960s. For health reasons, she confines her activities to San Antonio, though her poetry became widely known soon after the publication of *Arise Chicano!* in 1975.

Go Ahead, Ask Her

. . . . . . is it
not true
that when
a woman
cries
all the
gentlemen
console
her

but when
a wife
cries
she cries
alone?

Carmen Tafolla (Laredo)

"Scars and Three Daughters" and "and when I dream dreams . . ."

Scars and Three Daughters

she handed me a lotion
her grandmother had
handed her—this grown
daughter, strong and
armied, always smiling,
not born to me but rather
married to me, full with her brother
and her father—and her good
heart. "Concha Nacar," magic
cream, that "one light dab
touched on every day
will soften scars and make
them blend away."
I rush to put it on
the face of that black-diamond-eyed
power pack, my three-year-old
invincible returning hero

Carmen Tafolla was born in San Antonio. She received her B.A. in Spanish and French from Austin College in Sherman and her Ph.D. in bilingual education from the University of Texas at Austin. Her poetry was first published in the 1976 collection *Get Your Tortillas Together,* which also contained poems by Reyes Cardenas and Cecilio García-Camarillo. She has also worked as an educator, heading the Mexican-American Studies Center at Texas Lutheran College, and she is an associate professor at the California State University at Fresno. As talented for her dramatic work as for her poetry, Tafolla has been recognized by the National Association for Chicano Studies for her outstanding contributions to the arts and academia.

from a scratch of cat, a brush with tree,
her will untroubled by
the fear of scars,
I trembling take the potion,
pray the cream like incantations on
that face that I adore
want to preserve, protect, insure
yet I stare proudly at that thin white line
on hand that I have come to know as me,
that crooked intersection on the cheek
that I have loved to teasing say
came from a switchblade scar,
my "football knee" I brag
was an old "childcare injury"
while rushing to avoid a baby fall
as she charged forth, so ready to explore,
and that most precious line of all—
that now-pink redscar
where the firstborn love was passed,
still sleeping in her sac,
and left me only this
to touch her with—
I love my scars

AND WHEN I DREAM DREAMS . . .

when I dream dreams,
I dream of *YOU,*
Rhodes Jr. School
and the lockers of our minds
that were always jammed stuck
or that always hung open
and would never close,
no matter *how* hard You tried,
we messed up the looks of the place
and wouldn't be neat and organized
and look like we were sposed to look
and lock like we were sposed
                                        to lock.

yea that's right
I dream of *you*
degrees later
and from both sides of the desk
my dreams take place
in your two-way halls,
HallGuards from among us,
human traffic markers, bumps on the road
between the lanes,
to say, when we were sposed to say,
where to turn left, where right,
and how to get where you were going—
("You'll never get to high school
speakin' Spanish," I was told)
[nice of them, they thought, to not report me,
breakin' state law, school law, speakin' dirty
          (speakin' spanish)
and our tongues couldn't lump it
and do what they were sposed to do.
So instead I reminded others
to button buttons
and tuck shirttails in.]

I never graduated to a
Cafeteria Guard,
who knows how they were picked.
We thought it had something
to do
with the FBI
or maybe the Principal's office.
So we got frisked,
Boys in one line,
Girls in another,
twice every day
entering lunch and leaving
Check—no knives on the boys.
Check—no dangerous weapons on the girls
(like mirrors,
            perfume bottles,
               deodorant bottles,
                  or teased hair.)
So we wandered the halls
    cool chuca style
    "no se sale"
    and unawares,
    never knowing
    other junior highs were never frisked
    never knowing
    what the teachers said in the teachers lounge
    never knowing we were (sposed to be)
    the toughest junior high in town.

And the lockers of our minds
are now assigned to other minds,
carry other books,
follow other rules,
silence other tongues,
go to other schools—
Schools of VietNam,
Schools of cheap cafe,
Schools of dropout droppings, prison pains, and cop car's
        bulleted brains. »

Marcelino thought the only way
to finance college
was the Air Force
(G.I. Bill and *good pay!*)
War looked easy (compared to here)
Took his chances on a college education,
Took his pay on a shot-down helicopter
in a brown-skinned 'Nam,
with a pledge of allegiance in his mind
he had memorized through Spanish-speaking teeth
as a Hall Guard, "clean-cut,"
Now cut clean down in a hospital ward,
paralyzed below the lips,
that still speak Spanish
slowly.
Silvia thought no one had the right
to tell her what to do.
One year out of junior high, she bitterly bore
her second pregnancy,
stabbed forks unto cafe tables
and slushed coffee through the crowds
sixteen hours a day, and she was *fifteen*
and still fighting to say
"I HAVE A RIGHT TO BE *ME!*"
Esperanza with a needle in her heart, sucking *will,* wanting
junkies to say
"Hey, you're really okay."
And Lalo with a mind that could write in his sleep
growing epics from eyes that could dream
now writes only the same story over and over
until the day
that it's *all*
over,
as he's frisked and he's frisked and he's frisked
and they keep finding
nothing
and even when he's *out*
his mind is always *in*
prison.

Like Lupe's mind
that peels potatoes
and chops *repollo*
and wishes its boredom was less
than the ants in the hill
and never learned to read because
the words were in English
and she
was in Spanish.

I wonder what we would *do,*
Rhodes Junior School,
if we had all those
emblems of *you*
stamped on our lives
with a big Red "*R*"
like the letter sweaters
we could, never
afford
to buy.

I keep my honorary
junior school diploma,
from you
right next to the B.A., M.A.,
etcetera to a Ph.D.
because it means
I graduated
from you
and when I dream dreams,
—how I wish my dreams
had graduated too.

José Montalvo (San Antonio)

"Bicentennial Blues" and "El Barrio Revisited"

Bicentennial Blues

Well they waited and waited:
day and night for two hundred years
finally: llegó, vino, y se pasó
and it turned out to be . . .
Puro Pinche Pedo.

Señor Walter Cronkite
spent all day and half of the night
telling the audience about the:
"In celebration of U.S."
what he failed to mention was that:
it was not celebrated by all of "us"

The bicentennial minutes
kept coming and coming
like a pimpled faced teen-ager
masturbating for personal gratification
but not doing a damn thing for anybody else

José Montalvo received his "commuter education" traveling between Piedras Negras, Mexico, where he was born, and towns across the border in Texas. His family settled in San Antonio while he was a teenager, and after serving in the U.S. Air Force, he attended college there at St. Mary's University. Montalvo began working as a community organizer in San Antonio and became more involved with politics, which his poetry clearly shows. He ran unsuccessfully for state representative in 1974 as a member of La Raza Unida Party, calling himself an "ultra-nationalist." His first poetry was published in 1977 in *Pensamientos Capturados*.

People waving "old glory"
except of course:
the proud Red Men—
for he could not bring himself
to celebrate from a fenced-in
piece of desert called "reservation"

And the Black Men
yes the Black Men
who occasionally said: "Right On, America"
while remembering his relocation
from the old plantation
to the roach infested ghettoes

The Chicano community divided;
some demonstrating against 128 years of oppression
oyendo al juez Gutierrez repetir la formula, "P3"
y decia el hombre: "El American Dream" . . .
Puro Pinche Pedo . . . Puro Pinche Pedo"

All that going on
while the Mexican Americans were singing:
"This Land is Our Land"
Pendejos—todavía no se dan cuenta that
This land is not our land; for:
manifest destiny robbed us of it

Con lágrimas en mis ojos:
(tears that never reached mis cachetes
because they evaporated por el calor)
I saw Chicanos wanting to take a place
in the "Buy" centennial craze
next to smiling empty faces >>

And even I . . . as hard as I tried
could not escape the commercialism . . .
brought by the same bastards,
who are waiting for the second coming of Jesus Christ;
just to have another super giant "sale"

Wakened by the rockets red glare,
I found myself with a very hard problem
but my old lady who must have been dreaming
offered to help me to "work it out between us"
as, I tried to push the Bicentennial out of my mind

But this I could not do
for I was half drunk and half asleep
or maybe just plain clumsy—
But my revolutionary spirit was awakened
when my old lady said:
"O, José, can't you see"

And even I . . . as hard as I tried
could not escape the commercialism;
for at dawn's early light
I exploded in a Bicentennial
Red, white, and blue, "condón."

July 1976
San Antonio, Tejas

El Barrio Revisited

Laurel Street
corner with Zarzamora
and all the way
out west,
to the creek
just past Elmendorf.

Señor Murillo
beat up
Doña Margarita
because the unthoughtful wench
spent his beer money
on ice cream
for the children.

"Ture" got drunk again
and busted up
the car windows
of his nineteen-forty-nine
Chevrolet,
while Junior Moreno
cannot do
what he learned
in the Navy,
because he's too dark;
and Letty's house
was flooded when it rained,
but her father had no insurance.

And "Nona" lived to be 104,
but she still died
and Fred Mireles
moved to the north side
to get a better education,
just to die in Viet Nam
eight months after graduation.

And Rosita got pregnant
at fourteen,
and probably has
fourteen children
by now.
While Charlie is now residing
at the state hospital
and I can't think
of good things.

JOSÉ ANTONIO BURCIAGA was born in El Paso. He attended the University of Texas at El Paso, then studied at the San Francisco Art Institute. After college he found work as a graphic designer in Washington, DC. Once he moved to California, Burciaga began publishing poems, including his first collection from 1976, *Restless Spirits,* and also started the comedy group Culture Clash in San Francisco. He lived at Stanford University starting in 1985, where his wife worked as an administrator, and helped with the creation of several murals on the campus.

José Antonio Burciaga (El Paso)

"In Defense of the Jalapeño and Other Chiles"

A cartoon in the *New Yorker* shows a smiling Eskimo street vendor selling blubber in mid-town Manhattan, while a wrapped up Euro American walks by in the snow. Humorous though it may be, the cartoon also carries a clear and loud message about the infusion of exotic third world foods not only on the streets of New York but throughout the country.

As salsa outsells ketchup and Taco Bell outsells McDonald's, the latest wave is the introduction of more authentic Mexican restaurants. A little too smug and comfortable with the growing availability of the real thing, we should have expected the competition to come up with something.

So it was no surprise that a recent small article in the *San Francisco Chronicle* was headlined "Hot Chili Peppers May Be Carcinogenic." The Cox News Service article stated that some "epidemiologists" from Yale University and the Mexico National Institute of Public Health "had concluded" that chili peppers "may be" carcinogenic, cancer producing. Laboratory experiments with animals and cells in test tubes had already found that capsaicin, the hot producing agent in the peppers, is a carcinogen.

Dr. Robert Dubrow, a Yale Medical School epidemiologist, studied the incidence and distribution of stomach cancer and the eating habits of 1,000 residents in Mexico City.

Mexico City? It's the biggest city on earth with more than twenty million souls and over twenty-five million projected by the year 2,000. With all the smog, congestion, and earthquakes that afflict its residents, why they didn't study people in rural areas or a more sedate and relaxed Mexican town, like Brownsville or some other town on the border is a convenient mystery. They didn't have to go to Mexico City, unless they were after particular findings.

According to their studies, heavy consumers of hot chili peppers were seventeen times more likely to have stomach cancer than those who never eat hot peppers at all. Even people who considered themselves "medium" eaters were four times more likely to have stomach cancer. But what role did smog, earthquakes and big city nerves have in causing this?

Of course the two most interesting words in the headline and the article are "may be." The article stated their conclusion that chili peppers "may be" carcinogenic. Are they or are they not? The conclusion is "Maybe!" They weren't sure but felt compelled to broadcast their iffy conclusion.

How or why (two important questions for journalists) this study was thought up and who funded it should also be newsworthy. According to the article, per capita consumption of chili peppers in this country more than doubled from 1982 to 1992. "Pace Picket Chile Sauce," made in Santone, is a big seller in Mexico. Was this funded by a McDonald's or was the Ketchup Association trying to catch up? And so how many readers will believe and begin to boycott jalapeños due to this inconclusive study while they continue to consume carcinogenic California table grapes?

César Chávez had led a five-year boycott of California table grapes when he died. For years, the United Farm Workers have been sounding a warning about the danger of agricultural pesticides. Some 300,000 farm workers a year are stricken with pesticide-related illnesses. Childhood cancer and birth defects have reached epidemic proportions in many San Joaquin Valley towns. Yet you don't see Yale University epidemiologists coming to study this. You don't see the Mexican Institute for Public Health trying to protect their poor emigrant farm workers from the pesticides in this country Not until the mainstream majority in this country begins to feel the effects will any study be done. Until then, it's only affecting Mexican migrant workers, so who cares?

Meanwhile, a month after the inconclusive jalapeño scare, Florida legislators were trying to consider a bill that would give farmers the right to sue anyone who defames their crops. Criticize a cucumber, bad-mouth a bell pepper, insult a lettuce and you may have a day in court with possible jail time.

Under such a proposed law, farmers could slap a lawsuit on anyone who publicly states that a Florida-grown food product is unsafe for human consumption without reliable scientific facts to back up their claim.

A year before these two articles came out, there was a study out of Stanford University's Center for Research in Disease Prevention, which stated that the traditional diet of Mexican Americans is healthier than that of Euro Americans. That totally goes against the grain of what we have heard all our lives, but according to the study, Mexican Americans eat less cheese, fried foods, red meat and cured meat such as hot dogs, and add less fat to food after cooking. They also eat more healthy foods high in carbohydrates and fiber, such as rice, corn and dried beans.

According to the study, the more acculturated you become, the more you take on Euro American's bad habits. In July of 1994 yet another highly publicized study concluded that Mexican food is high in fat and cholesterol. The contradictions of these studies are confusing, but it appears that Americans can create Mexican fast foods that are less healthy by preparing beans cooked with lard, fried meats, and by adding an abundance of sour cream, guacamole, and cheeses. It seems untrue because this isn't really the authentic cuisine of Mexico. All these contradictory news items go to prove only one thing, with the right funding and an abiding press you can prove just about anything. Viva el jalapeño!

POST SCRIPT

Months after writing this, and a whole lifetime as a jalapeño consumer, aficionado, advocate and activist I was diagnosed with an abdominal tumor. (Pause for a last laugh, or you may want to read a more detailed account in the last essay of this collection.)

My alternatives here could have been to be obstinate on the unconvincing studies of 1,000 chile pepper eaters in Mexico City, a megapolis of 20 million. Natives of Veracruz, home of the Jalapeño, or people from the Northern state of Chihuahua who consume more hot peppers than Chilangos, Mexico City natives.

However, people will respectfully believe whatever they want to believe. Some friends pointed out that maybe it was the jalapeños that caused my tumor. Without dismissing that possibility, I'm also acutely aware of other probable causes. I even believe that Jalapeños have antioxidants that prevent cancer. However, "maybe" like radiation treatment for cancer, too much of a good thing or a bad thing can cause cancer.

I won't live my life observing all the "maybe" caution signs. So I will eat jalapeños again, but moderately and mildly. Besides, what kind of a Mexicano or Chicano would not love and defend jalapeños?

Reyes Cárdenas (El Paso)

"I Was Never A Militant Chicano" and "For Tigre"

I Was Never A Militant Chicano

I was never
like El Louie
and I am not Joaquín,
I never had
to worry
about surviving
in my barrio;
I never had
the driving force
to create
The Crusade for Justice
like Corky Gonzales,
I could never be
a César Chávez,
and reach down
deep inside
the earth
to find that
awesome inner strength.
Some of us
are just unable
to sacrifice ourselves.
I was never
like Raúl Salinas,
Alurista, or Ricardo Sánchez
creating a new
world of poetry
out of a white wasteland.
Some are leaders
and creators,
some are followers,
but the followers want
justice and liberty
and fairness, too.
I could never
shout like Tigre.
But inside
(right here) »

Reyes Cárdenas grew up in Seguin. At age sixteen he suffered from a bout of tuberculosis, which kept him in the hospital reading poetry for several months. He came back to school to find he was short of the requirements for graduation, and Cárdenas did not come back again. He began publishing in the journal *Caracol* in the early 1970s, and his first book of poems, *Chicano Territory,* was printed in 1975. His poetry is characterized by a sense of humor combined with a concern for the struggle of Chicanos to claim respect for their identity.

I guess I can
roar just as loud.
I never shot up
a federal courthouse
like Reies Tijerina
but I know
that the frustrations
won't stay
locked up forever.
I was never
really a pachuco
but I saw then what I still
see now—
that we're
getting nowhere,
that things
are worse
than they were
in the forties
and fifties.
I was never
the Che Guevara-type
but there's
nothing wrong
with revolution.
Everybody says
it can't happen here,
but, hell,
it can happen anywhere.
I was never
a militant chicano
but only because
I've always wanted
more than a revolution
can provide.

For Tigre

And Tigre's always talking about death.
There's no need to ask why, or how . .

There's too much death in Aztlán,
too many carnales shot down in the streets
because they won't surrender.

Shot down because they don't want to be slaves anymore.
Shot down because they want to unionize . . .
because they strike . . . because they picket . .

Carnales shot down because they tell the truth.
Children killed by pigs . . .
But Aztlán won't die!

Not with chicanos and chicanas fighting side by side,
fighting day and night until there's
nothing left but poetry.

Gloria Anzaldúa (Hargill)

"Entering Into the Serpent"

Sueño con serpientes, con serpientes del mar,
Con cierto mar, ay de serpientes sueño yo.
Largas, transparentes, en sus barrigas llevan
Lo que puedan arrebatarle al amor.
Oh, oh, oh, la mató y aparece una mayor.
Oh, con mucha más infierno en digestión.

I dream of serpents, serpents of the sea,
A certain sea, oh, of serpents I dream.
Long, transparent, in their bellies they carry
All that they can snatch away from love.
Oh, oh, oh, I kill one and a larger one appears.
Oh, with more hellfire burning inside!
—Silvio Rodriguez, "Sueño Con Serpientes"

In the predawn orange haze, the sleepy crowing of roosters atop the trees. *No vayas al escusado en lo oscuro.* Don't go to the outhouse at night, Prieta, my mother would say. *No se te vaya a meter algo por allá.* A snake will crawl into your *nalgas,* make you pregnant. They seek warmth in the cold. *Dicen que las culebras* like to suck *chiches,* can draw milk out of you.

En el escusado in the half-light spiders hang like gliders. Under my bare buttocks and the rough planks the deep yawning tugs at me. I can see my legs fly up to my face as my body falls through the round hole into the sheen of swarming maggots below. Avoiding the snakes under the porch I walk back into the kitchen, step on a big black one slithering across the floor.

GLORIA ANZALDÚA was born in a town in the Rio Grande Valley called Jesus María. Her family moved to Arkansas while she was in high school to work in the fields, but Anzaldúa returned to Texas for college, doing her undergraduate work at Pan-American University in Edinburg, then earning a M.A. from the University of Texas at Austin. She began teaching high school in Texas and then worked as a lecturer at colleges in California, including the University of California at Santa Cruz. There she established herself as a writer with the powerful perspective of a lesbian feminist, contributing and helping edit numerous collections of writings by women, including a 1981 volume, *The Bridge Called My Back: Writings by Radical Women of Color,* with Cherrie Moraga. She died of complications from her diabetes, shortly after completing a Ph.D. dissertation in Santa Cruz.

Ella tiene su tono

Once we were chopping cotton in the fields of Jesus María Ranch. All around us the woods. *Quelite* towered above me, choking the stubby cotton that had outlived the deer's teeth.

I swung *el azadón* hard. *El quelite* barely shook, showered nettles on my arms and face. When I heard the rattle the world froze.

I barely felt its fangs. Boot got all the *veneno* My mother came shrieking, swinging her hoe high, cutting the earth, the writhing body.

I stood still, the sun beat down. Afterwards I smelled where fear had been: back of neck, under arms, between my legs; I felt its heat slide down my body. I swallowed the rock it had hardened into.

When Mama had gone down the row and was out of sight, I took out my pocketknife. I made an X over each prick. My body followed the blood, fell onto the soft ground. I put my mouth over the red and sucked and spit between the rows of cotton.

I picked up the pieces, placed them end on end. *Culebra de cascabel.* I counted the rattlers: twelve. It would shed no more. I buried the pieces between the rows of cotton.

That night I watched the window sill, watched the moon dry the blood on the tail, dreamed rattler fangs filled my mouth, scales covered my body. In the morning I saw through snake eyes, felt snake blood course through my body. The serpent, *mi to no*, my animal counterpart. I was immune to its venom. Forever immune.

Snakes, *víboras:* since that day I've sought and shunned them. Always when they cross my path, fear and elation flood my body. I know things older than Freud, older than gender. She—that's how I think of *la Víbora,* Snake Woman. Like the ancient Olmecs, I know Earth is a coiled Serpent. Forty years it's taken me to enter into the Serpent, to acknowledge that I have a body, that I am a body and to assimilate the animal body, the animal soul.

Coatlalopeuh, **She Who Has Dominion Over Serpents**

Mi mamagrande Ramona toda su vida mantuvo un altar pequeño en la esquina del comedor. Siempre tenía las velas prendidas. Allí hacía promesas a la Virgen de Guadalupe. My family, like most Chicanos, did not practice Roman Catholicism but a folk Catholicism with many pagan elements. *La Virgen de Guadalupe*'s Indian name is *Coatlalopeuh*. She is the central deity connecting us to our Indian ancestry.

Coatlalopeuh is descended from, or is an aspect of, earlier Mesoamerican fertility and Earth goddesses. The earliest is *Coatlicue,* or "Serpent Skirt." She had a human skull or serpent for a head, a necklace of human hearts, a skirt of twisted serpents and taloned feet. As creator goddess, she was mother of the celestial deities, and of *Huitzilopochtli* and his sister, *Coyolxauhqui,* She With Golden Bells, Goddess of the Moon, who was decapitated by her brother. Another aspect of *Coatlicue* is *Tonantsi.* The Totonacs, tired of the Aztec human sacrifices to the male god, *Huitzilopochtli,* renewed their reverence for *Tonantsi* who preferred the sacrifice of birds and small animals.

The male-dominated Azteca-Mexica culture drove the powerful female deities underground by giving them monstrous attributes and by substituting male deities in their place, thus splitting the female Self and the female deities. They divided her who had been complete, who possessed both upper (light) and underworld (dark) aspects. *Coatlicue,* the Serpent goddess, and her more sinister aspects, *Tlazolteotl* and *Cihuacoatl,* were "darkened" and disempowered much in the same manner as the Indian *Kali.*

Tonantsi—split from her dark guises, *Coatlicue, Tlazolteotl,* and *Cihuacoatl*—became the good mother. The Nahuas, through ritual and prayer, sought to oblige *Tonantsi* to ensure their health and the growth of their crops. It was she who gave *México* the cactus plant to provide her people with milk and pulque. It was she who defended her children against the wrath of the Christian God by challenging God, her son, to produce mother's milk (as she had done) to prove that his benevolence equalled his disciplinary harshness.

After the Conquest, the Spaniards and their Church continued to split *Tonantsi/ Guadalupe.* They desexed *Guadalupe,* taking *Coatlalopeuh,* the serpent/sexuality, out of her. They completed the split begun by the Nahuas by making *La Virgen de Guadalupe/ Virgen María* into chaste virgins and *Tlazolteotl/Coatlicue/la Chingada* into *putas;* into the Beauties and the Beasts. They went even further; they made all Indian deities and religious practices the work of the devil.

Thus *Tonantsi* became *Guadalupe,* the chaste protective mother, the defender of the Mexican people.

El nueve de diciembre del año 1531
a las cuatro de la madrugada
un pobre indio que se llamaba Juan Diego
iba cruzando el cerro de Tepeyác
cuando oyó un canto de pájaro.

Alzó al cabeza vió que en la cima del cerro
estaba cubierta con una brillante nube blanca.
Parada en frente del sol
sobre una luna creciente
sostenida por un ángel
estaba una azteca
vestida en ropa de india.
Nuestra Señora María de Coatlalopeuh
se le apareció.
"Juan Dieguito, El-que-habla-como-un-águila,"
la Virgen le dijo en el lenguaje azteca.
"Para hacer mi altar este cerro elijo.
Dile a tu gente que yo soy la madre de Dios,
a los indios yo les ayudaré."
Esto se la cantó a Juan Zumarraga
pero el obispo no le creyó.
Juan Diego volvió, llenó su tilma
con rosas de castilla
creciendo milagrosamente en la nieve.
Se las llevó al obispo,
y cuando abrió su tilma
el retrato de la Virgen
ahí estaba pintado.

Guadalupe appeared on December 9, 1531, on the spot where the Aztec goddess, *Tonantsi* ("Our Lady Mother"), had been worshipped by the Nahuas and where a temple to her had stood. Speaking Nahua, she told Juan Diego, a poor Indian crossing Tepeyac Hill, whose Indian name was *Cuautlaohuac* and who belonged to the *mazehual* class, the humblest within the Chichimeca tribe, that her name was *María Coatlalopeuh. Coatl* is the Nahuatl word for serpent. *Lopeuh* means "the one who has dominion over serpents." I interpret this as "the one who is at one with the beasts." Some spell her name *Coatlaxopeuh* (pronounced "*Cuatlashupe*" in Nahuatl) and say that "*xopeuh*" means "crushed or stepped on with disdain." Some say it means "she who crushed the serpent," with the serpent as the symbol of the indigenous religion, meaning that her religion was to take the place of the Aztec religion. Because *Coatlalopeuh* was homophonous to the Spanish *Guadalupe,* the Spanish identified her with the dark Virgin, Guadalupe, patroness of West Central Spain.

From that meeting, Juan Diego walked away with the image of *la Virgen* painted on his cloak. Soon after, Mexico ceased to belong to Spain, and *la Virgen de Guadalupe* began to eclipse all the other male and female religious figures in Mexico, Central America and parts of the U.S. Southwest. "*Desde entonces para el mexicano ser Guadalupano es algo esencial*/Since then for the Mexican, to be a Guadalupano is something essential."

Mi Virgen Morena	My brown virgin
Mi Virgen Ranchera	my country virgin
Eres nuestra Reina	you are our queen
México es tu tierra	Mexico is your land
Y tú su bandera.	and you its flag.

—"*La Virgen Ranchera*"

. . .

Sueño con serpientes

Coatl. In pre-Columbian America the most notable symbol was the serpent. The Olmecs associated womanhood with the Serpent's mouth which was guarded by rows of dangerous teeth, a sort of *vagina dentate.* They considered it the most sacred place on earth, a place of refuge, the creative womb from which all things were born and to which all things returned. Snake people had holes, entrances to the body of the Earth Serpent; they followed the Serpent's way, identified with the Serpent deity, with the mouth, both the eater and the eaten. The destiny of humankind is to be devoured by the Serpent.

Dead,
the doctor by the operating table said.
I passed between the two fangs,
the flickering tongue.
Having come through the mouth of the serpent,
swallowed,
I found myself suddenly in the dark,
sliding down a smooth wet surface
down down into an even darker darkness.
Having crossed the portal, the raised hinged mouth,
having entered the serpent's belly,
now there was no looking back, no going back.

Why do I cast no shadow?
Are there lights from all sides shining on me?
Ahead, ahead.
curled up inside the serpent's coils,
the damp breath of death on my face.
I knew at that instant: something must change
or I'd die.
Algo tenía que cambiar.

After each of my four bouts with death I'd catch glimpses of an otherworld Serpent. Once, in my bedroom, I saw a cobra the size of the room, her hood expanding over me. When I blinked she was gone. I realized she was, in my psyche, the mental picture and symbol of the instinctual in its collective impersonal, prehuman. She, the symbol of the dark sexual drive, the chthonic (underworld), the feminine, the serpentine movement of sexuality, of creativity, the basis of all energy and life.

The Presences

She appeared in white, garbed in white,
standing white, pure white.
—Bernardino de Sahagún

On the gulf where I was raised, *en el Valle del Río Grande* in South Texas—that triangular piece of land wedged between the river *y el golfo* which serves as the Texas-U.S./Mexican border—is a Mexican *pueblito* called Hargill (at one time in the history of this one-grocery-store, two-service-stations town there were thirteen churches and thirteen cantinas). Down the road, a little ways from our house, was a deserted church. It was known among the *mexicanos* that if you walked down the road late at night you would see a woman dressed in white floating about, peering out the church window. She would follow those who had done something bad or who were afraid. *Los mexicanos* called her *la Jila.* Some thought she was *la Llorona.* She was, I think, *Cihuacoatl,* Serpent Woman, ancient Aztec goddess of the earth, of war and birth, patron of midwives, and antecedent of *la Llorona.* Covered with chalk, *Cihuacoatl* wears a white dress with a decoration half red and half black. Her hair forms two little horns (which the Aztecs depicted as knives) crossed on her forehead. The lower part of her face is a bare jawbone, signifying death. On her back she carries a cradle, the knife of sacrifice swaddled as if it were her papoose, her child. Like *la Llorona, Cihuacoatl* howls and weeps in the night, screams as if demented. She brings mental depression and sorrow. Long before it takes place, she is the first to predict something is to happen.

Back then, I, an unbeliever, scoffed at these Mexican superstitions as I was taught in Anglo school. Now, I wonder if this story and similar ones were the culture's attempts to "protect" members of the family, especially girls, from "wandering." Stories of the devil luring young girls away and having his way with them discouraged us from going out. There's an ancient Indian tradition of burning the umbilical cord of an infant girl under the house so she will never stray from it and her domestic role.

A mis ancas caen los cueros de culebra,
cuatro veces por año los arrastro,
me tropiezo y me caigo
y cada vez que miro una culebra le pregunto
¿Qué traes conmigo?

Four years ago a red snake crossed my path as I walked through the woods. The direction of its movement, its pace, its colors, the "mood" of the trees and the wind and the snake—they all "spoke" to me, told me things. I look for omens everywhere, everywhere catch glimpses of the patterns and cycles of my life. Stones "speak" to Luisah Teish, a Santera; trees whisper their secrets to Chrystos, a Native American. I remember listening to the voices of the wind as a child and understanding its messages. *Los espíritus* that ride the back of the south wind. I remember their exhalation blowing in through the slits in the door during those hot Texas afternoons. A gust of wind raising the linoleum under my feet, buffeting the house. Everything trembling.

We're not supposed to remember such otherworldly events. We're supposed to ignore, forget, kill those fleeting images of the soul's presence and of the spirit's presence. We've been taught that the spirit is outside our bodies or above our heads somewhere up in the sky with God. We're supposed to forget that every cell in our bodies, every bone and bird and worm has spirit in it.

Like many Indians and Mexicans, I did not deem my psychic experiences real. I denied their occurrences and let my inner senses atrophy. I allowed white rationality to tell me that the existence of the "other world" was mere pagan superstition. I accepted their reality, the "official" reality of the rational, reasoning mode which is connected with external reality, the upper world, and is considered the most developed consciousness—the consciousness of duality.

The other mode of consciousness facilitates images from the soul and the unconscious through dreams and the imagination. Its work is labeled "fiction," make-believe, wish-fulfillment. White anthropologists claim that Indians have "primitive" and therefore deficient minds, that we cannot think in the higher mode of consciousness—rationality. They are fascinated by what they call the "magical" mind, the "savage" mind, the *participation mystique* of the mind that says the world of the imagination—the world of the soul—and of the spirit is just as real as physical reality. In trying to be-come "objective," Western culture made "objects" of things and people when it distanced itself from them, thereby losing "touch" with them. This dichotomy is the root of all violence.

Not only was the brain split into two functions but so was reality. Thus people who inhabit both realities are forced to live in the interface between the two, forced to become adept at switching modes. Such is the case with the *india* and the *mestiza.*

Institutionalized religion fears trafficking with the spirit world and stigmatizes it as witchcraft. It has strict taboos against this kind of inner knowledge. It fears what Jung calls the Shadow, the unsavory aspects of ourselves. But even more it fears the supra-human, the god in ourselves.

"The purpose of any established religion . . . is to glorify, sanction and bless with a superpersonal meaning all personal and interpersonal activities. This occurs through the 'sacraments,' and indeed through most religious rites." But it sanctions only its own sacraments and rites. Voodoo, Santeria, Shamanism and other native religions are called cults and their beliefs are called mythologies. In my own life, the Catholic Church fails to give meaning to my daily acts, to my continuing encounters with the "other world." It and other institutionalized religions impoverish all life, beauty, pleasure.

The Catholic and Protestant religions encourage fear and distrust of life and of the body; they encourage a split between the body and the spirit and totally ignore the soul; they encourage us to kill off parts of ourselves. We are taught that the body is an ignorant animal; intelligence dwells only in the head. But the body is smart. It does not discern between external stimuli and stimuli from the imagination. It reacts equally viscerally to events from the imagination as it does to "real" events.

So I grew up in the interface trying not to give countenance to *el mal aigre,* evil non-human, non-corporeal entities riding the wind, that could come in through the window, through my nose with my breath. I was not supposed to believe in *susto,* a sudden shock or fall that frightens the soul out of the body. And growing up between such opposing spiritualities how could I reconcile the two, the pagan and the Christian?

No matter to what use my people put the supranatural world, it is evident to me now that the spirit world, whose existence the whites are so adamant in denying, does in fact exist. This very minute I sense the presence of the spirits of my ancestors in my room. And I think *la Jila* is *Cihuacoatl*, Snake Woman; she is *la Llorona*, Daughter of Night, traveling the dark terrains of the unknown searching for the lost parts of herself. I remember *la Jila* following me once, remember her eerie lament. I'd like to think that she was crying for her lost children, *los* Chicanos/*mexicanos*.

Max Martínez was born in the small town of Gonzales. He served in the Navy before attending college at St. Mary's University in San Antonio, then earning an M.A. from East Texas State University. Martinez tried out several careers, ranging from stockbroker to sailor, before returning to academic work. He began studying for a Ph.D. from the University of Denver but never completed a dissertation, instead turning to writing fulltime. His first book, *The Adventures of the Chicano Kid and Other Stories,* appeared in 1982.

Max Martínez (Gonzales)

"Portal"

Jerónimo Portal wore his usual black suit. He walked slowly, patiently, with the stability of habit, along the uneven sidewalk toward the plaza. The suit was well-worn, shimmering in a few places as it reflected light from the white-hot sun of summer. His walk was measured, almost cautious; but firm and still strong despite his eighty-two years. His eyesight was still very good. He avoided the drooping branches of the trees without having to bend over, dodging them as if they were a leafy obstacle course. Another much younger man would have made the walk to the plaza in thirty minutes or less. Jerónimo Portal needed just a few more minutes than that, but since he was in no hurry, he took nearer to an hour to make the walk. A younger man would have been going some place, would have been impatient to be at his destination. For Jerónimo Portal, the walk was as important as arriving at the plaza.

In the twenty years since his retirement, the plaza had become the center of his day. He calculated well the time it took him to walk there so that he could arrive a few minutes before noon. He timed his arrival to coincide with that of the workers from the surrounding buildings who would come to spend the last minutes of their lunch hour in the plaza. The plaza had become an impor-tant part of his daily life. Although he knew no one there and seldom spoke to anyone, he felt something sinister and disconcerting about finding it empty of people. Jerónimo Portal felt the same about entering a dark empty house late at night.

The buildings surrounding the plaza were tall, hiding the sun late in the morning and early in the afternoon. Jerónimo Portal remembered the not too distant past when the buildings were squat and broad, solid testaments to the self-assurance of the business expansion at the turn of the century. They were buildings made of wood, bricks and marble, with ornate façades and opulent lobbies. They were leisurely buildings blending in artificial symmetry with the square of reconstructed nature in the plaza. Now, as he sat there, the buildings were of a different order. These new buildings on three sides of the plaza were made with strange materials not in use or even invented when he worked with construction gangs. Only the glass seemed familiar to him. These were tall spires, trying to pierce the sky, tapered and lean, covered with mirror-like glass which reflected only the nearby buildings. These were also symbols of business; now narrow, specialized, temporary. They would not last beyond the children of the generation which built them.

Still, the trees remained in the plaza, undisturbed by the hurried activity around them. The white bandstand gleamed warmly in the spring. The granite statue commemorating a hero of Texas history whom he never bothered to learn about and who he finally decided was not very herioc at all was still there looking vacantly toward the subdued west. And the pigeons. Above all there were the pigeons, still coming to feed from the food he carried for them in a little brown paper sack with grease stains. It was the pigeons he loved. He came to think they could not survive without the crumbs he brought them each day. In a way, the pigeons provided Jerónimo Portal with the only urgency of his day.

During the time it took to destroy the fine old buildings and for the new sleek ones to go up, Jerónimo Portal thought of going elsewhere, to another plaza or park in the city, some place where he could rest and enjoy the quiet he came to feel he had earned with his life. He mused about the odd way of the society into which he had grown old. The strong, robust buildings were giving way to lean, anemic-looking ones. Human beings, he thought, cannot ignore, even in their artificial works, the rhythms of nature. They made time so that the old could make way for the new. But, search as he might for peace and quiet, things were not much different at other parks and plazas. There was only noise. If at one park there was too much traffic rumbling by, at another a band would play with amplifiers larger in size than some of the musicians. At still another place, there was the inescapable demolition and construction. He knew there were not many places for him to go and he preferred to keep to the routine to which he had accustomed himself. He reasoned, now with my wife gone, it is better to do the few things left to me to do and not change anything. Change is, of course, inevitable, but it can sometimes be avoided. Not forever, but long enough.

So, he endured the noise of the demolition crews and later of the construction crews. He was careful to move quickly when coming to the plaza lest some debris fall on him. The old buildings were quickly gutted leaving them like toothless, empty carcasses of once-fierce lions. Then, in a single afternoon, the shells of the old buildings cracked and crumbled in a swirling cloud of dust. In one swift, effortless motion, the buildings collapsed into a neat pile to the amusement and cheers of a gathered crowd. One by one the buildings went, until the plaza reminded him of the devastated cities he had seen during the Mexican Revolution.

The sleek buildings took so long to build that he became a familiar figure for the work crews putting them up. Eventually, he was a signal to them as they came to know his punctuality. His slow but steady walk, head held up high became a signal to the workmen to put their tools away, shut down equipment, and prepare for lunch. The workmen often sat near him. He had appropriated a bench for himself which they respected by leaving it to him. The workers seldom spoke to him, except to nod or grunt an off-hand sort of greeting. Despite more than sixty years of living in the United States, he had not learned English well enough to feel comfortable using it. He understood it much better than he let on. Gringos had always made him nervous and no matter how friendly they were or how long he came to know them, he could not be at ease with them. The few Mexicans on the construction projects only stared sullenly at him and seemed to refuse any acknowledgement of their common origins. He'd known that kind of Mexican already, he'd known far too many of them, and he sometimes wondered if they truly shared the bond of work with the gringos to the exclusion of any outsider such as himself or if they simply wanted to avoid the fact that they were Mexican.

Soon after the reconstruction of the plaza area began, he had to be absent for nearly a month. He had had a minor illness, nothing serious he told himself. The doctor felt he should stay in the hospital, fearing complications common to people of his age. After a few days in the hospital, his daughter, Marta, spoke with the doctor and arranged for him to come stay with her. She told the doctor she could take care of him and he would get well much sooner if he had his grandchildren near by. Jerónimo Portal agreed to the transfer, even though he was not delighted by it, because a hospital was not a fit place for a man to die. He thought his Marta might want an adult to talk to. Eduardo Macías, his son-in-law, had been dead for seven years. She must miss adult talk. Marta was a strong woman, past forty, who terrified her children and who had few friends. When he visited or she came to his home, with the children outside playing and laughing, she sometimes would speak suddenly. The sound of her voice would startle him, she sounded so much like his deceased wife. This troubled him. Marta became more and more like his wife each time he saw her.

Jerónimo Portal loved his wife in the way people unaccustomed to displays of affection do. He seldom told her of his feelings and almost never showed her he cared. When it was important that he demonstrate his love for her, both of them had been too busy trying to prove to the other who was the stronger. Later, much later, when which of the two was the stronger did not matter at all, they had fallen into those silences which say what words make redundant. It was then that he realized he had no life apart from her. He suspected his wife of continuing the struggle right up to the day of her death, but he never acknowledged nor accepted any of what he presumed to be challenges for fear they were not challenges at all. Women, he often mused, do not really want to understand men; or themselves, for that matter. They are as self centered. as men are. The kind of world we have created demands only strength The weak are soon brushed aside, made to serve the strong, or destroyed altogether. The buildings surrounding the plaza are like that, thought Jerónimo Portal. Age, or design, give them the appearance of weakness and so they are razed. New, taller buildings appearing strong and lean take their place. So it is with people. Jerónimo Portal shook his head in a bemused way. Men had so little imagination they could not create a world better than what they found around them. All of man's creations are an imitation of what they think they see. Hence, the strong must forever be posed against the weak. In each case, it is only the appearance of strength or weakness that finally matters.

Lately, Jerónimo Portal's daughter had taken to shouting at him. His hearing was as good as ever, but she naturally assumed that at his age it was necessary for her to speak in a loud voice to him. Marta, in imitation of her mother, perceived a situation at first glance, and then without unduly thinking about it acted resolutely on that initial perception. It was completely alien to her to have second thoughts. He had tried to explain to her, on a number of occasions, that it was quite unnecessary for her to scream at him or anyone when she wanted attention, that it was impolite and that well-brought-up people spoke in level and civil voices to each other. His even and patient words fell upon her deaf, uncomprehending ears as though he were trying to recite the poem of the Cid which he had memorized as a child. Just like her mother, he would say wistfully under his breath to himself and perhaps to his deceased wife.

Jerónimo Portal lived near the center of the city in an old neighborhood. The homes were sturdy frame and brick houses, surrounded by spacious yards. There were plenty of trees to absorb the heat of summer and to pose bleakly in winter. Marta lived further out, near the outer limits of the city where the buses did not go. He no longer drove his car, but he kept it nonetheless. It was necessary for Marta to come in her station wagon to pick him up if he was to visit her. For this reason, his trips to see her and the grandchildren lasted several days, even though the drive took less than half an hour. Marta worried about him living in what she called 'that neighborhood.' She was convinced he would be killed by a punk burglar some night. She had seen the television news reports aimed chiefly at people who lived far away from the inner city, depicting the viciousness of the poor people who lived around him. She implored him to sell the house and buy one in her neighborhood, where it would be safer and where she and Eduardo could be closer to him. She reminded him, what with his pension and the price he could get for his house, he could well afford it. He had explained to her that the economics of such a move were insane. He would be selling a perfectly good house made of perfectly good materials for a much lower price than the house he would be buying in the suburbs. Exasperated, Marta explained to him that it was much nicer where they lived and that was why the prices were higher. Patiently, he informed her that even at his age he could put his fist through the sheetrock wall of her home. In mock anger, he asked if she would like him to show her. Marta threw her hands up in the air and went to another room, leaving him smiling in the kitchen.

The last time he had visited Marta, he left her home sooner than planned. Over the years since Graciela, his wife, died, and especially since Eduardo died, she had taken to treating him as one of the children. The first morning of his visit, she had bustled—not just walked—into the spare bedroom, drawing the curtains with a flourish, permitting an immense gulf of sunlight to sweep over him. He considered himself an early riser, but five-thirty was too early. Marta, who had started working again, was up at five every day, not wanting to break with her weekly rhythms. At five-thirty, she was humming some tune that if pressed even she could not identify. Humming as though she were an alarm clock, she spread his clothes across his ankles. The night before, she had given him one of Eduardo's old robes and had made him take off his clothes. As the last act of the day, she put the clothes in the washing machine in the garage. In the morning, as the first act of the day, she transferred them to the clothes dryer where they would toss as the machine rumbled while she bathed. She draped his clothes, freshly ironed, across his ankles. While he was opening his eyes, she continued to hum—he imagined it to be a sound similar to a hen. He imagined she would stay in the room until he opened his eyes and would continue checking in on him until he was on his feet.

It was then she cooingly asked if grandpa would like to get up and have some nice nourishing breakfast. In a sing-song voice she gave him the menu, nice oatmeal with cinnamon sticks, orange juice and toast. And if he was real good and got up right away, he could have instant coffee, but not too much because we know very well what the doctor says. Jerónimo Portal, in the most formal Spanish he knew, firmly informed her that he, Jerónimo Portal, presently prone on the bed, was in fact her father, as far as he knew, and to his knowledge not at all her grandfather. To which she responded in English, grumpy this morning, aren't we. Jerónimo Portal did not know what 'grumpy' meant, but he knew enough English to realize it was useless. He finally asked her in Spanish to permit him to dress in private. Later in the day, over lunch, he told his daughter he was worried about a cat he did not have and had her drive him home.

That incident had occurred more than a year before. He was back to himself and glad to have his solitude. He had made his peace with society, and more importantly, with himself. In the years since his retirement, and in those following the death of his wife, he had become accustomed to himself as though he were encountering an old friend after many years of separation. The fade was there, the gestures, the mannerisms, the voice. The face he saw was his, the voice he heard was his, but this person he was discovering seemed strange, though vaguely familiar to him. It was as if this lost friend, himself, had been with him all along, alongside in fact, and knew of everything in his life, but there had never been any closeness or intimacy. In the solitude of retirement he had come to know and understand himself a little better—at least to the point where he enjoyed being with himself. He did not regret for one moment having to wait so long for the discoveries he was making. I have nothing to apologize for in my life to anyone, he thought. I have lived as I intended to live, as it was meant for me to live. This thinking about himself was new, of course. It meant he had to recover fragments of his past and he would think about them. But he did not think about his past in order to change things in his mind, in order to know the better way to have done something. Nor did he think of his past to make himself appear better in his memory than he had ever been in fact. What was done was done. Rather, he thought about his past because it was all he had, really, and he did not want to lose any of it. In the meantime, he had his repetitive house chores, his modest food which he learned to cook by campfire as a young boy during the Revolution, and he had the plaza.

The plaza, changed though it was by its new surroundings, soon returned to the way it was: a tranquil and quiet respite from the city expanding and rising on all four sides. Gradually, almost imperceptibly, the new buildings were becoming a natural part of the plaza landscape. Soon his mind no longer registered the time when they were not there. The new businesses that were coming into the new buildings were employing many young people. Life changed through them, he knew. The young were the true barometers of age and change. It would be interesting, he thought, to talk to them, to discover how life is changing through them, to know first hand the link which existed between the young and the old.

Occasionally, one or two of them would sit on his bench—despite the new people who now came to the plaza, it was still *his* bench. His attempts at conversation were invariably met with silence. Whenever he began by noting how nice a day it was, his listener would quickly assent and return to the private eating of a lunch or to the reading of a magazine. They were not interested in conversation nor did they seem to want to make new friends. None of them seemed to know one another, although many of them worked in the same buildings. He would see two or three of them walk together into the dark interiors of the buildings. It appeared to Jerónimo Portal that only inside the buildings did they know each other and once outside they became strangers.

He reasoned at first that it must be the age-old animosity of gringos toward Mexicans that prevented the young people from speaking to him. He had only recently been retired from the railroad when he noticed the situation. He had then only a tentative, wary, vague relationship with his solitude. He was not yet at the point where he reflected much. He needed to talk to human beings, to hear human voices. His silent communication with his wife was not enough. He simply accepted the reticence on the part of the young gringos as something he had been familiar with since coming over from Mexico. He knew gringos gave orders to Mexicans or exchanged work talk. Some spoke in friendlier voices than others. But there was never the true bond of intimacy between the two. Even on those occasions when the work boss treated the gang to beer alongside the railroad tracks, there was little affection between gringos and Mexicans. The more they drank the more hostility surfaced forcing the work boss to send the Mexicans away while the gringos drank the remainder of the beer.

In the years that followed, more and more Mexicans became part of the lunchtime crowd in the plaza. He noticed the faces and gestures of these young Mexicans They were no different from their gringo counterparts. They were reticent. It was then that he began to think about the situation. His wife was gone and he was at a point where he took care of himself automatically doing everything he had to do without thinking about it. He was aware of a new, aggressive generation of Mexicans. These were unlike the young men he grew up with or those of the following generation who left the farms and the barrios to fight the Germans and the Japanese for the Americans The dazed expressions on their faces were similar to those of the pachucos of an earlier day. Gone was the overt, seething menace that leapt at the world from the faces of the pachucos. Among this generation of Mexicans, there was an air of wanting success, almost craving it. They had clean, scrubbed faces, exuding confidence, intelligence. Their only imperfection was a tentative determination that made them seem like convalescents taking their first unsure steps.

The people all around the plaza shared the shade of the trees, the grass, the benches. They tossed the leftovers of their lunches into the white trash barrels. They looked at one another with the stern faces of statues, softer than granite perhaps, but hard nonetheless. During a brief period the plaza had been invaded—he thought about the word 'invaded' and decided he liked it even though it was not the right one—by unkempt, raggedly dressed young people. They gave him flowers and smiled a lot. The young girls with long, straight, blonde hair were especially friendly. There was something about the vacant, repetitive smiles that never left their faces which bothered him. He could notice their facial muscles tremble from maintaining the forced smiles so long. To them, he was not Jerónimo Portal, veteran of the Mexican Revolution, retired from the Missouri-Pacific Railroad Company, father of Marta, husband of Graciela—a man who had seen and done many things during his long life. He was instead a relic to them, someone who had survived far longer than they could imagine. He was a curiosity to them. They called him 'man,' which seemed to him disrespectful. They paid little attention—in fact, they became impatient with him—when he tried to explain about his life. For reasons which escaped him then, he felt it important to try to explain to them. His efforts to give them the details necessary to make of him someone besides an old man in the park made them nervous, angered them. It soon became clear to him that they took him to be a gentle, maybe foolish old man, who could share with them a rejection of society.

If they could only know, if only they could be genuinely interested, he thought. The opposite was true. They did make him discover that he had never thought very much about his life, had never tried to analyze the sort of life he had led for more than seventy years. When he considered everything, the major and the minor details, he judged his life to have been a good one. It had been good enough for him and now that he was quite well adjusted to his solitude, he expected the years remaining to him to be also good ones. He found pleasure in this discovery. The best life is the one not judged until it is nearly over. It is best to live as well as one can and not judge until there is sufficient evidence. He knew that there comes a time when one is compelled to make such judgments. His time came during his old age. It was not true for everyone.

Conjunto Aztlan (Austin)

"Yo soy Chicano" (I Am Chicano)

Yo soy Chicano, tengo color/Puro Chicano, hermano con honor.
Cuando me dicen que hay revolución, Defiendo a mi raza con mucho valor.

Tengo todita mi gente/Para la revolución.
Voy a luchar con los pobres/Pa'que se acabe el bolón.

Tengo mi par de pistolas/Para la revolución.
Una es una treinta y treinta,/Y otra es una treinta y dos.

Tengo mi par de caballos/Para la revolución.
Una se llama El Canario, /Y otro se llama El Gorrión.

Tengo mi orgullo y machismo,/Mi cultura y corazón.
Tengo mi fe y diferencia,/Y lucho con gran razón.

Tengo todita mi gente/Para la revolución.
Voy a luchar con los pobres/Pa'que se acabe el bolón.

Tengo mi orgullo, tengo mi fe./Soy diferente, soy color café.
Tengo cultura, tengo corazón,/Y no me lo quita a mí ningún cabrón.

BOTH TRADITIONAL AND NON-TRADITIONAL, CONJUNTO AZTLAN considers itself a spiritual and musical group of poetry and song, born into the Xicano Movement in 1977 Austin.

I am Chicano, of color,/Pure Chicano, a brother with honor.
When they tell me there is revolution, /I defend my people with great valor.

I have all my people/For the revolution.
I am going to fight alongside the poor/To end this oppression.

I have my pair of pistols/For the revolution
One is a thirty-thirty,/And the other is a thirty-two.

I have my pair of horses/For the revolution.
One is called The Canary/And the other is called The Sparrow.

I have my pride and my manliness/My culture and my heart.
I have my faith and differences/And I fight with great conviction.

I have all my people/For the revolution.
I am going to fight alongside the poor/To end this oppression.

I have my pride, I have my faith./I am different, I am of brown color.
I have culture, I have heart,/And no son-of-a-gun will take it away from me.

Gregg Barrios (Victoria)

"Puro Rollo (primera parte)" and "I Am an Americano Too"

Puro Rollo (primera parte)

Pues, ahí estábamos sentados
refinando muy despacio
cuando llegó la tía del jale
siempre con el tintineo
de sus botellitas de lone star

estaba puesto el aparato de televisión
estábamos viendo las noticias
en el canal cuarenta y uno
hablaban de unos jovenes SANTOS
se llamaba uno de ellos
una chota lo había matado bien sudas
con un balazo a la cabeza

'¡que relaje!' dijo mi carnal
y se pasó más sopa de arroz
la tía dijo que ella sí
estaba "muy cansada" y se abrío
otra botellita de bironga
y yo solamente pensaba en mi ruca
que me había hablado casi una hora antes

me levanté de la mesa
y me fui a mi recámara
no podía ver nada
estaba bien oscuro
mis blacklight posters
brillaban ¡de aquellas!
cerré la puerta

me puse a sonar un toque
el radio estaba diciendo
que "¡K.T.S.A. toca más
mú-si-ca!" ¡Qué Loco!

Gregg Barrios was born in Victoria and attended the University of Texas after serving as a medic in the US Air Force during Vietnam. In college he began writing film criticism and became involved with Chicano activism, interests that would combine in his work while he taught high school in Crystal City, where he produced plays that dealt with the political issues of this now famous Texas town. Barrios' major work of poetry, *Puro Rollo,* takes its title from reels of film (*rollos*) and its content from Barrios' interest in, as Tomas Rivera put it, "rescuing . . . the social life and culture of the Chicano community." A journalist, a playwright, a bilingual kindergarten teacher, a boxing publicist, an independent filmmaker, and the book review page editor for the *San Antonio Express News,* Barrios lives in San Antonio.

I Am an Americano Too

I am a poet of la plebe
I reflect what I know I am
aware of what I am not yet
I find hope and pride in all
that I know I can become
I am an americano, too.

If I speak in a different voice
it is because I have a choice
English or Español whichever
ancient or modern tongue I choose
my people will welcome the news
I am an americano, too.

I endeavor to stand firm
in the face of those that scorn
to watch my step or know my place
for I know how long the people yearn
to show the world our own unique grace
I am an americano, too.

If I refuse to stop dreaming
I know it's because god's will
prevails for he never gave his word
to make this life a suffering hell
something that only time will tell
I am an americano, too.

If I no longer hold rancor
against the prejudiced past
it doesn't mean I have forgotten
rather strive toward that unity
which signals a brave new world
I am an americano, too.

Aristeo Brito considers himself a native of Presidio, although he was born in Ojinaga, Mexico, where his father had moved his family during World War II. He attended college at Sul Ross State and then went on to earn a Ph.D. from the University of Arizona in 1976. A few years before receiving his doctorate Brito published his most famous work, *El Diablo en Tejas,* which helped him earn a grant from National Endowment for the Arts. He has taught Spanish and Chicano literature at Pima Community College in Tucson, Arizona, for many years.

Aristeo Brito (Presidio)

from *The Devil in Texas*

No one even knew how they got to Presidio, but the fact is that they were riding horses and shouting. They came from the south of Texas with one idea: to bury the people alive and to thrust them even deeper into hell. And even though the invaders had come to the darkest corners of the earth, they knew how to be creative. In Presidio they discovered that the land and the people had lucrative possibilities, but some of them had to be buried first. A few months later, they went straight down to the river to drown the launch operator, Don Pancho's son, in the water. First because he had struck Ben, and second because there were larger interests in the transportation of people. But the only thought on Jesús's mind was his sister Rosario. What business did that bastard gringo have dating her? Come on! Stay the hell away! So one night they buried Jesús under water, filling the launch and his body with dirt so the two would stay submerged. The stone hung from his neck would make sure of that. Meanwhile, his lawyer's diploma was only good for Don Francisco to wipe his ass with, since the case was thrown out of court. And the worst part was that his daughter ran off with the gringo before the year was out. Shit! Not only down, but out as well! But from now on, watch out, you bunch of bastards! Later, his brother Santamaría continued to ferry people across even after they said there would soon be an international bridge, and as soon as it was built, people would have to use it to get across. But Santamaría, armed with a carbine, ignored that law because people preferred the launch. Go through the checkpoint and show papers? Go straight to hell. The bridge was the work of the devil. (The bridge is the devil's rainbow: two goat's feet with each one planted in a graveyard. The bridge is a slide to make you die laughing, right, Jesús?)

"The Lynches have their history; the old people, anyway. They killed people like barbarians. There were some poor people working for them, and when they tried to leave after a year, they took their pay with them. Sure, I'll pay you, they would tell them, but then they would take them away and kill them. People didn't protest because there was nothing to eat. Things were very bad. Around here we had to get by on cups of atole or whatever. So what could anyone do about it? Sure, there were men like Papa who weren't bothered by having to kill someone. And so there were men like him who could do whatever they wanted to with anyone they wanted to, but they would think about not leaving the families all alone. Because anyone can be courageous. But Papa was all tied down with us. Otherwise, how long would the Lynches last? You could just chop their heads off and cross over to the other side. Because don't think there were only Lynches around here. I can still remember how that Captain Gray used to kick ass. He belonged at that time to the Texas Rangers. He was real mean."

Don Pancho couldn't understand the broken message that Chava the idiot was giving him, so he did his best to calm him down. Once he had calmed down a little, he opened the store's storage room and spread a sarape over the bags of beans so Chava could lie down. At least he won't spend the rest of the night wandering around in a daze, Francisco thought. Then he put the chain on the door and went home to his house-store-printshop, certain that truth would come out with the light of day.

But the night turned out to be a long one for Pancho. A few hours later a pair of eyes full of pure rage showed up at his door. Reyes handled the carbine as though it were made of paper; at the same time he poured out of the corner of his mouth the story of what happened at the fort. When he finished, the old man invited him in, but Reyes refused. He said he preferred to go find out the truth, since Chindo's word was often unreliable.

"Okay, but don't go doing anything foolish."

"That creep'll get his."

"Make sure first, Son, and be patient."

"That's what I'm going to do, make real sure."

"Then we'll talk about it. But don't forget, Reyes. It's never too late as long as you're still alive."

"Okay, old man."

Don Pancho went into his private office and there among books and piles of newspapers, he set about struggling against his cynicism. He meditated on his life and his career, which had been a real disaster. Nothing more. Failure, crashing failure, period. The dusty newspapers and books that surrounded him were the last vestiges of a fight he'd lost. Proof of his creative age? Even the question was stupid. He remembered how his own destruction matched the town's, how the two had been reduced to an insignificant microcosm, but one replete with history. For his part, he had been spurned by both governments because of his strong sense of justice. There was nothing left of the efforts he had made during his time to ensure basic human rights, and the only thing that consoled him was unearthing his truth buried under the dust. The issues of *The Frontiersman* he had saved in his office said it all. Perhaps someone would come someday and read them, but that would be after he was dead.

He remembered very well his first year of practice, because it was in that same year when the world he had built in the air during his studies collapsed around him. Reality, damn it, was something else. Life was lived by shouting and waving hats. He had soon realized that the career of a lawyer was not quite so illustrious, and even less when it was practiced in a town of impoverished conditions. Then he came to realize that the best way to help others and to help himself would be through journalism, and he immediately began to publish *The Frontiersman,* a small newspaper that was read not only by those who needed to read it but also by other publishers in the Southwest. His undertaking grew strong when to his surprise he began to receive newspapers from California, Trinidad, Colorado, Laredo, New Mexico, and from places where he never even suspected there were Mexicans. In time, the publication became a strong voice with one concern: polemics, denunciation, and protest over the life of Mexicans in these areas. Soon his words were being picked up by newspapers in Mexico, and the Mexican government did not take long to recognize Francisco Uranga's benefit to the country. He received his appointment as consul with great enthusiasm. The exact words? "To serve as representative of our citizens abroad as appropriate in the defense of their rights and principles as designated by the treaties between Mexico and the United States." Just as soon as he had received the appointment, he began to order by priority the tasks to be undertaken. First, the clarification of the question of properties that had been usurped in the Presidio valley and to discover how to validate claims on lands that had little by little been rolled away like a rug. (But he remembered that by that time it was already too late be cause the legal archives were written in another language and bore another seal.) Later, he would pursue the complicated question of citizenship, and for that he would have to contact the other consuls in the Southwest. And he would have to find quickly a more efficient way of arranging the repatriation of all those individuals who wished to go home, but who thought that the Mexican government had abandoned them. Another of the causes, and here he was emphatic, was the need to combat the insolence on the part of those who considered themselves the law, and crossed the border without prior authorization. This point was one of the touchiest, because he had seen numerous cases in which the person being pursued was taken out of Mexico in order to try him in a foreign court and in a foreign language. Yes, it was necessary to clarify the law of extradition so trammeled by the conqueror, although he knew that it was a very difficult task. On other occasions, the opposite occurred: the person accused by the Mexican authorities could not prove that he was a citizen of the United States, even when the treaty said that anyone not repatriated within two years would be considered a citizen. And the papers? They had vanished into thin air. Where are you from? From the land, sir. From wherever I can make a living.

It did not take long for Pancho Uranga to realize that he was in the same whirlpool. Between the accumulation of paper and the confusion, he lived as though sick and lost at sea. He ended up with his hands tied with frustration, transformed into one of those persons who know so much about how the world works that they smirk as if to say: Jerks, what did you expect? God's blessings wrapped in a blanket? Get it straight; humanity is rotten to the core. And each time the devil won out, the thorn dug deeper, and by the time he tried to extract it, it had already poisoned his soul. By then he had taken up the pen as a sword. His writings appeared in his own paper, *The Frontiersman,* in *The Tucsonian, The Spanish American, The Zurtian, The Voice of the People,* and forty other newspapers that were coming out at that time: "I roundly denounce the usurpation of the lands and I support the White Caps for having shown their weapons"; "I put my name to the resolution of the unified Spanish American press which condemns the governor of New Mexico for calling us 'greasers' in the English-language press of New York and who now has the nerve to threaten us"; "I protest the filibustering expeditions of opportunistic Yankees"; "I condemn discrimination in the workplace, in schools, and in public establishments"; "I support the defenses mounted by the Mexican Alliance"; "with anger and love I lament the dissolution of our people and I weep for its future"; "I am a partisan of the radical element of workers in San Antonio, California, and New Mexico, not because I know they have achieved something, but because it proves that we are still alive and that there will be something for us to fight"; "I am suspicious of the justice and the sentences meted out by judges that are guided by the opinions of prejudiced witnesses; moreover, I know that Manuel Verdugo was not guilty. I found out afterward that he was sentenced to die in El Paso"; "I condemn the sale of black slaves in Fayetteville, Missouri"; "for the information of the editor of the aforementioned rag in Guadalajara, my efforts to repatriate our people are genuine. And I do so because I know the sufferings experienced in a country that is considered the best example of democracy, and I also would have you understand fully, via examples, that our people here are not a bunch of tamale vendors, as you so grossly describe us. The survey I print here contains the number of persons of Mexican descent, and you should know that of all those who responded, only four are in the business of selling tamales, and not because they are lazy but because of the adverse fortunes they have experienced. I have on numerous occasions appealed to the Mexican government to provide the money to provide transport for those who want to be repatriated, as well as to allot them a parcel of land; otherwise, what guarantee is there that they would live any better if they returned to Mexico? The problem now has its roots in the fact that the Chinese are willing to work for less wages"; "I would have the gentleman, who speaks without any basis when he says that those of us who are from here are the poorest and uneducated, know that, if we concede that he is right that the working family lives poorly, that doesn't mean we are uneducated. We recognize our circumstances and do what we can about them. Now, explain to me, Mr. Publisher, why you believe that these working people are the ones who least seek to be repatriated? On another occasion I would like you, instead of spewing out nonsense, to set yourself to thinking a little more. We, my colleague, do not wish to move from this land that we have always considered our own, and if I make the effort to repatriate some people, it is because I am moved by the hope that the Mexican government will help us"; "I would remind the governor of Chihuahua that he made a big mistake by conceding vast areas of land to the settlement companies, since all they do is take over the natural resources. In time these companies will go the same way as the great overlords who now exploit the poor mercilessly"; "I denounce publicly the misguided deeds of the consul in El Paso, who cooperated with the sheriff in the extradition of Rufino Gómez. The hundred pesos they paid him under the table will not serve to calm his conscience after the accused has been sentenced"; "I would never have believed that one of our own (from Laredo) would comment so unfavorably on the poetry that we publish in the literary section, and even less so over its being written in 'bastard' Spanish. We regret very much that these attitudes are so deeply rooted. Why is our colleague so blind to the facts? Better, why doesn't the gentleman lodge his complaints with the educational system or the federal government., which promised to respect our language and our culture? If there were schools where our maternal tongue were taught, perhaps you would have no reason to complain. But this is an ideal. You'd be better off to spend your energies in assuring the well-being of your children, since God knows they need it, rather than showing the same attitude of superiority that we have experienced for so long."

Thus he pricked sensitivities with the tip of his pen, and it wasn't too long before both governments considered him an enemy of harmony. By the time he defended the cause of Catarino Garza, who provoked the uprising of workers in New Mexico against the landowners and the government of Chihuahua, he had ceased to be consul. It was a miracle he wasn't killed, although in those days he would have preferred it, because nothing mattered to him. The town he had defended with love now turned its back on him, and that was what hurt the most. Some, as soon as luck went their way, came down on him. "Old troublemaker, leave well enough alone. Things are going well, and you threaten our position with your stupidity. So either you shut up or . . ." *The Frontiersman* died a death without glory. People were right, history stops for no one. (History flows like water. Sometimes calm, sometimes with the devil riding it, making it swollen and rabid. Then it brings forth a deformed hand that stretches its fingers out to infinity. Then the water's hand withdraws and becomes a claw, leaving only a trickle in the bed of the Rio Grande. Then the people on their eternal migration return to form a twisted cross, a miserable cross of flesh and water.) And since the history of my race is that of the river, I thought, I am going to build a launch to ferry them across. This will help me support myself, but I will charge only those who can pay. It will also give me the opportunity to guide people by setting them on the best road. "Go this way and be careful with this and that, and if he doesn't give you a job, follow the river until . . ." But before I do that, I'll gather my belongings, my books, and move to Ojinaga. I will build a house near the river on the other side, in order for our history not to be washed away in the water. Many years after, when I lost Rosario and I found out they were going to build the bridge, I wasn't even surprised. Not even when I heard that they had drowned my Jesús. My wound began to bleed again when he was buried a mess, and I swore I would avenge him. But I couldn't, and I thought you would avenge him, Reyes, being his brother. I didn't want really to raise you to be an assassin. The weapons would come later, and these only as a last resort. What I wanted to give you first was book-learning, but not out of those that tell false stories. That's why I had you study with Mariana, my teacher, and not in that hovel of a school where they drill you with the idea that you should cut off the roots of the language that gave you birth. Then I would send you there to Presidio, but only after you knew the truth, why things are the way they are, when you would be proud to be a son of the people. But as you well know, you turned out a failure. I don't know why you were that way since childhood, Reyes. When I sent you to Mariana, after only a few days she came to tell me you had hit her back after she had struck you. I never even wanted to see your face. You didn't want to go to school, even though it earned you a lot of whippings; do you remember, Reyes? I still don't know how you learned what you do know. Perhaps from my books that you read on the sly, because I never saw you bother with anything. You're lazy and a bum. Busy yourself with the firewood so you can buy and sell or go help your uncle Santamaría with the launch, I told you, but no, you'd show up in the afternoon with food, firewood, and money. "And where did you get that money?" "I sold fish to the gringo down the bridge." "I told you not to go messing around with them! Damn kid!"

Carlos Cumpián (San Antonio)

"Armadillo Charm" and "'Bout to Leave the Barrio"

ARMADILLO CHARM

I.

Armadillos are flattened on roads every week,
ending up like some cold drunk Indians
who lie down on warm dark asphalt after
trips back from fiery-watering holes.

Smart armadillos amble jobless,
happy not to work in a zoo, they stroll
plush river grass and smooth red pebble paths,
far from fast two-legged foreigners.

II.

Armadillos want to be around when the earth smears
the last mad zigzag road from her body,
armadillos are patient, armadillos count
every wind stir roaring off solar coasters,
bringing layers of fine star dandruff to land,
that's why they look like dried-up

CARLOS CUMPIÁN was born in San Antonio, moving to Chicago as a teenager when it was impossible to find work in South Texas. In Chicago Cumpián became involved with the Chicano artistic movement coming to national prominence in the early 1970s, forming El Teatro del Barrio in Chicago. He also began working with the Movimiento Artístico Chicano as head of *Abrazo,* a journal published by the group. MARCH/Abrazo Press was the first to publish Sandra Cisneros. In Chicago he also began teaching high school as well as classes at Columbia College, and began publishing poetry in the late 1970s. Cumpián became more focused on teaching in the following years, but was still able to put together a collection of his works in 1996 called *Armadillo Charm.*

sailors or the last face of thirsty travelers,
armadillos are prone to tropical leprosy,
like lost botanists they go skinning themselves
raw while roaming hungry in the dark.

Before the sky master tossed sparks to bake all creation
with telltale universal panther carbon, nothing big had died
yet, truly a nadir niche for four-legged fossils, though not too
bad for fishes, it nearly killed calorie-starved armadillo.

III.
Armadillo, ugly craggy creature, with twenty tribes
across the hemisphere,
armadillo, with few friends from beginning to end:
the hairy tree sloth, and rapacious ant eater,
each claiming to be his pal, sharing a pre-Ice-Age pedigree
with the armored rascal, each sticking to the same survival
diet since making the Paleocene,
peg-tooth armadillo got hot under his sixty million year-old
scapular collar and became a cranium-hard tourist walking backwards—
going south to north, before entering borderland Texas.

Gringos discovered Armadillo in the mid-nineteenth century,
the indigenous people had always known him,
but history started with the newcomers ripe for independence,
Alamo insurance, Austin honky-tonks, accordion *conjunto*-polka suds,
salsa music, blue-eyed Baptists, plastic saints on dashboards,
chile-flavored beans and King Ranch cowboys trained by *vaqueros*,
raised on tacos of onion-soaked armadillo,
available only in south *Texaztlan,*
giving the chicken-colored meat cult status.

IV.
Armadillos are fond of colorful flowers, thorns pose no problem,
and armadillos love dark dirt body bugs, slugs and worms
on steamy leaves and bright powdery pistils-to-petals.
There are no obese armadillos. »

Armadillo has no patent on this diet, so some of us
wanting to slim down just might like to try it. You go first.

Armadillo kitsch means being flayed for book ends, salt shakers or
decorative baskets to please some schmucks passing through airports,
armadillos become rustic *canastas* filled with pecans and
pomegranates after eyes are shredded by twenty-two caliber bullets,
there's no graveside music for their passing,
no lead-lined casket for a charade with eternity,
not a moment of ritual magic,
nothing cushions armadillo death when shells, cars or trucks
splatter red guts like gastral litter on subtropical scrublands.

V.
Armadillo prefers his original name in Nahuatl, *Ayotochtli,*
a combination of turtle and rabbit,
looking like a hedgehog in an obsidian helmet,
sturdy enough to become an instrument,
complete with strings for *charango*-mountain music,
Ayotochtli, Ayotochtli, Ayotochtli,

"Ah, don't touch me," he seems to say,
balling up after he burrows away
at speeds pushing fifty,
armadillos have lived like charmed moving stones
for generations, so don't knickknack them to extinction,
be compassionate compadres,
adopt one.

'Bout to Leave the Barrio

A warm California breeze
lifts a cirrus cloud of smoldering
cigars and cigarettes, the gym's
cone lights cast spears down
where every bench is filled.
The crowd is gathered to see two
tight-lipped boxers stalk each other,

the fight is all for the spectators' pleasure,
who belch and bellow demands in
English, Spanish and Portuguese,
impatient for muscular *cholos* caged
in a dream to perform their
brown-skinned rooster routine.

Each two-legged *gallo* knows
he's a gambler taking
his chances at the
wheel.

One fighter is a *pocho* in red and gold,
he knows how to go toe-to-toe with
drunk *campesino* royalty and roughneck punks.
Barrio *cantinas* were his training grounds,
now, he wants to be a household name,
except the referee can't pronounce
"Villarreal."

Then there's the crop picker José "*Lechuga*"
Longoria in his lanky stance, robed in the green
promise of winning fast money, living proof
that crossing *el rio grande* was nothing
compared to this night's prospects.

Laced up, mouthpiece in place,
the timekeeper's bell propels
them forward, turning their
gloves into inflated lobes
of brick-colored leather.

Back and forth the boxers go
until a heliotrope of facial bruises
have blossomed in the third round.

Soon both men's gloves
are streaked with blood
and hair pomade.

In the sixth,
the ropes chafe arms and backs,
for courage, Longoria thinks of abandoning
his migrant tasks for the bright galaxy
of the ring, far
from all his mocking bosses.

Villarreal, "*nunca te aguitas,*"
he never quits, his buddies say.
Sweat covered, the hewed pugilist is
looking for his big break,
before the gallows of adulthood
bully him off to the army or
some other nit-picking job.

"*Dale duro pinche lechuga!*"
someone laughs,
then calling at an octave higher,
a woman in a tight white dress
offers her ocular breasts to the
fight's winner, a standing Odysseus.

This causes red and gold Villarreal
to galumph and with thunderbolt vision
launch a two-minute offensive,
to pummel Longoria,
the prune picker in green,
he wallops him inside his solar plexus,
leaving a curled-up, tired fetus
on the dirty canvas.

raúlrsalinas (Austin)

"La Loma" and "A Walk Through the Campo Santo"

La Loma

Neighborhood of my youth
demolished, erased forever from
the universe.
You live on, captive, in the lonely
cellblocks of my mind.

Neighborhood of endless hills
muddied streets—all chuckhole lined—
that never drank of asphalt.
Kids barefoot/snotty-nosed
playing marbles/munching on bean tacos
(the kind you'll never find in a café)
2 peaceful generations removed from
their abuelos' revolution.

Neighborhood of dilapidated community hail
—Salón Cinco de Mayo—
yearly (May 5/Sept. 16) gathering
of the familias. Re-asserting pride
on those two significant days.
Speeches by the elders,

Raúl Salinas was born in San Antonio and raised in Texas, but it was in California where his artistic consciousness was created. After moving to Los Angeles in 1956, Salinas spent over a decade in the California prison system. While there, he produced two prison journals, including *Aztlan de Leavenworth,* whose inaugural issue contained Salinas' most famous poem, "Un Trip Through the Mind Jail." After leaving prison in 1972, Salinas began attending classes at the University of Washington at Seattle. He later moved back to Austin, where he has become its premiere poet. He is the owner of Resistencia Bookstore.

patriarchs with evidence of oppression
distinctly etched upon mestizo faces.
"Sons of Independence!"
Emphasis on allegiance to the tri-color
obscure names: JUAREZ & HIDALGO
their heroic deeds. Nostalgic tales of war
years under VILLA'S command. No one listened,
no one seemed to really care.
Afterwards, the dance. Modest Mexican
maidens dancing polkas together
across splintered wooden floor.
They never deigned to dance with boys!
The careful scrutiny by curbstone sex-perts
8 & 9 years old. "Minga's bow-legged,
so we know she's done it, huh?"

Neighborhood of Sunday night jamaicas
at Guadalupe Church.
Fiestas for any occasion
holidays holy days happy days
'round and 'round the promenade
eating snowcones—raspas—& tamales
the games—bingo cakewalk spin-the-wheel
making eyes at girls from cleaner neighborhoods
the unobtainables
who responded all giggles and excitement.

Neighborhood of forays down to Buena Vista—
Santa Rita Courts—Los Projects—friendly neighborhood
cops n' robbers on the rooftops, sneaking peeks
in people's private night-time bedrooms
bearing gifts of Juicy Fruit gum for
the Project girls/ chasing them in adolescent heat
causing skinned knees & being run off for the night
disenchanted walking home affections spurned
stopping stay-out-late chicks in search of
Modern Romance lovers, who always stood them up
unable to leave their world in the magazines' pages. »

Angry fingers grabbing, squeezing, feeling,
french kisses imposed; close bodily contact, thigh &
belly rubbings under shadows of Cristo Rey Church.

Neighborhood that never saw a school-bus
the cross-town walks were much more fun
embarrassed when acquaintances or friends or relatives
were sent home excused from class
for having cooties in their hair!
Did only Mexicans have cooties in their hair?
¡Que gacho!

Neighborhood of Zaragoza Park
where scary stories interspersed with
inherited superstitions were exchanged
waiting for midnight and the haunting,
lament of La Llorona—the weeping lady
of our myths & folklore—who wept nightly
along the banks of Boggy Creek
for the children she'd lost or drowned
in some river (depending on the version).
i think i heard her once
and cried
out of sadness and fear
running all the way home nape hairs at attention
swallow a pinch of table salt and
make the sign of the cross
sure cure for frightened Mexican boys.

Neighborhood of Spanish Town Café
first grown-up (13) hangout
Andrés,
tolerant manager, proprietor, cook
victim of bungling baby burglars
your loss: Fritos n' Pepsi Colas—was our gain
you put up with us and still survived!
You, too, are granted immortality.

Neighborhood of groups and clusters
    sniffing gas, drinking muscatel
    solidarity cement hardening
    the clan the family the neighborhood the gang
                        NOMAS!
    Restless innocents tattoo'd crosses on their hands
    "just doing things different"
    "From now on, all troublemaking mex kids will be
    sent to Gatesville for 9 months."
    Henry home from La Corre
    khakis worn too low—below the waist
    the stomps, the greña with duck-tail
                        —Pachuco Yo—

Neighborhood of could-be artists

    the art form of our slums
    more meaningful & significant
    than Egypt's finest hieroglyphics.

Neighborhood where purple clouds of Yesca
    smoke one day descended & embraced us all.
    Skulls uncapped—Rhythum n' Blues
                        Chalie's 7th St. Club
    loud funky music/ wine spodee-odees/ barbecue & grass
    our very own connection man: big black Johnny B—

Neighborhood of Reyes' Bar
    where Lalo shotgunned
    Pete Evans to death because of
    an unintentional stare
    and because he was escuadra,
    only to end his life neatly sliced
    by prison barber's razor.
    Durán's grocery & gas station >>

Güero drunkenly stabbed Julio
arguing over who'd drive home
and got 55 years for his crime.
Ratón: 20 years for a matchbox of weed. Is that cold?
No lawyer no jury no trial i'm guilty
                    Aren't we all guilty?
Indian mothers, too unaware
of courtroom tragi-comedies
folded arms across their bosoms
saying, "Sea por Dios."

Neighborhood of my childhood
neighborhood that no longer exists
some died young—fortunate—some rot in prisons
the rest drifted away to be conjured up
in minds of others like them.
For me: only the NOW of THIS journey is REAL!

Neighborhood of my adolescence
neighborhood that is no more
YOU ARE TORN PIECES OF MY FLESH!!!!
Therefore, you ARE.
LA LOMA—AUSTIN—MI BARRIO—
            i bear you no grudge
i needed you then . . . identity . . . a sense of belonging
i need you now.
so essential to adult days of imprisonment,
you keep me away from INSANITY'S hungry jaws;
            Smiling/ Laughing/ Crying.

i respect your having been:
my Loma of Austin
my Rose Hill of Los Angeles
my West Side of San Anto
my Quinto of Houston
my Jackson of San Jo
my Segundo of El Paso
my Barelas of Alburque

my Westside of Denver
Flats, Los Marcos, Maravilla, Calle Guadalupe,
Magnolia, Buena Vista, Mateo, La Seís, Chíquis,
El Sur, and all Chicano neighborhoods that
now exist and once existed;
somewhere . . . , someone remembers. . . . .
14 Sept. '69
LEAVENWORTH

A Walk Through the Campo Santo

i walked through the Campo Santo of my ciudad tonight
visiting friends and relations playmates from childhoods
hurried/lived other mates from capitalist caves request stop
machinery for a while share in the sacred plants spreading the
presence of peace above/beneath the earth birthrights given
up the Spirit rusty nail at the heel locks the jaws locomotive
wheels become meat grinders the plague in the colony gang-
land guns coming and going family feud with his pistol in his
hand jazz trumpets blare flares catch the glimmer of the gun
running partner my blood of no more sounds no smoke-em-
ups narco hollow points riddled back .357 magnum reigns
stickpins in the skin pop poisonous veins 12 gauge shotgun
in the mouth scattered brains become wall designs life left
dangling on the old homestead backyard live oak tree elders
those who checked out caught the bus all on they own / popos
and grandpas grandmother gabriela dead not dead bracing up
temper the steel softening of the machine priestly eulogies
She Gave Birth to a Nation! an indio poet smiles and matriar-
chal voices set the tone as six generations sheep lonely in their
assimilation slump on cold, wooden church pews scratching
they heads wonder what it was the preacher meant bent on
knee i honor primos y tías compas & comrades shoulder to
shoulder laid out beneath caliche stones on sacred ground
i walked through the campo santo of my ciudad tonight.

—Austin, 1989

part eight

the 1980s

Laura Canales (San Antonio)

"Cuatro Caminos" (Four Roads)

Es imposible que yo te olvide,
es imposible que yo me vaya,
por donde quiera que voy te miro
ando con otra y por ti suspiro.

Es imposible que todo acabe,
yo sin tus besos me arranco el alma
si ando en mi juicio no estoy contento,
si ando borracho pa' qué te cuento.

Cuatro caminos hay en mi vida,
¿cuál de los cuatro será el mejor?
Tú que me viste llorar de angustia
dime paloma, ¿por cuál me voy?

Tú me juraste que amor del bueno
sólo en tus brazos lo encontraría,
ya no te acuerdas cuando dijiste
que yo era tuyo y que tú eras mía.

Si es que te marchas, paloma blanca
alza tu vuelo poquito a poco,
llévate mi alma bajo tus alas
y dime adiós a pesar de todo.

It's impossible to forget you,
it's impossible to go away,
wherever I go, I see you
I am with another, but I sigh for you.

It's impossible for everything to end,
without your kiss, I tear out my soul
if I'm in my right mind, I'm not content
if I'm drunk, well why say more.

Four roads are in my life,
which of the four will be the best?
You that saw me cry of anguish
tell me, dove, which should I take?

You swore that good kind of love
only in your arms I would find it,
already you don't remember when you said
that I was yours and you were mine.

If you leave, white dove,
lift your flight slowly,
take my soul under your wings
and tell me goodbye despite it all.

CALLED THE "BARBARA STREISAND OF TEJANO MUSIC" and "La Reina de Onda Tejano," Laura Canales, from San Antonio, was awarded both the Tejano Female Entertainer and Female Vocalist of the Year.

Lionel Garcia is from San Diego, Texas, and received a B.S. from Texas A & M and stayed to become a doctor of veterinary medicine. Between those degrees, Garcia also served in the U.S. Army. He contributed his first work to an anthology edited by Rudolfo Anaya in 1984, and since then has written several novels while continuing to practice as a veterinarian in Seabrook. Author of seven books, his first, *Leaving Home,* won the PEN Southwest Discovery Award in 1983.

Lionel G. García (Houston)

"Eladio Comes Home"

The large mahogany upright piano stood at the wall opposite from the entrance, a door to either side. The left door led into a hallway with several bedrooms. The right door went into the large elongated kitchen that ran from approximately halfway to the end of the house. On both sides of the room were seated women all dressed in black with black shawls. At the entrance wall were but a few chairs placed on either side of the door. The rest of the wall was taken over by the two large windows where the canaries lived. The woman who had raised Eladio sat to the right at the middle of the wall. She was a rather stout, short lady, with a large head with lots of dark hair with a white streak at the center combed severely back and pinned with a black ornamental comb. Her upper arms were pendulous and her dress, black also, was wet under her arms from perspiration although the two women on either side of her fanned her continuously for fear she may faint. Everyone knew her as Chata or Tía Chata. A black veil draped over the top of her head covered her face so that no one could see her cry or see the wrinkles of her face or see the forlorn look in her eyes. At that instant the priest across the street rang *la primera* for rosary. Outside, the children who had come with their parents were playing. Some had gone across the street to the parochial school playground to play to get away from parental, critically watchful eyes. The men who had come were scattered throughout the porch which ran completely around the house. They were talking in soft tones. Occasionally there was a short burst of laughter but then the solemnness of the occasion set in and all was muffled again. They had before spoken with the brothers and had gone through the dreaded chore of greeting all the women inside.

"How old was Eladio?" one of the men, the mayor, asked as he approached the brothers. He was a small penguinlike man, larger across the middle than he was tall. He took off his hat and wiped the inside with his handkerchief. He wore a wrinkled light grey suit, a white shirt with a bad collar and an old solid black mourning tie.

"Eladio was nineteen," his brother replied.

The mayor had parked his car on the side street and had come from almost behind the house. It was getting dark and the mayor offered his condolences when he realized it was the brother. The brother was dressed in an army uniform, as were his other three brothers who walked over behind him. One of them was smoking. He had a flask in his hip pocket.

The mayor said, shaking his head, "Too young. Too, too young."

The brothers did not answer but waited for the mayor to continue. The mayor, not one to be at a loss for words, said, "I tell you, this war is going to be the end of the young men of this town. How many have died?"

"I heard fourteen," said the brother who was smoking and drinking.

"Much. Much, too much," said the mayor and he excused himself to go inside.

The brothers watched him waddle his way to the front of the house and he disappeared from the porch by turning to his right. Then they could see him through the windows, through the canaries, going across the front of the house. They assumed he entered because in a short while they heard the women began to cry again.

A man, the tailor in town who had lost a son in the war, came to where the brothers were standing against the wall and shook hands. "*Les acompaño sus sentimientos,*" he said. "My son," he said, "was killed in Normandy. He is buried there. One day I hope to go see his grave. If God wants it and He gives me life." And with that, as if he had announced something unimportant, he apologized for taking their time and left to go inside to pay his respects to Chata. The mayor was on his way out through the front gate. He was on his way to the rosary when the priest rang *la segunda.* When the tailor entered, the women, realizing who he was, that he had lost a son in the war, wailed again. The tailor's wife had been there since morning and had taken her turn next to Chata, fanning her. The tailor shook Chata's hand and embraced her lightly and went around the room shaking hands, even his wife's. He stood by the piano momentarily. By now the wailing had reached a high pitch and the tailor excused himself. He stepped out and put his hat back on. He followed the mayor and went through the front gate. The cars were beginning to arrive at the church.

At the same time a car drove up to the front of the house and stopped. The driver, a thin young man in his twenties, got out quickly and came around and opened the passenger door. Mrs. Gonzales, the school principal, got off [*sic*] and walked slowly on her ponderous legs to the front gate with the help of the driver. This was her son, Robertito. She was a widow, a heavy woman with thick legs and a dark moustache and thick eyebrows. She had been born with a large chocolate-colored mole on her forehead from which thick, coarse white hairs grew. She had the look of perpetual disgust—the corners of her mouth turned down, her eyes fixed at some point beyond reason—as one would find in a school administrator-teacher who had been at it too long, seen it all, heard it all and didn't care anymore. The town was scared of her. She wore a black shawl over her head like the other women. The son opened the gate for her and escorted her to the front door. He knocked lightly and one of the women asked them to enter. Mrs. Gonzales caused even more wailing than the mayor and the tailor. She had brought with her the memories of Eladio and his school days. The son took her by the arm to where Chata was seated and she bent down to embrace Chata. She went slowly around the room shaking everyone's hand, exchanging greetings, fixing everyone with her stare. Her son followed meekly. She finally came all the way around and the son was asked to go into the kitchen to get an extra chair. In the kitchen he saw the women he knew, his mother's friends, who were cooking and preparing coffee for the wake. He noticed Carolina there and he smiled but she was busy and she returned his smile with a look of indifference. He came back, set the chair by the piano and stepped behind his mother.

Mrs. Gonzales looked back over her shoulder at her son and said, "I imagine the boys are outside. Why don't you go offer your condolences to them?"

The son excused himself went to the door, and left.

"What a beautiful son," the tailor's wife said.

"God keep him from going to the war," said the mayor's wife.

Mrs. Gonzales said, "Fortunately, he has a heart condition."

Chata's cat came out from behind the piano, stretched, and went around the room rubbing itself against the women's legs.

"They say a cat is bad luck," the butcher's wife said.

"Not true," Mrs. Gonzales, a cat lover, said very sternly. Everyone remembered she was the principal and that she was above the butcher's wife and that ended the conversation. The butcher's wife looked blankly at the wall, as if she had not said what she said.

Chata, behind her veil, was lost in thought. She was thinking that perhaps this was a dream, a bad dream, and that she would awaken before long and she would tell her canaries what she had dreamed. The canaries would make such a sound that she knew they were laughing. And then someday she would be laughing, playing the piano, singing with her canaries and Eladio would come in. He would be in uniform. A sergeant at such a young age. She would embrace him so tightly and then she would say that she would never let him go. How much love she had for him and the others. They had been very young when their mother died and they had come to live with her. She couldn't remember the time and it bothered her enough that her lower lip trembled. How foolish and sacrilegious of her, their aunt, not to remember when her sister had died.

"Chata hasn't been herself since this happened," whispered the mayor's wife.

"Of course not. She's stunned," Mrs. Gonzales replied, again killing the conversation.

The mayor's wife pursed her lips as though she would cry and then bit her tongue.

It was time for the canaries to sing and they filled the room with whistles. Chata did not hear them. Mrs. Gonzales stood and went to the windows and unfurled the drapes held to one side by a hook. In doing so she covered the windows and the canaries slowly quieted down.

At that moment the priest sounded *la tercera* and Chata awoke from her thoughts and began to wail and talk at the same time. The others did not lose the opportunity to cry out also. Only a few of Chata's words could be understood: church, bells, rosary, priest. They were incoherent enough to trigger even more cries from the collection of women. Ultimately the sound reverberated through the house with so much force that it appeared the house would burst with the intensity of so much sorrow. The weakest part of the house was the chimney. The top fell harmlessly at the rear of the house where no one could see it.

Mrs. Gonzales had the presence of mind to get up and tiptoe into the kitchen where she noticed the dust coming from the hearth. She looked up the chimney and saw the empty night sky. The other women were so preoccupied that they had not noticed. Carolina, whom Mrs. Gonzales hated, caught her eye kneading dough for biscuits. She would be sure that Carolina did not speak to Robertito. She left the chimney as though nothing had happened. She did not want to say that the top of the chimney had fallen. There was enough pain in the house as it was. Instead she poured herself some tea and one for Chata, which she carried into the parlor but not before turning her nose up at Carolina.

The tea satisfied Chata as she drank it under her veil. The others took the opportunity to rest and go into the kitchen to eat and drink. Chata was left alone with Mrs. Gonzales.

"You know that Mr. Gonzales would have been heartbroken over this," Mrs. Gonzales said.

Chata nodded her head.

"This would have been a horrible blow for him to take," she added. "You know how much he admired the boys. Well, you know how much Robertito admires the boys."

Chata put her cup down, rested it on her lap and looked over to the canaries and Mrs. Gonzales, her gaze following, saw the five stars on the window over the cage. She got up and removed one of the stars and handed it to Chata.

Robertito had found the brothers on the porch at the east side of the house. He approached them slowly, timidly, hoping they would not move before he got to them. Most of the men who had been outside had gone to the church for the rosary.

"What time does the body arrive?" Robertito asked. He could not help but feel a sense of guilt not being in uniform.

"Eight," said one of the brothers.

"In one hour," said Robertito checking his watch. "I can't begin to tell you guys how sorry I feel that Eladio was killed. I heard it was Iwo Jima?"

Three of the brothers excused themselves and went into the kitchen by the porch door. The remaining brother, the one with the flask and cigarettes, said, "He was killed in Iwo Jima."

Robertito said, "Maybe I can go with you to get the body."

"We already have enough men," the brother said.

"Maybe, if you would allow me, I can stand guard over the casket."

"No. It's not necessary," said he. "Listen, we don't want too much for him. You understand?"

"I understand. It was just that I felt that I could help in some way by guarding the casket."

"No."

"Whatever you say. I was just volunteering in case you needed someone to guard the casket."

"No, we don't need anyone."

"I just thought I'd ask. You know that if you don't ask then you don't find out. Now I know how you feel."

"Would you just leave me alone? Please?"

"All right. I was only trying to help."

"I know. I appreciate it. We all do. You want a drink? A cigarette?"

"No. I don't drink or smoke. Eladio drank, didn't he?"

"Yes. Eladio drank and he smoked. We all drink and smoke. What else is there to do?"

"I've never had a drink in my life. Never had a cigarette."

"You ought to drink. You ought to smoke. How can you stand it?"

"I just can. I don't even have the desire. I'm not even curious."

"What about women?"

"What about them?"

"I saw you making eyes at Carolina in the kitchen. I could see from here inside through the window."

"She's just a friend."

"You don't love her?"

"No. I don't love anyone. I'm not like Eladio. Eladio loved all the women."

"He sure did. He loved women and women loved him."

"But Eladio was handsome."

"Yes. He was handsome. You sure you don't want a drink?"

"No."

"I hate to end this but I'm going inside to eat something now that the crowd has thinned out. About you guarding the casket, you can do it if you want to. I've changed my mind."

"And your other brothers?"

"They won't mind."

"I can just sit by the casket. That's what I meant. I don't have a uniform or anything like that. I'll sit by the casket."

"That's good of you."

"Thank you for letting me. I was feeling real down. You don't know what it feels not to be going to the war. Staying behind."

"Keeping all the women satisfied."

"Oh, no. Nothing like that."

"Why didn't you go?"

"I went but they turned me down. I have a bad heart."

"Well, you're lucky. Having a bad heart. I sometimes wish I had something wrong with me."

"I wish I could have gone. But my mother was glad I came back. I was only gone for one night. She missed me so much you would have thought I had been gone for a year."

"You don't have to be telling me all this."

"I'm sorry. If I don't tell it to someone, then who's to know?"

"Tell it to somebody else. Carolina. Some woman. This is woman talk. I want to know if you want a drink."

"No. Thank you.

The mayor left the rosary early. He was at the front of the house waiting for the delegation of men to accompany him and the brothers to go get the body at the depot. He was standing by the front gate smoking a cigarette when he heard the train. He counted the number of men he had available. Now all they had to do was wait for the hearse.

The men were waiting when the priest left the rectory and crossed the street. The priest greeted them and went through the gate. At the sidewalk he greeted some of the men standing there and he kept on to the porch. He knocked on the door and was let in by the mayor's wife who had seen him at the porch. He embraced Chata and went around the circle as all the others had done. He shook hands and then said, "We will never understand the ways of our Lord Jesus Christ and God. Let us pray." He lowered his head and said, "Dear God, I know that at these times it is very hard to understand Your wisdom. But we must trust in You and Your plan for our lives. Bless Chata and the boys. May they be safe from now on. Protect them, dear God." The priest raised his head and looked around. He felt that his presence was an impedance to the whole affair so he proceeded into the kitchen where he saw Carolina at the table. She offered him some coffee but he chose tea. As he sipped, the smell of the old soot from the fallen chimney caught his senses. He went to the hearth and looked inside and up through the flue. He said, "I can see the sky. The chimney seems to have fallen. But that is the least of our worries."

The hearse arrived while the priest was contemplating the fallen chimney. Robertito came into the kitchen to get him to go with the men. Robertito saw Carolina again and went over and extended his hand. Carolina cleaned her hand before shaking. He tried to speak to Carolina but the priest hurried him along.

The men had collected at the front of the house and the mayor appointed who should go and who should stay. No one wanted to ride in the hearse so two cars were needed. The rest of the men, according to the mayor, would stay to move the piano into the kitchen. The casket would go where the piano now stood.

By the time the men arrived with the casket the piano had been moved and placed in the kitchen in front of the chimney.

As the men manhandled the casket into the parlor, the wails reached such a force that one would have thought the house could not take any more. The pitch, the noise—almost inhuman in its intensity—curdled the blood and made the hair stand on end. The frightened children playing outside and at the parochial school ran away. It would not have seemed unusual for one of the pallbearers to run out in fear of so much sorrow. The house bulged in pain. The canaries, used to more pleasant sounds and by now agitated from the previous wailing, were now all aflutter, flying desperately about, trying to hide from the noise the women were making. But there was no escape and the canaries were forced to hear, to be bombarded with the pitch and intensity of a sound so alien, an experience so bizarre, that it tore into their little hearts. They flew into the window sill, smashed into the windowpane and eventually, instead of reaching freedom, killed themselves from fright.

In the kitchen, the women began to hear the gradual song of the piano strings as the strings began to resonate with the cries. The piano had taken a life of its own. Now the mahogany wood reverberated along with the strings. It was a crescendo with its own lament, its own sorrowful story to play. And yet, Chata's voice could be heard above all else.

At the same time, as the casket was pushed against the wall, with the force of so much emotion, the rest of the chimney fell and the sound in the kitchen, along with the piano's cries, was unbearable. The people ran out, fearing the whole house would tumble.

Once outside, the priest, who had followed the gathering, circled them around him and began his own rosary, one eye on the missal and one eye on the house. Only Chata and the brothers and Robertito remained inside but the noise stayed in the house as though it could not leave and the people outside could hear their own voices trapped within. The piano, moved by the ever-increasing sounds of sorrow, reached a fortissimo that pierced the ears. The vibrating strings from the piano disturbed the soot from the downed chimney and the ashes came through the kitchen door as a dark cloud looking for relief and they spread slowly throughout the porch, completely surrounding the house, which finally let out a moan so full of pain and sorrow that the women and the men and the priest ran to the church to hide from the intensity of the moment. The house, they could see from across the street, had taken a pale color. Unknown to them, it had begun to die.

Rosemary Catacalos (San Antonio)

"La Casa" and "(There Has To Be) Something More Than Everything"

La Casa

The house by the *acequia,*
its front porch dark and
cool with begonias,
an old house, always there,
always of the same adobe,
always full of the same lessons.
We would like to stop.
We know we belonged there once.
Our mothers are inside.
All the mothers are inside,
lighting candles, swaying
back and forth on their knees,
begging The Virgin's forgiveness
for having reeled us out
on such very weak string.
They are afraid for us.
They know we will not stop.
We will only wave as we pass by.
They will go on praying
that we might be simple again.

Rosemary Catacalos grew up with Greek and Mexican grandparents in San Antonio. Her heritage was very important in her first book of poetry, *Again For the First Time,* published in 1984. In addition to her poetry, Catacalos has worked on bringing poetry to a wider audience, organizing an international book fair and helping to produce television shows for San Antonio audiences. She lived in California during the 1990s, much of the time as a Wallace Stegner Fellow in Poetry at Stanford University, before returning to San Antonio to work for the arts organization there, Gemini Ink.

(There Has To Be) Something More Than Everything

"Oh, everywhere. All around. Trees are harlequins, words are harlequins. So are situations and sums. Put two things together—jokes, images—and you get a triple harlequin. Come on! Play! Invent the world! Invent reality!"

—Vladimir Nabokov

But there are things that have been torn away.
From all of us. And we need to collect the shadows,
the pain as it ghosts along the soul in faded fragments.
We need to put as many old pieces as we can together
to make something else entirely.
As many times as we have to and as long as it takes.

There is for instance this mourning
I've been running from for six years.
My blithe floating off to Mexico
sure that time was in abundant supply
and leaving Albie showing the nurses
how to find the veins in his arms.
Showing them access to the bloodstream
the way only a junkie could know it.
Leaving him with a splendid view
of the Texas hill country and his own
short-lived certainty of harlequins and
most of his heart that would soon fall apart
trussed up into a series of blips
staggering across a hospital monitoring screen.
Leaving him knowing which words are the last
and how they should be spoken.

The story of death is infinite in its variety
but the end is always the same.
This time it comes with the impersonal
scratching of a long distance line,
someone saying, *Sit down and listen. Albie's gone.*
I clutch the edge of a hard bed in a hot hotel room »

in an ancient country where there is nothing
at this moment except a senseless dead-end present.
No past. No future. Downstairs in the courtyard
a woman with a face older than the first sun forgets
and shapes corn into cakes intended only for the living.
The jaguar leaves his temple stone and his godhood behind
and lets his claws and teeth go soft with mortality.
The orchid suspends its sweetness
high in the canopy of the jungle
as if there will be no tomorrow
as if yesterday the young bride had not
fixed love into her hair.
To have come this far to see time snag and eddy
around my closest cousin's still-warm body.
To have come this far to watch him finally
drain away in that slow-motion torrent
he had always claimed as his own rhythm.

Today is six years to the day he was buried.
I know because Albert just called to tell me
that he's a little bit drunk and
that he's cooked up a batch of chicken creole
and why don't I come on over
and the damn calendar never just folds its hands
and waits like the rest of us
and yesterday was Father's Day
this year an even uglier black mark
precisely setting apart the hours
between the Sunday his firstborn died
and the funeral on Monday.
And we talked about growing old
and how the body begins to falter
and about the new camper
that sleeps two comfortably
and when not in use can fold down
to only six inches on top of the car.
And about taking Lupe and Sister Julia

to their hometown in The Valley
to visit an old aunt.
And about how electrical engineers have impatiently
taken over the functions of real watchmakers
without having an inkling of how to order
the true passage of time.
And about the sons who are left.

And suddenly there it is.
Something more than everything.
Everywhere. All around.
In the mundane inventions of our living
and laughing and grieving.
In the way we are somehow bound together
by this thing called family
that each of us celebrates so differently
but sometimes not so differently after all.
Just one stop on the way
to pick up a loaf of French bread
to go with the chicken.

SANDRA CISNEROS was born in Chicago, visiting Mexico often because, as she has said, her father was homesick. She attended Loyola University and then moved on to the Iowa Writers' Workshop for an M.F.A. She worked as a teacher in Chicago before coming to San Antonio. The enormous appeal and success of her 1984 book *The House on Mango Street* led Cisneros to become the first Chicana to be published by a major publisher with *Woman Hollering Creek* in 1991. Cisneros received a prestigious MacArthur Foundation fellowship in 1995. She lives in San Antonio.

Sandra Cisneros (San Antonio)

"The Vogue"

Not class like Frost Brothers, but definitely not cheese like the Kress.—Verrry rrritzy, verrry fancy, verrry Vogue, Viva says in a snooty fake accent she makes up from I don't know where.—Formals, shoes, gloves, hats, hose. Whenever you shop for a special occasion, head over to the Vogue, corner of Houston and Navarro Streets, downtown San Antonio, Viva says breathlessly as she swirls through the doors like a TV commercial.

—We're shopping for the prom, Viva says to the saleswomen trailing us. Not true, but that's how we get to play dress-up for an hour, trying on beaded gowns we can't afford. Viva pulls a purple crocheted number over her head and shimmies until it falls into place, the pearl spangles sparkling when she moves, the neckline plunging like an Acapulco cliff diver.

—Oh, my God, Viva, you look just like Cher!

The Vogue saleswomen have to wear prissy name tags that say "Miss" in front of their first names, even if they're a hundred years old! Miss Sharon, Miss Marcy, Miss Rose.

Viva asks me,—And when you're on your period, do you get real *cacosa?*

—Shit, yes!

—Ha! That's a good one. Me too.

Miss Rose hovering about, knocking on the dressing room door too sharply, and asking a hundred times,—Everything all right, honey?

—Gawd! Can't we have a little privacy here? Viva

says squeezing her *chichis* into a serve-'em-on-a-platter corset gown.

The Vogue is Viva's choice. Mine, the Woolworth's across from the Alamo because of the lunch counter that loops in and out like a snake. I like sitting next to the toothless *viejitos* enjoying their grilled tuna triangles and slurping chicken noodle soup. I could sit at that counter for hours, ordering Cokes and fries, a caramel sundae, a banana split. Or wander the aisles filling a collapsible basket with glitter nail polish, little jars of fruit-flavored lip gloss, neon felt-tip pens, take the escalator to the basement to check out the parakeets and canaries, poke around Hardware looking for cool stuff, or dig through the bargain bins for marked-down treasures.

Viva says who would ever want to shop at the Woolworth's when there's the Kress. She has a way of finding jewels even there. Like maybe picking up thick fluorescent yarn for our hair over in Knitting. Or a little girl's purse I wouldn't ever notice in a thousand years. Or the funkiest old ladies' sandals that turn sexy when she wears them.

But it's over at the Vogue that Viva's happiest. I can't see the point in spending so much time in a store that sells nothing for less than five dollars.—But who cares, says Viva.—Right? Who cares.

We try on every formal dress in the store till I complain I'm hungry. No use. Viva pauses in Jewelry and tries on a pair of gold hoop earrings almost bigger than her head.

—Gold hoops look good on us, Viva says. She means Mexicans, and who am I to argue with the fashion expert. We do look good.—Never sleep with your gold hoops, though, Viva adds.—Last time I did that I woke up and they weren't hoops anymore, but something shaped like peanuts. I'm going to write a list of twenty things you should never do, *nunca*, or you'll be sorry, and on the top of that list will be: Never, never, never sleep with your gold hoop earrings. I'm telling you.

Number two. Never date anyone prettier than yourself Viva says, trying on a rhinestone tiara.—Believe me, I know.

She still has to pester saleswomen to help her get her hands on a felt fedora, fishnet pantyhose, pearl hair snoods, strapless bras. I'm slumped on a bench over by the elevator when she finally reappears, sighing loudly and snapping,—Number three. Never shop for more than an hour in platform shoes. My feet feel like zombies, and this place bores me to tears. Let's cut out.

—I was hoping we could stop at the Woolworth's for a chili dog, I say.—But it's late. My ma will be pissed.

—Quit already. We'll tell her . . . we were at my house bathing my mother.

Viva is braying over the genius of the story we're going to tell, exaggerating worse than ever, yakking a mile a minute when we push open the heavy glass doors of the Vogue and step out onto the busy foot traffic of Houston Street.

And then the rest, I don't remember exactly. Some big clown in a dark suit behind us barking something, a dark shadow out of the corner of my eye, and Viva's yowl when one grabs her by the shoulder and the little one hustles me by the elbow, escorting us real quick back inside the Vogue while a bunch of shoppers stare at us, and Viva starts cussing, and me mad as hell saying,—Take your hands off her! It happens so fast I really don't know what's happening at first. Like being shaken awake from a nightmare, only the nightmare is on the wrong side.

The two guys in suits say we've stolen something. I mean, how do you like that? 'Cause we're teenagers, 'cause we're brown, 'cause we're not rich enough, right? Pisses me off. I'm thinking this as they shove us downstairs to the basement and trot us down to their offices, where there are mirrors and cameras and everything. Who the hell do they think they are? We haven't done a damn thing. Jesus Christ, lay off already, will you!

Viva is looking really scared, pathetic even, making me feel sick. I would say something to her if they'd leave us alone, but they don't let us out of their sight, not for a minute.

—Take everything out of your bags and pockets.

Viva plucks things out of her purse like she's got all the time in the world. Not me; I dump my backpack right on the cop's desk so that all my books and papers spill out. I'm so mad I can hardly look anybody in the eye. Then I empty my pockets. I wish I had something really badass to toss on the desk, like a knife or something, but all I've got is two wads of dirty Kleenex, and my bus pass, which I flick down with as much hate as I can gather, like Billy Jack in that movie.

I wonder if they'll force us to undress, and the thought of having to undress in front of these old farts makes me pissed.

But I don't finish the thought because of what Viva tugs out of one of her pockets. A pair of gold lamé gloves, the kind that go up to your armpits, the price tag still spinning from a cotton string.

Swear to God, that's when I get really scared. Then Viva does something that's pure genius.

She starts crying.

I've never seen Viva cry, ever. Seeing her cry scares the hell out of me at first. I'm thinking maybe we should call a lawyer. There must be somebody we could call, only I can't think of anybody's name except Ralph Nader, and what good is that?

Viva begs with real tears for the store cops not to call our parents. That she's already on probation with her dad, who is Mexican Methodist and the worst, and if he finds out about this, she won't get to go to her own prom. And how she had to work after school to buy her dress, and how she only needed the gloves because she was short on cash, and she couldn't ask her dad because he didn't want her to work anyway, and go ahead, call. Her mom's dead, died from leukemia last winter, a slow, horrible death. And I don't know where she gets the nerve to make up such a bunch of baloney, but she does it, all the while sniffling and hiccuping like if every word is true. Damn, she's so good, she almost has me crying.

I don't know how, but they let us go, toss us out of there like trash bags, and we don't ask questions.

—And don't come back here.

—Don't worry; we won't.

We bust out of the double doors of the Vogue on the Navarro Street side. I mean bust out, like the Devil's on our ass. The fresh air makes me realize how hot my face is. I feel dizzy and notice this weird smell to my skin, like chlorine. I'm so relieved, I just want to break into a run, but Viva is hanging on my arm and dawdling.

—Oh, my God, Lala. You better not tell anyone. Swear to God. You promise? Promise you won't say nothing to nobody. You gotta promise.

—I promise, I say.

One minute she's scared, and the next minute I look and she's laughing with her head thrown back like a horse.

—What? I ask.—What is it? Tell me already, will you?

—Number four, never . . . , Viva begins but stops there. She's laughing so much she can't even talk.

—What? You better tell me, girl!

She pulls out of her blouse a cheap memo pad she lifted from the detective's desk.

—Shit, Viva, honest to God, you scare me.

Viva just laughs. She laughs so hard, she makes me laugh. Then I have her laughing too. We have to hold on to the building. We laugh till we're doubled over, our stomachs hurting. When we think it's finally winding down, the laughing rolls back in all over again even stronger. Viva's braying has me snorting like a pig. Till the knees give out. Till Viva has to genuflect right then and there on the sidewalk, on busy Navarro Street, I'm not kidding, and hold it in, pivoting on one foot. She's laughing so hard she can hardly talk.

Then Viva rises to her feet like an actress about to deliver her lines. For a fraction of a moment, like the eye of a camera, I catch a Viva I've never seen before, a sadness she's carried around inside her all this time, years and years and years, since she was a little kid, its silver shimmering, every bad thing that ever happened to her I see in her face, but only for a slippery second, and then it's gone.—Number four, Viva says, dead serious.—Never. Ever get arrested when . . . when you've really gotta piss.

And then it's me dropping down to the sidewalk, and Viva tottering beside me, laughing and laughing, the thin bone of an ankle wedged in our you-know-what holding back a flood, our bodies shaking, and the citizens of San Antonio walking by and thinking—What the hell?—and probably thinking we're crazy, and maybe we are. But who cares, right? I mean, who the hell cares?

Arturo Islas (El Paso)

from *Migrant Souls*

After the war, their mother took to raising chickens and pigeons in order to save money. Josie saw their neighbors enjoying life and thought that her mother had gone crazy. Eduviges had even bought a live duck from God knows where and kept it until the Garcias next door began complaining about all the racket it made at night. Josie and Serena had become attached to it, so much so that when it appeared piecemeal in a *mole poblano*, both of them refused to eat it.

"It's too greasy," Josie said, holding back her tears and criticizing her mother's cooking instead.

"Then let your sisters have your portion. Eat the beans," Sancho said from behind the hunting magazine that was his bible.

"I don't want it," Serena said, her tears falling unchecked. "Poor don Pato. He didn't make that much noise. The Garcias are louder than he ever was."

Ofelia was dutifully, even happily, chewing away. "I think he's delicious," she said.

Josie glared at her and held her hands tightly under the table and away from the knife next to her plate. In her mind, she was dumping its contents into Ofelia's lap.

Eduviges stared at her husband until the silence made him glance up from his magazine. "Well," she said, "if your little darlings won't eat what I raise, slaughter, and cook with my own hands, let them live on beans. I know Josie likes chicken well enough. And pigeon stew. From now on, she can do the

ARTURO ISLAS was born in El Paso. He attended Stanford University, starting out with a plan to become a doctor, but switched to studying literature. After earning his degree, he never left the University, earning an M.A. and then a Ph.D. in 1971, when he joined the faculty. His literary fame began with his first novel, *The Rain God*, published in 1984. He taught in the Stanford English Department until his death from AIDS in 1991.

killing before she eats them. Let's see how she likes it."

And then speaking to Josie directly, she added, "This is not a restaurant, young lady. You have to eat what I serve you. And that's that." She said nothing to Serena, who was blowing her nose loudly into a paper napkin and not glaring at her in an accusing way.

"Leave her alone," Sancho said, meaning Josie. "The child liked that dumb duck, that's all. She doesn't have to eat him if she doesn't want to." These words caused Josie to leave the table in tears, followed by Serena, now struck by another fit of weeping. Ofelia kept eating and asked that her sisters' portions be passed to her.

"Of course, darling," Eduviges said. Sancho returned to his magazine.

In their bedroom, Josie and Serena held each other until they stopped crying. "I'll never forgive her for killing him," Josie said.

"Oh, Josie, don't say that. I was crying because of the way you were looking at Ofelia and Mother. We can always get another duck."

After don Pato's transformation, their mother stuck to chickens and pigeons. Atoning for her harshness toward Josie, she cooked omelets and looked the other way whenever Serena slipped Josie a piece of chicken. But for Thanksgiving in 1947, Eduviges, in a fit of guilt, decided to bake a turkey with all the trimmings. She had memorized the recipes in the glossy American magazines while waiting her turn at the Safeway checkout counter.

Because the girls were in public school and learning about North American holidays and customs, Eduviges thought her plan would please them. It did and even Josie allowed her mother to embrace her in that quick, embarrassed way she had of touching them. As usual, Sancho had no idea why she was going to such lengths preparing for a ritual that meant nothing to him.

"I don't see why we can't have the enchiladas you always make," he said. "I don't even like turkey. Why don't you let me bring you a nice, fat pheasant from the Chihuahua mountains? At least it'll taste like something. Eating turkey is going to turn my girls into little *gringas.* Is that what you want?"

"Oh, Daddy, please! Everybody else is going to have turkey." The girls, wearing colored paper headdresses they had made in art class, were acting out the Pocahontas story and reciting from "Hiawatha" in a hodgepodge of Indian sentiment that forced Sancho to agree in order to keep them quiet.

"All right, all right," he said. "Just stop all the racket, please. And Serena, *querida,* don't wear that stuff outside the house or they'll pick you up and send you to a reservation. That would be okay with me, but your mother wouldn't like it."

Serena and Josie gave each other' knowing glances. "They" were the *migra,* who drove around in their green vans, sneaked up on innocent dark-skinned people, and deported them. Their neighbor down the block—Benito Cruz, who was lighter-skinned than Serena and did not look at all like an Indian—had been picked up three times already, detained at the border for hours, and then released with the warning that he was to carry his identification papers at all times. That he was an American citizen did not seem to matter to the immigration officers.

The Angel children were brought up on as many deportation stories as fairy tales and family legends. The latest border incident had been the discovery of twenty-one young Mexican males who had been left to asphyxiate in an airtight boxcar on their way to pick cotton in the lower Rio Grande Valley.

When they read the newspaper articles about how the men died, both Josie and Serena thought of the fluttering noises made by the pigeons their mother first strangled and then put under a heavy cardboard box for minutes that seemed eternal to the girls. They covered their ears to protect their souls from the thumping and scratching noises of the doomed birds.

Even their mother had shown sympathy for the Mexican youths, especially when it was learned that they were not from the poorest class. "I feel very bad for their families," she said. "Their mothers must be in agony."

What about their fathers? Josie felt like asking but did not. Because of the horror she imagined they went through, Josie did not want to turn her own feelings for the young men into yet another argument with her mother about "wetbacks" or about who did and did not "deserve" to be in the United States.

In the first semester of seventh grade, Josie had begun to wonder why being make-believe North American Indians seemed to be all right with their mother. "Maybe it was because those Indians spoke English," Josie said to Serena. Mexican Indians were too close to home and the truth, and the way Eduviges looked at Serena in her art class getup convinced Josie she was on the right track.

That year on the Saturday before Thanksgiving, their mother and father took them across the river in search of the perfect turkey. Sancho borrowed his friend Tacho Morales' pickup and they drove down the valley to the Zaragoza crossing. It was closer to the ranch where Eduviges had been told the turkeys were raised and sold for practically nothing. Josie and Serena sat in the front seat of the pickup with their father. Eduviges and Ofelia followed them in the Chevy in case anything went wrong.

Sancho was a slower, more patient driver than their mother, who turned into a speed demon with a sharp tongue behind the wheel. More refined than her younger sisters, Ofelia was scandalized by every phrase that came out of Eduviges' mouth when some sorry driver from Chihuahua or New Mexico got in her way.

"Why don't they teach those imbecilic cretins how to drive?" she said loudly in Spanish, window down and honking. Or, "May all your teeth fall out but one and may that ache until the day you die" to the man who pulled out in front of her without a signal.

Grateful that her mother was being good for once and following slowly and at a safe distance behind the pickup, Ofelia dozed, barely aware of the clear day so warm for November. Only the bright yellow leaves of the cottonwood trees reminded her that it was autumn. They clung to the branches and vibrated in the breeze, which smelled of burning mesquite and Mexican alders. As they followed her father away from the mountains and into the valley, Ofelia began to dream they were inside one of Mama Chona's Mexican blue clay bowls, suspended in midair while the sky revolved around them.

To Josie and Serena, it seemed their father was taking forever to get to where they were going. "Are we there yet?" they asked him until he told them that if they asked again, he would leave them in the middle of nowhere and not let their mother rescue them. The threat only made them laugh more and they started asking him where the middle of nowhere was until he, too, laughed with them.

"The middle of nowhere, smart alecks, is at the bottom of the sea and so deep not even the fish go there," Sancho said, getting serious about it.

"No, no," Serena said. "It's in the space between two stars and no planets around."

"I already said the middle of nowhere is in Del Sapo, Texas," Josie said, not wanting to get serious.

"I know, I know. It's in the Sahara Desert where not even the tumbleweeds will grow," their father said.

"No, Daddy. It's at the top of Mount Everest." Serena was proud of the B she had gotten for her report on the highest mountain in the world. They fell silent and waited for Josie to take her turn.

"It's here," Josie said quietly and pointed to her heart.

"Oh, for heaven's sake, Josie, don't be so dramatic. You don't even know what you are saying," Serena said. Their father changed the subject. When they arrived at the ranch, he told Eduviges and the girls that the worst that could happen on their return was that the turkey would be taken away from them. But the girls, especially, must do and say exactly as he instructed them.

Their mother was not satisfied with Sancho's simple directions and once again told them about the humiliating body search her friend from New Mexico, *la señora* Moulton, had been subjected to at the Santa Fe Street bridge. She had just treated her daughter Ethel and her granddaughters, Amy and Mary Ann, to lunch at the old Central Cafe in Juarez. When *la señora* had been asked her citizenship, she had replied in a jovial way, "Well, what do I look like, sir?"

They made her get out of the car, led her to a special examining cell, ordered her to undress, and made her suffer unspeakable mortifications while her relatives waited at least four hours in terror, wondering if they would ever see her again or be allowed to return to the country of their birth. Then, right on cue, Josie and Serena said along with Eduviges, "And they were Anglos and blond!"

While their parents were bargaining for the bird, the girls looked with awe upon the hundreds of adult turkeys kept inside four large corrals. As they walked by each enclosure, one of the birds gobbled and the rest echoed its call until the racket was unbearable. Serena was struck by an attack of giggles.

"They sure are stupid," Josie said in Spanish to their Mexican guide.

"They really are," he said with a smile. "When it rains, we have to cover the coops of the younger ones so they won't drown." He was a dark red color and very shy. Josie liked him instantly.

"How can they drown?" Serena asked him. "The river is nowhere near here. Does it flood?"

"No," the young man said, looking away from them. "Not from the Rio Bravo. From the rain itself. They stretch their necks, open their beaks wide, and let it pour in until they drown. They keel over all bloated. That's how stupid they are." He bent his head back and showed them as they walked by an enclosure. "Gobble, gobble," the guide called and the turkeys answered hysterically.

Josie and Serena laughed all the way back to the pickup. Ofelia had not been allowed to join them because of the way their mother thought the guide was looking at her. She was dreaming away in the backseat of the Chevy while their father struggled to get the newly bought and nervous turkey into a slatted crate. Eduviges was criticizing every move he made. At last, the creature was in the box and eerily silent.

"Now remember, girls," Sancho said, wiping his face, "I'll do all the talking at the bridge. You just say 'American' when the time comes. Not another word, you hear? Think about Mrs. Moulton, Josie." He gave her a wink.

The turkey remained frozen inside the crate. Sancho lifted it onto the pickup, covered it with a yellow plastic tablecloth they used on picnics, and told Serena to sit on top of it with her back against the rear window.

"Serena," he said, "I'd hate to lose you because of this stupid bird, but if you open your mouth except to say 'American,' I won't be responsible for what happens. Okay?" He kissed her on the cheek as if in farewell forever, Josie thought, looking at them from the front seat. She was beginning to wish they had not begged so successfully for a traditional North American ceremony. Nothing would happen to Ofelia, of course. She was protected in their mother's car and nowhere near the turkey. Josie felt that Serena was in great peril and made up her mind to do anything to keep her from harm.

On the way to the bridge. Josie made the mistake of asking her father if they were aliens. Sancho put his foot on the brake so hard that Eduviges almost rear-ended the truck. He looked at Josie very hard and said, "I do not ever want to hear you use that word in my presence again. About anybody. We are not aliens. We are American citizens of Mexican heritage. We are proud of both countries and have never and will never be that word you just said to me."

"Well," Josie said. Sancho knew she was not afraid of him. He pulled the truck away from the shoulder and signaled for his wife to continue following them. "That's what they call Mexican people in all the newspapers. And Kathy Jarvis at school told me real snotty at recess yesterday that we were nothing but a bunch of resident aliens."

After making sure Eduviges was right behind them, Sancho said in a calmer, serious tone, "Josie, I'm warning you. I do not want to hear those words again. Do you understand me?"

"I'm only telling you what Kathy told me. What did she mean? Is she right?"

"Kathy Jarvis is an ignorant little brat. The next time she tells you that, you tell her that Mexican and Indian people were in this part of the country long before any *gringos*, Europeans (he said 'Yurrupbeans') or anyone else decided it was theirs. That should shut her up. If it doesn't, tell her those words are used by people who think Mexicans are not human beings. That goes for the newspapers, too. They don't think anyone is human." She watched him look straight ahead, then in the rearview mirror, then at her as he spoke.

"Don't you see, Josie. When people call Mexicans those words, it makes it easier for them to deport or kill them. Aliens come from outer space." He paused. "Sort of like your mother's family, the blessed Angels, who think they come from heaven. Don't tell her I said that."

Before he made that last comment, Josie was impressed by her father's tone. Sancho seldom became that passionate in their presence about any issue. He laughed at the serious and the pompous and especially at religious fanatics.

During their aunt Jesus Maria's visits, the girls and their cousins were sent out of the house in the summer or to the farthest room away from the kitchen in the winter so that they would not be able to hear her and Sancho arguing about God and the Church. Unnoticed, the children sneaked around the house and crouched in the honeysuckle under the kitchen window, wide open to the heat of July. In horror and amusement, they listened to Jesus Maria tell Sancho that he would burn in hell for all eternity because he did not believe in an afterlife and dared to criticize the infallibility of the Pope.

"It's because they're afraid of dying that people make up an afterlife to believe in," Sancho said.

"That's not true. God created Heaven, Hell, and Purgatory before He created man. And you are going to end up in Hell if you don't start believing what the Church teaches us." Jesus Maria was in her glory defending the teachings of Roman Catholicism purged by the fires of the Spanish Inquisition.

"Oh, Jessie—" he began.

"Don't call me that. My name is Jesus Maria and I am proud of it." She knew the children were listening.

"Excuse me, Jesus Maria," he said with a flourish. "I just want to point out to you that it's hotter here in Del Sapo right now than in hell." He saw her bristle but went on anyway. "Haven't you figured it out yet? This is hell and heaven and purgatory right here. How much worse, better, or boring can the afterlife be?" Sancho was laughing at his own insight.

"If you are going to start joking about life-and-death matters, I simply won't talk about anything serious with you again," their aunt said. They knew she meant it. "I, like the Pope, am fighting for your everlasting soul, Sancho. If I did not love you because you are my sister's husband, I would not be telling you these things."

"Thank you, Jessie. I appreciate your efforts and love. But the Pope is only a man. He is not Christ. Don't you read history? All most popes have cared about is money and keeping the poor in rags so that they can mince about in gold lamé dresses."

"Apostate!" their aunt cried.

"What's that?" Serena whispered to Josie.

"I don't know but it sounds terrible. We'll look it up in the dictionary as soon as they stop." They knew the arguing was almost over when their aunt began calling their father names. Overwhelmed by the smell of the honeysuckle, the children ran off to play kick the can. Later, when Josie looked up the word "apostate," she kept its meaning to herself because she knew that Serena believed in an afterlife and would be afraid for her father.

That one word affected her father more than another was a mystery to Josie. She loved words and believed them to be more real than whatever they described. In her mind, she, too, suspected that she was an apostate but, like her father, she did not want to be an alien.

"All right, Daddy. I promise I won't say that word again. And I won't tell Mother what you said about the Angels."

They were now driving through the main streets of Juarez, and Sancho was fighting to stay in his lane. "God, these Mexicans drive like your mother," he said with affection.

At every intersection, young Indian women with babies at their breast stretched out their hands. Josie was filled with dread and pity. One of the women knocked on her window while they waited for the light to change. She held up her baby and said, "*Señorita, por favor. Dinero para el niño*" Her hair was black and shiny and her eyes as dark as Josie's. The words came through the glass in a muted, dreamlike way. Silent and unblinking, the infant stared at Josie. She had a quarter in her pocket.

"Don't roll down the window or your mother will have a fit," Sancho said. He turned the corner and headed toward the river. The woman and child disappeared. Behind them, Eduviges kept honking almost all the way to the bridge.

"I think it was blind," Josie said. Her father did not answer and looked straight ahead.

The traffic leading to the declaration points was backed up several blocks, and the stop-and-go movement as they inched their way to the American side was more than Josie could bear. She kept looking back at Serena, who sat like a *Virgen de Guadalupe* statue on her yellow plastic-covered throne.

Knowing her sister, Josie was certain that Serena was going to free the turkey, jump out of the truck with it, gather up the beggarly women and children, and disappear forever, into the sidestreets and alleys of Juarez. They drove past an old Indian woman, her long braids silver gray in the sun, begging in front of Curley's Club. And that is how Josie imagined Serena years from that day—an ancient and withered creature, bare feet crusted with clay, too old to recognize her little sister. The vision made her believe that the middle of nowhere was exactly where she felt it was. She covered her chest with her arms.

"What's the matter? Don't tell me you're going to be sick," her father said.

"No. I'm fine. Can't you hurry?"

Seeing the fear in her face, Sancho told her gently that he had not yet figured out how to drive through cars without banging them up. Josie smiled and kept her hands over her heart.

When they approached the border patrolman's station, the turkey began gobbling away. "Oh, no," Josie cried and shut her eyes in terror for her sister.

"Oh, shit," her father said. "I hate this goddamned bridge." At that moment, the officer stuck his head into the pickup and asked for their citizenship.

"American," said Sancho.

"American," said Josie.

"Anything to declare? Any liquor or food?" he asked in an accusing way. While Sancho was assuring him that there was nothing to declare, the turkey gobbled again in a long stream of high-pitched gurgles that sent shivers up and down Josie's spine. She vowed to go into the cell with Serena when the search was ordered.

"What's that noise?" the patrolman wanted to know. Sancho shrugged and gave Josie and then the officer a look filled with the ignorance of the world.

Behind them, Serena began gobbling along with the bird and it was hard for them to tell one gobble from another. Their mother pressed down on the horn of the Chevy and made it stick. Eduviges was ready to jump out of the car and save her daughter from a fate worse than death. In the middle of the racket, the officer's frown was turning into anger and he started yelling at Serena.

"American!" she yelled back and gobbled.

"What have you got there?" The officer pointed to the plastic-covered crate.

"It's a turkey," Serena shouted. "It's American, too." She kept gobbling along with the noise of the horn. Other drivers had begun honking with impatience.

The patrolman looked at her and yelled, "Sure it is! Don't move," he shouted toward Sancho.

Eduviges had opened the hood and was pretending not to know what to do. Rushing toward the officer, she grabbed him by the sleeve and pulled him away from the pickup. Confused by the din, he made gestures that Sancho took as permission to drive away. "Relax, *señora.* Please let go of my arm."

In the truck, Sancho was laughing like a maniac and wiping the tears and his nose on his sleeve. "Look at that, Josie. The guy is twice as big as your mother."

She was too scared to laugh and did not want to look. Several blocks into South Del Sapo, she was still trembling. Serena kept on gobbling in case they were being followed by the *migra* in unmarked cars.

Fifteen minutes later, Eduviges and Ofelia caught up with them on Alameda Street. Sancho signaled his wife to follow him into the vacant lot next to Don Luis Leal's Famous Tex-Mex Diner. They left the turkey unattended and silent once more.

"Dumb bird," Sancho said. With great ceremony, he treated them to *menudo* and *gorditas* washed down with as much Coca-Cola as they could drink.

La Sombra (Corpus Christi)

"Sancho"

Pero de dónde llegó ese Sancho?
Pues todos dicen que bajó del rancho
Dicen que usa bota y sombrero
Pero caramba será ranchero

Botas coloradas, pantalones verdes
Saco amarillo que parece gorrioncillo
El sombrero negro con rayas de plata
Pero si lo pezcan lo van a tirar al río

Tiene a la comadre bien emocionada
Y a la tía Juana desaquilibrada
Tiene la coyota, que es la más chiquita
Tan enamorada que nadie se fija

Pobre Reinalda, la de la minifalda
Dicen que al Sancho le lavaba las espaldas
Pero muy sola ya se quedó
Porque el Sancho pegó y corrió

María Cantú, la del shampoo
Dice que el Sancho le robó su juventud
María Cantú, la del shampoo
La culpa no es de él, la sonza eres tu »

As Tejano music boomed in the 1980s, the group La Sombra, from Corpus Christi, who'd gone away to Chicago, came back to be celebrated in Texas for its cumbia rap style.

But where did that Sancho come from?
Well everyone says he came from the ranch
They say he wears boots and a hat
But caramba is he a rancher?

Red boots, green pants
Yellow coat that makes him look like a bird
Black hat with silver stripes
But if they catch him they'll throw him in the river

He has la comadre very excited
And Aunt Juana is riled up
He has la coyota, who is the smallest
So much in love that no one notices

Poor Reinalda, the one with the miniskirt
They say the Sancho washes her back
But already he left her all alone
Because Sancho hit and ran

Maria Cantu, the one with shampoo
They say the Sancho stole her youth
Maria Cantu, the one with shampoo
It's not his fault, the dumb one is you >>

Y todas las hijas de don Simón
Ya todos se lo saben que son un montón
Y se las trae el Sancho con un cordón
Ellas se lo reparten y no hay fijón

La mujer casada, la ropa le lava
Nada se lo niega pues está enamorada
La mujer casada, se quedó sin nada
Lo gastó en el Sancho y quedó bien amolada

Quién es el Sancho, pues quién sera?
Nadie sabe de donde vino ni a donde va
Así de repente llega y aparece
Luego lo descubren y se desaparece

Nadie lo conoce quien pudiera ser?
Puede ser tu compadre, o tu amigo más fiel
Puede ser un cualquiera, a lo mejor tu vecino
O si no un extraño, a la mejor tu padrino

No dejes tu mujer, no la dejes sola
Porque el Sancho se da cuenta
Y luego la enamora
Quiere a tu mujer y no le amargues la vida
Porque será del Sancho, la más preferida

Con esto ya terminó, ya dije la verdad
Si no cuidas tu mujer, el Sancho la cuidará.

And all the daughters of Don Simón
Everyone knows they are a bunch
and that Sancho has them on a rope
They all share him and they don't care

The married woman, washes his clothes
She can't say no to him, she's in love
The married woman, is left with nothing
She spent it on el Sancho and it left her broken

Who is el Sancho, who can he be?
No one knows where he came from or where he's going
He just suddenly comes and appears
Then they discover him and he disappears

No one knows him, who can he be?
It can be your compadre, or your most faithful friend
It can be anyone, or even your neighbor?
Or if not a stranger better your godfather?

Don't leave your woman, don't leave her alone
Because el Sancho will give her a story
And then he will make her fall in love with him
Love your woman and don't make her life bitter
Because she will be el Sancho's favorite

With this I end, I have told the truth
If you don't take care of your woman, el Sancho will.

Dagoberto Gilb (El Paso)

"The Señora"

The view from the señora's building was handsome—below its height on the Franklin Mountains sat a wide, manly expanse of land, from the buildings downtown, over the river to Juárez, past its colonias, to the emptiness of the Chihuahua Desert. In the day, in the summer, the land below never budged, and the blue sky would hang above it without end, everywhere, while in the evening the same sight was an ocean mirroring a black, starry air above it. No doubt it was this which attracted the señora to the spot here on the mountain so many years ago when she was young, when she and her husband, who survived only a year back on this side, moved north, wealthy from Mexican mines. So maybe her building wasn't the most plush in the city, but expenses weren't spared either. This could have been a matter of chance—that is to say a matter of history, because it was built in the days when property and labor were especially easy to come by—though it could equally be argued that for someone of her wealth and position, life had always been cheap in El Paso.

Maybe cheap, but never easy. Anyone who had lived here knew this. Jesus knew, and Jesse had learned it. They both knew this woman—the señora was all they ever called her—wouldn't for one moment let them think it could have been another way. Not that they would mention this to her, not that she'd have to remind them of it, or even bring it up once. Not that they thought about it all.

They did think about her, though. Maybe for the obvious reasons. Like that Jesus, a national without documents, often got work from her, both here and on her ranch in New Mexico, and that his wife, who was also undocumented, was her maid. Like that

DAGOBERTO GILB was born in Los Angeles and spent as many years of his life in El Paso, where his children were raised. A graduate of the University of California, Santa Barbara, he earned bachelor's and master's degrees in philosophy and religious studies. He spent the next sixteen years making a living as a construction worker, twelve as a journeyman high-rise carpenter and member of the United Brotherhood of Carpenters. His reputation as a writer began in 1983 with a first of many publications in *The Threepenny Review.* Among the national awards for his writing is the 1994 PEN/Hemingway for his first book, *The Magic of Blood.* He teaches at Texas State University in San Marcos.

Jesse rented one of the guest houses, in these times called a furnished apartment, for practically nothing, even when he paid, which he hadn't every month because the señora didn't always notice. But there was more to it than that. They thought about her because it would be impossible not to.

In the four months he was a tenant, Jesse seldom came out of his apartment. When he did, he always had a shirt off and dark glasses on. Since there was no one around to ask him what he was doing in El Paso, why, how, no one but Jesus made a question of anything, and his was only where Jesse was from. California, Jesse told him, the Bay Area. And even that was answered with a caution Jesus could read. But despite first appearances, Jesse was gentle and soft-spoken, friendly toward Jesus, who was as kind as the name of the village he'd come from, La Paz.

"Coffee?" Jesse asked with a leg outside his screen door. His shirt was not on, and a blue tattoo of an eagle spanned his hairless chest.

"Of course," said Jesus, pleased. He rested his roller in the bucket of white paint and wiped his hands on the brown cotton pants he worked in. Then he adjusted his paint-splattered Houston Astros baseball cap and waited at the steps near Jesse's door.

Jesse came back and stepped outside with two mugs of hot instant coffee he'd already sweetened. "You keep going as fast as you are and you'll paint yourself out of the money." The arm with the black widow tattoo held out a mug for Jesus.

"The señora told me when I finish with this she has more for me, like the rooms inside, and some other things too." Jesus had been defensive ever since he perceived that Jesse didn't approve of the wage he'd accepted for the work.

"It's hot," said Jesse.

"I think it's just right," Jesus said, referring to the coffee.

"I'm talking about the sun, the heat. That it's already hot."

"Oh. Yes. A little." He hadn't thought about it.

They drank the coffee under the wooden eaves of the building while the chicharras, the cicadas, clicked on and off like small motors.

It was always quiet when the señora wasn't there. She wasn't physically loud when she was around, but even her unseen presence filled what was silence otherwise. So the noise she made the day she died wasn't surprising. Both Jesus and Jesse heard it from the beginning and neither thought anything peculiar about it. She was throwing a tantrum at a nurse—the woman, anyway, who wore a white uniform. The señora fired her, screamed at the woman as she was helping the señora into the wheelchair. The señora told her to get back in her car and to go and to not come back. The nurse obliged and drove down the unpaved alley, popping her tires off the rocks, dusting the air. The señora rolled herself across the rocky path until she got to the smooth cement sidewalk. Neither Jesus nor Jesse moved to help her, instinctively knowing better. When the señora got to her door she began screaming about that nurse still having the keys. She stood with her cane, and then, standing on her old legs, heaved that cane into the glass panes of the door. That's when Jesus came over. He couldn't understand all she was wailing about in English, but he broke out a square of glass and reached inside and turned the deadbolt. When the door still didn't open, the señora tensed again and screamed more. She was not sweating, but she was breathing with a loud hiss. Jesus couldn't get it opened, and the señora hollered. That's when Jesse came over. He positioned himself, then kicked the door. It splintered the jamb and sprang into an arc. The señora did not thank them as she went inside, and left behind the wheelchair and the two men. She screamed and complained from within her home. Jesus and Jesse returned to what they were doing, which is to say Jesus rolled white paint onto the plaster walls and Jesse went to the other side of the screen door where he couldn't be seen.

It got hugely quiet. Jesse stepped out of his apartment, and Jesus looked over to him.

"We better see," Jesse told Jesus.

"Yes. It's what I'm thinking."

They entered the señora's home, the mahogony and crystal and silver sparkling with cleanliness. She was sprawled on her rug, the stem of a rose in the carpet's pattern seeming to hook between her teeth. Her eyes were closed, but an ornery scowl kept the señora from looking peaceful. The combination suited her death. There was nothing at all sad about seeing her like this, and neither man felt a twinge of sentimentality. They simply respected the finality of it.

Later, after people had come for her body, Jesus tried to finish the section of wall he'd started, while Jesse went back to his apartment. In those hours, the chicharras, hundreds of them, drilled without pause at the sky. They were the reason the memory of that day became so inexhaustible, and they were what both men, in their separate lives, talked about from the moment they moved on and told this story.

Pat Mora (El Paso)

"Elena" and "Now and Then, America"

Elena

My Spanish isn't enough.
I remember how I'd smile
listening to my little ones,
understanding every word they'd say,
their jokes, their songs, their plots.
Vamos a pedirle dulces a mamá. Vamos.
But that was in Mexico.
Now my children go to American high schools.
They speak English. At night they sit around
the kitchen table, laugh with one another.
I stand by the stove and feel dumb, alone.
I bought a book to learn English.
My husband frowned, drank more beer.
My oldest said, "*Mamá,* he doesn't want you
to be smarter than he is." I'm forty,
embarrassed at mispronouncing words,
embarrassed at the laughter of my children,
the grocer, the mailman. Sometimes I take
my English book and lock myself in the bathroom,
say the thick words softly,
for if I stop trying, I will be deaf
when my children need my help.

Pat Mora was born in El Paso and received her B.A. from Texas Western University (now University of Texas, El Paso). She earned an M.A. and began teaching in El Paso, switching to an administrative position in 1981, when she began to focus on her writing. A mother of three, she finally began publishing in small journals and, in 1984, *Chants,* her first book of poetry, was published. In 1989 she moved to Cincinnati and became a full-time writer, receiving fellowships from the NEA and the Kellogg Foundation. She has since published several books of poetry as well as twenty-five books for young readers. She lives in Santa Fe, New Mexico.

Now and Then, America

Who wants to rot
beneath dry, winter grass
in a numbered grave
in a numbered row
in a section labeled Eternal Peace
with neighbors plagued
by limp, plastic roses
springing from their toes?
Grant me a little life now and then, America.

Who wants to rot
as she marches through life
in a pin-striped suit
neck chained in a soft, silk bow
in step, in style, insane.
Let me in
to board rooms wearing hot
colors, my hair long and free,
maybe speaking Spanish.
Risk my difference, my surprises.
Grant me a little life, America.

And when I die, plant *zempasúchitl,*
flowers of the dead, and at my head
plant organ cactus, green fleshy
fingers sprouting, like in Oaxaca.
Let desert creatures hide
in the orange blooms.
Let birds nest in the cactus stems.
Let me go knowing life
            flower and song
will continue right above my bones.

Plate 1: *Transition of Government in Texas from Spanish to Mexican* by Jose Cisneros. Courtesy of Serie Print Project printed at Coronado Studio in Austin, Texas.

Plate 2: *Chula* by Luis Jimenez. Courtesy of Luis Jimenez and Segura Publishing Company.

Plate 3: *Bato Verde* by Cesar A. Martinez. Courtesy of Cesar A. Martinez.

Plate 4: *Soldaderas* by Santa Barraza. Courtesy of Santa Barraza.

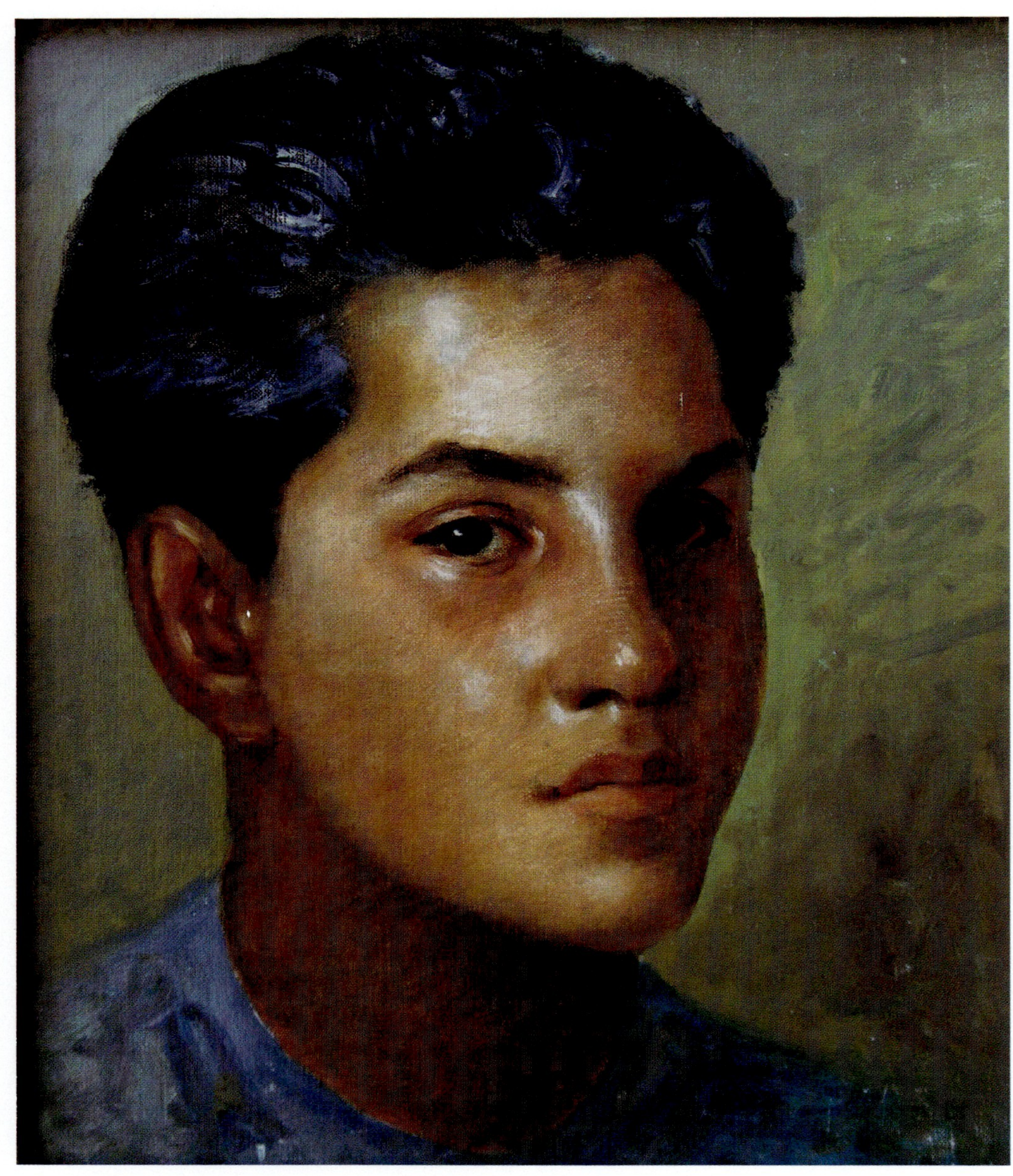

Plate 5: *Chavo* by Manuel Acosta. © Hal Marcus Gallery 2006, www.halmarcus.com.

Plate 6: *Tamalada* by Carmen Lomas Garza. Courstesy of M. Lee Fatherree, Collection of Paula Maciel-Benecke and Norbert Benecke, Aptos, California.

Plate 7: *Pan Dulce* by Sam Coronado. Courtesy of Self-Help Graphics, 1988.

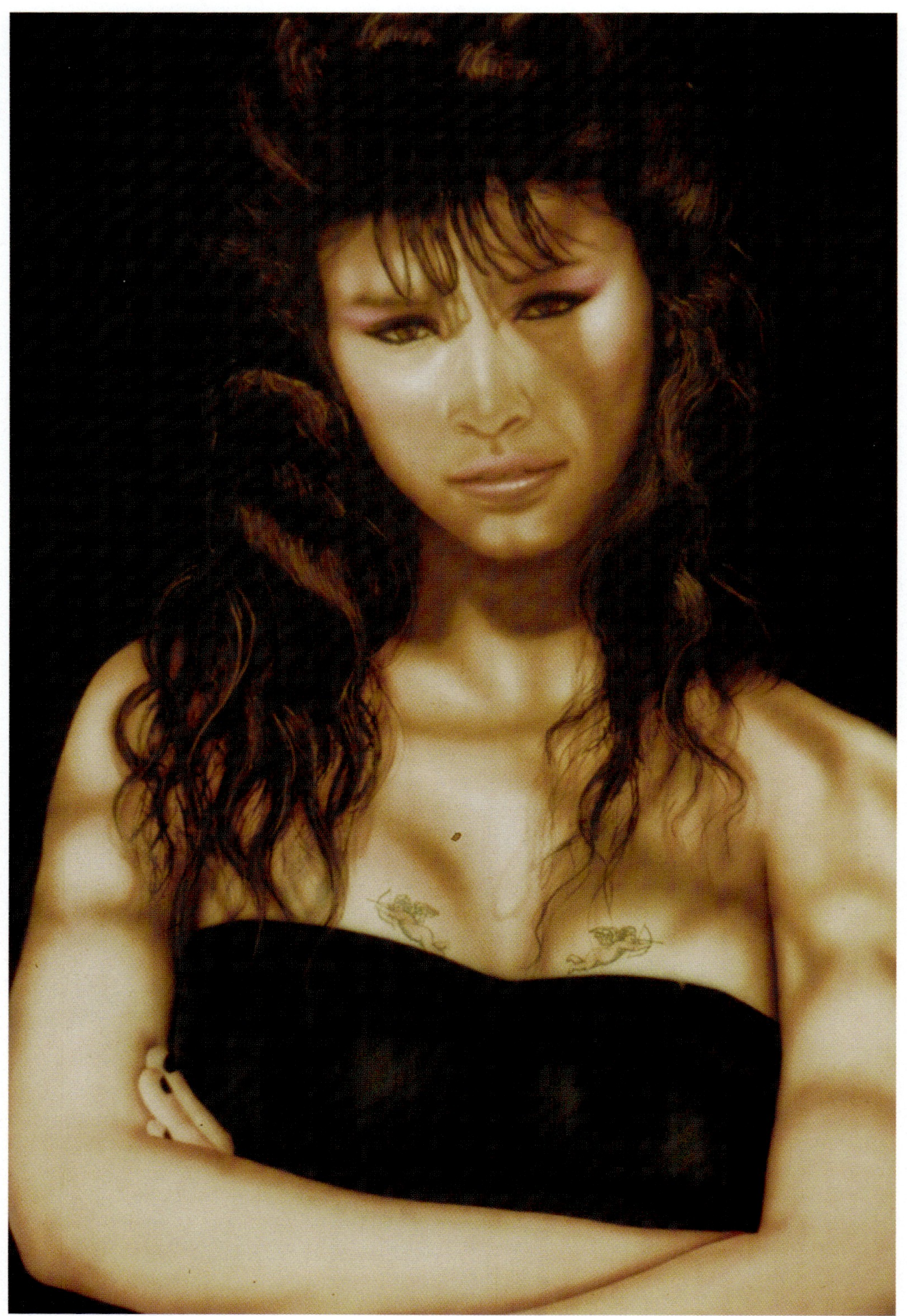

Facing page / Plate 8: *Maria de los Angelitos Negros* by Gaspar Enriquez. Courtesy of Gaspar Enriquez.

Plate 9: Joe Lopez, *The Spirit of Machismo*, 2003, oil on canvas, 60" x 36". Collection of Arizona State University Hispanic Research Center.

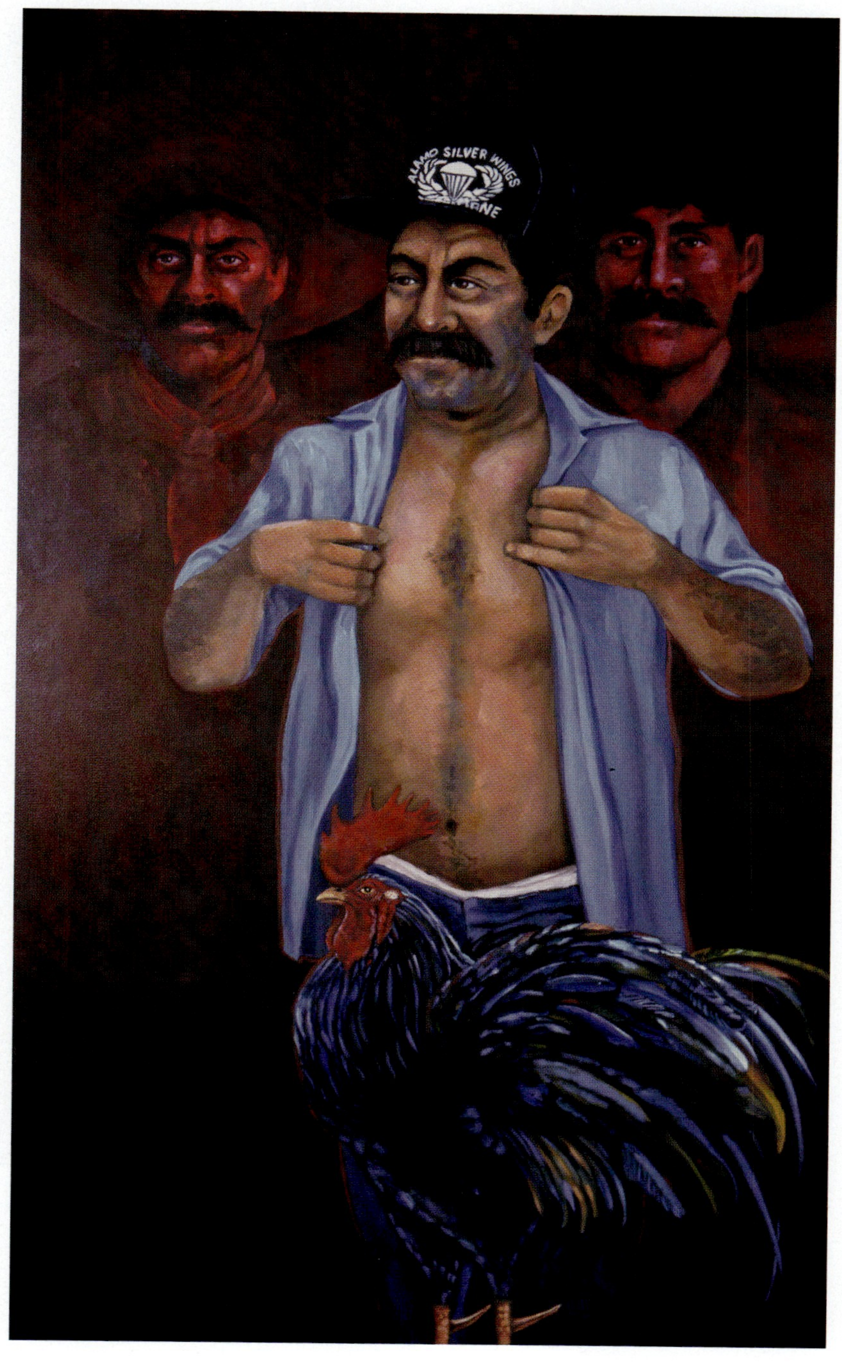

Plate 10: *I Was Little*, 1998, hand-colored iris print by Kathy Vargas. Courtesy of the Wittliff Gallery of Southwestern & Mexican Photography, Texas State University-San Marcos.

Plate 11: *I lost her to El Diablo, He can have her, I don't want her anymore* by Vincent Valdez. Courtesy of Serie Print Project at Coronado Studio in Austin, Texas.

Plate 12: *El Spider* by Alex Rubio. Courtesy of Serie Print Project at Coronado Studio in Austin, Texas.

Plate 13: *El Niños Santos* by Amado Pena. Courtesy of Amado Pena and Gregorio Barrios Jr.

Plate 14: *Sweet Nothings* by Celia Alvarez. Courtesy of Serie Print Project at Coronado Studio in Austin, Texas.

Plate 15: *Las Rosas de Mi Uelita* by Candace Briceño. Courtesy of Serie Print Project at Coronado Studio in Austin, Texas.

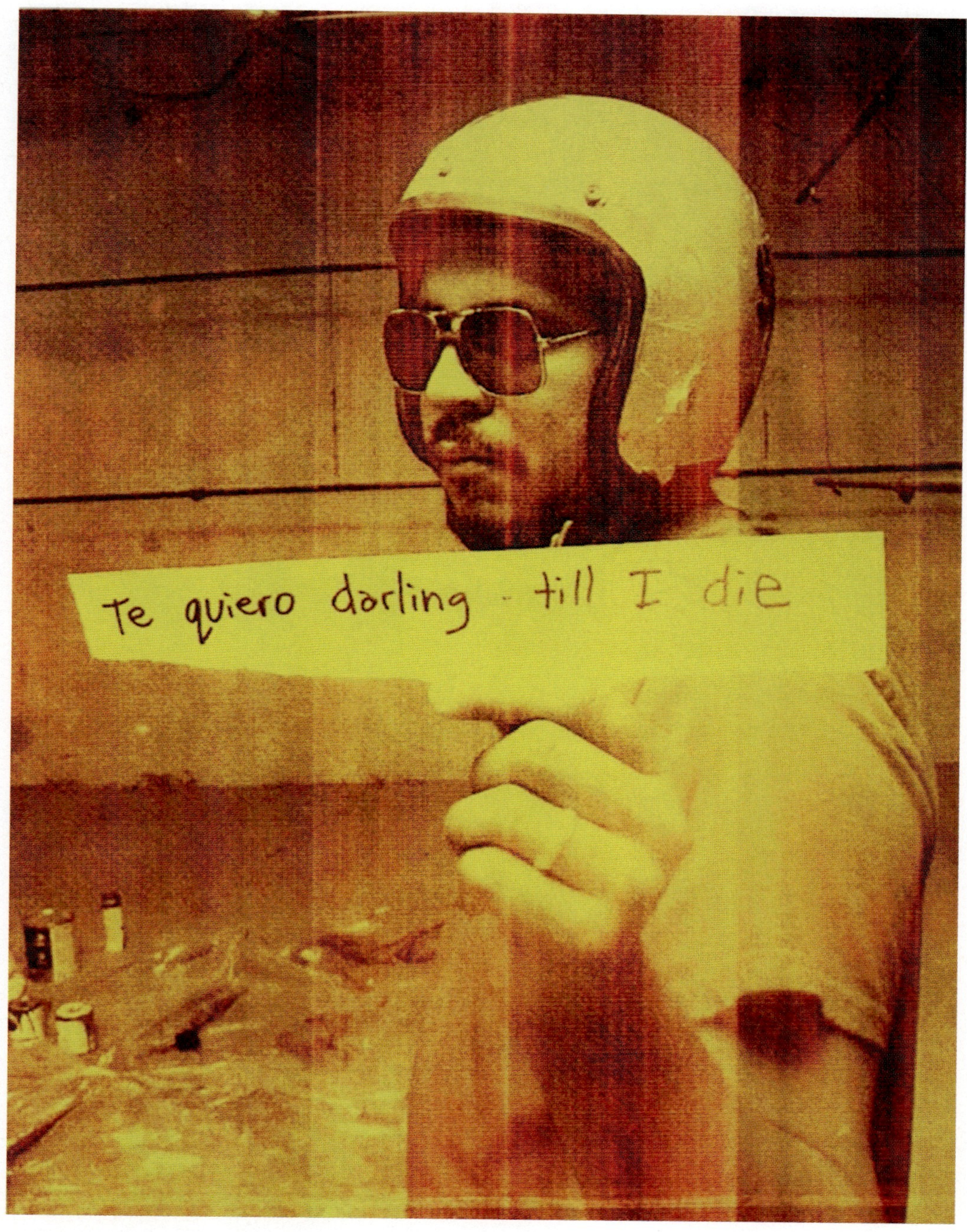

Plate 16: *Darling* by Cruz Ortiz. Courtesy of Serie Print Project at Coronado Studio in Austin, Texas.

Plate 17: *Bicultural Tablesetting* by Rolando Briseño. Courtesy of Serie Print Project at Coronado Studio in Austin, Texas.

Plate 18: *Ladder* by Connie Arismendis. Courtesy of Serie Print Project at Coronado Studio in Austin, Texas.

Plate 19: *1936 Ford* by Maria Almeida Natividad. Courtesy of Maria Almeida Natividad.

Plate 20: *Guerra de flores hijo* by Roberto Sifuentes. Courtesy of Roberto Sifuentes and Herlinda Sifuentes.

Genaro González (McAllen)

"Pruning the Family Tree, Grafts and All"

Returning from Mexico, I get the usual inquiries from Manos and a couple of Anglo coeds in my honors group, asking how everything went. I'd like to tell them it was an enlightening experience, but in truth I'm only more uncertain, trying to sort out the good *mexicanos* from the bad. It's obvious where the students who protested in the streets stood, but the government and press seem to want it both ways. The official publicity during the Olympics appeared to push for the same things MANO stands for: pride in our culture and a suspicion of gringos. And when some black athletes were criticized by the American press for protesting U. S. racism, many of the Mexican papers took their side. Even as I walked along the main avenues of Mexico City, I was impressed by all the monuments to revolutionaries. Government offices displayed posters in their windows of Zapata, Villa, and lesser-known heroes. I remember thinking, *This is fantastic.*

Now I'm beginning to think it was propaganda, just as the Mexican media's support for American minorities was using somebody's else's crap to clean their own hands. It was nothing more than papering over the cracks. The revolutionary posters look down on the paperwork of bureaucrats who talk of radical reform, then stall. From the little I know of the Mexican Revolution, Zapata was gunned down just as the posters on the street said—by the same ones who now murder students.

So I'm not as enthusiastic as other Manos about

GENARO GONZÁLEZ grew up in McAllen and began his college studies at Pan American University until he transferred to California to complete his studies. He received a B.S. and Ph.D. in psychology from the University of California at Santa Cruz. González came back to Texas to teach, but when he had trouble getting tenure, he turned to writing. In 1988, he was both offered tenure by Pan American University and his novel *Rainbow's End* was published. A Dobie-Paisano and NEA fellow, he writes and teaches psychology in Edinburg.

Mexico, at least its government. Even when I ask those same Manos what their older relatives have to say about the Revolution, what I get is a romanticized version. "My grandfather? He was an officer with Villa's Dorados. And my grandmother was an Adelita with Zapata." Since Villa's front was in northern Mexico and Zapata's in the south, you try to imagine that sort of long-distance marriage, each catching a supply train to meet halfway in Matehuala for the weekend.

At first, being naive, I was impressed by such accounts. But after hearing similar lines sixty different times, you can't help but wonder: Against those odds, how come the *federales* finally won? Who was left on the side of the bad guys? Moreover, so many of our grandfathers were right-hand men for Villa that I doubt the man was the Centaur of the North; he must have been an octopus.

The trouble with revising history is, it's hard to stop with modest gains. Once you realize that Indian blood is something to be proud of, you decide that yours is premium Aztec grade. One goes for the best-known brand, and makes it blue blood for good measure. Of course, even the average Aztec was a peasant who toiled for the religious elite, but why stop there when the titles of chieftains are out there for the taking? Who'll prove otherwise? Just one look at those. Mexican calendars with a sullen, muscular warrior defending his Aztec maiden, and your undernourished ego whispers, "This is me."

Yet mention Villa's exploits to my maternal grandfather, and he'll counter with anecdotes of incredible cruelty from the man and his underlings, which is partly why he left Mexico. Being dirt-poor proved no immunity from indiscriminate sadism.

We create myths of our ideal ancestors as well. My father was smuggled out of Mexico as a newborn after his mother died in childbirth. After he finished his Army tour and applied for G.I. benefits, a bureaucratic background check showed that he was neither American-born nor a De la O. An uncle he occasionally visited in Mexico was his real father. The discovery didn't help bring them closer.

So my family portrait, like our history, doesn't fit the neat frame the movement wants to create for us. Yet we, like many families, perpetuate our own myths and half-truths as much as the gringos do. We insist that our family roots in the Southwest go back hundreds of years. That's true for a few but not for most That's why if someone tells my grandfather, who never owned property until he got here, about "our land" being stolen by the gringos, he won't get the same indignation as from the landholding families whose lands were actually taken.

You even have Manos who want it both ways. "Why, the Alvirez clan has lived in these parts for three hundred years. Longer, if you count our Indian blood."

"So then they didn't fight in the Revolution?"

"Oh, they did. All the Alvirez menfolk went to Mexico to help Villa."

"Wow. Talk about swimming against the current."

"That's our family motto: A man's got to do what a man's got to do."

Actually, a Mano has to do whatever it takes to look good—even when our romanticizing the Revolution is lost on the *mexicanos* who actually lived during that time. While life under the Anglo yoke has not left them with fond memories, the despots in Mexico were an equivalent evil. And given the famine and killing in Mexico at the time, for some the United States was the lesser evil. A grand-uncle who recently heard me glorifying the Revolution sat me down to set the record straight, at least about his own experience.

He was too young to fight, so he became a human deadweight: He gave the troop hangman a helping hand whenever "justice" lingered too long. Any traitor who twitched too long on the noose made the captain squeamish, so he'd yell for the piñata boy, and my grand-uncle would run over, tackle the victim's legs with a death grip, and hang on for dear life until the man stopped kicking. If the bootheels were too high, he snared them with a short lasso then dangled underneath, jerking his own legs to humor the men until the captain gave the slit-throat sign to signal a job well done.

They called him *el niño de las piñatas.* After each hanging they congratulated him on another birthday. By that yardstick, the captain once calculated the piñata boy was already pushing eighty.

At first he enjoyed his work, especially when the captain would make a second slitting gesture, this time above his head, to cut the corpse down and let him pick the dead man's pockets. He would add, like a doting uncle fond of hiding treats for his nephews, "See if he left you a going-away gift" Most did, since the men were often the former overlords in the region. He almost never saw the thick tongues and popped eyes that the regiment's mimic entertained the troops with afterwards, only their anonymous boots, the same boots that had once been at the throats of the poor.

One day another officer arrived at camp with orders from a Colonel So-and-So to hang the captain for treason. The captain, who was the colonel's *compadre,* chalked up the charges to their mutual and macabre sense of humor. He even played along with the practical joke by hoisting a rope over the closest mesquite and slipping the noose around his own neck. He then called the piñata boy to his feet, like a mascot that brought good luck.

That same instant the officer thanked him for lightening his load and immediately signaled two of his men to yank him high off the ground, while the rest kept the captain's men at bay. Another of the officer's men put a pistol to the boy's head and forced him to hang on to his captain's boots. In the haste no one had tied the captain's trouser bottoms, so in his death throes he let go his last shit on earth. It might even have been a fitting final touch—fertilizing the very soil he had fought for—except that the load landed on the piñata boy's head.

"Good God!" howled the officer. "You hit the jackpot this time!"

"He tore open that piñata, sure as shit!" said the soldier with the pistol, laughing so hard that he accidentally fired a shot past my grand-uncle's ear, causing him to piss in his trousers.

He deserted the troop that same night, but the stench stayed in his hair and followed him until he reached the border. There he scrubbed himself compulsively with lye soap, until his hair fell out in clumps. By the time new growth came out, the stench was a thing of the past. But the memory remains to this day, even though the years have added a self-mocking irony. "The Revolution freed some peasants," he tells me. "Some of us paid for it with their blood, others with our piss."

Memories like his are why MANO's simple view of our history—good guys versus bad—usually gets us nowhere with the older *raza* except out the door. So we're left with the younger generation to organize, but even here things aren't any easier. The younger immigrants who come here to make it are here to help themselves to the American cornucopia, not to help others. In their eyes America can do no wrong, especially when they compare their lot to what they left back home. They don't recognize the racism until later, but even then they're reluctant to protest. Many remain Mexican citizens, partly because gringos try to keep it that way, partly to show they haven't turned their backs on Mexico entirely, and partly as a way to hedge their bets in case they're forced to go back. Yet by remaining Mexican citizens they also remain powerless here. On top of all that, they come from a country where being political can be suicidal, so they leave activism to those of us born here.

But we native-born *raza* have our own dilemmas, including questions about our loyalty. Whenever Anglos hear us speaking Spanish they must feel something like how Lizard says he felt in Nam, never really knowing which Vietnamese were friends and which foes. They probably figure that if there were trouble on the border we'd either head south or else stay put and do a variation of "What-do-you-mean-*we,* white-man?" when the Mexicans show up.

Sadly, Chicanos around here often respond to this doubt by trying even harder for acceptance. Esteban becomes Steve, Genoveva becomes Baby. Yet the ghosts continue to haunt them, whispering through the trace of an accent. So Esteban/Steve and Genoveva/Baby try to cover up their accent by layering another on top, as if a Texas drawl is the high point of one's achievements. For many it is.

Evangelina Vigil-Piñón (San Antonio)

"por la calle Zarzamora" and "el mercado en San Antonio where the tourists trot"

POR LA CALLE ZARZAMORA

entro a una cantina
y como ciega busco mi lugar
eso es muy importante
luego ordeno una cerveza
y me acomodo

allí están sentaos
los batos y señores
on bar stools like pájaros cansados
periqueando y pisteando
y de rato a mi presencia se acostumbran
y siguen con su onda natural

entran por la puerta dos mujeres
muy arregladas—
o como decían más antes, bien 'jitis'
con olores de perfume
y de aqua net hairspray;
pues, se ven bien

pregunta el bato
"¿de dónde eres?"
contesta ella
"¡yo soy del Westside y no trosteo
ni a mis hermanos, bro'!"

responde él
"¡pues, jijo!
¿te compro una cerveza, babe?"

dice ella
"no"
pero se sonríe en secreto
y le dice a su amiga
"'horita vengo" >>

EVANGELINA VIGIL-PIÑÓN was born and raised in San Antonio. Her first book, *Nade y Nade,* was published in 1978, and she has since then published three more books, including one for children. A translator for Arte Público Books and editor of *The Americas Review,* Vigil-Piñón has a successful career as a broadcast journalist, hosting television shows in Houston. She is also a lecturer at the University of Houston and leads a Latin Jazz ensemble. Her poetry has been the winner of an American Book Award and a National Endowment for the Arts Fellowship. She is now the producer of "Viva Houston" and "Visions," television programs focusing on Latino and Asian-American public affairs at KTRK-TV.

se para, componiéndose la blusa
bien, over her pants, y él viéndola
"¿a poco ya te vas?"
él dice
dando esa mirada conocida
"no, voy al restroom"

side glance
side smile
swaying hips and curves
jingle jangle of her bracelet

sonriéndose se empina el bato la botella
and wagging chapulín legs in-and-out
le dice algo a su camarada
y los dos avientan una buena carcajada
y luego siguen platicando
mientras la amiga, unaffected
masca y truena su chicle
viéndose por un espejo
componiéndose el hairdo

EL MERCADO EN SAN ANTONIO WHERE THE TOURISTS TROT

el otro día
me levanté yo bien temprano
y una buena caminata di
por la plaza y el mercado
y en una banca de madera me senté
a desenmarañarme el pelo
y, hijo, que sí batallé

y luego como casi media hora
me pasé entretenida
viendo por entre vidrieras
aterradas y pañosas
de tiendillas y boticas
ya abandonadas
pero nunca olvidadas
donde en años del pasado
se vendían comics
anillos importados
y velitas y novelas
santitos y rosarios

y de repente me di cuenta
qué tan hondo me encontraba
en recuerdos del pasado
cuando una voz tan de repente
tan cerca que se oyó—
voz que penetró mi espacio
voz que me espantó
me estremeció

dice la voz artificial
oiga, señorita,
perdone la molestia
pero por casualidad
¿no traerá usted un nicle
que me pueda dar?
me sorprendo
y volteo
y veo al señor
barbudo, flaco, hambreado y crudo
adicto del licor
vagabundo solitario
perdido al mirar

y la realidad absurda
me estruja
y obedezco mi impulso—
pero ay, pregunto yo,
dígame, señor,
¿en qué le va a servir un solo nicle?

con ojos brillosos como espejos
me da una mirada penetrante
y como entre sonrisa y dolor
la voz artificial me informa:

pues nunca sabe uno
un poquito aquí
un poquito acá
quién diga quizás junte
suficiente pa'—

and I smile from heart
comprendiendo que's verdad
y le doy una peseta
y el comprende el respeto
y yo la claridad cristal

el mercado queda
por la calle Produce Row
y la plaza queda
en el corazón del centro
por la calle de Comercio
de Comercio y Soledad

Selena (Corpus Christi)

"Como la flor" (Like the Flower)

Yo sé que tienes
Un nuevo amor
Sin embargo
Te deseo lo mejor

Si en mí no encontraste
Felicidad
Tal vez alguien más
Te la dará

Como la flor (como la flor)
Con tanto amor (con tanto amor)
Me diste tú
Se marchitó
Me marcho hoy
Yo sé perder
Pero ay, cómo me duele
Ay, cómo me duele

I know you have
A new love
Nevertheless
I wish you the best

If in me you found no
Happiness
Perhaps someone else
Will give it to you

Like the flower (like the flower)
With so much love (With so much love)
You gave me
It withered
Today I leave
I know how to lose
But oh, how it hurts me
Oh, how it hurts me

CONSIDERED THE MODERN REINA DE TEJANO MUSIC, Corpus Christi's Selena Quintanilla Perez began performing at an early age, was awarded Female Vocalist of the Year in 1987, and won a Grammy in 1993. She was in the process of recording an all-English album when she was murdered in 1995.

Si vieras cómo duele
Perder tu amor
Con tu adiós te llevas
Mi corazón

No sé si pueda
Volver a amar
Porque te di todo el amor
Que pude dar

Como la flor . . .
Como la flor . . .
Ay, cómo me duele

If you were to see how it hurts
To lose your love
With your farewell you take with you
my heart

I don't know if I'll be able
To love again
Because I gave you all the love
I could give

Like the flower. . . .
Like the flower. . .
Oh, how it hurts me

Ray González (El Paso)

"The Past" and "Pancho Villa Invites My Grandfather to the Revolution, Mexico, 1914"

The Past

I quit depending on the smell of the earth
to give me an idea about what was there,
what happened, how I could read
the marks in the arroyos to pronounce
the ones that became mouths
to startle villages,
as if the world knew how to take me apart
and call me by my name.

If I am haunted by my past,
I don't know how to get rid
of the beggar in the mercado
who tried to trip me
as I walked by lost, trying to find
my way back to El Paso.

Ray González started out in El Paso, attending college at the University of Texas at El Paso. In Denver, González worked with *La Voz,* the Latino newspaper of Colorado, and he became poetry editor of *Bloomsbury Review.* He returned to San Antonio and became director of the Guadalupe Cultural Arts Center, and has continued to edit and help publish many other Chicano writers. The prolific author of nine books of poetry, twelve anthologies, and two books of nonfiction, he received the Border Regional Library Associations Lifetime Achievement Award in 2003. He is a professor at the University of Minnesota.

He whispers in my ear,
holds out his dirty foot to press it
into the small of my back, drag me down
to tell me I can't return without
remembering every lost friend,
river, or mountain.

When I make it home,
buildings are spray-painted with welcoming letters
written by young boys who don't know
what I did yesterday,
how I was able to read their words
without accusing them of loss.

I tell them about the Arizona shadows
of my grandfather, my mother admitting
she lay on his deathbed as a little girl,
watched the blood drip out
of his mouth as he died.

I write with the melting candle,
try to interpret the falling wax
that drips and says
I will move from my past
the day and night I am able to say,
"This is how it happened.
This is how it happens.
This is how it is going to be."

Pancho Villa Invites My Grandfather to the Revolution, Mexico, 1914

He offers Bonifacio a pistol and a woman,
promises of land to fight the Federales,
my grandfather at fourteen never seeing the blood
of change before the battle for the border town,
fear growing inside his pounding heart.
Villa invites my grandfather to sit and eat with him,
stacks of warm tortillas, frijoles, and jalapeños
offered to the volunteers as the reward for liberation.
Bonifacio eats in silence, looks timidly at the great hero,
wonders if this will be his last meal,
if he can kill for the first time.

Villa rises from the table, toasts the young boys
with tequila, laughs because many will die without
knowing how many of their mothers, wives,
and sisters his men will take in the name of freedom.
Bonifacio stands with his *compañeros*,
drinks the tequila and is told to leave.
He is given an old rifle and a few bullets,
told where to gather for the assault.

He never sees Villa again, only fires his rifle
four times before the battle is over.
He doesn't shoot anyone, stares at the fourteen
Federales who are lined up and executed,
the five whose heads are cut off.
Dropping his rifle behind a burning wagon,
Bonifacio runs toward the river where Julia,
my grandmother, waits in El Paso.
He tries to cross at nightfall,
hears the cries of men in the water.

He clings to the bottom of the low, wooden bridge,
thinks of his meal with Villa.
Three bodies float by as gunshots flash behind him,
horses splashing violently downstream.
Bonifacio closes his eyes to the dream he had last night,
where they served him his head on a wooden plate,
set it on a table for the laughing men
who occupied Bonifacio's town.

My grandfather dreamed this ten years before
the hero was gunned down, the assassins molding
the death mask of Pancho Villa, cutting off his head,
only to lose it somewhere between Chihuahua
and the bridge where Bonifacio crossed to meet Julia,
black waters of the Rio Grande foaming
toward the other side of the world.

Alicia Gaspar de Alba is originally from the border region of Juárez and El Paso. She received a degree in creative writing from the University of Texas at El Paso and won the first Premio Aztlán award for her novel *The Mystery of Survival.* In addition to her writing, Gaspar de Alba has an academic career. She received her Ph.D. in American Studies from the University of New Mexico, and helped found the Chicana/Chicano Studies Department and César Chávez Center for Interdisciplinary Instruction at UCLA, where she has been an Associate Professor.

Alicia Gaspar de Alba (El Paso)

"Literary Wetback"

When Bostonians hear me speak Spanish and ask me what country I'm from, I say I come from the border between Tejas and Méjico. Nobody asks me what side of the border I'm talking about, and I don't tell them, mainly because, to me, the border is the border, and it would not make any sense to divide it into sides. It is the place that it is, the country that it is, because of the influence and the inbreeding of the Mexican and North American cultures. As proud and grateful as I am about having grown up in La Frontera, I do recognize its problems, cultural schizophrenia being the one that most concerns me in my writing. By way of explaining what I mean by cultural schizophrenia, I would like to share with you some of the highlights of my formative years.

I was born into a strict, Mexican-Catholic family that treasured, above everything else, all of its ties to *el* Méjico: *real* customs, values, religion, and language. That this strict Mexican-Catholic family had its residence in the United States was a question of economic circumstance rather than personal preference.

At home, I was literally forbidden to speak English, and any of my aunts or uncles could rap me on the head if they heard me disobeying the rule. At school I could only speak Spanish in my Spanish class, otherwise I would be fined a quarter for each transgression. At the same time, we ate Mexican food in the school cafeteria. Most of the women who worked in the kitchen were from across the river, and cheap labor is especially appealing to convent schools.

As you can see, cultural schizophrenia set in early. At home I was *pura* Mejicana. At school I was an American citizen. Neither place validated the idea of the Mexican-American. Actually, I grew up believing that Mexican-Americans, or Pochos, as my family preferred to call them, were stupid. Not only could they not even speak their own language correctly (meaning Spanish), but their dark coloring denounced them as ignorant. Apart from being strict, Mexican, and Catholic, my family was also under the delusion that since our ancestors were made in Madrid, our fair coloring made us better than common Mexicans. If we maintained the purity of la lengua castellana, and didn't associate with prietos or Pochos, our superiority over that low breed of people would always be clear.

To safeguard me lest I become infected by that kind of people, my grandparents enrolled me in a private Catholic girls' school—a luxury which they were certain Pocho families could not afford or even aspire to. To make sure that my Spanish remained "pure," my grandmother had me do two hours of Spanish lessons at home every evening. "Forgetting my Spanish"—meaning not just the language, but the accent as well—was the equivalent of losing my virginity.

But I had no intention of forsaking either my mother tongue or my cherry; both were integral to my survival in the family. English, on the other hand, the forbidden tree of knowledge that I could diagram with my eyes closed, was a reward that my family could never give me, and, therefore, a rebellion. My brother and I used to sneak conversations in English, even swear words, behind my Grandma's back. I would write hour after hour in my journal/portable confessional, playing with the forbidden words and sentences as if they were a hieroglyphics that only I could read. I wrote and performed my first play in the fourth grade, and in the eighth grade I had my first essay published. Neither of those pieces had anything to do with cultural schizophrenia (although the play was about racial discrimination), but they had everything to do with my becoming a writer.

I don't know when I decided that I was a Chicana writer, or if I decided at all. It must have happened during my junior year in college, when I was enrolled in a Chicano Literature class, which, of course, I kept a secret from my family. Until I took this class, I had seen myself adamantly as Mexican. Chicanos, in my illuminated opinion, had no language, no country, and certainly no culture. They all wore zoot suits and lived in the tenements of the Second Ward; their graffiti did to buildings what their dialect did to the Spanish language. I was no goddamn Chicana!

How was I to know that zoot suits comprised a culture of their own? That graffiti was symbolic expression, a language of the barrio, as intricate and full of meaning as poetry itself? Who could have told me that Chicanos practiced the same rituals, listened to the same music, believed the same superstitions, ate the same food, even told the same jokes as my purebred Mexican family? Needless to say, my cultural schizophrenia transcended the realm of my unconscious and became a conscious demon, grinning over my shoulder at every turn.

But it wasn't until the Chicano Literature class exposed me to poems and stories about La Llorona, the mythic Weeping Woman of my own childhood fears who more than once had peeked into the windows of my darkest nightmares, that I really started to locate myself within La Raza. Chicanos did have a heritage after all, and I was living it! At home I was Mexican and spoke only Spanish, and yet we celebrated Thanksgiving and the Fourth of July. At school, my language was English and we pledged allegiance to the American flag, and yet we prayed to the Virgen de Guadalupe. Naturally, imperceptibly, this bilingual/bicultural identity became the controlling image of my life, and nowhere did it manifest itself more than in my poetry.

Chicanos are lucky because our heritage straddles two countries and feeds off two traditions, but Chicano culture feeds tradition as well, with change, with individual history, with contemporary vision. In an essay I wrote in the mid 1980s about the place of Chicana literature in the wide, white world, I explained the Chicana writer's role as "historian, journalist, sociologist, teacher, and, activist," like this:

> The Chicana writer, like the curandera (medicine woman) or the bruja (witch) is the keeper of the culture, keeper of the memories, the rituals, the stories, the superstitions, the language, the imagery of her Mexican heritage. She is also the one who changes the culture, the one who breeds a new language and a new lifestyle, new values, new images and rhythms, new dreams and conflicts into that heritage, making of all of this brouhaha and cultural schizophrenia a new legacy for those who have still to squeeze into legitimacy as human beings and American citizens.

So you see, I have always been a Chicana, and I have always wanted to be a poet. The bridge between my identity and my writing has become a symbolic border that I cross at will, without a green card, without la migra or el coyote.

Now there is another bridge to cross, one I have migrated far away from home to find: the invisible bridge between the marginal and the mainstream literary worlds. Like any frontera, this one requires the "right" credentials or the right coyote to get me across. Without either one, all I am is a literary wetback, but that, too, has its own magic.

Tish Hinojosa (San Antonio)

"Las Marías" (The Marias)

Dedicada a Elena Poniatowska por su obra profunda e inspirante
Dedicated to Elena Poniatowska for her insightful, inspiring written works

Me llamo María de Luz
Mil años de cuna a cruz

Mil voces que tengo en el alma
Son cantos en alas de la juventud

Yo soy de manos ajenas
mis hijos no saben de mí
Aquí escondida en los barrios de americanos
Guardo mi sufrir

Aquí en esta planta ruidosa
Mis dedos aplican su bien
No pienso en hogar ni futuro
Sólo me conformo con lo que me den »

My name is Marie de luz (of light)
A thousand years from cradle to the cross

A thousand voices I have in my soul
Are songs on wings of youth

I am of stranger's hands
my children don't know of me
Here hidden in the neighborhoods of Americans
I keep my suffering

Here in this noisy plant
my fingers apply their good
I don't think of home or future
I content myself with what I am given »

Performed in both English and Spanish, Tish Hinojosa's music is a blend of country and folk, and critics describe this San Antonio native's greatest talent as bridging the gap between cultures.

Aquí en esta cocina
en esta cuidad donde estoy
qué nombres tan más complicados
les dan a los tacos de donde yo soy

Risa y también tristeza
la vida del norte me da
los sueños que traigo conmigo
quizás algún día se me cumpliràn

Recuerdo ranchito y ganado
sonrisa y orgullo de ayer
Mi altarcito salado de llanto
por tantas Marías que hemos de ser ▣

Here in this kitchen
in this city where I am
what complicated names
they give the tacos of my homeland

Laughter and also sadness
the life up north gives me
the dreams that I carry with me
perhaps someday will come true

I remember a little ranch and livestock
smiles and pride of yesterday
My little altar salty with tears
for all the Marías we must be ▣

Benjamín Alire Saenz (El Paso)

"The Unchronicled Death of Your Holy Father" and "Fences"

The Unchronicled Death of Your Holy Father

For the record: there is no record
of your father's death. He died
of a disease that is today
                                        preventable.
In the land where you were
born, the current century has not
arrived—not so much as one damn gangrene
foot in the goddamn door—and so

If your old man were alive today,
He'd live the same. He'd die the same.

Since there is no record, I have elected
myself as chronicler. I have inherited
the unhappy task of representing
your father's death. It falls to me
to pick a name for your disease— >>

Born in Picacho, New Mexico, Benjamín Saenz had a unique education. After high school in Las Cruces, New Mexico, he attended St. Thomas Seminary in Connecticut, received an M.A. in theology from the University of Louvain in Belgium, intending to enter the priesthood. At the University of Texas at El Paso, he earned an M.F.A in creative writing. A winner of the prestigious Lannan Award, his first publication, in 1991, was a book of poetry, *Calendar of Dust.* Since then he has written collections of short stories, novels, and works for young audiences. He teaches creative writing at University of Texas at El Paso.

we cannot live in the country
of vague generalities. (In my chosen vocation,
lying is permissible—encouraged
but the lies must be specific).
Cholera perhaps? Yes,

Cholera will do—it's in the news again.
A common fate? Why not? He was a common man.

As you well know, I know little
of your father, since you never spoke
to me—except to shout. Grandchildren
were not your forte. My natural inclination
is to write about our failed friendship
But this is about you—so let me
sympathetically continue:

You loved him, your father, loved him
to the point of obsession. You loved
the way he struggled with his Spanish,
spoke it like a child because he came
from a place
                                        of another language.
You saw his country in his green eyes
and hated *hated* your mother. The villagers
told you he married beneath his station. It was
not his fault. That dark Indian orphan
bewitched him with powder and herbs.
It was clear his love was unnatural.
It was common knowledge
she came from a family of witches:

The color of his skin won great respect
But where your mother walked, the people spit.

You watched him grow weaker. Your mother stood by
and did nothing. Where were her

herbs and powder? She could have saved him.
You watched him taking his last
breath, and still she refused
to work her magic. All she did was pray
before a worthless cross. She saw you sad,
and tried to comfort you:

"Have faith, have faith, the saints won't let him die."
He died. Inside you screamed: "She lied! She lied!"

When she wept over his cold corpse,
you refused to believe in her tears.
Can it be that witches cry? You
walked away from her:

"Stupid Indian woman, you told me he would live."

Her grief was hers. Your grief was
yours. Separate in your sorrow, you ran
to that river where
he taught you to swim and fish.
There you slammed your dark
body against the stones and howled
like a wolf in a trap: *Why*
did he die? Why did he live?
Me? Is that his great gift
to the world? Me? You looked
at your reflection in the water
of the river that you loved. You saw
your mother—Indian and dark—nothing
of your father in your face—and after a night
of howls, you locked his image
in your heart and never again
let him out. And so, I your grandson,

Who never learned your father's name,
Sit here writing of your boyhood pain.

Fences

I was six.
The fence was high and as I leapt
the barbs wrote perfect lines
straight across my chest.
My skin ripped easy as a rag.

I dangled there
my blood was thick and red.

That was when
I first began
to know the price
of jumping
over fences.

✲

In love with women
and men, he says they're both
the same: "I could close
my eyes and groan and groan
all night. Hands are hands.
And when they knead
my body like bread
I rise to meet the touch."

✲

Sad and old, she opened her house
to elders knocking at her door.
They promised to visit her
daily. She agreed to join
their church. She was asked
to rid herself of statues
saved on altars in her room.
She told them she was ready
to renounce. Next day, when they
returned, she told them how she'd
thrown her statues out: "I beat
them into nothing." Each day
when the elders left her home,

she took her statues from a closet
and raised them back to life.

A drink in hand, she talks:
"When I have sex
my mind dissolves.
In the everything of touch,
the nothingness of language
disappears. When thought
returns, I am left with sadness
and with words. I want to live
on the silent side of speech."

I stood before
the Torah. I searched
for Yahweh's name whose face
cannot be seen, whose name
cannot be said.
    When I found
letters that stood
for his name, I touched them
trembling. Lines on fragile
parchment: what about them
takes us close to God?

I write in English, dream
in Spanish, listen to Latin chants.
I like streets where
Chicanos make up words.
Sometimes, I shout
Italian words to wake
the morning light.
At dusk, I breathe out
fragments of Swahili.
I want to feel words
swimming in my throat
like fighting fish
that refuse to be hooked
on a line.

part nine

the 1990s

Roberta Fernández (Laredo)

"Intaglia"

As I opened the door I heard Father Murphy reciting the prayers of Extreme Unction and saw him blessing the small body on the hospital bed. My mother leaned towards me and whispered as she put her arm around me, "I'm so sorry. She died about fifteen minutes ago."

I felt everyone's eyes on me as I walked up to the bed. As tears streamed down my face I kissed the smooth sallow cheeks, then looked at the body for a long time without saying anything. It was useless for me to remain there, I thought, and slowly I began to envision what it was I had to do.

In my sister's car I drove across the border to the church by the first plaza, then walked towards the adjacent small shop which sold religious articles. As I had hoped, its window display was full of saints with tin *milagros* pinned to their clothing. Inside I found hundreds of *milagros* for sale in many dif-fer-ent shapes, sizes and materials. Immediately I by-passed the larger ones and the gold ones which I could not afford. Looking at the half-inch tin offerings, I carefully selected from those in the shape of human profiles, hearts and tongues of fire. The volunteer at the shop seemed surprised when I said I wanted five dozen of each, then waited patiently while I made my selection. Eventually, she divided the offerings into small plastic bags.

With the *milagros* on my lap I drove a few blocks to the flower market. There I purchased bunches of marigolds and asked the vendor to divide them up

Roberta Fernández is originally from Laredo. She received her B.A. and M.A. from the University of Texas at Austin. After getting her Ph.D. in Romance Languages and Literatures from the University of California at Berkeley, she began teaching in Texas and working as an editor for the publisher Arte Público. Fernández has explored the relationship of cultural identity and literature in her literary work, which includes editing an anthology of Latina writing and curating an exhibit of Hispanic literature, and through the fine arts, working at the Mexican Museum in San Francisco.

into small bouquets which he tied together with white ribbons. They took up most of the back seat, making the custom inspector remark on my collection of *flores para los muertos.* My next stop was the stationery shop where I bought a small box of red cinnamon-scented candles. Then, on my way to the funeral parlor I passed by a record shop. Slamming on the brakes, I double-parked and ran in to inquire if they sold small 45's that were blank. The clerk thought they had three such records left over from an old special order. As soon as he found them I rushed back to the car and made my way to the funeral parlor. The administrator listened rather dubiously to my plans, then reluctantly gave me permission to do as I wished.

I went home to rest for a while, then at the agreed-upon hour I returned to the funeral parlor and for the next three hours I carried out my task. My back hurt from being bent for so long as, between tears, I carefully sewed the *milagros* on the white satin which lined the inside cover of the casket. Applying three stitches through the tiny hole on each tin sculpture I made a design of three arcs—the faces were on the outer row, the tongues in the middle and the hearts on the inner row. Once I finished with the *milagros* I stepped back to get a better view. Seeing how pretty they looked, each with its accompanying tiny red ribbon, I cried once more, yet felt a little relief from my sorrow knowing that when the lid was closed *the milagros* would be a lovely sight to behold from inside. Then, with the marigolds, I created a halo effect on the space above the corpse, hoping its spirit could savor the smell of the flowers. I arranged the candles in a row in front of the casket and felt myself tremble as I placed the three records on the left side of the body. "*Llénalos con tus cuentos favoritos,*" I whispered. "Fill them with your favorite stories."

For a long time I sat in the semi-darkness, mesmerized by the smell of the flowers and the perfumed glow of the candles. Recalling the many *cuentos* which had inspired my youthful imagination, I felt I could stay there forever. But I knew I did not want to see anyone tonight, and soon someone would be coming to sit out the early morning vigil.

Slowly, I got up and walked to the coffin once again. The *milagros* and the flowers looked splendid but I wondered what the rest of the family would say when they saw them. I touched the dear figure for the last time, then walked out into the night knowing I would not be going to the burial ceremony the next afternoon.

Instead I went home and immediately began to write in my journal. For two days I wrote, filling all its pages. Then I gave my thick blue book to Patricia so she could read what I had just finished.

She started reading right away and did not move from her chair for hours. At times I would see her shake her head and make almost audible sounds. Finally, when she finished, she closed the book but kept her hand on its cover.

"*No,*" she said. "*No fue así.*" A stern expression crossed her face. "It's not been at all the way you've presented it. You've mixed up some of the stories Mariana and Zulema have told you, which might not even be true in the first place. I've heard other versions from Tía Carmen and, in fact, from Zulema herself. Mariana would never even recognize herself if you ever show this to her."

"I'm not sure what you are trying to do," Patricia continued, but what you have here is not at all what really happened."

"*Lo que tienes aquí no es lo que pasó.*"

I smiled at Patricia, then took my journal back. As I did so, I remembered that my mother always said that her own memory book had been a collection of images of our family's past both as it was and as we all would have liked that past to have been.

"You know," I responded. "*Uno cuenta de la feria según lo que ye en ella.* Each of us tell it as we see it."

Alejandro Escovedo (Austin)

"Wave"

Wave goodbye
Everybody waves goodbye
Climb aboard the train
Turn and wave goodbye again
Some go north, some go south
Maybe east, some left out
Some are rich, some are poor
But everybody's got to wave

Wave goodbye
They've headed for the other side
The sun shines brighter there
And everyone's got golden hair
They went north, they went south
Maybe east, some left out
Some are rich, some are poor
Some want less and some want more

My cousin said
We are going to find the ones that left
The boy climbs aboard the train
Never to wave bye again
He went north, he went south
Maybe east, some left out
Some are rich, some are poor
But everybody's got to wave

Proclaimed his "own genre" by *Rolling Stone*, Alejandro Escovedo's musical career began with the 1970s San Francisco punk band The Nuns, and rose to stardom in Austin.

Norma Cantú (Laredo)

"Halloween" and "Santa María"

NORMA CANTU came to live in Laredo a year after being born in Tamaulipas, Mexico. She graduated from Texas A & M and received a Ph.D. from the University of Nebraska in Lincoln. She returned to teach at Texas A & M in 1983 and a decade later began work on her first book, *Canícula,* which was published in 1995. Her interest in folklore led her to serve on a National Endowment for the Arts task force on folk art in school, and it has caused her to think of her literary work as "ethnographic," showing the traditions of an entire culture. She lives in San Antonio and is a professor at the University of Texas at San Antonio.

HALLOWEEN

It's Halloween, but we haven't donned costumes—we didn't yet believe in that strange U.S. custom; only my younger siblings did many years later. Mamagrande and her oldest daughter, Tía Lydia, have come to visit, to clean the lápida in Nuevo Laredo where Mamagrande's dead children are buried, to place fresh flowers in tin cans wrapped in foil, and hang beautiful wreaths, they've come to honor the dead. But it's the day before, and Mami and Papi and Bueli leave me alone with our guests and the kids; I'm fixing dinner—showing off that I can cook and feed the kids. I've made the flour tortillas, measuring ingredients with my hands, the way Mami and Bueli do, five handfuls of flour, some salt, a handful of shortening, some espauda from the red can marked "KC." Once it's all mixed in, the shortening broken into bits no bigger than peas, I pour hot water, almost boiling but not quite, and knead the dough, shape it into a fat ball like a bowl turned over, I let it set while I prepare the sauce I will use for the fideo. When it's time, I form the small testales the size of my small fist; I roll out the tortillas, small and round, the size of saucers, and cook them on the comal. As they cook, I pile them up on a dinner plate, wrap them in a cloth embroidered with a garland of tiny flowers—red, blue, yellow—and crochet-edged in pale pink. We eat fideo, beans, tortillas quietly because Mamagrande and Tía Lydia watch us. We drink the cinnamon tea with milk. I look outside and see a huge moon rising;

it's the same color as the warm liquid in my cup. Later, Tino and Dahlia wash the dishes, and even later, the kids are watching TV quietly, without arguing. Mamagrande rocks in the sillón out on the porch and can't understand why some kids all ragged and costumed as hoboes and clowns come and ask for treats. I try to explain, but it's useless. My siblings want "fritos" so I cut some corn tortillas Mamagrande has brought from Monterrey into strips and heat the grease in an old skillet. I'm busily frying the strips and soaking the grease off on a clean dishrag when all of a sudden the skillet turns and I see the hot grease fall as if in slow motion. My reflexes are good, but the burning on my foot tells me I wasn't fast enough. At first it doesn't hurt, but then I feel it—the skin and to the bone, as if a million cactus thorns—the tiny nopal thorns—have penetrated my foot, I scream with pain. Mamagrande rushes and puts butter on the burn. I cry. The kids are scared. Later, Doña Lupe will have to do healings de susto–they're so frightened. And when Mami and Papi return they scold me for not being careful.

I miss school for two days. When I go back, my foot and ankle wrapped in gauze and cotton bandages attract attention. I'm embarrassed. When my social studies teacher, Mrs. Kazen, the wife of a future senator, concerned, asks I tell her the truth.

"Did you go to the hospital? Did a doctor examine the burn?"

"No," I answer, knowing it's the wrong answer, but not wanting to lie.

She shakes her head, so I know not to tell her how every three hours, day and night for three days, Mami, remembering Bueli's remedios, has been putting herb poultices on the burn and cleaning it thoroughly. She's punctured the water-filled ampula with a maguey thorn and tells me there won't even be a scar. And there isn't.

Santa María

On quiet evenings, Santa María, the highway to San Antonio, was our entertainment as we sat listening to the radio and watching cars go by. One Saturday afternoon Papi is showing off his new apple-green Ford to Compadre Daniel, Tino's padrino. The two families, Comadre Mary, and Compadre Daniel, their kids Danny and Memo; Mami, Papi, my brother, and I, get in the car. Papi drives back and forth on Santa María. All huddled, feeling the thrill of speeding in the car. A siren scares us. Papi stops and yes, the police officer asks for his license. But Papi sweet-talks him into letting him go with a warning—"Andamos estrenando carro, so we were testing it," he says.

"Bueno, if you say you're estrenando and you're only testing it, but be sure not to drive that fast, okay?"

We're only two blocks from the house. In silence Papi drives on the side street and parks the car. Later they're all laughing at how we were testing the car. For many years later when Mami wants to make him slow down on the road she'll remind him that he isn't estrenando anymore.

That was the same green Ford Mami was driving when she accidentally backed out without shutting the passenger door. Papi was screaming. His anger turned the veins along the neck so big and purple I thought they would explode right out of his skin. And from that day on Mami said she wouldn't drive and he would have to take her everywhere. And he has for these forty-odd years, driven her everywhere from long trips to visit family in Monterrey and to the beach in Corpus to short everyday kind of trips—trips to the mall or the grocery store and to her "distracción," bingo games. First at San Luis Rey Church where Papi as a member of the Holy Name Society gets to call out the numbers loud and clear, while we play a la rona and fall asleep on the folding chairs, underneath light bulbs strung along thin wires lighting the outdoor games. Now to Border Bingo, the commercial hall, where hundreds from both Laredos play, sitting solemnly side by side at tables set row upon row. Before the games begin or between games while the ushers verify the winning card, Mami jokes and chats with her comrades; Mine confides her son is getting divorced; Susana's daughter just found out she's got cancer; Tina's son-in-law was caught with drugs; Concha comes by to say hello, catch up on things, players all around eat frito pies, bemoan their bad luck, and rearrange good luck charms—ivory, jade, bone, wooden elephants of all sizes but always with their trunks up, Buddhas in all sizes, "fixed" garlic cloves tied with red ribbons, images of St. Anthony, or personal favorites such as Santa Teresita or San Martin de Porres, or good luck rosemary and lavender herbal oils sprinkled on themselves and the cards. Amulets—some wrapped in soft red felt, others just stashed away in plastic baggies—put away in pockets, purses, or tote bags until the next time. And Papi waits for the Bingo Monster to spew out the patrons like used fodder every night at ten, and drives her home.

TONY DÍAZ was born in Chicago and came to college at the University of Houston, where he received an M.F.A in creative writing. Much of Díaz's success has come from his humor, which led to his first published pieces as well as being the source f his first novel, *The Aztec Love God,* about a young Chicano who wants to be a stand-up comedian. In 1998 Díaz founded the organization Nuestra Palabra: Latino Writers Having Their Say, the nation's premiere forum for Latino literature. He hosts a radio show and is a professor at Houston Community College.

Tony Díaz (Houston)

"Casa Sánchez"

Hot vapor enveloped us when I shoved open the front door. My mom was boiling beans in the kitchen, and we would boil with them. I slammed the door twice to get it to close. Because of the house's crooked frame, the door did not fit just right. My folks most likely barely noticed the slam because it was a regular occurrence and because the television blared a Spanish dubbed commercial for underarm spray. *Sobacos* means "arm pits" in Spanish. On entering, there was a painting of Jesus bleeding as he prayed in the garden of Gethsemane. Under it, roses from my mother's garden; a wooden rosary holder with short protruding sticks high enough to let dangle the blue, red, white, silver beaded strings and crosses, each an abacus of prayers, a strung out prayer wheel, dried string beans with the knuckles protruding through the skin worn away from so many syllables aimed at Heaven. My mom always prayed just as hard as He did in the garden but would never insult Him by out-bleeding Him.

I never brought outsiders home.

Besides the fact that I knew we would seem strange to most anyone, on top of that, one side of the house had different colored walls, different size windows, and did not perfectly connect with the rest of the house. It felt odd more than looked strange right away.

Cliché, familiar enough looked the hall, the living room, and the room designated for the preparation of food to consume. And inside this kitchen sat this device which caught airwaves and translated them into moving images, like a phone taking constant one-way calls, describing, dressing, telling us what the wave after wave of messages travelling through the air, passing right through us, not under our nose, through our heads, through our milking cows, washing over our cars, spraying traffic, coursing through the city, over the skyscrapers, what wave after wave after wave was saying. The TV in the kitchen pulled in the images of "Telemundo"—a new Spanish soap opera, previews for MTV Internacional, Spanish beer-commercials starring Spuds Mackenzie, the beer guzzling pooch (which was why Bud Light tasted like dog piss).

Father, home early from his imaginary job, dissected jalapeños under the glow of "Telemundo" while Mom stirred the beans. Bright red sides of skirt steak lay on the table, out-lined in dull white fat. "Goo afterr nooon," my mom said, smiling, exaggerating her accent. That was her best bit, flinging English words at us when we didn't expect it. Then my father shocked me by greeting me. "*Buenas tardes,* Junior." When he was home at what he considered an "unmanly" hour (many soap operas on TV was a good indication of the femininity of a particular hour), he did not like to acknowledge my existence which would thereby acknowledge his own existence. I kinda nodded my head at him, scared he had watched some talk show on parenting, wondering if he would try to hug me, or ask me how my day went.

Rosie tossed her jacket on the couch in the living room, walked into the killing room to the refrigerator and pulled out lemons. She grabbed a knife from the sink and quartered the lemons. She rubbed them on the raw meat. My parents smiled. I think they both came. "Eskoot ober," Mom said to Dad, and Rosie moved between them. I get a nice long shot of them together at the table, the new Cleavers, just a regular Fuck'n family.

I sauntered through the swinging door (It was my favorite door because it worked fine.) and into the living room and grabbed the newspaper to search for topical jokes hidden between the headlines. I needed to write six more jokes for my twenty for that day, but it was so damn hot from the boiling beans that I felt as if I was having lemons rubbed on ME.

I plopped down on our leather couch, unwrapped the toilet paper on my hand, and switched my brain to three track, mixing the conversation between my producers and Rosie; the musical transitions and the screams of the telenovela; and the headlines, story previews, sub-headlines, blurb boxes, ads, pictures.

"You know, Rosie," my dad said. "I learneda English froma the television. My verbal skills havea dramatically increased by 30%—almost over night." Rosie laughed while I read about a televangelist who'd been caught with a hooker, accepting a donation in-kind, the congregation would get their cut later. "Rosie," Mom said in Spanish with the English subtitles I think in, "can you please put these potatoes in *el pica le i pica le,*" the poke-it-here-and-poke-it-there. Most mothers would just say "nuke this for me" if they were feeling nutty. But the scary part is that Rosie knew what Mom meant. She stuck the potatoes in the microwave for 10 minutes while a prisoner on death row sued the state for not providing him with a color TV. Maybe he'll settle out of court if said televangelist takes his confession and hears his last prayer. I stared at the women modeling bras in the ads under a story about the rising, skyrocketing, boner of inflation. And the musical crescendo accented the realization of the wealthy family's most arrogant son—he was given birth by the maid! Poor Lefty, poor, poor Lefty.

Then dinner was served.

We sat around the table, my dad, my mom, me, Rosie, and we ate.

In all honesty, I remember it as very nice.

Then the phone rang in the living room, and my dad almost knocked the table over to answer it, but I was closer, younger, faster, and programmed to answer it during meals. "Relax, Pa," I said, as he caught himself acting strange. "I'll get it, Pa. I always do."

I let it ring three times to let my pop fidget. Whatever he was acting strange about had to do with the phone. Maybe he was having an affair and tried to break it off, and she said she would call and blow the whistle. We didn't really know where he went during the day for his pretend job. When I picked up, the caller on the other side started breathing heavily, but it sounded like a man. "Stop calling here, Wally!" I shouted, and the guy hung up. I was the only kid in high school who got prank calls from his principal. I caught him once after we'd been getting a string of prank calls. What I did is pick up the receiver right after the first full ring, but I didn't say anything. I just listened. So that when the second ring should have rolled around there was a noticeable silence, and a thicker silence after what should have been the third ring, and Wally couldn't take it 'cause he said, "Hello?" And I could recognize the mutherfucker's voice in a crowded auditorium.

"Who called, Son? You took an awfully long time," my Dad said in a fat-television-father-at-the-dinner-table-voice with-out an accent.

"That wasn't a long time. It was a prank caller. Why you lookin' at me funny?"

He shook his head and shook on his normal face. "What do joo mean?"

"You look like that time you were trying to tell me where babies come from."

He laughed. "Thee boy ees funny. *Muy curioso.*"

As I crunched through the dark brown skin of the skirt steak, I taste the tiniest tang of lemon. "*Maravilloso, Mama. Esto me encanta, Rosie.*" My mom blushes as if I had said she was pretty. Rosie smiles.

"I sent a tape of you to 'Star Search,'" says Dad.

"What!" I throw my meat onto my plate. "You're a . . ."

"Don't talk to your father like that," mother shouts.

"He shouldn't treat me like that . . . Ed McMahon's an idiot."

"Dat man's gone a long way for a sidekick. Hee'z struggled and won."

"Why do you do this shit to me?"

"Don't curse in this house," Dad shoots up from his chair for dramatic effect. "I doan want ju speeking like that at the table, with your mother and Rosa present. Why don't you listen to me for once. Jour life would be new and improved if you had let me take you to the Menudo auditions like I wanted to."

"I'd be a washed-up transsexual from a teen band." I grab Rosie by the arm. "Come on," I tell her. "Show's over."

She handles it perfectly and says nothing to me in the car. I wonder just how much my mom and Rosie have seen, what they do with all those secrets.

Dropping her off, I ask her if this weekend she wants to try and get into this nightclub called Faces. She's quiet, then says maybe we could go roller-skating instead. She tells me about other things juniors from her school do.

Not me. What I'd always wanted to have was a prime-time night on the town: dinner at a great restaurant, a carriage ride downtown, some club hopping, maybe a car chase—hell a carriage chase, maybe solving a murder then spending the night in a fine hotel, sexing in so many different positions that it takes us weeks to recover.

Of course, we both had curfews and neither of us had money. But even if we didn't and we did, these weren't things Rosie wanted to get bold for anyway.

I get a kiss when I drop her off.

I could never go straight home. When I was in high school, I spent a lot of nights circling and circling our block before pulling into the driveway, nervous like the first time I waited behind the curtains on the stage of "The Tonight Show," the spotlight waiting for me, the set ready.

I always entertained thoughts of leaving, just driving away, making it on my own, like I knew I could. But home was where the food was, where my mom was, the TV, my bed, cable. And my dad.

It is tough to explain who my father was because the different men he was are always filtered through the different men I have been. And thus he is always changing.

My father was an actor.

There was a time, when I was a very young man when I liked to say that, and then pause.

I would let the word "actor" unfold in your head as your experience has come to define it, let you picture a show or two, a face from a show, someone with Hispanic features. Do you see a handsome Latin Lover, a bandito, a gang banger, a man with a large mustache? Can you imagine my father as a leading man?

I never could.

Which still did not ease the disappointment of finding out that he was not a leading man.

My father was an actor in *carpas,* tent shows performed in Spanish and Spanglish.

He let the word "actor" build in my mind and in my stories about him, at the same time as the word "*pelado*" for me developed into a synonym for "punk."

And then one day when I was in 5th grade, he told me that when he acted he had been a *pelado.*

I don't know why he hadn't told me before then, or why he had told me that day in a practiced and nonchalant way as if we had just met and he was simply explaining what he did for a living.

There were times when my life would have been more merciful as a sitcom. Spending only a half hour picturing my dad as a punk on stage, grappling with what that word really meant, having in my mind as a definition only pictures of the kids who I had thought were punks, imagining what I must have looked or acted like when I was called it, looking for similarities, and placing them on my dad, in a suit, on some stage with a spotlight on him. Hoping that "I was a punk" could also be an idiomatic expression I had never heard that meant something like "I was a bad ass."

And I would compress, depress, and express all those wonderful moments that had led up to my life at that point, and there were certain scenes that I always went back to, I think triggered by each, maybe certain buildings I would pass in my drives around the block, past Bill and Betty's Bar, the abandoned Lithuanian Bakery, Tony's Supermarket, Unique Thrift Store, The Golden Dragon Chinese Take-Out, Jimmy's Barbershop, a turn of the corner, the alley and then homes.

And it takes years, and stories, and tidbits of information, and other peoples' recollections for a bit of history to resurface for me, for me to find out that the *carpas* were the Mexican version of vaudeville. And *el peladito* was a stock character. Plucky, living by his wits (which were sometimes questionable) and luck. He was part clown, part fool, part wise man, part court jester, all underdog. He was especially funny because of his use of Spanglish; and he was at times a caricature, at heightened moments, a symbol for the new breed of people who were growing up between the U.S. and Mexico, a new breed of half-breeds.

And maybe, just maybe my father was telling the truth, and he was one of the best *pelados* ever. And maybe it was just a matter of timing that Cantinflas and Tin Tan became famous. Maybe my father was born too late to do much with being a great, maybe even a wonderful *pelado.*

By the time his performances must have peaked, vaudeville and *carpas* had been almost wiped out by film. The earliest, most well-known performers had gone into film and even radio. And my father, perhaps, honed his craft alone. Thinking he could bring back the movement himself.

I can respect that, now.

But I also have to wonder how good he really was.

There are clips of him. From two newspapers, one from San Antonio, one from Phoenix. And he enjoyed explaining the details of the picture of him in costume. "Part of thee presentation ees thee tradition. The other part eeees my flare." Puddle-jumper, wide, flared pants—his innovation. A very short tie instead of the traditional long one. (And I'm sure this also afforded him a large store of phallic jokes.) A painted-on mustache and thin beard. Shoes with holes in them, long white stockings showing "because you have to stick to some of the old ways." And mittens hanging from his back pocket. "I was famous for my mittens."

He does not speak for the other picture. He simply shows it. He is dressed in a black, pin-striped suit, black thin tie; he is square jawed, hair slicked back, looking away from the camera and over our left shoulder, looking at something not too interesting, perhaps just resting his gaze there.

His name is under both photos, and if there were related stories, he didn't save them, or he didn't show them to me at least.

So I assume that he was either given a scathing review, a review so vicious, even *he* could not make it sound good by interpreting it for you, or he was a side shot, a side bar, just an incidental picture. Which might be even more tragic.

These, however, were not the end of the clippings.

When I was a baby, depending on the time of year, he'd dress me up like a pilgrim, a turkey, an elf, and create photo opportunities for the local newspapers, no matter how great or small, and sometimes local news shows or programs. There were many of these frozen moments. But then I got old enough to talk.

When he wouldn't listen to my protests, I started to swear on camera or shoot the finger at photographers like the older kids at school shot at me.

His next wave of clips were because of the house, but he also made the news for stopping a fleeing burglar, returning lost money, shaking Jimmy Carter's hand. There was a gold-framed photo of Dad when he was a contestant on "The Price Is Right" (He won a set of skis, which he sold. He didn't make the final showcase showdown.) and a framed personal rejection from "Jeopardy," signed by Alex Trebeck. Dad highlighted the key phrase: "We would lose too much money with you as a contestant." And all those pictures of Ed McMahon.

Then there is my father who won the lottery. Not *the* lottery. But *a* lottery.

I never even knew he bought tickets. And then one day, there was money.

Then there existed brochures on certificates of deposit, mutual funds, and stocks. I had to translate them. I was in 6th grade. He never let me see the official papers from the lottery, though. "I doan want jew 2 know zometing that could get jew keednapped," he told me with a straight face.

One day he looked like he'd cashed a hundred thousand dollar check. Not a million. I never saw that look on his face. And the way I thought of him then, I figured he *could* win a million dollars but never get or keep his hands on the prize. He said he would keep his job "because work made the man." This was before he got the brochures. He got together my college fund then quit his job. Then he bought the set of "Leave It to Beaver" and turned it into our house, using my college fund.

I figured he bought the house so he could get back in the public eye, which seemed slightly un-insane.

And sometimes Pop would forget he won the lottery and tell people that he'd won Publisher's Clearing House Sweepstakes and that Ed McMahon had delivered him a fat check. I didn't mind that lie. I got a kick out of picturing McMahon cruising through our neighborhood in a van with a million bucks, like a visitor from outerspace.

No one had a Neilsen Ratings Box where we lived. Cabs didn't cruise for fares. There weren't any Automated Teller Machines or health food stores, and *el carnicero* had dead, skinned animals hanging in his shop window. At the end of our block was a run-down abandoned bungalow whose graffiti evolved with the neighborhood: The Latin Disciples, The Latin Kings, Bishops, Saints—a regular Vatican IV.

Since I'd stopped helping him and our neighborhood had gotten too run-down and dangerous for even the bravest tourist to stop by and take a picture (the house was getting run-down too), Dad hadn't been in the news for a long time. This meant he was becoming a little too interested in my stab at comedian-dom. But I was gonna be as selfish as he was.

When I was a kid, he'd have heart-to-heart monologues with me and say, "Joo gonna haff to make it on jour own sum day. Joo know dat, Yoon-yer. There's no money for joo after I die. Thee money that fell on my lap is evaporating as we speak. Eeetz flying out the fridge when joo leave the door open too long, spraying out thee lamp that's on when no one's in thee room. Joo gotta make money after joo get out of high school." And this he told the kid who busted his skull trying to correctly translate the complicated forms he showed him. I would stay awake at night, worried that my dad would get in trouble because I interpreted something wrong. He never let me even look at the lottery papers. All I knew was that there was money, and I knew where it was going to disappear before it would get to me.

"I know you smart," he'd say to me, "I know you know someteeng about thee money. But you doan know that eets all a trick on us. The lottery says they goin' to give you one million dollars. They make you think you a millionaire, like you can buy a manshion, beautiful cars, go on glamorous vacations, but they only going to give you fifty thousand dollars a year for twenty years. And then they going to take out tax, even though it's all run by the gobernment anyway, the gobierno still wants tax—that's seventy-five-hundred dollars. And you can't keep jour job because the other workers think you're a big shot then. They say you should give your job to someone who really needs it. They say they don't believe you won the lottery 'cause they never heard about it on the news. You tell them you just don't want your kids kidnapped. They say you're lying one way or another. You either always been rich or you're still poor. You can't keep working. So if you want a little more than forty-two thousand five-hundred a year, you gotta sell part of the pot. You get more upfront but less later, so the checks get smaller and smaller and then boom—you back to middle class."

But my dad didn't have middle-class obsessions or vices like smoking, drinking, a little whoring. No, I remember him blowing money on installing real plumbing into his dream house 'cause the toilets were props. Adding the cooling and heating systems that the actors hadn't needed.

My dad thought the den would be a perfect room for me because it was the room on the show with the books in it. "My son should be smart," he used to say to me and pat my head when I would still let him get that close.

My father gives me a heart-to-heart monologue when I get back home, in the Cleaver's den with the corroding bookshelves that Jerry Mathers leaned on between takes, the original prop books on the shelves: Victorian poetry, Charles Brockden Brown, Nathaniel Hawthorne. Someone's written "Stinky" under Sonnet #152 in a Shakespeare book. I think it was The Beaver.

"Eeet ees our destiny to be famous. I wish it was not too dangerous to tell you who my father was, Junior," my father says. "He put stars in my eyes, cha-cha-cha in my head, zoom lense in my heart. He must have already been famous when he fell in love with your young, poor, grandmother—so beautiful, her long, black eyelashes, capuccino skin, her little hands scrubbing the floor, selling matchsticks. He married her and gave up his fame. He preferred happiness with a poor, young Mexican girl, until he was murdered by the forces that be. The forces that could not deel weeth their hero mixing his semen with such a lowly woman. And we have been happy so long that it is time for us to rise again, to reclaim our fame."

And what kind of son am I to have to wonder if he was telling the truth or acting? To suspect he was confessing that he was the bastard child of Ward Cleaver? Or just illegitimate? Was he telling me Gram had been raped? Or that he ripped her off for the money for the house? Maybe he robbed a bank, peddled drugs? What kind of kid was I to think this stuff? What kind of son was I to not believe the shit about the lottery unless I could see the paperwork? And even then . . .

I'm the kind of son who can't write two more jokes after that. I'm the kind of kid who promises and *will* write 22 the next day.

And if I had found out that night, two years before I investigated the issue and found out that the house was a fraud, that in fact, the two sets that had been used for "Leave It to Beaver" were accounted for, one on the Universal movie lot, the other having become the house for "Marcus Welby, M.D.," if I had found out that night that even my suffering was not as glamorous as I had hoped, I would not have been able to write those almost two dozen jokes. But I was spared that. I learn that truth when I am ready, when my suffering has been better put into perspective.

So instead, I slip to sleep in the den, flipping off in my bed. My thumb automatically pumping the arrow-up button, switching to pre-set channels. There in the dark, alone, the TV projecting on my wall, I slip between sleep and waking, not sure when one ends and the other begins, mixing in my head the frequencies of the dreams and the subconscious of the TV. Killing time between performances.

Arturo Longoria (Mission)

"El Cuervo"

My father, Ramon J. Longoria, purchased a ranch twenty miles east of San Fernando, Tamaulipas, Mexico, in 1959. He called it *El Cuervo.* The ranch—a montage of thickly wooded hills and steep gullies—stretched north from the lethargic San Fernando River for seven miles.

I first visited El Cuervo in the summer of 1959 during the time when my father was having a stone-walled cabin built on a hill that overlooked the San Fernando. We camped beneath a simple *portal:* four *barretta* trunks stripped of limbs and leaves and held in place by small limestone boulders, on which structure was placed a mat of grass and dried twigs to provide an anemic shade.

Though I was no stranger to the brush, when I awoke on that first morning—a pink sun emerging from behind a monolithic plateau in the east—and I saw the thick stands of barretta trees braced stoically on a surreal stage, the sky and clouds painted on a soft canvas behind it, I felt for the first time that feeling of awe and adventure that was to carry me, wrapped within its leafy blanket, through life.

Mine was not the ghetto story—the child raised in the barrio, the farmworker's son, the Mexican immigrant overcoming the challenges of a new land. I was raised speaking English, the son of a fifth-generation Texan father and a Texas-born mother whose parents had fled to the United States when revolution swept Mexico.

I was the progeny of ranch people. For them, life's epicenter was not any specific language or country but instead *el monte,* that untamed woods of twisted

ARTURO LONGORIA is a sixth-generation Texan who grew up in Mission. Now a teacher of biology at South Texas Community College in McAllen, he is a former newspaper reporter and stringer for *Time* magazine. He has also written numerous articles for *Texas Parks & Wildlife* and *Texas Highways* magazines. Author of *Adios to the Brushlands,* he is a trained biologist who has been recognized by the National Audubon Society for his investigative articles on the environment. He shares his time between homes in McAllen and the Hill Country.

trees and briary shrubs from which warmth and sustenance, and other blessed gifts emerged. My father's father had driven horses from Edinburg to San Antonio in the days when pronghorn antelope still roamed the eolian sands and oak motts of northern Brooks County and mes- quite and nopal lay across Hidalgo and Starr counties like wool on an unshorn lamb. My mother's father, too, had spent his life close to the brush, raising his children in a house on an almost forgotten road, four miles from a nearly forgotten town in northern Starr County.

So what if El Cuervo was in Mexico? The country in which it lay was of no importance. It was simply an extension of the brush that rose from the foothills south of the Mexican town of Jimenez along the banks of El Rio Soto la Marina and sprawled north, crossing the great Rio Grande until it dissolved amidst the mountain laurels, oaks, and pecans of the Texas Hill Country at the Nueces River. The land remained unaware of the concept of boundary lines; borders are the projects of politicians and bureaucrats, and El Cuervo and all the brush that surrounded it could never be truly possessed. They could only be understood. But understanding comes from growth, and growth evolves from exposure. What exists as foreign and wild in the beginning becomes natural and tranquil within the subtle revelations of nature. Tenuous at first, that path reveals itself not by way of its gentle contours but from the very obstacles and deterrents that border it.

One moonless and cloudless summer's night the ranch foreman, Don Teodoro, came to my father and said that a cow was lost. He said we should go to an isolated spot on the ranch and listen. He said the cow wore a bell that could be heard from a great distance. Squatting on a gravelly road, embraced by penetrating quiet and baffled by the radiance from a million stars that gathered in clusters and streams and stretched from horizon to horizon like luminous dust and sparkling pebbles, we waited.

Don Teodoro and my father spoke in low, nearly hushed tones. I assume they were discussing cattle and such, but I could hear only the phonetic melody of their voices. Why it came to mind, I cannot recall, but I realized at that moment that without my father there to protect me, I could never have sat on that lonely road, surrounded by the unknown, listening patiently for the gossamer clang of a wooden clapper on a brass bell. It was okay as long as Dad was with me. I the child, he the father: one who was afraid but found solace through his parent, the other undoubtedly experiencing fear but deriving appeasement from within.

In the distance, a mockingbird volunteered a fusillade of falsetto sounds, mimicking the avian calls of the region. And now and then a solitary coyote cried out, searching for a mate, or a friend.

"*Ay esta,*" Don Teodoro mumbled, his finger pointing slowly in the direction of the faraway sound that coalesced into a feeble clang. "*Mañana entramos con los caballos.*"

We walked carefully back to the pickup, always watching for the rattlesnakes that might lie coiled on the warm road bed. Tomorrow, Don Teodoro and his *vaqueros* would ride in the direction from which the bell had sounded and return the lost cow to the herd. But all I could think of was how I treasured those fleeting moments with my father.

El Cuervo was where I first ventured into the woods alone. At the time I did not consider it a milestone. But things would never be quite the same after that. The absolute trust I had placed in my father to protect me was now, in some nebulous way, transferred to me.

The transference came, as it often does, without fanfare. One morning I simply grabbed the Savage .30–30 bolt rifle kept handy at the stone-walled cabin and I walked into manhood. The year was 1962, or thereabouts. It was late spring; the leaves were wet with dew and freshly green. The trail I chose was dense with foliage, overgrown and obscure—a preamble of the life to come, perhaps. It was also the day I discovered the great benefits of woods roaming.

Woods roaming is more than mere walking. It is a form of meditation, a way to the intrinsic self. It allows one to see conceptually. It reveals. But it is not a form of physical exercise, though undoubtedly the soma benefits. Woods roaming is a state of mind.

The .30–30 I carried that day was a crutch: a long arm reaching back to my father, protecting me in the uncharted maze that lay ahead. Like a yearling deer, I stepped cautiously, unwilling to blunder head-long into the unknown.

I walked unhurried, dewy-wet from the knees down, reveling in my solitude. I saw as I had never seen before. Now I alone would provide for my safety. I heard everything—the raspy whistle of a scaled quail, the snapping flutter of large, green grasshoppers, the swaying of ancient barretta limbs.

As I walked a strange energy began coursing through me, filling me with sensations that, until then, I had never known. I studied the trees—the speckled-white barretta, the crenulated bark of massive black ebonies, the smooth emerald limbs of palo verde, the mottled gray branches of the brasil—all the while a gentle breeze fluttering across leaves sparkling green and gray, and tempting me onward.

Midway through the walk, I spotted a chachalaca perched on the limb of a Mexican olive tree. Since that first summer when Dad built the stone cabin, I had heard chachalacas many times. At daybreak their galloping calls echoed up from the San

Fernando River like trumpets stuck on a staccato cadence. But now was the first time I had seen a chachalaca up close. The bird stared at me, I stared back—a long moment—restless brown eyes winking and shifting, one spindly leg held up, nape feathers flared. I stepped back. With determined wing thrusts the bird was gone, lost in a mesh of thorns and branches.

As I walked farther, time passed of its own accord; the sun marking its endless journey overhead; the morphology of burgeoning clouds and waning shadows bathing the land in hues too numerous to recount. At last, I sauntered up to the stone cabin having followed the rocky wash that crept down the hill on the northwest side. I was thirsty and hungry. The gathering clouds seemed to reinforce the feelings of tranquility that ushered me along, that had filtered up from the earth in a delicate osmosis working its way through my body like an ethereal mist. I stepped into the cabin, having been gone but a couple of hours, yet at the same time having transcended one stage of my life to enter another.

In early fall, we caught butterflies in wire-rimmed mist nets that were fashioned into large socks. There were millions of butterflies at El Cuervo. I spent hours trying to match my specimens with the pictures in the field manual, *Butterflies of North America.*

Mostly, however, the fall was reserved for hunting. El Cuervo was where I shot my first deer: a fat doe that appeared one foggy morning a hundred yards down a *sendero* that Petroleos Mexicanos (Mexico's national oil company) had cut through the brush. Dad heard the boom of the .270 rifle clear back at the cabin. When he arrived I was too nervous to join in the search, so he and Don Teodoro went looking for the deer. Dad found it; the animal had traveled only a few yards.

Another milestone. A father's proud smile. The young brave could now feed the camp.

Then there was New Year's Eve of 1965. Dad had brought me to El Cuervo deer hunting. A frigid norther had blown through, and we hadn't bathed in several days. We slept in the sheet-metal-roofed brick lean-to that braced the stone cabin's north side, because though cool in the summer, the cabin's high thatch roof allowed heat to escape in the winter. A cramped ten by twenty feet, the lean-to served as kitchen and dining room. And on that cold New Year's night, it was the only place to keep warm.

Windows shut tightly, a glowing propane flame issuing from the blackened burners in the corner, I huddled in one sleeping bag and Dad ensconced in another, shared laughter helping us ignore the ripe smell of feet gone unwashed.

On hot summer days I would sit atop the water tank on the west side of the stone cabin. From that vantage place—some ten feet above the highest point on the hill

—I could see plainly the blue mountains to the west, which we called the Victoria Mountains. Sometimes I would sit for hours, watching turkey vultures climb invisible thermals, listening to the soft cooing of white-tipped doves, and gazing at the mosaic of greens that rippled into the distance. Something told me that I should swallow every angstrom of this beauty, commit it to memory, and hold it firmly in my heart. It was an education that might someday serve me well.

On lazy afternoons I would follow the trails that paralleled the slothful San Fernando. I'd find a spot on the cool, damp earth—places where the river was no more than fifty yards across, and where tall trees hunched over the water's edge like old men—and observe the dark green current as it reluctantly inched its way to the coast. Now and then a group of *cuervos* (the crows from which the ranch got its name) would fly over me, screaming hoarsely *mari, mari, mari,* as if it were a blasphemy. I shot a few crows. I was young and ignorant.

Occasionally, my cousins would accompany us to El Cuervo. The first thing they wanted to do was ride horses. I could not see the fascination. There was no direct contact with the earth. Besides, the horses made too much noise. They scared animals away. They could only traverse well-marked trails–never *through* the brush, never up steep banks or down narrow ravines. Sometimes horses had minds of their own. I swore I'd never ride atop anything that could think for itself.

I'd let my cousins mount their steeds and go their way, talking loudly, silhouetted against the bright sun, trot noises reverberating into the woods like rimfire rounds shot from a pistol. It didn't occur to them to whisper; they never learned to tiptoe lightly; they weren't interested in watching birds or lizards or deer.

I was unprepared for my last visit to El Cuervo. In retrospect, I imagine it was just another prelude to so many instances in later life where no proper goodbyes were said, the assumption being that there would always be another day.

That final journey came during the Easter vacation in 1967. It was supposed to be a three-day trip. It turned into a one-day tour. By then Dad had become a wheeler-dealer businessman, too busy to enjoy the brush. I was into varmint calling at the time. I wanted to try my calling skills at the ranch. Because Mexican soldiers operating along the roadways often confiscated guns, even when permits had been issued, we hid a Remington model 600 .222 rifle and a pouch full of calls—Burnham, Herters, Olts—in the Jeep Wagoneer and headed south. We arrived at El Cuervo in the early morning. I roamed the lazy trails as I had done so many times before. By late afternoon, I'd collected two bobcats. I enjoyed the hunt, but the real treat was to be at the ranch, and with Dad. I looked forward to a couple of nights in the stone cabin, its straw roof layered over the vaulted rafters, cool Gulf air steering the sounds of pauraques and screech owls through the windows. But it wasn't to be. As we watched one of the vaqueros skin out the cats, Dad said: "Let's head home. You've shot a couple of bobcats—that should do it."

I don't remember what I said, if anything at all. We loaded the Jeep and that was that. Dad sold the ranch a few months later because the Mexican agrarians were threatening to take it away—by force if need be.

But the memories persist. Now, when I am in one of my sunken, teary moods, I sometimes close my eyes and find myself sitting on the old water tank next to the stone cabin. I look west at the far-off mountains, and I hear the white-tipped doves, their soft coos filtering from the barretta woods. I watch the turkey vultures flying high overhead, and I smell the clean air. For a long, wishful moment, I sit on that old, red water tank, remembering. It was an education indeed.

Octavio Solis (El Paso)

"The Day of Whack"

(VICKY slams the suitcase shut and stands apart as WILLIS, MIKE, PEGGY, FELECIA, GONZALEZ, and the JUDGE enter. MIKE stands with a deck of bingo cards. During the following sequence, PEGGY and FELECIA provide props for the JUDGE as WILLIS observes the action with stopwatch and binoculars. The JUDGE walks to designated areas to indicate movement within time and space.)

WILLIS

This is the Day of Whack.

TOMAS

Phase one.

PEGGY

The Judge wakes at 6:00 every morning.

JUDGE

But today, a vivid dream stirs me at 5:57.

TOMAS

The exact time I open my eyes.

PEGGY

He gets up, fetches the paper from the slot in his door.

OCTAVIO SOLIS was born and raised in El Paso and educated at Trinity College in San Antonio, where he received his B.A., and at the Dallas Theater Center, where he received an M.F.A. With his numerous plays about the Chicano experience, often set in the border region of Texas, Solis has become perhaps the best-known Chicano dramatist in the country. His work has been produced around the country. Solis lives in San Francisco.

FELECIA

He showers, dresses, makes breakfast for him and his biddy.

JUDGE

I read my daily passage from the Book of Psalms.

TOMAS

I read mine from Judges.

WILLIS

And he goes to his car. He uses an automatic garage door opener.

JUDGE

I drive in silence, the faint remembrance of the dream filtering through my mind.

TOMAS

As he drives south, I drive north to Vicky's house for the money.

MIKE

In the jail, Camacho and me wager for our souls in a game of *Loteria.*

GONZALEZ

I prepare the opening statement for the trial.

TOMAS

Phase two.

PEGGY

He goes down Broadway and arrives at the parking garage downtown at 7:45.

FELECIA

And he ain't wearing no bulletproof vest.

JUDGE

On this day a comely young creature is bending over the open hood of her car. The security officers are helping her out.

VICKY

I bring the money in my suitcase and we count it.

PEGGY

He parks in his assigned space and goes through an underway to the Federal Courthouse.

FELECIA

While the cop is with me, Pappy slips inside and goes to his car.

WILLIS

I quietly break in and take the batteries from the garage door opener. Then I replace it, lock the car, and stroll away.

MIKE

La Corona.

PEGGY

His first case is at 8:00. He comes five minutes early every day, barring weekends and holidays.

WILLIS

He sees both misdemeanor and felony cases all morning long.

JUDGE

There is a faint ringing in my ears during some hearings.

TOMAS

It's the breach. I hear it again getting louder.

GONZALEZ

I am going to win this case.

MIKE

El Catrin.

TOMAS

Phase three.

FELECIA

At 9:32 I fly out to Midland where I check into a Best Western.

WILLIS

(as PEGGY enters with a rifle and ammo)

And I prepare the hardware Peg bought me three weeks before.

PEGGY

This here's a Mauser 98 Bolt-action Rifle. Mostly used for deer, this baby has a sweet-as-pie adjustable trigger. It's real light, real smooth, and real strong. It's chambered for the 7mm Magnum cartridge, and I bought me the 100 grain hollow-point. I also picked out a top-of-the-line Leupold 10x Silver scope. With these crosshairs you can shoot the head off a sparrow at 300 yards.

WILLIS

Peg, you know I would never do that. Birds are sacred.

PEGGY

You know what name I bought it under? Ida B. Lyon.

WILLIS

Damn, I dunno which I like better: my guns or my women. (NENA comes on to take the suitcase from VICKY.)

TOMAS

Phase four. When we are done counting, Nena comes over and takes the load.

NENA

Me pongo mis sunglasses and catch me a plane to Midland.

MIKE

El pajaro.

GONZALEZ

I am going to bring down Santos & Santos.

FELECIA

I lie in bed in my panties eatin' fajita-pitas and watchin' HBO.

PEGGY

At 11:30 he breaks for lunch to Joseph's Deli, usually in the company of other jurists or big-time city politicos.

JUDGE

I take a chance on the combination Mexican plate.

WILLIS

He has two cocktails with lunch and tips like a woman.

PEGGY

He goes back at 1:00 and resumes his hearings and the like, until 3:00 which is when he's done for the day.

JUDGE

This dream is nagging me on the way to my car. It has bedeviled my whole day.

TOMAS

Phase Five. VICKY closes the store early and joins me at her house.

MIKE

La mano.

GONZALEZ

The only way now is up. I'm going to score.

WILLIS

He drives back Alamo Heights way to the Country Club, where he's a standing member, and suits out for a game of tennis.

PEGGY

He plays hard with any one of a small circle of geezers with overdeveloped calves.
JUDGE definitely likes to win.

JUDGE

But this day I lose when a face from the dream seizes me for a flash and makes me miss the ball. My insides are burning.

TOMAS

Phase six.

FELECIA

At 4:00 I get a call. Then a knock at 4:05.

NENA

(with the suitcase)
Where's your father?

FELECIA

Out.

NENA

Where's your mother?

FELECIA

Out.

NENA

I'm suppose to leave this with you?

FELECIA

That's my understanding.

NENA

The key's inside.

FELECIA

How'm I supposed to open it?

NENA

You're not.

(NENA drops the suitcase. FELECIA takes it.)

PEGGY

I get a call shortly thereafter.

TOMAS

Phase seven.

WILLIS

At 5:30 he showers and phones his wife from the lobby.

PEGGY

By 5:50 he's headed home. Takes a left out of the driveway, goes right, then right again, then left, then straight, then left.

TOMAS

In the evening with all the lights in the house out, we sit in front of a TV neither of us have the nerve to turn on.

MIKE

El Diablito.

WILLIS

He pulls into his garage at 6:00 on the nose. A creature of meticulous habit.

JUDGE

The garage won't open. Push the pad again and wait.

TOMAS

We wait.

PEGGY

The second he pushes the garage door opener, I'm packing our stuff into the car.

FELECIA

I'm over Ft. Worth on Southwest Fl. 401.

WILLIS

I'm on the roof of the Victory Arms Apartment Complex aiming the Model 98 Mauser rifle with the high power telescopic sight across eight clean manicured suburban lawns.

JUDGE

The garage won't open. Then in a great fit of gas, it occurs to me. The entire dream.

WILLIS

He gets out of his car. An abstract look on his face that I really hate to mess up.

PEGGY/FELECIA

He walks to his front door.

GONZALEZ

Then I hear it on the news.

MIKE/NENA/VICKY

El Corazon.

TOMAS

Now.

JUDGE

The dream. The middle of this narrow street, cobbled with greasy stones that shine like exposed ulcers in the green light of the streetlamp. Overhead the night opens its mouth to me with a sound like steam. Old crumbling buildings with the shutters drawn. No-one out. One doorway has a sheet draped over it. I peer inside. There, on a stinking mattress, lit by a candle, Paloma. Her knees drawn up to her chin, her black hair falling over her face. She's young all over again. With a look, she draws me to her and we are in each others' arms, kissing and groping under worn sheets. I am aware only of her muffled cries, but when I finally come, I feel something like a single burning heartbeat shoot through my spine, shoot, shoot right through, and it comes out the small of my back and I am suspended in air. Then I look up beside me, and standing over me, I see him. I see him with the eyes of judgement pressing into me.

TOMAS

What time is it?

VICKY

I don't know.

TOMAS

Don't turn the light on.

VICKY

What's happened?

FELECIA

The phone rings.

TOMAS

Final phase. Yes.

WILLIS

To-weee. To-weee.

TOMAS

Is it done?

WILLIS

I rang his bell. Once for you.

(WILLIS fires his rifle. A tremendous crack. The JUDGE falls to the floor with a cry.)

And once for me.

(He fires again. The JUDGE groans and is still.)

It was a pleasure to serve you.

MIKE

La muerte.

(Everyone goes, but VICKY, TOMAS, and the JUDGE.)

VICKY

Who was it?

TOMAS

JUDGE Benton is dead.

VICKY

Is this . . . is this what I paid for?

(He starts to take his clothes off.)

TOMAS

These are the wages of brotherhood.

VICKY

Tommy. . . . have you . . . have you murdered this man?

TOMAS

(moving toward her half-undressed)
These are the wounds that bind us.

VICKY

TOMMY!

TOMAS

Our blood is now blood of the house.

VICKY

WHAT DID YOU MAKE ME DO! OH DEAR GOD IN HEAVEN!

TOMAS

(taking her in his arms)

Now we are fully made. Familia. Santos.

(BLACK OUT. She cries in the darkness. End of Act 2.)

Richard Yañez (El Paso)

RICHARD YAÑEZ is from El Paso and went to college in nearby Las Cruces, New Mexico, at New Mexico State University, as well as Arizona State University. He has taught at Colorado College, Saint Mary's College, and New Mexico State University. He is a founding member of the Con Tinta, a coalition of Chicano/Latino poets and writers. Yañez's first collection of short stories, *Paso del Norte,* was published in 2003. He teaches at El Paso Community College.

"I&M Plumbing"

Apolonio had passed the courtyard of the nursing home many times before, but today was the first time he stopped and entered.

In the courtyard's center, there was a cement fountain with a statue of an angel-faced boy. He carried a pitcher from which water once poured. The fountain wasn't working, and judging from the boys chipped limbs and the condition of the round base—drowned with leaves and dirt—it had been abandoned for some time.

Taking a break from his third daily visit with his wife, the retired plumber studied the figure in the fountain. "Qué lástima," he mumbled and imagined a happier boy if water would only come out of his pitcher.

He went back inside the disinfectant-smelling hallway that led out to the courtyard. He passed storage closets full of sheets and towels and rooms 82 through 86, two hospital beds to each room, and entered the room near the facility's main entrance.

The first thing he heard was Mrs. Mercedes calling for Eva. Esta mujer está loca, he thought. He wasn't being mean. It's just that he knew from personal experience what this so-called rest home could do to one's mind. He wanted to go over to the Mexican woman and tell her that Eva, her only daughter, had left hours ago after feeding her lunch. But he decided he'd better not or he'd risk having to hear many questions for which he didn't have answers.

On the other side of the room, his wife slept, or so it seemed. It was hard to tell, since she hadn't spoken or moved voluntarily for many months now.

He examined a face he better recognized in yellowed photographs and gripped his wife's well-lotioned hands. He began to rub her fingers like the physical therapist had shown him. Pressing knuckles and squeezing joints, he shut his eyes and prayed the rosary, starting where he'd left off before walking into the courtyard.

Dios te salve, María
llena eres de gracia,
el Señor es contigo,
bendita tú eres entre todas las mujeres . . .

When he opened his eyes, it was dark outside the room's only window. Reaching in his pocket, he sorted through loose change and aspirins until he retrieved a watch with a busted band. He realized that evening Mass at Cristo Rey was already under way. If he hurried to San José, he could catch the later Mass, but he decided to pray another rosary at home instead. He'd be up a little after dawn and after feeding the gatitos—some his and others strays from around La Loma—morning Mass would put him back on schedule.

Before he left, he made sure his wife was tucked well under the sheets and blanket he'd brought that first night she was transported to the nursing home from the hospital. Hope it doesn't get too cold, he thought as he put dirty tissues, a Spanish *Reader's Digest,* and an empty mason jar in a Kmart bag.

Trying to make as little noise as possible, he inched his way toward the door. No luck. Mrs. Mercedes opened her glazed eyes and called for Eva once again: "Venga mijita, ayúdame. Ándale, no seas mala." She repeated this several times, while managing to bravely raise one of her puny arms in his direction. "Eva, hija . . . ayúdame." Her voice was a scratchy phonograph.

He knew she'd keep it up if he didn't do something to comfort her. From his shirt pocket, he pulled out his rosary and placed it in the woman's palm. As if she were a baby and the string of beads a pacifier, Mrs. Mercedes's otherwise blank face grew what appeared to be a smile.

He decided that if he wanted his wife to get some sleep tonight her roommate would need to be quiet. He left the rosary that Padre Islas had blessed the day of his wife's stroke. The business-like nursing staff would remove the rosary in the morning during the changing of soiled sheets and giving of sponge baths. They wouldn't care if the lonely woman cried for Eva, or God, for that matter, he thought. Mrs. Mercedes was one body among the hundred-plus at the nursing home, so they would stick something in her mouth if she made too much of a fuss. He never forgot his fear of the morning he'd found Mrs. Mercedes gagged with a sock.

In a way he didn't fully understand, he was glad that his wife couldn't speak. Or else she would also be victimized by nurses who confessed that they worked long hours and were underpaid.

The nursing home's superintendent, Mrs. Hennessey, appeared surprised when he offered to fix the courtyard's fountain. She said they'd always meant to get it repaired but never had the funds. He told her he would take care of everything. Most of the materials, he already had.

After getting her blessings, he went to his truck. He always carried his plumbing tools behind the seat. "Nunca sabes cuando va haber un trabajito" he'd told his grandson many times. Along with his toolbox, he got a flashlight and dragged out a rooter that he used for clearing out drains. "La Víbora Negra," his grandson named the long metal coil.

In his worn army-green overalls, he crouched over—his shrunken size held together by a life of labor—and put his bare hands into the pipe behind the building. From the way it felt, the fountain's drain hadn't been cleaned in a long while. And if his experience with the plumbing of other, newly built buildings was any sign, he knew that the cheapest materials had been used. He would rely on his twenty-eight years with El Paso county maintenance to finish the task.

He felt good to be working on the fountain. Finally, after what seemed like a lifetime of witnessing his wife's decline, he faced something he could fix. The longer he strained at clearing the pipes, replacing all the corroded fittings, and hauling heavy tubing from the back of his truck, the more absorbed he became in his work.

Padre Islas would ask him at Sunday Mass why he hadn't joined him recently for a cup of coffee, not knowing that one of his most loyal parishioners had taken a vow outside of church.

As a compromise, Apolonio had taken to saying his daily rosary while he worked. The time passed quicker. He found that gripping crescents and pliers, tightening the pipes and fittings, was like handling a rosary. He was most at peace when his hands were working.

After another day under the sun, tired and achy, he went home somewhat satisfied. He didn't look in on his wife before he left the nursing home. While his thoughts were of her on his drive home, completing the work on the fountain was his immediate priority.

First thing in the morning, he would drive to I&M Plumbing for some needed materials. The store was out of the way, but he thought that he would enjoy the smell of alfalfa on North Loop Road. And he looked forward to seeing an old friend even more.

Manuel, his partner from his days with county maintenance, always had the right supplies for any trabajitos he took on. Having contact with someone who didn't feel sorry for him, he decided, would also do him good.

Before he went to sleep that night, unlike other nights, he didn't ask God why He hadn't just taken his wife that Sunday afternoon rather than prolonging her ascent. After praying on his knees before his dresser—lit velas rested next to a faded print of La Virgen—he fell asleep and dreamt that the boy from the fountain came to La Loma.

The laborer welcomed the visitor into his adobe home. He drank when the boy offered him water from his clay jarra. The boy then went over and gave water to a woman in a hospital bed. Apolonio first thought she was his wife, but when he hurried over to her, he realized it was Mrs. Mercedes. She stood after drinking the water and walked off with the boy.

Apolonio was content on sleeping that night—not feeling too alone—and for quite some time after, he awoke without being thirsty for answers.

The next day, a full coffee cup warming his hand, he listened to Manuel speak of a trabajito he'd done for his compadre's son. The way his old friend explained it, the kitchen sink would continue to leak no matter what he did.

"I'm a good plumber, tú sabes eso," Manuel said, "but when they don't pay me, pos, I replace the washer y me voy."

Apolonio smiled and sipped his coffee, which Manuel had served him although he'd said no thanks.

"Next time he calls, I'll just say my arthritis is acting up." Apolonio shared in Manuel's laughter.

Every few minutes a customer would come to the counter and pay for some materials. If they didn't know what it was they needed or where to find it, Manuel would help them. But only after making a fuss about having to put down the pan de huevo he was enjoying with a cup of coffee, his third since Apolonio's arrival.

I&M Plumbing on Alameda Avenue was one of the few places left in the border city that had everything you needed for a plumbing job. Yes, other stores had recently opened nearby and were bigger and more modern, and maybe even cheaper, but these flashier stores made you wait up to a week for some things you needed right away. Like the model of water heater a man was describing to Manuel.

"I don't have it here, but come back tomorrow y te lo tengo listo." Manuel winked as if to assure the man he'd come to the right place.

"Really, is there an extra charge for that?" the customer asked.

"Qué extra charge?" Manuel pursed his lips. "Oiga, joven, just come back." He wrote down the man's name and the water heater's model number.

"Thank you. My family's been taking cold showers for two days."

"And if you need a good plumber to put it in, this is your man." Manuel patted Apolonio on the shoulder. "He's the best I know. Next to me."

The three men grinned.

The customer said thanks but that he would try to install the water heater himself. Apolonio was embarrassed by his friend's flattery but silently agreed that he was one of the two best plumbers he knew.

Manuel took out a notepad and phoned the person who could get the water heater he needed. Apolonio didn't keep a notepad with names and phone numbers anymore, but he, too, knew from who and where in El Paso-Juarez he could get what he needed for any trabajito. That was why he was here today visiting Manuel. Well, at least, that's what he'd told his friend, who he hadn't seen since around the time of his wife's stroke.

"¿Miraste los Dodgers?" Apolonio asked Manuel after he got off the phone.

"No. When they play?"

"El otro día."

"¿Quién les jugaron?"

"Los Padres, no, los Giants. Dodgers won, seis a dos."

Silence filled the next moments. Apolonio liked that they didn't have to talk all the time. This silence—unlike the one with his wife—was comforting.

"Polo, ven, te quiero 'señar algo." The two men walked out from behind the front counter to the sales area. In front of rows of bins filled with pipe fittings of various sizes, PVC and brass, was a display: KING SPEED ROOTER—"GETS THE JOB DONE FAST."

Apolonio pulled on the metal coil and stroked the chrome casing of the electric rooter. If he'd had one of these, he thought, he could've finished unclogging the fountain's drain in no time. The manual rooter he used did the job, but he had to take frequent breaks because his arms, especially around his shoulders, tired from cranking it. Ever since he started fixing the fountain, he had to rub Ben-Gay on himself before he went to bed.

"'sta suave. But too much money." Apolonio stood back and admired the King Speed Rooter, certain it was a better machine than the ones hooked up to his wife.

"The salesman who brought it in told me to put it here, right as you walk in the store," Manuel said. "If it doesn't sell by the end of the month, he said he'd take it back. He gave me some free washers, fittings, and this calendar."

He took the calendar off the near wall and showed it to Apolonio. A redhead in only overalls was posed among assorted colors of sinks, bathtubs, and commodes. Apolonio put his hand under his cap and scratched his balding head. When they'd worked together at the County Coliseum, Manuel had decorated the tool room with pictures from magazines he thought the other workers would like—women in bikinis, new pickups, Carlos Palomino, Fernando Valenzuela.

"Casados" was what the supervisor used to call them. In their marriage, Apolonio was the worker and Manuel the thinker.

Apolonio had always been thankful that Manuel had taught him patience. When they'd met, right after Apolonio came out of the army, his approach to every job was finish it as fast as he could. He felt proud when he did twice as much as other plumbers and his superiors, like Lieutenant Jarvis at Fort Bliss, praised him for it.

"It's no good if you do it fast and you have to go back and do it again in a few months," Manuel had told Apolonio on their first job together, installing the urinals at Western Playland Amusement Park. He learned to listen, take his time, and eventually it worked out to where they would always be partners. Twenty-five years, second only to his forty-three-year marriage.

Behind the counter, they finished their coffees and watched customers enter the store. They would comment on all the purchases, and they agreed that nothing was as good as it used to be.

"When are we going?" Manuel made a drinking motion with his hand, a big grin on his face.

"Cuando quieras." Apolonio didn't like lying to his oldest friend. He knew that he couldn't go drinking like they used to every payday, and he didn't know how to say this without sounding like less than the man he once was. Anyway, his friend wasn't supposed to drink anymore. After his operation a few years ago, the doctors told him to stop drinking and smoking. From the full ashtray near the coffee machine, Apolonio guessed that Manuel had said to hell with the doctors' instructions.

"I could use a cervezita right now." Manuel took a long swallow from his "Viva Las Vegas" mug. Apolonio wondered what his friend kept cool inside the refrigerator in the back room.

They talked about their children. Manuel had always been jealous of Apolonio because he had only one, a son. In Manuel's own words, he'd been cursed with bad luck—four daughters. One was a dancer at the Tropicana, another was married to un Americano and lived on the other side of the freeway, and the other two attended the local college. After Apolonio told his friend that he didn't see his son much anymore, his friend joked that he wished his two youngest would go on and get married and leave him alone.

"I know when they want something. They call me 'Papi' and put their arms around me and tickle my stomach." Manuel went into an adjacent bathroom, left the door open, and kept talking. "They don't like sharing a car, but that's all I can get them. I told them one could drive my truck. 'Yonque' they call it. ¿Lo crees?"

Apolonio found it almost unbelievable that Manuel could still be driving the truck he'd had since before they started working together. It *was* a piece of junk, and he'd told him many times before.

"Comprate otra."

"¿Polo, 'stas loco? Esa troquita es mi sweetheart—together forever."

Manuel walked out of the bathroom and over to a window. The body of the Chevy truck was more rust than blue paint, the hubcaps had been stolen, and cardboard was taped over a broken window. The only thing that had kept it from completely falling apart all these years, Apolonio thought, was the rosary hanging from the rearview mirror.

Shaking his head, he remembered Manuel was as dedicated to Iliana, his wife. After she died about fifteen years ago, work was the only thing that Manuel seemed to care about. Often, Apolonio would get home late because his partner wanted to answer another call, or after clocking out early, he convinced him to. go to Zaragoza, across the bridge, for a few beers. Apolonio never had to explain his lateness to his wife. She'd said his best friend needed his company now more than ever.

Apolonio told Manuel that he had to go. The drive to the nursing home was a long one, and he wanted to see if the hose and valves were right for the fountain. Manuel assured him that they were, but if not, he'd be here tomorrow—"Como siempre."

The soon-to-be widower took comfort in this. And he didn't feel as guilty that he'd skipped his morning visit to the nursing home. I&M Plumbing would remain the one place that always had what he needed.

A few days passed before news of the working fountain made its way to every room of the nursing home. No longer were the residents satisfied with being placed in front of a talk-and-game-show-happy TV set in the facility's lobby. Even ones that couldn't—or wouldn't—speak somehow managed to communicate to the nurses that they'd rather be outside in the courtyard. Mrs. Mercedes, for one, had Eva wheel her out every morning and evening to see the fountain, or else the mother refused to eat.

The courtyard's centerpiece was not the only object that had been resurrected. Encouraged by Apolonio's success, Mrs. Hennessey had put some staff people to work on the landscape: Flowers from the nursing home's front lawn were transplanted, plump bushes were trimmed into matching shapes, and, in a few weeks, the grass would be alive again with color.

Inside the faded blue walls of room 89, Apolonio only hoped that his wife could imagine the courtyard from his simple descriptions in Spanish. But many doctors were positive that she couldn't hear or see anything, and if she did, she most likely didn't understand it. The stroke, along with her already weak heart and chronic diabetes, had completely wrecked most of her brain. When Apolonio tried to speak with her or get her to move a hand or a foot, he considered a blink a cruel settlement.

To make it easier for Apolonio to understand, a member of the hospital staff had tried to explain his wife's condition in terms he might recognize. The male nurse told him in Spanish that his wife had suffered a stroke, which is like when a machine short-circuits.

Staring at his wife's lifeless face, he remembered thinking that if the stroke she'd suffered was like a machine breaking down, then there must be someone who could provide repair. Doctors are like electricians and mechanics and plumbers, he thought. They can fix whatever's broken. The following months changed how his own mind understood and registered things. His wife's physical state was more than a trabajito.

He placed a new box of tissues and a mason jar on the table next to her bed. Twisting off the cap, he put his fingers in the holy water and made the sign of the cross on his wife's forehead, then did the same for himself.

Intending to pray a rosary before he visited the courtyard, he searched his pockets, then remembered that he had never gotten his rosary back from Mrs. Mercedes. All he had in his pockets were some fittings that he'd replaced on the fountain. Rather than throw them out, he was taking them home, where he had buckets of brass and copper materials among an altar of sinks and commodes in his cuartito.

Sitting on a corner of his wife's bed, he shut his eyes and began a rosary. While the string of recited words comforted him, he winced as he prayed. The sharp edges of the metal fittings stung and creased his fingertips.

Tammy Gomez (Fort Worth)

"Mexicano Antonio" and "On Language"

Mexicano Antonio

Mexicano Antonio tugged on his crampons
and proceeded up the lanky Laney
my tall gringa friend
so blonde and elevated
dancing tight revolutions
while the pool ball vaqueros
squeezed out another side pocket hit
in tight-fitting leather jackets
and crusty nightclub shoes,

and I refuted the wound-up boys
swooping at me like earnest wine porters
or Tampico-bound Canadian geese,
begging their unanswerable questions.

"¿Quieres bailar?"
"¿Tienes esposo?"

Until I could say yes, I said nothing,
even as the synthesized banda brass tunes
worked up my chakras and
wore down my resistance to
high speed circle dancing
until at last I chose a partner,
with whom I danced in awkward flow, >>

Tammy Gomez was born in Stamford and is known for her performances as both a poet and the lead singer-guitarist in her band. She is also a radio producer, talk show host, events organizer, educator, activist, publisher, and rabble-rouser. Gomez's first children's play, "El Conejito Verde," based on a Mexican folktale, has been performed in public schools throughout the Fort Worth-Dallas area. She lives in Fort Worth.

he squeezed my hand so soft
to his heart
to his memory
of something that I could never be
of something lost and catalog wear—
his western shirt so thick and rough,
a vintage not of my world.

he: well-cleaned and dry
me: dry-cleaned and wry

Men like him are December daguerreotypes,
traditional holidays in copper frames,
blurred by my urban digital viewpoint
and fading as sepia sentiments. Ni modo.
All I wisht was cumbia merengue footwork
and to be early weekend tipsy, or
to be amused
by the Mexicana mae west,
78 and skin-tight dressed
in a mini that matched
her perfect ruby nails and
a well-tested smile.

Endlessly wondering as she winked our way.

"¿Do you like the drink?"
"It's estrong. Strong."

And I finally spoke, to them who asked.

"No, no quiero bailar."
"Yes, I like the men."
"But no dance, not tonight."

about Friday night at Recuerdos de Kansas cantina,
Fort Worth, Texas
January 4, 2004

On Language

No Spanish at home. No hablamos Spanish at home.
Even so, my English was deemed inferior,
incorrect, and irreverent. In school.

So off I was sent to speech class, singled out
in front of my classmates for special therapy . . .

sh instead of ch
sh instead of ch
ch en vez de sh was my main problem. I couldn't tell them apart.

If I wanted to sit, well then I would find a 'shair,'
but if I wanted to compartir algo contigo, well that was 'chairing.'
I was poked fun of and embarrassed in front of my classmates,
so, after that, I vowed to speak it, English, better than anyone else.
I would no longer be singled out for intimidation.

Bee—geen—eeng ov thoe—row ah—seem—ee—laa—shun
Bee—geeneeng of tho—row ahseem—eelaa shun
Beginning of tho—rough assi—mila—tion
Beginning of thorough assimilation.

And so began my separation from my native tongue,
the family language—Spanish, no more, no mas,
the distance between me and my cultural heritage
grew larger and larger, as the ethnic roots of my familia
faded and blurred in the distance behind.

I was so keen on being blended in, whitewashed into the landscape
and not being discerned as diferente, me entiendes?

Because if you noticed that I was different, then you might treat
me different, and the way I viewed this, historically speaking,
different meant worse. Treating different means treating worse. »

Yeah, I've been called nigger. I've perceived prejudice.
You can tell when the teachers don't know how to talk to you,
how to pronounce your last name, your weird name.
How to act with a foreign species, illegal species.
You can sense their discomfort.

And a chota once told me, when we first met in person,
"Funny, but you didn't sound MEXICAN on the phone."

So I tried, always tried, to keep myself invisible and mute,
be low-key. Don't rise and shine. Lay low, be dull.
Don't stand out, don't risk the put-downs and humiliations.
But that's hard when you're also overcompensating
for your wrong history, wrong accent, skin color . . .
. . . to keep up with the rules of Gringolandia U—S—A, vato,
the biggest theme park in the world today.
Gringolandia, U.S.A.

So me, la over-compensating, over-achiever:
I made sure I had the cleanest hands
(They weren't going to call ME a 'dirty' Mexican!).
I had the straightest posture and the straightest As
(You weren't going to call ME a 'lazy' Mexican!).

Pretty soon, the kids in my class started to not like me
as much, because I was so good at playing the game,
their game, by their rules, that I made them look bad.

Oh, I retro-fitted so well, I must have assimilated too much.
I even sent myself to an uppity women's college in the northeast.
Why? To prove again, as I never stopped trying to prove,
that I could toe the line with daughters of
wealthy white professional men.

I'm talking about
progressive whitening of Latinos.
The gradual whitening of Chicanos, Chicanas,
and eventual whitening of Tejana Mexicanas.

You start off speaking Spanish, coming in with shy,
but respectful, gentle nature. And as that gets stripped away,
you become more anglicized, speaking a baby's English.
But don't worry, you can take remedial classes.

You begin walking the American pace, with rigid posture,
always in a hurry, but never on time. All the time for work
and none for familia. Until one day, you glance in the mirror,
and you don't even know who that person is looking back at you.

But hey, I don't wanna think about that, I'm here to party.
I'm here to celebrate my AmericanISM.

I'm ready for the red, white, and blue.
I'm ready to be red, white, and blue.
So long, Mexico. Farewell, Cuba.
Never mind, Nicaragua. Piss off, Peru.

I'm WHITE now. I'm RIGHT now. I'm MIGHT now.

So, what has this cost?
And what have I lost?

Randy Garibay (San Antonio)

"Barbacoa Blues"

I went down Nogalitos, looking for some barbacoa and Big Red

I could have had menudo, but I got some cabeza instead

Give me two pounds of regular 'cause I like a little fat

You might like la pura carne but for me, fats where it's at

Give me four gorditas so I can put some meat inside

I love my barbacoa with a Big Red on the side

I went down Nogalitos, looking for some barbacoa and Big Red

I could'a had menudo
    but I got some tortillas,
    and I got some carnitas,
    and I got some gorditas,
    and I got some chili,
    I got some chile,
    and I got some cabeza instead.

Recognized by his peers as the "godfather" of San Antonio blues, Randy Garibay's career spanned over forty years, garnering a wider audience with his 1997 release of "Barbacoa Blues."

John Phillip Santos (San Antonio)

from *Places Left Unfinished at the Time of Creation*

By the time I was born in 1957, my grandfathers were already long gone. When their names were mentioned, once in a long while, by parents or aunts and uncles, it was always with great ceremony and formality. There were never disparaging words of any kind. My mother's father, Leonides, owned a dry goods store in Cotulla, Texas, and my father's father, Juan José, with the same name as my father, was a gardener and laborer in San Antonio. Both were remembered as men of few words, prone to meting out family justice in swift and unwavering fashion. I hadn't seen pictures of Juan José, but in an old photograph of Leonides, taken when he was already in his early fifties, he is sitting next to a great desk in his store, stacked high with papers weighted by horseshoes. A big man with a bald head, and light-complexioned for a Mexicano, he is dressed in a suit and vest, with a shiny watch fob hanging, and his demeanor is serious, with a forceful gaze as direct and unyielding as an old judge's. If the stories are to be believed, both grandfathers were exemplars of virtue, honesty, and integrity, beloved by their families and communities alike. *Los Abuelos* never indulged in alcohol. Both Juan José and Leonides were said to be teetotalers who rarely drank, even at weddings or during holidays. There are no tales of drunkenness or recklessness among them. Yet neither lived to meet a single one of their scores of grandchildren.

JOHN PHILLIP SANTOS, a native of San Antonio, attended the University of Notre Dame before studying at Oxford as a Rhodes Scholar. He has written for a variety of national publications, and has been a documentary film producer for the Ford Foundation and twice nominated for the Emmy Award, once for his "Exiles Who Never Left Home," about Mexican-American spirituality. His memoir *Places Left Unfinished at the Time of the Creation* was nominated for a National Book Award. He lives in San Antonio.

Did they leave anything behind? Was there anything of the memory of *los Abuelos* left for us, their progeny, to share? It felt as if their legacies had been completely extinguished, perpetually lost to their descendants.

Perhaps the answers lay in the words of Tundama, the powerful Chibcha Indian *cacique,* or king. In 1541, in the part of Latin America that is present-day Colombia, Tundama rejected a peace overture made by Quesada, the Spanish conquistador, with a warning that prophesied the invincibility of the past, even in the face of imminent defeat and death:

> *You desecrate the sanctuaries of our Gods and sack the houses of men who haven't offended you. Who would choose to undergo these insults? We now know that you are not immortal or descended from the sun. Note well the survivors who await you, to undeceive you that victory is always yours.*

Grandfather Leonides used to help people in Cotulla by using his horse-drawn wagon to transport corpses from their homes to the undertaker to be prepared for their final rest. Many of the Mexican families of the town would ask him to speak at the funerals since he knew everyone and, as one of my aunts put it, "He always spoke so pretty."

Once, just before he died, Grandfather Leonides awoke Uncles Leo, Lauro, and Lico in the middle of the night. Without telling them where they were going, he put their jackets on and led them down a side street until they were just out of town, where the railroad tracks passed through a large, flat, dry pasture. There were other people there, holding candles, singing and praying softly in the moonlit indigo evening. Uncle Lauro remembered how it felt as if hours went by before everyone heard the sound of a slowly approaching train, heading south for Laredo. The three-car procession was decked with brass torches and great ribbons of black bunting that waved in the warm night breeze like banners.

"It is the body of Anfitrio Mendiola!" Grandfather whispered to my uncles, who struggled through the crowd to get a clear sight of the funeral train.

Mendiola was one of the most acclaimed Mexican stage actors of the time, and Grandfather had seen him perform in classical Spanish plays on buying trips to Monterrey. He had died while working on a silent movie in California.

Now his body was being taken home to Nuevo Leon, and all along the route through south Texas his fans had come out to the tracks to offer their *despedida.* The glass-walled car, like a traveling shrine, passed them, and the candlelit, draped coffin was visible to the small group of the devoted from Cotulla who had been keeping vigil half of the night. They crossed themselves and waited until the train fell below the horizon.

Then they made their way back home as dawn was coming on.

"Within a month, he was gone, too," Uncle Lauro said, speaking of his own father.

"An ordinary day, working in the store, talking to everyone, then, in the afternoon, a massive cerebral hemorrhage, and he was gone."

"He was in his underwear, on his bed, and there was silver froth on his lips. And not a doctor to be found."

Even in our own homelands, our traditions were fragile, and without *los Abuelos* to serve as their guarantors, many of them have been lost in the translation between the worlds of Mexico and Texas, Mexican and Anglo. Great-uncle Frank, Uela's eldest brother Francisco, was like a grandfather to me. He lived with my grandmother for many years before her death. If *las Viejitas* showed me how the world of spirits worked amidst the world of the living, Uncle Frank, a naturally gifted inventor, engineer, and metallurgist, tried to teach something to all of us about how to act in the world, how to conduct ourselves in the proper Mexicano way that his father, Great-grandfather Jacobo, had taught him.

He told me that Mexicans born in the United States were different from the Mexicans of Mexico. They acted differently. Uncle Frank felt they had lost the long-held Mexican traditions of courtesy and love for others. Worse, they had lost respect for their elders, and for the dead. If he was on a sidewalk in the middle of town and a chain of cars in a funeral cortege passed by, he would stop, even if he was the only one doing so, to stand erect, take off his hat, and cross himself, waiting until the procession went by. Uncle Frank worried that, once lost, these traditions would never again return.

"When we were on the other side, in Mexico, they taught us to respect the older ones. This is gone now. No one respects the old people."

Whether we're born north or south of the border, rich or poor, proud or contrite, we decide whether we will continue to abandon the often beautiful, sometimes terrifying stories of the past by small degrees, or, against the drift, to remember, to salvage—to conjure and resurrect them anew. Every Mexican lives this destiny out by either embracing, or falling further, from the sources of hidden light left behind in the past with *los Abuelos.*

Great-grandfather Jacobo Garcia, Uela's father, was a perfect twin, absolutely identical, except for a large brown mole, a lunar, in the middle of his brother Abrán's cheek. A hand-painted photograph of the two hangs on a living room wall in Tía Pepa's house, with the two of them looking like a mirrored reflection, their hands to their hearts, and crabbed expressions on their mustachioed faces. They looked so much alike that it is said that Jacobo once found himself holding a conversation in a full-size mirror when he thought he was talking to Abrán. And they stayed identical, until their deaths in their nineties.

In addition to Jacobo and his twin, there were twins in the next generations—Jacobo's sons, Manuel and Valentín, now dead, and my brothers, George and Charles. There were other twins, elsewhere in the family, as if there was a regular doubling pulse in the bloodline. As the Garcias moved through time, this pulse resulted in the presence in every generation of people who lived with their mirror image. With so many doubles around the tribe, it made the rest of us more aware of our own solitariness.

Uncle Frank, like most of the Garcias, lived into his late nineties. His long, lanky frame and enormous hands could make him seem like an intimidating old gentleman, but his limpid eyes and gentle mien showed a tenderness that he shared with the rest of his siblings. He remained lean, disciplined, and active to the end. When Uela died, Frank was already in his late eighties. But on the way to the cemetery, we spotted him along Colorado Street, with his thumb out, hitchhiking. Somehow, everyone had left the funeral parlor without him.

By then, he had been alone almost twenty years. In the 1950s, his only son had died young, suddenly and mysteriously, in a motel in Laredo where he was on business. Uncle Frank's wife never got over that loss, and she also died a few years after their son. As the eldest of the Garcias, Uncle Frank had been the one who came alone to Texas and eventually helped to bring the rest of the family north. The Garcias had left their life in Mexico behind. He saw his two greatest inventions—a dump truck and an industrial pecan sheller—stolen by dishonest business partners. Yet, despite all the sadness that he had experienced in his life, he was content. Years later, after being blind for nearly twenty years, he had a cataract operation, and suddenly he could see again. Living with Madrina and Uncle Manuel, he spent the last several years of his life reading historical novels about the time of Jesus, mowing the lawn, making drawings of new inventions, such as motorized drying racks for clothes and garage doors that opened sideways. When we frequently talked together, he saw all of the lives in our family as part of one continuous story one mission, one journey.

Great-grandfather Jacobo's father, el abuelo Teofilo Garcia, had lived to be one hundred years old, and Uncle Frank remembered him vividly from his youth in Coahuila. As a young child on a farm outside of Palaú in the middle of the nineteenth century, Teofilo was kidnapped and raised by the Kikapu Indians in the Coahuila sierra. By then, the Kikapu had been roaming in the nearby mountains for decades, occasionally raiding the Mexican frontier settlements when food was scarce in the wild. It was said they had once been a part of the Cherokee nation, but in the nineteenth century, when Texas Republicans expelled all the Indians to the nearest border, the Kikapu were repelled across the Rio Grande. President Benito Juárez later granted them a rich piece of territory on the headwaters of the Sabinas River high in the mountain range called the Serranía del Burro. The land was named *el Nacimiento,* "the birthplace," where the Indians remain to this day.

Uncle Frank recalled that el abuelo Teofilo had grown up with the Kikapu, under the name Tibú. "*Qué curioso,* for a name, no?" he always began, as he prepared to tell the story again.

It was years later, on a dawn raid against the town of Múzquiz that Abuelo Teofilo was wounded and left behind. According to Uncle Frank, he was rescued and cared for by a couple who found him, shivering, hysterical, and bleeding from a gunshot wound to the leg, by the banks of the Rio Salinas. While his wounds healed, he stayed in their home, eating and sleeping "like an animal" on the floor in the corner of a room, unable to speak Spanish or to communicate in any way.

Then, there came a day when the woman who had rescued the young man heard him singing after breakfast while he lay on the floor looking at the ceiling. It was a lullaby that she remembered teaching her own child eleven years before, when he had been kidnapped by the band of Indians. She began to sing along with him. Suddenly, from deep inside of himself, he recognized her voice from where it still burned for him as faint as starlight.

Uncle Frank relished telling the end of the story, sitting upright in his chair.

"And from this moment on, Abuelo Teofilo was reunited with his parents, and stayed thereafter in town with them, later bringing home a Kikapu woman he had already married, with whom he later fathered Jacobo, my father, and Abrán, my uncle—absolutely identical twins.

"Abuelos can be lost and found," Frank would say about his grandfather Teofilo.

"*Somos de los abuelos perdidos y los hallados.*"

We are of the grandfathers lost, and of those found.

It was late afternoon one May day in 1974 when the distant voices of *los antepasados* were in the parched Texas scirocco wind that blew through San Fernando Cemetery feeling like a breath the planet exhaled thousands of years before. It was the same wind that had always been blowing through our lives and the lives of all those we had brought there in so many long, slow automobile corteges down Culebra Street, past barrio *taquerías* and hubcap shops, to the great Mexicano necropolis of San Antonio. A wind of story, a wind of forgetting, a perpetual wind, through storms and droughts and *calorones* that is a blessing from our ancestors.

It was Mother's Day and we were visiting Uela's grave. In San Antonio, Mother's Day is like the *Día de los Muertos* in Mexico. It is a day when it is necessary and honorable to revere all of *las Viejitas,* whether living or departed. Earlier that week we had driven to Laredo, on the Texas horde; where my mother's mother and father were buried. We washed the cracked headstone, clipped the overgrown Bermuda grass, and pulled the weeds with dull flowers. I remembered a sunny autumn day many years before, seeing Grandmother Lopez, with a wry, almost pathetic little smile, standing proudly in a great caramel-colored fur coat next to that headstone with her name already etched into it, as Mother snapped her photograph. In that picture, Grandmother has an almost haughty expression on her face, as if to mock the death that awaited her, and to show that she had no fear about her destiny in that place.

Back in San Antonio, standing by the graveside of my father's parents at San Fernando Cemetery with my parents and two brothers, one scraggly mesquite tree offered sparse shade, and the scent of Mother's Day chrysanthemums wafted across the grounds like a narcotic spell.

It had been only nine months since "the great *despedida,*" as we all came to refer to that season of the sudden exodus of the family's grandmothers. *Despedida* means a "fare thee well." The September before, in the space of sixty days, just as if it were a scheduled embarkation, most of the remaining grandmothers from around the extended tribe took their leave from this world. Both my mother's and father's mothers. Uncle Richard's mother. Aunt Minnie's mother. For decades, they had known one another as *comadres,* sharing tamales and a discreet cerveza or two at Christmas parties—polite, regal, but aloof from each other.

They left as a departing chorus would, each one carrying off their own veiled and unspoken secrets from the past with them. Their passing on left us that much further from all the Mexican stories, a little more engulfed by a world increasingly taken up by expressways, shopping malls, and the news of Vietnam and Watergate. In the end, resilient and fierce as each of them were, they had been vexed by this caterwauling century of revolutions and wars, and most of them died in fitful sleep, exhausted and confused by much of what they saw around them in their final years. In this way, they had joined *los Abuelos.*

That afternoon, looking at the headstone on my grandparents' grave, I noticed for the first time the dates of Abuelo Juan José's life:

1890–1939

I was seventeen, and I thought I knew all there was to know about the family's past in Mexico and Texas. I had gone to the dusty *pueblitos* in the Coahuila foothills of the Sierra Madre. I knew the stories of la Tía Fermina Ferguson, Mother's clairvoyant albino aunt. On my father's side, there was el Tío Santos Garcia, the evangelist, who had prophesied the end of the world would begin with a great tidal wave in the Gulf of Mexico. There was the Lopez dry goods store in Cotulla, where a young schoolteacher had listened to grandfather Leonides's jokes and accepted gifts of cabbages and potatoes in exchange for giving Aunt Lydia English speech classes. The teacher was Lyndon Baines Johnson.

All the faces, the few keepsakes, the shoeboxes of sepia-tinted photographs, were a Mexican Book of the Dead, with the shards of a story that had remained untold. Yet, the stories had always seemed to fit together like a brightly colored mural that, taken collectively, might tell the saga of a family. But I had never known that my father's father among so many others who lived to virtually biblical longevity, died at age forty-nine.

I rehearsed what I knew.

Abuelo Juan José was one of six children in his father's second family. He had crossed the imaginary threshold of the Rio Grande, heading into Texas in the time of the revolution. Like the Garcias, he had come from the Serranía del Burro in the northwestern mountains of Coahuila. Settling in San Antonio, he had tended a network of subterranean floral greenhouses connected by tunnels on the large estate of Col. George W. Brackenridge, the onetime prince of the city's business, social, and military gentry. Later my grandfather had worked in one of the local foundries, Alamo Iron Works, from which we still have two exquisitely crafted metal bookends in the shape of the Alamo and a polished bronze sculpture of two hands clasped in prayer, both of which he made.

That day, I realized that no one had ever spoken about his death.

I asked my father how his father had died.

He fixed me with a quick, hard stare, strange for his usually gentle temperament. "He died too young," he said, with a conclusive snap that told me he wasn't going to say anything further.

My brothers darted their eyes to me, and Mother gave a stern look. We had just come from a long *Misa de las Madres,* a "Mass for the Mothers," and we were already getting uncomfortable in our church trappings in the bright Texas heat, but I asked again.

Growing more exasperated, my father promised to tell me someday. His voice trailed off, indicating that this was the absolute last word on the matter, and burying the first secret we openly held from each other. I could tell he wasn't really angry, though. It was more a feeling of a hidden sadness and fear, as if the act of forced remembering might bring with it an uncontrollable rush of despondency.

I had seen this before in him.

My father, usually a quiet man, often decorated his silences with his guitar. He could retreat into it for weeks. In the evenings, after dinner, off on his own, he sometimes strummed in a dream, staring distantly across the living room. At night, against sheets of cascading cicada song from outside, he leaned forward and down, with his head bowed, wrapping his arm around the instrument, throwing flamenco curls off the battered face of the guitar. In those evenings, he seemed to draw his breath from deep out of the lost world of his own past. Daddy slowly drew his hand up, backward against the strings, singing slowly.

Ma-ala-gue-ña-a Sal-e-rosa-a-a . . .

Days later, I still felt a gnawing curiosity about Grandfather's death. Maybe it was a hunting mishap, I thought, or maybe an accident during one of the days I had heard about when the whole Santos-Garcia family had worked as pickers on one of the farms surrounding San Antonio.

Then, Mother told me. She closed her bedroom door behind her, and spoke in a hushed, whispered voice. She wanted me to know my father's outburst at his parents' grave had come from a very deep place.

Abuelo Juan José had committed suicide.

She said that on one morning in 1939, Abuelo had been missing, and everybody was out looking for him. Uncles and aunts, even neighbors. Apparently, it was Daddy, along with his uncle Chale, who found him dead, floating, drowned in the San Antonio River where it crosses Roosevelt Park, near the old Lone Star brewery, on the south side of town. My father was twenty-two years old.

Standing there with Mother, the windows bright with Texas sunlight, the air of the house chilled with air-conditioned calm, all the decades seemed to telescope into a moment. Perhaps my father, along with the rest of the family, felt it was their *encargo* to bear the story in silence, as if we might vanquish something dark in our hearts by breaking the webs of telling and retelling that told us who we were, where we came from, and why we were here.

In that moment, I felt a pang of the fear of drowning I had always had deep inside of me. Suddenly, it swept through me like the shadow of an unknown memory. The first time I had felt it, I was swimming in the Guadalupe River, in New Braunfels, north of

San Antonio. My legs had gotten tangled in the long, undulating plumes of weeds in the green water by the bank. I felt myself falling and falling, as if from an enormous tree that stretched up into the deep blue ether of the sky. I saw ribbons of vivid colors coming out from every part of my body, the faces of family members, Padrino Julín who saved me once from choking on a gumball, friends, and some faces I did not recognize.

The Aztecs believed there was a separate part of paradise, Tlalocan, that was reserved for the souls of those who died by drowning. Now I was falling into that ageless heaven of the drowned. It was as if this trace of my grandfather had been left inside of me—a flash of lightning behind my eyes, my brain hungry for air in the murky water. And before a friend pulled me out of that river, I had a glimpse of a borderless fog as old as night.

I did not know then that Grandfather had dwelled there, that inside the fog was also a hidden time, a lost song, a secret archive of the soul of our family.

SERGIO TRONCOSO grew up in Ysleta, which became part of El Paso while Troncoso was young. He graduated from Harvard magna cum laude and, after a year of study in Mexico City on a Fulbright Scholarship, went to Yale and obtained a master's degree in international relations. He spent a brief period as a labor economist and then returned to Yale to get a second master's degree, this time in philosophy. His first collection of short stories, *The Last Tortilla,* was published in 1999 and won the Premio Aztlán Award. He lives in New York City.

Sergio Troncoso (Ysleta)

"A Rock Trying to Be a Stone"

We took Chuy to the ditch behind my house, Joe, me, and Fernández, and tied him up. We tied him up tight with a rope I found in the shed. It must've burned his wrists 'cause as soon as Joe yanked on the square knot, Chuy yelped and started blubbering in the way he does when he's hungry, but I know he wasn't hungry. It hadn't been more than ten minutes since I had given him the Heath bar in front of his porch, right under his mama's eyes. Hell, I could smell the frijoles she was cooking in the kitchen just as I dangled the shiny wrapper under those stupid eyes. He followed me like a puppy, and then we tied him up secret-like.

Chuy wiggled his shoulders and stood up, his hands dangling in front of him like flippers, but Joe pushed him down hard into a tumbleweed still green from the rain. Nobody could see us in this thicket of mesquite, cattails, and garbage, the best of which was the rusted frame of El Muerto's Buick station wagon lying near the bottom of the ditch. When that stupid pothead had driven into the ditch drunk, he had left us a great place to wait for the bullfrogs to jump out of the mud when the rains came in the summer. And he also punched a tunnel through all the overgrowth and junk in the ditch, a tunnel that ended up at the station wagon with the tinted moonroof, a tunnel we hid from the other pendejos in the neighborhood by covering it with dried-out tumbleweeds. This was our place, only the three of us knew about it, and we swore we wouldn't tell anyone else. Anyway, Joe would have kicked the shit out of anybody who told. He loved that tunnel more than anything else, more than being in his own house. Now we had a prisoner in our tunnel, too.

"Now what?" Fernández said, staring at the slobber dripping down Chuy's lips. "I hope he isn't sick."

"Shut up. Get me that other wire over there," Joe demanded and pulled Chuy up to his feet and pushed him down the ditch tunnel toward the station wagon and the slimy green water full of tadpoles and such. "We're gonna tie the re-tard to the Buick, we're gonna tie his legs." Joe slapped Chuy on top of his head, but it wasn't a hard slap.

"What for?" Fernández asked. "What are we gonna do with him?"

"So he can't run away. What good's a prisoner if he runs away?" I said, grabbing the tumbleweed stems behind me and closing up the entrance. The morning had been way too hot already. There weren't any mosquitoes buzzing yet, but the ditch was full of big black shiny flies, the kind that land on dogshit and eat it. Two of 'em buzzed my head, and I jumped back. Hell, I didn't want any shit flies on me.

"Araaaayia! Araaaayia! Araaayiump!"

"Shut up, damn it. Shut the fuck up," Joe said.

"Araaaayia! Araaayiump!"

"Turi, shut him up! Somebody'll hear him," Joe said. He was getting angry. He had that bored look in his eyes, the one before he lunged at whoever was in his face. Steady eyes above a slight smile, his shoulders and arms straight like a tight coil.

"Araaaayia! Araa . . ." The last one died just after it left his lips. His eyes became distracted by the cinnamon jawbreaker I waved in front of him. I pushed it into the fat open mouth, and slobber got all over my fingers. I wiped myself on Fernández's T-shirt, and he slapped it away. Too late. The white saliva slobber was on him, a big foamy wet spot on his chest. I dragged my fingers through the desert dust to get the rest of it off me. I had six more jawbreakers in my jean pockets.

Chuy was sitting in the back seat of the Buick, red foam dripping down his mouth. He seemed happy looking around the bottom of the ditch through the shattered windows, gawking up at the sun through the moonroof. He bounced his tied-up hands on his lap and looked at Joe fiddling with the copper wire around his legs. The wire wasn't long enough to fasten around both legs and the front seat frame.

"Just tie up one leg to the bar," I said, "'cause if he can't run with one leg he can't run with two." Joe looked up and glared at me, but he tied a one-legged tie. We had ourselves a prisoner, if only a happy moron at that.

"Now what?" Fernández asked again, sitting up on the slope of the ditch with his hands on his lap.

"Shut up with your 'now what.' Can't you say anything else?" Joe said, exasperated, just about to pop Fernández one. "I have an idea."

"'What?" I said, cutting a cattail off its stalk. It was about the longest I'd seen this summer, longer and thicker than the ones I already had drying on our garage roof for the Fourth of July. As long as a giant Cuban cigar and about as good for lighting firecrackers.

"Let's read the pecker his rights," Joe said, smiling widely.

"His what?" Fernández asked, stupefied. He didn't get it. When he didn't get something, he put on this scrunched-up face as if we were responsible for his mind not grasping what a normal one would. Fernández didn't have much on Chuy, nothing much at all.

"His rights, idiot. Like *Dragnet,*" I said.

"Fuck *Dragnet,*" Joe said, standing up next to me and reaching for something in his wallet. He was bigger than both of us, older too. No other boys in the neighborhood were friendly with him. My mother had warned me not to hang around Joe. He was a cholo, she said, his family was cursed with the malignant spirit. But I knew he was lonely sometimes, and I knew I was his friend. "I'll read him his Miranda shit."

"What's that?" Fernández asked, standing up and peering at a piece of paper in Joe's hand.

"You have a right to remain silent. . . ."

"It says 'Miranda Rights' on top," I said.

"Anything you say can and will be used against you in a fucking court of law. . . ."

"Who the hell is Miranda? Is it the chick who wrote that?" Fernández asked with his scrunched-up face again. "Who is it?"

"You have a right to an attorney, you have a right to be a re-tard, you have a right to be my slave forever."

"Araaaayia! Araaaayia!"

"Give him another one, Turi. Shut him up. You don't have a right to breathe unless I say so," Joe said loudly, stunning Chuy into silence with a raised index finger in his face. I popped another jawbreaker into the fat mouth, a lime-flavored one, and Chuy's face turned up toward the moonroof in beatific happiness again.

"I'm gonna start a fire. I need a smoke," Joe said, stepping away from the station wagon, bored with the game. He strode to an open space among the weeds in the ditch and put his lighter to a dried-up tumbleweed. He threw a piece of cardboard on it and a plank and some scraggly branches. Soon there was a blaze in the open space of our tunnel, about waist-high. Fernández threw rocks at the puddles of slime in the ditch, aiming for two empty beer bottles floating next to a dead frog. I watched Joe roll out a tiny sheet of paper on his knee, sprinkle a sliver of marijuana from a plastic zip-lock bag onto the sheet, and roll it back up tightly into a crooked, lumpy roll. He licked the edge of it before pressing it together.

"Ese Turi, do you want some?" Joe asked, taking his first long inhale of the lighted weed.

"You know I don't. I don't like it," I said. I felt a little stupid myself.

"Well I thought you changed your mind," he said.

"No I didn't," I said.

"I'll smoke it, give me some," Fernández said, looking at me with a smirk. Now I felt ashamed. Fernández was usually a coward.

"Since when are you smoking pot?" Joe challenged, almost like a big brother.

"Since about a week. Roberto Luján gave me some behind the stadium, when I went to play basket at Ysleta High," Fernández said triumphantly. All of a sudden the little thirteen-year-old I knew from down the street, the runt I used to pound into submission with my fists, seemed older, worldly, threatening. I popped a cherry jawbreaker into my mouth.

"Here then," Joe said, holding up the crude cigarette. He didn't seem to care one way or another. Joe was content to sit under the sun, quietly smoking his cigarette with or without company.

Fernández put the cigarette to his lips and expertly inhaled the acrid smoke slowly into his lungs. He didn't move his face on purpose, like a rock trying to be a stone. Fernández handed the cigarette back to Joe, who didn't even look up from scrutinizing the fire. Joe took a toke and suspended the weed between his fingers. Fernández tried to suppress a cough, but he still coughed up a huff of air. I gave him a big smile.

"I know. Let's torture el pinchi Chuy. Let's torture the re-tard," Fernández said, striding down the ditch toward the station wagon. Chuy seemed asleep, his head against the seat, his eyes closed.

"Leave him alone," Joe snapped, his eyes still on the fire. "If he wakes up and starts hollering again, I'm gonna tie *you* up."

I heard my mother calling me from our backyard. The ditch was behind it, running alongside San Lorenzo Street. I could see her peer over the rock wall and search for me up and down the banks of the ditch. My mother went back into the house, and I heard the screen door slam shut.

"I better go. La jefa is calling me," I said, turning to Joe. I could see Fernández stalking the perimeter of the station wagon, jumping over the puddles of water. His eyes were fixed to the ground.

"Ese Turi, can you give me some of your mama's enchiladas again? Just like last week?" he asked quietly, glancing up toward the station wagon to see where Fernández was.

"Well, we might be having flautas tonight," I said.

"Hey, I love flautas. Anything, you know. Just through the back of the fence, just like last week, okay?" he said.

"No problem," I said. I saw that Fernández had gotten a stick, about three feet long, and was taunting Chuy with it, poking him in the stomach.

"Mi jefe beat the crap out of me last night," Joe said, his head down again, his eyes on the fire. "Estaba borracho." I had noticed the welts on his face, his black eye, which was blood red and terribly swollen. I had thought that Joe had been in a fight again, that the other guy must've been dead 'cause Joe could be tough, muscular, mean. I knew Joe always carried a knife in his boot pocket.

"What did you do?" I asked stupidly.

"I let him hit me. He's my father," he said. "I just tried not to get hurt too much. I'm staying here tonight."

I heard the screen door slam shut again. "I'm going. Around seven, okay?" I said and started up the ditch toward the tumbleweed entrance of our tunnel. I remembered, as I walked out onto the ditch bank, that I didn't even know if Joe had a watch. I didn't know if he had *ever* had one.

Now I didn't see firsthand what happened between the time I left the two of them with Chuy and when I heard the commotion in the ditch behind our backyard, with the ambulance siren wailing in the late afternoon and the police cars roaming the neighborhood until dark. Joe told me about it later. This is what he said, as near as I can remember it.

After I left, Joe got up and went to buy a six-pack at Emma's. That's about a twenty-minute walk round-trip from the corner of San Lorenzo and San Simon. That is, if old man Julian isn't asleep in the back room and answers the door right away. Joe didn't say anything about the old geezer, so I assume he was sitting on the porch waiting for anyone to show up. Joe showed up, and he bought what he always buys, a six-pack of Coors. By the time he got back to the tunnel in the ditch, he had already drunk a can of beer and stopped to piss it off behind the Gonzalez house. I think he had once gone out with Leticia Gonzalez, and maybe the place seemed familiar to him. Anyway, that's where he pissed.

So he returned to the tunnel in what couldn't have been more than an hour. And guess what the idiot Fernández had done? He had set fire to the tumbleweeds and the grass around the station wagon, he had thrown wood and shit onto it to make it as if he were roasting poor Chuy alive, like a luau pig. He was just fucking pretending, he said, pretending to put the fire all around the other idiot and burn him up. By the time Joe was walking down the tunnel of brush toward the station wagon, Fernández was trying to stomp the fire out. His sneakers were melting, his pants caught fire, and Joe pushed him away and into the slimy water. Then Joe tried to beat the fire with an old coat somebody had left behind. Chuy was screaming wildly. He screamed and shrieked although the fire still wasn't on him. But it was all around him. The fire was burning up the front seat. The moonroof cracked in the heat and crashed down on Chuy's face. Joe took an empty paint can and was pitching water into the blaze in the back seat, as much as he could with each canful. Fernández stumbled up the ditch bank and ran home. Chuy was jumping up and down and holding his tied-up hands to his face, against the flames in front of him. Jumping up and down and yelling a long scream that Joe said sounded like a freight train's whistle. Joe reached in and pulled Chuy's tied-up foot for a second, pulled it so he could free the other idiot and maybe snap the goddamn wire, but he couldn't. The fire scorched Joe's hand and forearm, burned it like a steak so that his skin wrinkled up and hissed and stung with such a deep pain that he wanted to cut it off to free himself of the agony.

Chuy must've felt the tug at his leg. For as soon as Joe fell back and dunked his fiery arm in the algae water, Chuy jumped off the back seat and discovered his legs and took a step out of the station wagon as if someone had tied his shoe laces together secret-like. Plop. Chuy fell right on top of the blaze outside the car door, his leg still tied up to what was left of the front seat, and the poor bastard wiggled crazily on top of the fire, and hissed and screamed until his burned-up flesh stunk so much that you couldn't smell the slimy water in the ditch anymore. Then he stopped moving and fired up like a Duraflame.

Joe walked home holding up his arm just as the fire raced up the ditch banks in a cloud of black smoke high above Ysleta. The neighbors had seen the smoke and called the fire department, and they had seen Joe but didn't pay him no mind then. That ditch went up in flames at least once a year for as long as I can remember, so whoever happened to junk his cigarette in the tumbleweeds just started what was going to happen sooner or later anyway. It's just that the ditch never burned with some idiot in it before. So after the firemen rode in from Alameda Street with all of their commotion, they started hosing down the grass and the pile of tires and the like. The little cabrones in the neighborhood probably ran after the fire truck like they always do, and climbed on the truck when the firemen weren't looking. And the gringo firemen patted the kids on the head and went about their business stomping the bushes and spraying their waterhoses with that deafening drone from the fire truck. Then, at the bottom of the ditch, I'm sure one of them got real curious. Next to El Muerto's station wagon was something round and blackened and wearing sneakers. They didn't know it was Chuy yet. They just knew it wasn't a charred-up Michelin man.

Joe said he went home. His father wasn't there; the house was empty. With his free arm, Joe broke open a couple of eggs in a dish and patted the egg whites onto the burnt skin on his arm. This made the pain recede. He said he wrapped it up in gauze and sat down to drink a beer before he packed up some clothes in a Safeway bag, his father's Raven MP-25, and whatever cash he could find. Joe never showed me the Raven, but I didn't think he was lying. He didn't care enough to lie. He just did what he did, and that's how he said it. He hid for a while in the ditch behind Carl Longuemare Road. *That* ditch is actually an irrigation canal for the cotton fields on Americas Avenue and for the fields beyond the maquiladoras, unlike the ditch behind my house, which is mostly ornamental, good for draining off the two or three summer downpours we get in the El Paso desert. But ours is still a good ditch to play in, even after Chuy got himself killed in it.

I knew the police were looking for Joe. They knocked on all the houses on San Lorenzo Street, including mine. Luckily my mother wasn't there. Doña Maria had called her, and together they had walked down the street to see Doña Lupe, who was hysterical, my mother said later. She loved her little re-tard. So the police came, and I walked out to the fence with Lobo growling and jumping against the chainlink, and I told them my mother wasn't home. They asked if I had seen a José Domínguez of the neighborhood, and I said I hadn't. They went next door with that shithole Don Eugénio, who never returns any of my baseballs, and so on down the street. I never told them anything, and that includes my mother. I should've told them that there was still another stupid idiot in the neighborhood and that his name was Horácio Fernández. But I didn't.

After I ate dinner, I went out back with a plateful of flautas, frijoles, and rice. My mother didn't see me, and my dad was watching TV. I also took some scraps for Lobo, mainly a thick round bone from the brisket for the flautas. This way the dog wouldn't keep begging for what I carried up high on the plate. That was for Joe, if he was still alive and not with a bullet in his chest. I waited out there for a long time. I waited in the dark until I couldn't smell the frijoles anymore, until everything was dead cold. Nothing. I figured the police had already arrested Joe for the fire, but I didn't want to believe it. So I waited some more until I got tired. Then I started feeding a flauta to Lobo in the dark, and the stupid mutt gnawed on one end of it as if it were a giant jawbreaker. The wetness of the muzzle reminded me of Chuy's slobber. I heard "Ese Turi" from behind the rock wall. It was Joe, just another shadow in the darkness. I handed him the plate, and he told me what happened, and I told him that the cops were looking for him, and he said he knew that already. "Munch Munch Munch" I heard from somewhere just beyond me, over the fence. I didn't tell him anything about the half-eaten flauta, and he didn't seem to notice 'cause he left the plate clean. I figured I didn't want to add to his troubles. Anyway, he said he was starving, and the dog already had a bone.

That's the last time I ever saw Joe. I don't know what happened to him after that, whether he got to Mexico like he said he wanted to. I'm gonna be a reverse wetback, he said, a mojado without a country. He said that he had some cousins in Delicias who had a farm, that the Chihuahua girls he knew were extra nice. I don't know if he ever got himself a Chihuahua girl. I never saw him again. But I did see el pinchi Fernández again. About a week later. The runt had been playing basket behind Ysleta High again. He was sitting smoking pot behind the stadium with another idiot I didn't recognize. I walked up to him, and he was inhaling the stub of a cigarette. The fire glowed brightly in the afternoon shadow of the stadium. His stupid face was lit up. I punched him right in the mouth with my fist exploding with a hardness I don't remember ever having again. Fernández rolled in the dust and still didn't recognize me. He couldn't even stand up, lost in the stupor of the drug. After that, I never talked to him again either. But I still have a neat round burn scar between the middle knuckles of my left hand, right where I crushed the cigarette on his face.

MANUEL MARTÍNEZ is a native of San Antonio. He received a Ph.D. from Stanford University in 1997 and soon afterward published his first novel, *Crossing,* which was selected as one of the ten outstanding books by a writer of color by the PEN American Center. He is a professor at Ohio State University where he teaches twentieth century American literature, Chicano/Latino studies, and creative writing.

Manuel Luis Martínez

(San Antonio)

from *Drift*

We're rolling around the northside, looking for some place called Arturo's. It's this club that Nacho says we can get into without ID. I don't really want to go because this place is for old people, but Nacho's hot for some chick he met at the mall and she told him she'd be there tonight. She sold him some ugly sunglasses and he spent an hour trying to look cool for her. He even put the fucking things on right after he bought them. I kept laughing at him standing in front of that Sunglass Hut cubicle, but he didn't pay attention because I was sitting at one of the benches behind him as he talked to this girl. He looked like a clown, wearing those shades and trying to convince her to give him her number. But she did it. "So fuck you, fucker," he said, waving it at me. He didn't even have the smarts not to wave it around in front of her.

I know Arturo's will be lame, but I didn't want to stick around the house with Grams another night. Tonight this new kid, Leo, is riding around with us. He's alright, but he's real quiet. An unsettling kind of quiet, a *Christopher Walken* kind of quiet. He's from L.A. and his parents sent him to the academy to keep him from doing the shit he was doing in Califas.

After half the night, we find the place. It's worse than I thought it would be. I like joints that are shitholes but know that they are shitholes. This place is a shithole that thinks it's not. There s a bunch of older people prancing around in suits and tight dresses.

They have a band playing, but they suck. They're trying to do an imitation of Sonny & the Sunliners, playing these old fifties love ballads one minute and then the faggy lead singer going into an Engelbert Humperdinck routine, shaking his fat ass up on the stage. Even the Mexican music sucks. No *cumbia* or *polka.* Just some tired *orchestra* shit.

Nacho finds his girl. I have to admit she looks kind of hot. She's wearing this tight, short black dress, showing off her thinness and her nice legs, long and all shapely. I try not to look at her too much because I'm high and I'm a little paranoid. So Leo and me are sitting at a table watching Nacho dance to the corny music, but he's doing a good lob. That motherfucker can dance. Leo's not much of a conversationalist. He's more the cold-blooded starer, with an almost stalker type of intensity. I don't feel much like talking, anyway. So we drink rum and Coke and chill.

"Wanna dance with Diana?" It's Nacho and he's trying to be cool, like, "You fuckers don't threaten me." I say sure and I take her out for a spin, only I'm not too coordinated at that moment and I'm bumping into people. Thing is, this girl's kind of grinding me. Maybe I'm *imagining* it, but my *pingo* knows what's up. I can't lie to him. The way I look at it, I got no choice. I didn't ask to dance with this chick and Nacho took his chances trying to be suave, so I go ahead and lean into it a little bit. The band goes off for a break and by accident the DJ puts on a nice slow groove. I spin her around a little bit and notice that Nacho is watching us, but I don't care and I feel her put her arms around my hips. So I go with it and slide them around and she's holding me loosely so that I can feel her hands gliding down around my ass. I put one of my hands on the back of her head and she puts her face on my shoulder, only she's facing my neck and I can feel her breath, her lips so close that my *pellitos* stand up around the edges of my mouth. *So what's all this about,* but before I can finish the thought, the song goes off and the DJ puts on some old heavy metal song, so I walk her back to the table. Nacho's looking at me funny, but I play it off and just shrug my shoulders. "She's hot, motherfucker." He seems to be satisfied with that. He takes her back on the floor without skipping a beat.

After a few drinks, with nothing else to do, I find myself almost missing my pops, regretting that I've never heard him play at a club. I wonder where he is. I never ask Grams anymore. It makes her feel bad that her son doesn't call very often. He does send some dough, but Grams needs it all to help out with the tuition.

Elena shows up and she says, "Hey," but I'm not in the mood to talk. I sit at the table and drink up, all the while Nacho and even Leo, who's loosened way up, lead the girls around the floor. "Come on, get out there. Diana's a good teacher," Nacho says, grinning. He's good at picking up heavy vibes.

"Nah," I say. I don't want to go out there. I'm bummed now and I feel like going home. "I'm fine right here. This isn't my bag. This stuff is for old folks."

"C'mon, sad boy," Diana says, grabbing me by the hand. She leads me out on the floor again. She's a little drunk now and I get the sense that she's tired of Nacho. Having my arms around her makes me sad and excited. She smells sweet, her breath like the wine we've been drinking at the table. We go around in a circle, and I realize that I am hot for Nacho's girl.

After, we decide to go to the park. First thing Nacho does is roll a joint. He steps outside the car with Leo to smoke it. I'm about to go out, too, but Diana holds me back and whispers, "Why don't we stay here and talk." Nacho doesn't seem to care. He's tripping by now anyway and he's more concerned with whirling Elena and Leo around a merry-go-round, laughing like all hell is breaking loose. "He's a maniac," she says, but not like it's a compliment. "You're already older than him, I can tell just by the way you look at me." She leans over and kisses me. "Watch out," I say, backing off even though I don't feel like it. "Nacho's been talking about you all day since he saw you at the mall. It wouldn't be cool for him to come back and find his boy messing with his dream girl."

Diana acts mad. "I'm nobody's girl. I'm just here to see what's what. I like you better already, but suit yourself." I look back at Nacho and he's acting a fool now, lying on the grass singing and laughing. I look over at Diana. She really is beautiful, light brown hair and smart, playful eyes that make me want to be with her. I reach over and pull her to me again, this time kissing her without thinking about anything but how good her lips taste, how warm her tongue is as I smooth my tongue over her slick teeth. I'm crazy, I know, but I'm into her already.

A couple of weeks later, I find out that Diana's father owns this *barbacoa* joint called Los Reyes Molino. And she tells me that he always needs part-time workers there, especially on the weekends. I'm not that interested, but I agree because it's kind of hard to say no when she's rubbing my belly, lying in my bed. Plus, the sixty bucks for two days' work doesn't sound so bad, either.

I show up at five in the morning feeling hung over. I didn't want to come. I'd changed my mind, but Diana called me up this morning to wake me up. I guess her dad has had too many workers who've blown it off when they feel that morning hammer come down at four A.M. when they try to drag themselves out of bed.

The building is a squat beige deal with an ugly tin roof and a tacky white sign that says LOS REYES MOLINO: BARBACOA, TAMALES Y TORTILLAS. I can't imagine any king wanting to eat that shit, but I don't have too much time to consider the irony. Once inside, Diana's mom, this fat, short woman who seems to be moving constantly and talking at the same time, throws an apron in my direction.

"You Robert?"

She doesn't seem to know who I am. Diana's been sneaking around behind their backs. She's only sixteen and not supposed to be going out, let alone fucking *cholitos* like me. That's why her parents send her to Incarnate Word High School for girls. They've made the mistake of thinking that being around the nuns and the Virgin will make her good.

"Yes, I'm Robert," I say, already getting a vibe that this isn't gonna work out. She makes me nervous flapping her jaws like she is, not bothering to look at me while she busies herself looking around for something to give the new boy to do.

"Yeah, well, *m'ija* told me you're a hard worker, that right?"

"Uh-huh," I say, tying the white apron around my waist.

"Well, we'll see." She gives me a suspicious look, already sizing me up. "You know I take care of my boys so long as they work, but you gotta be busy all the time. You won't believe how busy we're gonna get today. You just wait."

I don't know whether to wait or get busy, but she doesn't give me much time to think about it. "Okay, you take one of those washcloths, dunk it in that water with the bleach in it, and start cleaning the counters."

I take one of the cloths and start shining up the stainless-steel counters, which are streaked with congealed grease. The bleach smells strong and it covers up the whiff of corn that's barely hanging in the air. "Smells good in here," I tell her, but she doesn't say anything and I decide that will be the end of my chitchat for the day. After a while, maybe about fifteen minutes, this other kid comes in the door. He's thin but wiry and he has big teeth that make him look kind of goofy except for the fact that he doesn't look too happy about anything.

"Who are you?" he says none too friendly.

"Who're you?" I say without even looking at him.

"I'm Renaldo, *vato.* And I've been here a long time." He keeps staring at me while he ties on his apron. "Yeah, that's right. Been here for two years. So, who are you? Some goddamn relative?"

"I'm a friend of Diana's."

"That lazy *puta?*" he says with contempt. "I hate that little bitch."

"Watch your mouth," I say, "it doesn't sound like you know her well at all." He gets this look on his face, like he just discovered a Jerry Springer-type secret.

"Oh, you're *that* kind of friend. You bangin' that *nalga?*"

"Hey, *vato,* I told you to watch your mouth," I'm getting ready to clock this motherfucker.

He turns back toward the bucket with the washcloths and I decide to ignore him because I can see that he's a punk, anyway.

After a few more minutes this other guy comes in. I like him better than Renaldo right from the beginning. He's a body-builder type, but you can tell he's cool. He walks in humming some song or something and he says hello to everyone with a smile. He comes up to me and offers me his hand right away. "I'm Jorge. You new?"

"Yeah, I'm Robert." He shakes my hand Chicano style—thumb-grip, to hooked fingers, and ending with the palm-to-palm. But he doesn't do it corny like some of those old-timers who try, only they're so drunk they get it all wrong.

"I gotta do my stuff in the back," he says, "I'll talk to you later." As soon as he splits, Renaldo comes up to me.

He hates Jorge. "That son of a bitch thinks he's strong," he says. "He ain't so fucking strong. He thinks he's bad, always taking off on those body-building contests, trying to win, coming in here bragging about how he placed." He watches him walking across the store. "He don't got shit. I got more muscles than him. Look at this." He lifts his shirt up and shows me his stomach, which I have to admit has no fat, just a pretty defined six-pack. "And this," he says, flexing his shoulders and biceps at the same time. This is getting a little gay, but I nod. "You see, I just don't go showing it off."

I find out that Renaldo lives in the Alizondo Courts, a housing project close to the stockyards, *La matanza.* That place stinks so bad that coming in from town, when you have to pass the yards where you get off the highway to get to the westside, you have to roll up the windows and hold your nose so as not to smell that sick-sweet stench. Fucking slaughterhouse makes you want to throw up. People usually drive fast to get past the yards. But they drive even faster through Alizondo, or Tripa Courts. Motherfuckers get dropped there. It's known as the most violent spot in San Antonio. Me and Grams live on the westside, but I don't go near that place. The courts are surrounded on one side by the stockyards, on the other by a huge length of drainage canals to keep the area from flooding in the rainy season. Renaldo has to walk to work on the weekends, maybe an hour in the dark, cold morning. He tells me he doesn't care; in fact he prides himself on it. "I'm no fucking punk-ass, man, Lots of pussies in the courts, dude, but I'll walk around by myself and shit. I don't need a fucking gang to watch my back like some punk bitch." He flashes a set of knuckles that's got a Phillips screwdriver head attached between the middle two rings. "I'll fuck anyone up with this. I always got my hand in my pocket, too. Once, this *pendejo* tried to jump me on my way home. I punched him in his eye. Motherfucker's walking around like a cyclops now."

Jorge lives on the westside, too, but in the neighborhood, and he goes to Kennedy High School, which is the best in the area. That's part of the reason that Renaldo hates him, I think. Renaldo dropped out of La Techla, the worst high school in the city. But more than that, it's like some westside *East of Eden* setup, the two of them competing for Diana's mom's attention and approval, only Jorge knows he has it, and skinny, shifty Renaldo knows he doesn't. I don't guess that he's got a mom, either, but I'm lucky that I don't have to consider that crazy-assed manic midget my moms.

The three of us make sure everything is ready for opening, sweeping and mopping the cement floor, wiping the counters, counting the register money. And then Diana's mom opens the doors for the people lined up outside in the gray dawn. The crowd never lets up on Saturdays or Sundays. People line up holding their four or five dollars, buying the meat and a couple of dozen tortillas, ready to take the food home for their families to eat together on the only day they can spend with each other since the old man probably works like a dog during the week, and the mom, too. What's behind this *barbacoa* thing is that the family can just hang together, eating some tacos, making that goddamned hard week bearable.

Hardly anyone drives to the *molino.* Most people walk since they live in the neighborhood and most of them don't have their own ride. This is the westside and if you can afford the bus, you're lucky. The cars around here are mostly big-assed, rumbling, beat-up pickups or station wagons, driven by some poor, tired-looking migrant type wearing a sweat-stained cowboy hat. Those guys come in, sometimes in twos, *compadres,* talking in Spanish, laughing every once in a while while they talk shit about the new *pendejo* foreman or some white fuck who took a fall or stepped through a ceiling. They order a pound of this and a pound of that.

Women come in, too. They come in wearing rollers and *chanclas,* the cheapy terry-cloth ones you buy at HEB for two dollars. Those shits come in three colors: baby blue, pretty pink, and vanilla white. The women don't care what they look like at this time in the morning. They're there to pick up some food for their kids and husbands, and anyway, they only live down the block, and who the hell is there to impress?

We work fifteen, sixteen hours straight. No official lunch. Just a few breaks in the back where you can eat anything you want for free. I try everything. Hot pork *carnitas* wrapped in a corn tortilla. Tamales from huge tin cans that hold twelve dozen. *Barbacoa,* always the "all-meat" for me, which I comb through back there, making sure it is the leanest I can get. I stay away from the *menudo.* That shit smells good, like warm corn, but its full of *tripa* and I'm not into eating intestines. There's *pan dulce,* too, and Mexican candy, and sodas and juices. Eating is not going to be a problem, but we do it fast because always there's *pinche* customers waiting.

Diana lied to my ass. She said it was an easy job, just take the money and give the customers the food. But she didn't tell me all of them would be ordering in Spanish and fast Spanish, too. "*Dame dos libras de barbacoa, toda carne. Dos dozenas de tortillas de maiz. Un cuarto de menudo, doz regalitos, y dame un ojo.*" They say it quick and I'm trying to process that info, write it down on a little slip of paper and weigh that shit out, and they're holding on to their rolled-up wad of ones looking impatient. There's this *mojado* type who's looking like he wants to fuck with me because he can tell I'm a *pocho*. "*Andale muchacho, chingado, que tienes?*" I don't like his face, so I give him my "Fuck you, motherfucker" look and slow down. Everybody's in a hurry and I got all this *barbacoa* grease on my face and hands and leaking all over my clothes. They keep the *barbacoa* in two huge metal tins, and when someone orders it, I go scoop it out onto some butcher paper, weigh it, wrap it. The "all meat" isn't as popular as the "regular" because it's more expensive, but I wouldn't want to eat the regular. We're always pulling chunks of cow lips out of that shit. I find big-assed cow teeth in there, too. I put them in my pocket so I can freak out Nacho when he's stoned.

The thing of it is, I don't mind the *barbacoa.* It's the other stuff that the Mexican cooks in the back scrape off of the cow head that makes me want to throw up. Those guys get to the store Friday night and start cooking up the heads. They load them into this huge metal pressure cooker that looks like an atomic bomb or something. It takes a while to load those heavy heads in there and arrange them just right. They take hours to cook and then those guys go to work, scraping all the meat off. They take everything that's edible off, too. First, there's the *lengua,* a six-pound cow tongue that looks like it's ready to take a big lick even though it's been cooked. It grosses me out to have to serve that shit, but these westsiders love it. "*Dame una libra de lengua.*" I hate to hear that. It means cutting into the big tongue and it gives me the willies. After a couple of times, I don't even bother doing it. It doesn't matter to me how much a customer orders, I give them the whole damned thing, being careful not to let it slide off the big fork as I plop it into a cardboard basket and wrap it up before it leaks all over the fucking place. A close second as far as nausea factor is *sesos.* A big pile of cold, gray brains sitting in a metal tub. I'm like, what the hell is that shit? Jorge laughs and says, That's *sesos,* you know, brains. "People eat that?" I'm amazed at the idea.

"It's good for your thinking, man.

"Fuck that," I say. "I mean, if I was some sort of starving Aztec son of a bitch, I might eat that, but right now, I wouldn't give it to Grams, and she'll suck a chicken wing till it flies."

But the people order it. I've seen a big meat-eatin' Mexican order a pound of it and say, "Hey, don't wrap it up just yet." And he'll pull out a corn tortilla and spread some of that gray gook on it and munch the brain taco down in three bites flat. I guess my face contorts into a look of disgust, because the guy smiles at me with brain goo on his teeth and he says, "Mmmm, that's damn good."

But *ojos* are the worst. They pop those eyeballs loose from the cowheads and toss 'em in a pan, cow pupils all which a way, staring at nothing and everything at the same time. This dude, Pedro, his job is to sit in front of that pan on a stool with a filet knife and cut the brown pupil away. He takes a fork and pulls out the ocular nerve, also gray and looking like a big mushroom. He's about thirty years old and he's got a fat wife who comes in at about nine in the morning. She goes through the back door and takes home this garbage bag full of the shit that was rejected from the morning's cowheads. "For the dogs," Pedro says when he sees me checking out his hefty wife struggling with about thirty pounds of the most heinous "meat" I've ever seen. It looks like somebody just dismembered a couple of murder victims, or like an autopsy. "Dogs love it. It's good for them," he says, smiling at me.

"Yeah," I say, wondering how long it'll be before his dogs jump his ass for making them eat that nasty slop.

After a few trips back to the cook room, I notice the guys are talking shit about me. They're looking me over, cracking a joke or two, but I try to be cool and join in the conversation during break, but they want to put me to the test, Finally, Pedro looks at me, giving me an "Are you a pussy?" look.

"Ay, Beto," he says, shortening my name, "ay, we got a question for you."

I stand there with a fifteen-pound tin of tamales in my arms. "What's up?"

"We wanna know one thing, *vato.*" He looks at his pals to show me that they all really want to know. "Are you a man?"

"What?" I know that he's up to something, but I'm kind of unclear. It's a weird question. I think maybe I'm gonna have to fight someone.

"Are you a man, that's all we want to know. Do you have *huevos* or do you have *huevitos?*" It's a provocative question but I don't think about it too long.

"My balls are big enough," I say, trying to sound sure of it.

"Come here, then," he says. I put down the tin and walk closer to them. They're all smiling at one another. Pedro reaches into the aluminum bin and pulls out a big round eyeball, bigger than a golf ball. He holds it out, looking into my eyes. "Let's see you eat it."

Everyone is looking at me. Brown eyes everywhere, even the eyeball in Pedro's hand is staring up at me, all dull and wrinkly, like maybe it would wink if it still had an eyelid. I take it out of his hand. It's heavier than I thought and it feels like a peeled, boiled egg. "You gotta cut it first, *m'ijito,*" Pedro says, goading me. He hands me his dirty filet knife. So I take it and slice the pupil clear off. Then, with my thumb, I dig out the mushroomy nerve, pluck it free, and plop it in my mouth. I chew it a few times, and just about the time I think I'm gonna puke, I swallow the whole damned thing. Those fuckers are all laughing. "Damn, dude, I wouldn't have done that. You're gonna choke on that *ojo.* That was gross, man. *Me dió asco.*" They've had their fun, but fuck 'em, I figure, they'll chill now.

The day passes quick after that and I'm bone tired by five P.M. Now it's time to dean up, and it's nasty work, but I'm so anxious to wash the grease off my body and hair that I rush through it. Diana's mom is impressed, mistaking my speed for initiative. We're done by seven and she gives us a big smile as we leave. "You come tomorrow. Tomorrow's the big day. Pay tomorrow," she says all loud.

Grams is out there waiting for me and I watch Renaldo take off into the dark. It doesn't occur to me to give him a ride. "You look tired," Grams says. "*Apestas de pura graza,*" she says, wrinkling her nose at my greasy, smelling self. "It's not me," I say, trying to defend myself. "It's the meat. I brought us some for dinner." And I hold up the grease-shined paper bag for her to see. "It's the all-meat."

Elva Treviño Hart (Pearsall)

from *Barefoot Heart*

Mestizo educado, diablo colorado.
An educated mestizo is a red devil.
—(Mexican dicho from the colonial days)

On the morning of my first day of high school, I sat on the porch and waited for my friend Manuela to walk by so we could go to school together. I wore a new outfit that I had made with Diamantina's help, and I also wore white bobby socks and canvas sneakers. My mother had scrubbed the bobby socks on the washboard to get the red Pearsall dirt out. She had bleached them and rinsed them in bluing. They blazed startlingly white against my brown legs. She had scrubbed my canvas sneakers too, trying to get them white again after I had walked through the mud in them.

When Manuela came by, I fell into step with her and her two sisters. On the next block, Irene joined us. Two blocks later, we picked up Rosemary. We walked a mile to school because buses were only for the farm kids and for the kids who came thirteen miles from Moore, an even smaller town than Pearsall. Except for two of the main streets, the streets on the Mexican side were not paved. I was glad that the weather had been dry lately, because when it rained, the streets ran like muddy red-brown rivers, making deep rifts. The cars picked their way slowly around puddles of unknown depth. When it dried, the city grader tractor came and leveled the dirt streets somewhat. Of course, no storm drains existed, so the really big storms caused major damage.

Elva Treviño Hart was born in Pearsall but has moved all over the country. She spent part of her childhood as a migrant worker in Minnesota, returning to her native state to earn a B.S. in theoretical mathematics at the University of Texas and, has an M.S. in computer science/engineering from Stanford University. Only after many years of professional work did she write her first book, *Barefoot Heart*, a memoir published in 1999 about her childhood in Texas and Minnesota. Her current home is in Virginia.

Our little group walked across the railroad tracks to "el otro lado," the other side of town. The railroad tracks divided the town like the Rio Bravo. It might just as well have been the Rio Grande River because Pearsall was really two towns. The gringos lived on the east side of town and the Mexicans lived on the west side. That's just the way it was. The Mexican side of town was euphemistically referred to on surveys as "Spanish Acres." The downtown, the junior high school, the high school, and the post office were all on the gringo side.

The downtown consisted of a few stores, the bank, and the post office. There was no mail delivery on the Mexican side, so Mexicans had to have post office boxes. Our whole family shared Tío Alfredo's post office box. I had gone with my father to the bank often. He went there to borrow money every time we went north again. We bought cheap trinkets at the dime store. And we liked the clothes store downtown because we could buy on credit. For the rest of our needs, we stayed on our side of town. We had little grocery stores called "tendajos," except for the big one owned by my father's oldest brother, Tío Bias. We also had the Mexican movie theater, the big Catholic Church, and lots of cantinas.

In Pearsall, even the cemeteries were segregated. There might have been one or two Mexicans buried in the gringo cemetery, but the Mexican cemetery was pure. No gringo in Pearsall would allow his body to rot for eternity among the Mexicans.

The halls of the high school were shiny with new summer wax. The students were shiny with a first-day-of-school polish: scrubbed faces, new clothes, new shoes. The inside of the dark school building felt cool in the south Texas September morning.

At the end of the previous school year, at the eighth-grade graduation, I had gotten the "High Point Mexican Girl" award. In Pearsall, there wasn't just one award for having the highest grades. There was "High Point Girl," "High Point Boy," "High Point Mexican Girl," and "High Point Mexican Boy." No one ever said whether the grades of the other winners were better than mine or not. I determined to do well in high school also, even though my parents had low expectations for me. They signed the back of my report card without looking at the front. My "A+'s" and my angst over the one "B+" meant nothing to them. They couldn't read the English or understand the grading system. They hoped I wouldn't get pregnant and that I stayed in school long enough to get a job that didn't involve dirt or being someone's servant.

At the high school, benches surrounded the trees. No one told us to, but we segregated ourselves on the schoolyard, waiting for class to begin. The white kids had their set of benches and we had ours.

Teachers in Pearsall came in two basic flavors. One was the out-of-town teachers, who frequently came only for a year and were never seen again. Most of the imports were just well-meaning teachers who couldn't find a job anywhere else. The other variety consisted of locals: farmers' wives, bankers' wives, and male teachers who had family in town. The great majority of the teachers were white; you did not need all the fingers on one hand to count the Mexican teachers in the entire school system.

My first class in the morning was freshman English. When the late bell rang, our teacher walked into the classroom, sat on top of the desk, and looked at us. I had never seen him before, so I assumed he must be one of the one-year imports. We looked at him. His dark eyes examined us out of a shiny, dark brown face. His clothes, a brown coat and tie and brown pants, were unusual in Pearsall, especially in the hot months. He looked the way I expected my college professors would look someday.

When he had had a good look at us, and we at him, he went to the perfectly clean blackboard and wrote "Mr. Derderian, English Composition and Literature." He said he was from Brooklyn and had gone to NYU.

"Now, if you'll take out a clean piece of paper," he started. Rustle, rustle, rustle.

"Ey, Elva. Can I borrow a sheet of paper?" It was just like Robert to come to the first day of class with no paper.

"And for the next ten minutes, tell me about the last book you read," he continued. I waited for someone to say, "But what if you haven't read a book?" But no one did. Maybe they said it on paper. We all scratched away for ten minutes.

My favorite book then was *Bulfinch's Mythology.* I read the tales over and over. Persephone and I descended into the underworld together even as I grieved with Demeter. Every time I killed a spider, I thought of Arachne. I flew with Icarus every time he got too close to the sun and melted his wings. I despaired with Sisyphus. In my dreams, I flew heavenward with Pegasus, the horse of the Muses.

When the time was up, I wasn't done. But I wrote a closing sentence and passed it in.

"Next, I want you to tell me a fairy tale on paper. Any fairy tale—your favorite will do. But I don't want you to use perfect English to write it. Tell it using Mexican slang words, black jive, teenager parking-lot words, business memo language, or Bible verse language . . . For the rest of the class, write down some ideas for this project—or even write the project."

We sat there stunned. What happened to diagramming sentences? Subject, predicate, verb, adverb? Mexican slang? Anathema in the Pearsall schools. Worse than profanity. Obviously this guy was new. He probably wouldn't last the year that most of the non-resident teachers did.

I wrote the Three Little Pigs using King James Bible language. It was as far out as I could go. Then, within the new bounds he had set for me, I had a good time with it. Writing the fairy tale felt like eating candy. I felt a sweet excitement when I turned it in the next day. I knew it was good. It had come from a place in my soul that was joyful and free and that rarely found expression in my Pearsall life.

The following Monday morning, he walked in and sat on his desk as usual. He laid the stack of papers next to him and asked, "Which one of you is Elva?"

I flushed red as everyone turned to look at me. He took my fairy tale off the top of the stack and handed it to me. "Will you stand at the front and read this, please?" He looked at me with that half-smile of his. All the blood had gone to my head and was making my face burn. My legs and arms were filled with molasses. I got up to the front and someone started reading my story.

"In the beginning, God created three little pigs. Now their minds were formless and empty. Darkness was over them . . ." It didn't seem to be me. It was a Bible scholar reading at the lectern at church, except she was reading about pigs.

When I finished, the class clapped. I looked up and everyone was smiling. My story had made people smile. And their smiles were the same as the smile I felt when I was writing the story. Transference had happened.

Mr. Derderian clapped too and smiled broadly now. He asked me to tell the class my "experience" of writing the story. But the experience was over for me; I was tongue-tied and nervous now. I said I didn't know and sat down fast. He seemed disappointed. The class kept looking back and forth between us. Desperately, I wished I was somewhere alone with a book instead of here. He left me alone and went on.

Later, as we were working quietly at our desks, I looked at him out of the corner of my eye. He wasn't handsome at all, at least not to me. But he was very alive. He seemed to be thinking and creating every second and he pulled us along with him.

Our next assignment was to write a diary entry for someone we admired: a famous person, a family member, or a character in a novel. My heroes then were dancers, especially ballerinas. They practiced until their toes bled. Bathed in beautiful music, they danced through their pain, making their movements look effortless and graceful.

Being tall for a Mexican girl, I rarely got asked to dance. When I was ten, I wanted to take dancing lessons, but my mother said we couldn't afford the shoes or the two dollars a week for lessons. I wrote all my longing into my piece, along with my admiration for and love of hard work and beauty.

At the end of the period, I walked out of English and down the hall to algebra. In math there was only one right answer. Mr. Jiles would have a hard time giving Ruth a better grade than he would give me if we both had the answer right. At least this way, I could come out even. I made sure there was no possible way he could take off points: I copied the problem down neatly, showed every single step neatly, and put a box around the answer neatly.

In math I could always make 100% if I just worked hard enough, long enough. My history teacher could judge me less than the white kids, as could my English and band teachers, but I could fight the system in math and win.

So, even though I loved English and reading best, I gave my all to math. Nothing would satisfy me except to get every single problem right on my homework and on my tests. I hated to fight for grades. In math, if I just did my very best, then I didn't have to fight, and I could get the best grade. I had finally found a place where being Mexican didn't matter.

During math, Mr. Jiles was telling us about the previous night. He had been visiting a friend. Mr. Jiles, his friend and his friend's daughter, Marjorie, had watched as a mare delivered her foal. Marjorie, blonde, beautiful, and talented, was two years older than I. Her family was wealthy by Pearsall standards; they could afford pregnant mares and veterinarians. Mr. Tiles was singing Marjorie's praises, saying she had such a strong stomach, she was so brave, so calm, so . . . I gritted my teeth and thought that I would be brave, strong, and calm too if I had a stable of horses and a rich daddy.

The next day Mr. Derderian wasn't there. The top of his desk was clear and empty. My dancer piece burned in my notebook. Toward the end of the period, the principal came to our room. He said he would be announcing some terrible news over the loudspeaker about Mr. Derderian. He wanted to tell us first because we were his class. Mr. Derderian had been found dead at the side of the major highway between Pearsall and San Antonio. This was all he knew. Further details would be forthcoming.

I never knew the real story. Rumors were that he was naked and several miles from his car. There was evidence that someone else had been with him—there was possibly foul play, possibly he had been hit by a car, possibly he was homosexual.

The desk sat empty for several more days. We did math homework in English class. A local matron replaced him. She asked us to read *Great Expectations* and write a book report. She had us write about our summer vacation. Ruth wrote about going to summer camp and swinging from a rope into the cool water of the Blue Hole at Wimberley. I wrote about visiting my sister at the edge of the Arroyo del Alazán, deep in the Mexican west side of San Antonio, and the joy of playing with my new baby nephew, even though it was among the broken glass and weeds. I was afraid the subject matter would influence the grade, but anything else would have been fiction.

Mrs. Ballard, my sophomore-year geometry teacher, was the best. She was severely handicapped, which is probably the reason she ended up in Pearsall. She walked slowly, moving her deformed legs and arms carefully. But this didn't stop her from much. She was cheerful, married, and had two babies. She couldn't make her arms work to write on the board, but she could make her hands work on an overhead projector.

She loved geometry teaching, and kids, and she pushed us to the limit. But my limit was miles above that of anyone else in the class. Working geometry problems in clean bobby socks and a dress was trivial compared to working for my father in Minnesota. The perfect logic and symmetry of geometry proofs appealed to my sense of order.

Her grading method was to give everyone longer tests than anyone could possibly finish in a one-hour class. And then she graded on a curve. I worked at home for days before a test as if training for a marathon. Every problem in the previous chapters, even all the ones that had never been assigned as homework, became practice exercises for me. Changing the most difficult ones, I worked those. I pushed myself to work harder and harder geometry proofs faster and faster.

By the time the test was handed out on test day, every single problem was trivial to me; the only thing that mattered was speed. I worked like a madwoman.

I beat her system. I finished her monster tests and still got every single problem correct. If she graded on a normal curve, I would get 100% and everyone else would fail.

She asked me to separate myself from the class. She asked me to work ahead in the book alone. She would get James, a teacher's son in another class, whose only interest in the world was math, to work with me.

I tried it. The work itself continued to be no problem, but I was paying the lonely price of succeeding too well. Before this, my friends would ask to see my geometry homework in the morning before class. They copied my answers to the problems they hadn't been able to work on their own. Now they looked at each other's work. In the past, I could amaze everyone and get huge satisfaction by proving a complicated problem on the board. Now I was no longer part of the class.

I couldn't do it. The loneliness of the new regime devastated me. I requested permission to go back to working with the class with the understanding that I would be graded separately from them.

The truth was that what I loved was not so much the geometry. What I loved was clearly being the best—not in anyone's opinion, but in fact. I had finally found a place where I could not only be equal to the gringos, but clearly better.

It was at this time that my first writing muse came to me. I called her a muse because she inspired me to write, but she was really more of a mentor, mother, and supporter all in one. She came to me through the written page and very much encouraged me to write about everything. Her name was Soledad (Solitude). I addressed all my diary entries to her. She comforted me in my aloneness. She understood everything I said in English, but she answered me mostly in Spanish, which I loved.

Journal entry:

Me: Soledad, where are you? Here I am alone again, looking for you, as always.

Soledad: Aquí estoy, Preciosa. Ya no estás sola. Ven aquí, cuéntame donde has estado, cuéntame tu vida. Aquí estoy. Solo para ti, mí amor. Cuéntame.

Me: Today my Algebra II teacher invited me to be on the Number Sense team to compete in the InterScholastic League.

Soledad: Ay qué bueno, mija. Ha de pensar muy bien de ti. Cuéntamelo todo. Dime qué es "Number Sense" y cómo van las cosas.

Me: Well, to participate in Number Sense competitions, you learn how to do math problems in the shortest amount of time. You learn hundreds of shortcuts and clever ways to do math in your head. The more shortcuts you learn, the faster you can work math problems in the Number Sense competitions.

Soledad: Qué bueno, hija. ¡Eso lo podrás usar toda la vida!

Me: Yes, I know, but I'm afraid. I prefer to think on paper, the way I do with you, rather than just figuring out everything in my head. And also, I have to come to school half an hour early and only take twenty minutes for lunch. That cuts out most of my social time with my friends.

Soledad: Mira en tu corazón. Allí está la respuesta.

Me: Yes, I see. I have to do it. Thanks for talking it out with me.

Soledad: Aquí, en el otro lado del papel, estoy siempre para ti. Háblame seguido.

Sometimes at night, after my homework was done and my parents were in bed asleep, I wrote to Mr. Derderian, telling him how much his half-smile and his encouragement had meant to me. When he had smiled at me, he had looked straight into my face. I was a real person to him, not a Mexican, not a non-gringo, but a real person with a life, hopes, dreams, and expectations. I had things to say, unspoken opinions, and creative juices. He saw all of that in me, and his seeing it made me bigger than I was.

As a tribute to him, I wrote journal entries for him. In them I described why I had left Brooklyn and come to this dusty south-Texas town. I told how I had come by my dark, shiny brown skin. I described my death.

So my sleeping parents wouldn't hear, I cried quietly into my pillow. I cried for all the affirmation I wouldn't get, for all the hopes, fears, and opinions I had inside that no one would ever hear.

One afternoon after school, Tío Manuel came to talk to my father about some business at the Buenos Aires Cantina that Apá managed for him. But my father was out, so he sat in a lawn chair to talk to me instead.

"Your father tells me you're an excellent student," he said.

"Everyday I fight the good fight, Tío."

"What's your favorite subject?" he asked.

"I enjoy English best because I like reading and writing, but my best grades are in math."

"Is that so? I'm starting a big new job soon, and I'm going to use a lot of math. Maybe you could help me figure some of it out."

I quailed deep in my stomach. I was great at academics but poor at life.

I remembered a time when the whole family had been in the car going to visit some farm relatives. The farm gate had been latched and I had begged to be the one to jump out of the car to open it. This was normally Rudy's job. Apá let me go. I jumped out and ran to the gate. I fumbled with the latch until Apá lost all patience. He yelled something about "muchacha inútil" and sent Rudy to open the door. I walked back to the car in disgrace, knowing I would never be as good at life as my brother or my father.

Another time, when Rudy was out with friends, Apá had asked me to dice the jalapeños for the salsa. Normally Rudy diced jalapeños, onions, and tomatoes for the salsa. In the midst of the job, I accidentally rubbed my eyes and they caught fire. I ran, crying and half-blinded, to the faucet. I tried to wash my eyes with the backs of my hands. All I succeeded in doing was turning up the fire with soap in my eyes. Everyone in the kitchen laughed.

"¡Qué muchacha más inútil!" Apá had said amid guffaws. It was only one of many times he had called me a useless girl. In my father's eyes, Rudy was the useful one. He was the one who got to work with Tío Manuel on Saturday as a carpenter's apprentice. When Apá had a job that required dexterity and common sense, he gave it to Rudy. I was sent to fetch water when he was thirsty, and I was the go-for-this and go-for-that one.

If I failed at this project Tío Manuel wanted help with, he too would think of me as a muchacha inútil. This hurt particularly because Tío Manuel was my favorite uncle. He was the man I most admired.

Tío Manuel was Apá's most successful brother. The two of them grew up in Mexico and no one in the family had gone to school past the fourth grade, but Tío Manuel had wanted to very badly. In his school days, he had boarded in town with a childless couple. They grew fond of him and recognized his potential. Finally this couple went out to the ranch and tried to convince Manuel's parents to let them adopt him and send him to school in Monterrey. Alarmed at the prospect of losing him, his mother Santa pulled him out of school and put him to work on the ranch.

So Tío Manuel educated himself. He learned enough math and reading and business to be a prosperous carpenter who bought plots of land, built houses, and sold them at a nice profit, which he then reinvested in more land. When we visited him at his house, he was frequently reading with a dictionary at his side, or filling pages with sums and figures for his work.

On weekends, Rudy and Luis went to work with Tío Manuel as carpenter's apprentices. His apprentices buzzed around him amid mounds of fragrant sawdust. He insisted that the workers around him hum with activity, that they work as hard and as consistently as he did, which was at a furious, nonstop rate. He barked out orders to his minions, wanting it done pronto! And they got busy, running, not walking, to their tasks, the way he liked it. Sawhorses were set up everywhere at his work sites. The sounds of hammers and saws filled the air. Biting into the wood. Making it into a dwelling. Slackers could expect a clod of dirt to hit them hard as a reminder to pick up the pace. Pearsall dirt is soft, sandy loam, so the indignity hurt a lot more than the blow.

I've heard of a Protestant work ethic. I've heard Mexicans are lazy; they'll do it mañana. But I never saw anyone work harder, more diligently, or with more ganas than my Tío Manuel.

My two brothers learned carpentry at Tío Manuel's side, as did his children and grandchildren. He drove them hard. "Want me to cut it off'?" he would ask Rudy if he held the hammer by the middle of the handle, instead of by the end of the handle, which is the correct way. He made me want to be a carpenter. It seemed like the most honorable, clean profession in the world.

I didn't like housework, laundry, the hot kitchen. Watching my Tío Manuel sharpen his flat carpenter's pencil and then whip out figures and sums right on a wooden plank, I became envious of his apprentices.

"Don't get too close, mija; you could get hurt." A building site was no place for a girl. I was the one who got out of the car to deliver the hot lunch. The bringer of hot tortilla tacos and cool salsa.

Tío Manuel finally brought me the problem he was having trouble with. It had to do with cone-shaped holes in the ground, cubic yards of dirt, and the amount of cement needed for the job. It was a huge job he was estimating, probably the biggest of his life. He was to build the Morales feedlots. They would be massive cement cattle feedlots, where hundreds of cattle would be fattened. The cow manure would be mixed with water and fed out through giant sprinklers to fertilize the surrounding pastures.

But what I had learned in school was plane geometry. Solutions for a two-dimensional world. He was working in the real world, with real shovels and real money to be estimated for the job. I couldn't solve his problem. Oh, I worked at it mightily. Research at the library. Ciphering into the night. But it seemed my brain wasn't big enough to hold all the parameters of his problems.

The disappointment on his face devastated me. What good are math whizzes then, if they can't figure out everyday practical problems? No, he didn't say it, but it was written on his face. He never asked for help again. And he figured it out. The best he could. By trial and error, partial figuring, and a lot of intuition, he learned and did things his fourth-grade education didn't help him with.

By the following spring he had finished the project successfully. The meadows around the Morales Farm turned a deep, lush green, dotted with yearling calves.

Even in math, where I was most successful in school, I had failed in the world. I really was a "muchacha inútil." Well then, I would focus my attention on academics even more. I had wanted to go to college since the fourth grade. Now I decided everything I did would be aimed at that goal.

part ten

the 2000s

David Garza (Austin)

"Compassion"

all the gardens died in the early freeze no more two-headed roses or
candy apple trees chuck taylor's hanging from a phone wire if you wanna
play the prophet you gotta learn your lines

compassion
compassion flowin' in and out of me

i ache all monday morning i sin all sunday long where the whores hustle
and the freaks moan i got the men scared now the cops watch me 'cause i
raise the dead for kicks and heal the sick for free

compassion
compassion flowin' in and out of me

i broke into the sacristy after mass
and i got down on my knees when i found the cash there was no in
the altars and no one in the pews just sister barbara frances playing
pallbearer's blues

compassion
compassion flowin' in and out of me

Born into a family of musicians, Garza grew up with traditional cumbias, waltzes and rancheras, but is now known for his alternative style and sensual vocals.

CECILIA BALLÍ was born in Woodland, California, and attended college there, studying Spanish and American Studies at Stanford University. But her interests come from growing up in Brownsville, where both of her parents families had lived for centuries, and where she began working as a journalist interested in border issues, especially about the women murdered in Juárez, a project growing out of an article she wrote for *Texas Monthly*. She is finishing a doctorate in cultural anthropology at Rice University.

Cecilia Ballí (Brownsville)

"All About My Mother"

She was 21. She was, as they say in Matamoros, *del rancho,* from one of the scrappy ranches on the outskirts of town, which should have meant she was so shy she wouldn't even eat in front of strangers. But the boys she met at the dances in the city were always surprised to learn that she had been raised on a ranch, because she wore the most fashionably daring clothes and liked to converse and go to the movies.

He was 23. He didn't know too much about her, only that he wanted to dance with her that night. You see, he was from a ranch too, but from a real one farther down the same road, where agriculture had paid off in big wads of cash that were traded for gaudy furniture. Although they had attended the same elementary school, their backgrounds had set them worlds apart. It wasn't until he was a young man with a trim mustache that he would watch her across the aisle of the bus from town. He was so smitten with her that when she got off, he would take the spot where she had sat, just to feel what was left of her. Sometimes, when he drove by Rancho San Pedro on his way home, he would honk in case she was sitting by the window or wandering about outside and might turn to look.

But she was oblivious. She had promised herself that she would not date any of the young men from the ranches, whose small-town ideas about the world frustrated her. She had grown up admiring the city lights. From her family's property, she could see them winking in the distance if she walked far enough into the fields, and they stood for all the things that couldn't be hers on that little patch of dirt. There, for six years of schooling, she had squeezed an old rag late at night through the top of a petroleum can and lit it, devouring the facts and numbers she had printed as her teacher dictated them aloud, because too many of the schoolchildren couldn't pay for textbooks. She rose to the top of her class and even got to carry the Mexican flag once during an end-of-year assembly, decked out in her cousin's pink quinceañera dress since she couldn't afford a school uniform like everyone else.

Then it was over: no free education after the sixth grade in her country, and the young women—especially *las del rancho*—had to get a job or help watch their younger brothers and sisters. But she kept on daydreaming, thrilled when she sat by the radio and listened to it murmur of all the great things man did, like walk on the moon. On infrequent trips to the hospital in Matamoros, she would idolize the nurses in their crisp white uniforms. One day, she believed, she too would live in the city and wear a white uniform—maybe a chemist's lab coat. All she knew about her future was that she wanted to discover new things.

So naturally, when this young man offered her a goofy, hopeful grin from across the dance floor that night in 1969, she didn't understand. And she didn't really care for it either, despite his good looks and his reputation as a charming guy. What could he want? she wondered. To dance, he confessed. She hesitated. But then—who knows why—she said yes.

"I like the word 'wi-dow,'" my mother told me recently. She was speaking in Spanish, the only language she knows well, but she allowed the precariously pronounced English word to teeter on the tip of her tongue. Then, aware of the stigma of being a woman alone, she added, almost defiantly, "I'm not ashamed. It gives you personality."

She had slipped on her black-rimmed glasses to inspect the naturalization certificate she had just received. At the age of 53, she had finally become a citizen of the United States. Always on the fringe—that had been her biography. I had thought about this as a solemn woman opened the ceremony with a dramatic rendition of "America the Beautiful" and the robed judge thanked the inductees for representing the very best of this country. Even though I, an American citizen by birth, have in some ways become jaded about the meaning of U.S. citizenship, that morning I found myself swelling with pride for my mother. She herself had been a little distracted during the ceremony, flustered by the way everyone raced through the Pledge of Allegiance. But when the vocalist took the microphone one last time and filled the auditorium with glass-shattering strains of "God Bless America," she blinked rapidly and began to fan herself.

It wasn't until we were outside, walking toward her silver pickup under the warm South Texas sun, that she began dabbing sloppily at her red eyes. For the first time, she told me that when she was about eight, she had briefly attended an elementary school in Brownsville, just across the Rio Grande from her Mexican hometown. She wasn't supposed to be there, of course, a child whose family had tiptoed across the border *sin papeles,* "without papers." She and her parents and her little brother, Raul, had squeezed into a one-room, rat-infested shack. At the American school the students had sung "Ten Little Indians" and "God Bless America." She was crying now because the song had brought back bittersweet memories of how tough things had been then for that bony, dark-skinned girl who didn't belong.

Indeed, for most of her life my mother has been only a partial member of her own world. She was taught how to be a woman in rural Mexico during the fifties and sixties. As a daughter, she was expected to shoulder responsibility without questioning. As a wife, she was expected to serve without resenting. As a mother, she was expected to sacrifice without looking back. Soon it was difficult for her to remember the days when she had indulged in making plans, in thinking about what might make her happy.

The cancer was eating him up, chewing him from head to toe like an impatient dog. His hair was the first casualty. The chemotherapy left it lying in clumps on his white pillow, so much that you could soon see his pale scalp under the few sad strands that remained. Gone were the days when he would spend hours before the mirror gelling it all in place, even though he would be spending most of the day sitting under a palm tree next to his yellow cab as he waited for customers. The tumor was lodged behind his nose, and all the radiation on his face had made him extremely weak. Now our dad used the mirror to watch himself as he performed the daily jaw exercises the doctor had ordered, forcing him to make exaggerated, contorted faces. Plus, something was rotting inside him, we were convinced, because his disease made him smell very bad. Every morning in the hallway, my mother would have to coax me, quietly so that his feelings wouldn't be hurt, to walk to his bed and kiss him good-bye, as my sisters and I had always done before running off to school.

Our father had just turned 36 when we made that fateful trip to a Harlingen clinic, where the doctor announced that he was seriously ill. Our parents received the news together, and though they said little, they understood that in too many cases cancer meant death. "So much for building my credit," Papi muttered as they walked out glumly. When he saw his three daughters, though, he tried to appear cheerful, and since fast food was considered a special treat, he announced that he felt like eating a really big hamburger.

In reality, he was devastated. He was immediately given a dose of radiation and then went to Houston every few months for checkups at M.D. Anderson, where he could get free treatments. In between, he drank himself to sleep and laughed in cancer's face. "*El cáncer me hace los mandados,*" he would brag. It was the cancer that took orders from him. Once, on his way to a bar after he had been drinking at home, he lost control of his car and took down the fence of our elementary school. He would curse and slam doors and throw things when he felt like it, then try desperately to make amends the next morning. It was his way of coping with his downfall, with the fact that, deep down, he understood life was cruelly slipping away.

For five years our mother bore it all stoically, calmly even. She made the long trips to Houston with him, spending hours embroidering Mother Goose pillows for us while he slept. She was forced to quit her job, leaving us with no income at all. But she tried to stay focused on helping our dad feel better, especially since the doctor told her that he cried when she wasn't with him. One day, when he said he wanted some *caldo de pollo,* she rode the only bus route she knew to a Mexican neighborhood on the other side of Houston, where she found the chicken broth he was craving. "The patient prefers Spanish foods," the doctor had noted in his file. By the time she returned, four hours later, the patient had fallen asleep.

As he lay dying, he wept regretfully and pleaded for forgiveness. Then he was gone, just moments before my sisters and I arrived to see him. A few hours later we were riding back to Brownsville in the darkness, my mother embracing me silently as we nodded in and out of sleep. She asked the mortician to dress him in the only suit he owned—the brown one he had bought at the Salvation Army store he often rummaged through to kill time on his trips to Houston. Though she wept a little, she made sure to greet the many people who came to the funeral home to pay their respects. Even when she closed the coffin, she was surprisingly, almost embarrassingly, composed.

It was weeks later, when she was home and we were off at school, that she cried, letting her pain fill the walls of her empty brick house. She cried for the times the nurses had poked him blue in search of a vein, cried for the days his anxiety attacks had gotten so bad he had sworn his flesh was falling off his bones. In those tears went the long nights by his hospital bed, the hot trips to California, the evening he had asked her to dance. Seventeen years later it was just her, her and three daughters and an undetermined future. No husband. No job. No guarantees. She was so young to be left alone, so old to be starting her life. She was 38.

But after all the sadness had been emptied and God had answered her prayers for peace, my mother's anxieties turned into resignation—then into exhilaration. For the first time in her life, she began to feel like an independent adult, and the sensation was liberating. She knew immediately what she would do: She would work hard and take care of her daughters. That was what she already knew how to do, only now it would he on her own terms.

Slowly, she began to piece herself back together. She had applied for a job cooking in the public schools after my father died; nearly a year later, she was hired. One day she noticed a line of people outside the school district's offices. When she asked them what the line was for, they said they were signing up to take the general equivalency diploma exam. On a whim, she put down her own name, and although she hadn't sat in a classroom in nearly thirty years, she took the test in Spanish and received a high school diploma.

I remember when she bought her first car and posed with us for a Polaroid that would be tacked up on the dealer's wall—four smiling women and an equally proud 1988 charcoal-gray Plymouth Reliant, her first new car. In her name. That car was her little mobile home for the next six years, the place where she spent many hours in a school parking lot waiting for us to emerge from a late choir rehearsal or student council meeting. When we had a concert or an awards assembly, she always sat near the front, making every effort to appear interested despite the ungraceful sounds of our awkward sixth-grade band. She made only about $7,000 a year working full-time, so when I cried to her that I would be the only clarinet player at the all-state band tryouts with an old, second-rate instrument, she made mental calculations for days. Finally, she charged my $1,300, top-of-the-line Buffet clarinet on a credit card.

"When you three began to learn is when I began to learn," my mother once told me, oblivious of the fact that the reverse had also been true. In our family, almost everything is a group project, and one person's accomplishment belongs to everyone else. Our mom didn't get to be a chemist after all—didn't even get to middle school—but she has three college degrees hanging on her wall and several graduate degrees coming. And they are all hers as much as they are ours. She is a social worker, a journalist, a lawyer. Even as young adults, we continue to seek her help and her company. It is not just that her experiences help us put our own challenges in perspective; it is that they reside deep within us. It is that a little part of her is with us always, making us the women we want to be.

She has had to swallow the consequences of choosing a different life for her daughters. When Cristina insisted that she had to leave Brownsville to get a degree in social work, our mom was afraid to let her go, but she halfheartedly packed up the Reliant and drove her firstborn to San Antonio. Her heart sank when, walking into the dorm where my sister would be spending the next several years, she saw the students sitting around the lobby, The scene was painfully familiar: They reminded her of sad relatives in a hospital waiting room. Two years later she forced a smile and waved good-bye from the tiny

Brownsville airport as her twins flew away to New York and California, She later told me that she had wept the night before as, for the last time, she ironed my long-sleeved cotton shirts just the way I liked them. The way my father had liked them too.

But a new kind of life, one that she had longed to know as a child, opened up to her when we left. In endless late-night phone conversations, she sympathized with our registration hassles, asked about our new friends, reminded us to eat well and sleep plenty. She came to visit me in California, where we climbed the sloping streets of San Francisco and revisited the migrant camp in Davis that had been her first home in the United States. When I spent a semester in Puebla with a Mexican exchange program, she made the eighteen-hour bus trip with me, exploring places she'd never known in her own country. She took lots of pictures, later carrying them in her purse to show her co-workers.

Then, in 1996, Celia took her to New York. She was horrified by the crazy driving and the subways where people stared, so she insisted on walking dozens of blocks at a time to see the city. On a sticky July morning, they decided to visit the Statue of Liberty. Our mom knew little about the scores of immigrants who had passed by the monument for generations, but as a child she had glimpsed it in books and on television, and it had represented the glitzy life of New York—a cosmopolitanism this little girl from the ranch had always wished for herself.

Standing there in her broken-in walking shoes, her unruly black curls dancing as the ferry glided across the cold blue waters to Ellis Island, Mami choked up and tingled all over as she contemplated that majestic woman for the first time. Miles away from the fringes of Matamoros, Antonia Hinojosa felt she had seen the world.

Erasmo Guerra comes from Mission. He has lived for many years in New York City while working for a stock market analyst. He began his education at West Point, attended University of Texas, Pan Am, and graduated from The New School. He has received writing grants from the Vermont Studio Center in Vermont and the Fine Arts Work Center in Massachusetts. His first novel, *Between Dances,* won a Lambda Literary Award in 2000 for Best Small Press Novel. A frequent contributor to *The Texas Observer,* Guerra is a member of Sandra Cisneros's writing collective, Macondo.

Erasmo Guerra (Mission)

"Once More to the River"

Each summer, as a young girl, Maria Guadalupe crossed the Rio Grande into Mexico to spend the long months at the ranch that belonged to her mother's family. They rode to the river bank by taxi, steered by her tío Garcia. "He was fat," she says, which is about all she remembers about him and the drive to the Los Ebanos Ferry, which she calls *el chalan.* Her father never went. None of her older brothers who still live remember ever going, though she insists that they went, too. It may have just been the women: Maria and her older sister Belsa, their mother, Victorina, and their aunt Petra and cousin Elvita. The taxi left them at the river and they boarded the hand-pulled ferry on foot.

The Los Ebanos Ferry is named after the surrounding community, which itself is named after the Texas Ebony, a thorny tree with horned moon husks; white wing doves nest in its branches; the black-brown seeds are eaten by wild tusked pigs. The Los Ebanos town square is a sun-scorched baseball field, and from behind the aluminum bleachers St Michael's Catholic Church stands empty.

This is one of those communities that upstate folks cannot resist calling "sleepy" and "quiet." The truth is that everyone else must be at work, in the bigger towns, miles away, on the weekday Maria Guadalupe (no longer that young girl of summer, but my mother, a woman in her late fifties who suffers from high blood pressure and too much free-floating anxiety) drives us through Los Ebanos. Most houses are made of clapboard or cinderblock. The smaller, mud brick and straw *jacals* seem slumped over with the pain of calcified bones. The local cemetery, where the decorative arch reads *La Puerta,* the sagging chain-link fence is decorated with pink and aquamarine funereal bows.

My mother turns off at the next sign for the ferry and the gravel road turns to dirt. Up ahead, a line of dusty, window-tinted Crown Victorias and Chevy pickup trucks wait on the downward slope toward the river, where the greenish water flows, opaque and shimmering, like memory itself.

The ferry boat is banked on the Mexican side. The people who wait on this side have come out of their cars and trucks to talk to those they know. We aren't driving across. We haven't risked that since the late seventies on a trip to visit my father's relatives in San Juan, Nuevo Leon.

We park under the shade of a mesquite and walk to the toll booth, which is nothing more than a wooden shack, where a guy, waist tied with an apron heavy with coins, charges the fifty cent toll for the ferry.

"Before it used to be a quarter," my mother gripes.

"*Pues ya no,*" the man says. "Now it's fifty cents."

I hand over the dollar for the both of us.

Across from the shack are the barracks for the Border Patrol. At a separate, smaller booth that seems more like a hunter's lookout, two agents sit outside in their khakis and wait for the next load from Mexico.

As my mother and I wait for the cars to disembark, and the cars from the United States to pull up (the ferry takes no more than three cars per trip), we spot a pair of swim trunks discarded under the thick brush nearby. The drawstring is knotted, the mesh lining bunched and crawling with ants. This happens to be the same summer that a handful of Mexicans smuggled into the US suffocated in the back of an unventilated rig outside of Victoria, Texas.

The Mexico-bound cars start their engines and nose down the dirt bank. My mother hurries alongside, covering her nose and eyes against the up-churned dust, threatening to take a misstep and go head-over-tennis shoes into the dirt or the river. She says "*Uenas*" to the men as we set foot onto the metal ramp.

Down river, a flat-bottom boat floats between the banks of the two countries and cuts a silhouette against the glare off the water. This is the Border Patrol—*La Migra.* The agents are motionless as they watch us drift.

According to one of the ferrymen, we are drifting on the river current, which, in this bend, sends us toward Mexico.

"How many cars pass back and forth each day," my mother asks.

The one guy asks the others for their estimate, "How many?" When none of them reply, the guy concludes, "Maybe around fifty."

"Now why do you stop service at four o'clock?"

"Because that's a full day," he says. "From eight in the morning to four o'clock in the afternoon that's eight hours."

"Right," she says, and then she looks at me with an arched brow to make sure I got that. My mother, still plays the sometimes meddlesome, forever helpful and self-sacrificing mother who does for her kids what she thinks they are too embarrassed to do, like ask questions, get the story. But, really, she likes this. She tells the ferryman that she used to ride this thing as a girl, on summer trips to the family ranch in Santa Gertrudis.

The guy nods and then joins the others who have distanced themselves from our leisure life. This is just another work day for them. They are Mexican-Mexicans in middle-age, which comes as early as your teens when you weather a life of hard labor. They are sunburned brown, wear baseball caps and T-shirts, except for one guy in a sweat-stained straw hat. These are the kind of men who do not miss a day of work unless they wake up and find out that they have died during the night.

At the end of the day, after being driven around town by a taxi, my mother finally thinks to ask the driver his name. "*Pa' la otra,*" my mother says, though I can't imagine "a next time."

Perhaps, even if we never come back, she cannot let go the idea of having someone, even a taxi driver named Acosta, forever waiting for her on the other side. He says he's not always at the river. Six taxis operate in Diaz-Ordaz. Between them they take turns working out of the ferry. Two cars park there two days out of the week. The remaining five days they cruise the town streets.

Driving past the fields, the river visible alongside the road, he tells us that many people drown trying to swim across. "They don't know how strong the current can be. You get a cramp. You stall in a whirlpool. That's it." He also tells us about the ferry accident in the late fifties, when a taxi, carrying four women, dove into the river and drowned everyone. Every published story about the ferry mentions this tragedy, sometimes reporting four women died, other times three. According to Acosta, one of the women panicked, startling their driver and causing him to hit the accelerator and send the car into the river.

Arriving at the ferry station a soldier nods us through. Off to the side, a truck with Texas plates is being searched. Acosta parks his taxi under the faded billboards, behind the other taxi, a shiny Jetta.

A band has set up under the trees opposite a snack and drink vendor, where on the way in I bought a Topo Chico. A snare drum sits on its stand. A bass drum takes up part of the bench where the rest of the family of musicians sits in the swelter. One of the girls seems choked by the saxophone hanging from her neck. A boy holds a battered and scaly trumpet across his lap. Still no music.

I pay for the return toll, but it is a while before we can get back, since the ferrymen are taking their lunch break on this side. My mother and I sit at one of the covered picnic tables.

Two middle aged women who seem headed for the other picnic bench to wait out the ferrymen, stop in front of my mother and tell her that they are going to divine her luck and tell her the future.

My mother shrieks, getting up from where she's been sitting. She lets out a string of NOs, shaking her shoulders and stamping her feet as if to shake off a chill. "*¡Que susto!* Those things make me scared," she says, ignoring the women and giving them her back.

"There's nothing to be afraid of," the second woman reassures. "It's nothing bad."

The first woman eyes me. "How 'bout you *joven?*"

My mother pulls me away. "*¡Ya! vamonos d'aqui.* I don't need nobody to tell me my future if I already have God." My mother is a born again Christian.

As my mother and I take the steps down to the ferry, the band starts playing Las Mañanitas, The Little Mornings, which is a song traditionally played in the early morning of a person's birthday.

My mother doesn't need to know the future when she has the past to keep her happy. She recalls the early morning errands for the nixtamal to make corn tortillas. She also remembers the house, the kitchen with the dirt floors and the walls made of dried mud, the wool blankets for the night chill. On weekend nights the boys from the neighboring ranches came to the windows to sing *Las Mañanitas* to the girls.

Of the family who lived at Santa Gertrudis, she recalls the bachelor uncle, Augustin, who liked to play the accordion and guitar. "They say that a woman left him and he never wanted another," my mother says.

Her aunt Virginia didn't marry until she was so old that most of her teeth had already fallen out and she kept wads of cotton in her withdrawn mouth to look full-cheeked. That's what my mother says. She also says that the new husband would shut Virginia in the house and with a snapped-off tree branch he brushed the dirt around the front door so that he could later check for tracks. He didn't want anyone coming in and out of the house while he was gone.

My mother stopped going to Mexico when she became working age. "Around thirteen," she says. She spent her summers picking cotton and clearing fields. She never returned to school either, dropping out after the sixth grade at Alton Elementary, so that she could help pay for her mother's increasing medical bills. If my mother went back to the ranch it was only for the funerals.

The last time she'd been to Santa Gertrudis, she was an adult, married, with children, for the funeral of her aunt Virginia.

"Over there the caskets are fitted with glass," my mother tells me. "You see them dead, but you don't touch them."

You don't kiss their cold cheek or their liver-spotted hands. Which my mother forced me to do at the funerals on this side. Until now I always thought it was a Mexican thing. It must be my mother's way of sending off our loved ones with the hope that they will be waiting for us on the other side of whatever lies beyond this life.

With the ferrymen back on the job, the first U.S.-bound truck is waved forward a few more inches to make room for a beige pickup the men call La Guerita, referring to its pale color, or the light-skinned, bleached-blond Mexican woman at the wheel. Another truck has a Spiderman piñata face down on the rear flat bed. My mother and I stand on the ferry and face upriver. The green murk swirls and eddies. We watch dragonflies disturb the river surface with the dip of their tails. La Migra is nowhere in sight, as if the whole idea of borders never existed, as if this *norteño* homeland was still undivided and left us free to not be afraid of ourselves.

The ferrymen pull us across. The four, in tandem, lean forward and pull on the rope with their gloved hands. A pulley squeaks against a greased guide rope. The water slaps the lip of the ferry, pushing aside leaves and twigs and trailing a delicate wake of foam. Except for the grunts from the ferrymen, the complaint of the gears that guide us across the river, there is no other sound in the world. The ferry ride has been clocked at anywhere from three to five minutes. For my mother it must feel like a lifetime passing.

It isn't until we're almost midway across the river that she and I notice Acosta, our cab driver, on the other side of the ferry, standing against the railing that faces downriver. My mother calls and waves to get his attention. She hollers that she just remembered that a cousin of hers died in the nearby river of Comales. "Her car fell into the water and she drowned," my mother says out loud.

Acosta nods without comment—what could he say—and then, when the ferry docks, he walks ahead as if to get away. A bald spot gapes through the back of his cap. He is fatter than I remember, white shirt too tight, the epaulets ready to pop their buttons.

The trucks that come across are gone by the time the three of us on foot arrive at the checkpoint. A sober, vaguely antagonistic sign, in the parched colors of emotional drought, welcome us to United States of America. The immigration agent checks Acosta's "papers," a single laminated card that he pulls out halfway from his wallet and then puts back into his worn back pocket, where there's a shotgun-sized hole.

The agent, a Mexican-American like us, asks my mother and me if we're American citizens. I say yes. My mother says, as proud as when she said she was Mexican, "Yessir, I'm an American!"

My mother always served as the ferry between our "American" lives (with its public school English) and those of my immigrant grandparents. She supplied the more sophisticated words we didn't know in Spanish. We asked: "How do you say honor roll?" "How do you say cheerleading? Drama Club? Drumline? How do you say I got accepted to college?" My mother invariably gave it back to us unchanged except with rolled R's and in a lower register. My grandmother insisted she understood, though all she knew in English were bad words, to hurl against my grandfather, who knew what she meant by the tone of her voice.

They have been dead for more than a decade. But the story goes that when she was four years old, my maternal grandmother, Victorina Magaña, was floated over the river in a tin washtub. My mother doesn't know at which point in the river, but more than likely, and perhaps not at all, it was around this area of Los Ebanos, where all of history seems to have splashed through. In the 1700s, Spanish explorers and colonists first crossed this point in the river in their move north. From then on it has been a free-for-all. As the Texas State Historical Commission plaque reads: "The ford was used by Mexican War Troops, 1845; by Texas Rangers chasing cattle rustlers, 1874; by smugglers in many eras, especially during the American Prohibition years, 1920s and 30s. The ferry and inspection station were established in 1950."

For years there have been plans to build a bridge. Ever since President Dwight D. Eisenhower was in office and granted the ferry owners a permit for an international bridge there have been plans. Though nothing has come of it. Every ten years the local papers report that construction will start soon and it will be the end to the ferry. What won't end will be the constant back and forth, whether by car or foot, by inner tube or swim trunk or tin washtub.

Tonantzín Canestaro-García (Houston)

"Cave-Woman I," "Cave-Woman II," and "Perfection"

CAVE-WOMAN I:
I abuse echoes (I abuse echoes)
because they deserve it (because they deserve it)
because they are just empty space
with more empty space behind them
that I fill them
that I use them

echoes
    echoes
        echoes
    because they deserve it
        serve it
    sever it

& they would be nothing without my abuse
you would be nothing without my abuse
you would never cry as much
& you would never be as twisted
you would never feel as much
or think as much
or write poetry

TONANTZÍN CANESTARO-GARCÍA was born in San Antonio but became well-known as a daring and original performance poet in Houston while a member of Nuestra Palabra, the Latino Arts advocacy organization based at the Teatro Bilingüe. She has also been a student at University of Houston. Featured in several documentaries and videos, Tonzi, as she calls herself, made her early work public with a CD of her poetry, *Cave Woman.*

or question death & therefore life
& therefore learn as much
you would be invisible & leave no trace
unhistorical as an animal
only live outside & you'd be a professional giggler
& testickler
conditioned to eroding curiosity
for perpetual bikinis.
You would never contemplate killing me as much.

CAVE-WOMAN II:
I would never have contemplated killing you as much.
I would never have charted or graphed you weekly, daily, at half-hour intervals.
I would never have tested my medicine out on you
& I don't think you could stand deprivation of my special cookies.

I would never have whispered things to you as you slept
& you never would have woken up screaming

"Same reoccurring nightmare again?"
"Yes."
"Warm milk & cookies?"
"Please."
& then you would never have seen a doctor
& you would have never gotten a prescription for double triple sleeping pills.
(They were blue. My favorite color.)
& then I would never have become interested in chemistry of the mind
or have volunteered at the hospital & stolen thirty hypodermic needles
or purchased a video camera
or thrown a party for all of my friends
or filled the blue cups with anti-depressants
or green with anti-psychotics
red with amphetamine-phetamines
yellow with mood stabilizers (for relatively stable individuals)
purple, anti-love
silver, anti-celibate. >>

& I was in the attic this whole time documenting us.
& when someone came into the bathroom (alone)
I would flick on the new surround sound system
(the bathroom walls were covered in egg-cartons pocket-texture
but really to keep the room roughly sound proof)

& turn the volume to minimal level (but still eerie)
& whisper to my beloved altered-state-of-mind friends
how someone was against them
or that I was God with a secret mission

or The Devil, depending;
or that they truly were invincible & imperceptible.

Sometimes I would just laugh & laugh

for minutes & minutes until they joined
on account of they couldn't know where the echoes were coming from
because I was invisible & left NO trace.
(Usually their heightened paranoia allowed them to assume
it was company from inside themselves)

& so I abused them
because they did sever it, did serve it, deserved it
& they would be nothing without my abuse
& I would be nothing without your abuse
of my echoes

Because I do save them
save them
save them
& they are not empty space with more empty space behind them.
Because when they fill me full of sound (sound of waves)
full of sound (sound of waves)
I go to the most open land & set them free
uncave my throat, howl with the echoes

Perfection

p/p = perfection over patience

She sat me down.
"Impatience,"

She called me her child.
"My child, Impatience,"

She said so softly
"My child, Impatience,"

With a queer quiver in her throat
"Mmmy~y~y~y child, impa~a~a~a~tience,

will get you~u~u~u~ no~o~o~o~w~wher~r~r~

bu~u~u~u~t-t-t-t fetal positions

& puddles on the floor

of your hyper-venta-inhale-inflation

due to exhale-liberation

of your hyper-venta(why didn't you tell me?)

of your hyper-venta-venta-venta

oh, my ch-child, deeper breathe now

for perfection is key to attack(no)

for panic is the key to attack (NO)(we have to leave now)

for key perfection IS an attack (NO!) >>

(we have you now)

inhale very softly

exhale not too deeply

for . . .

____VOW!______
_______________________________HOW!________perfect_________
______________NOW!______prevent________high____________
______stressed_________hy____________________________
hyper____
____

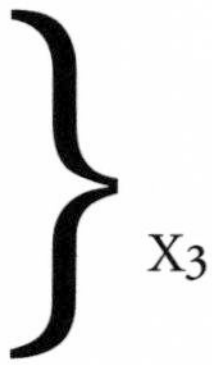 X3

high precision ((NOW)) hyper vision((HOW))

Diana López (Corpus Christi)

from *Sofia's Saints*

DIANA LÓPEZ was born and raised in Corpus Christi and studied creative writing at Southwest Texas State University in San Marcos, where she received an MFA degree. She lives in San Antonio, where she taught eighth-grade English for many years until she took a faculty position at St. Philip's College. A winner of the Alfredo Cisneros del Moral Award, her first novel, *Sofia's Saints,* was published in 2003.

THE MARKET

I draw with fire. After all, isn't it in fire and through fire, the fire of that strange bush that will not be consumed, that God speaks His one absolute truth? I AM WHO I AM. My fire is not so mystical, is no more than the hot iron tip of a pyroelectric pen. I draw my own interpretations of saints—St. Anne, St. Dominic, St. Jude. Instead of in the blazes of hell, St. Lucifer stands in the oil refinery flames that stink up the edges of Corpus Christi. Instead of a child on his back, St. Christopher carries the Harbor Bridge and the Intercoastal Highway. Here in the musty building of the Trade Center Flea Market my woodburnings hang on the walls of my best friend's booth—For Sale.

"Sofía, you need to diversify," Susie says, her wispy mouth fattened by thick red lipstick. She's pretty in a girlish way, a prettiness that would be nice without the sexy attempt at makeup, without the bangs splayed upright like a fan. "You need logos. Pizza Hut or Budweiser. Spanish surnames written in calligraphy."

"Logos?" I say.

"Or a gimmick. Second one at half price or free gift wrapping like those people over there." She points to bins of Tupperware and Slim Jims across the aisle, her fingernail sculptured and drippingly red.

Susie is always thinking about maximizing profits. This whole flea market booth is her idea. She rents the space. She posts a sign above the doorway: Church Things. She sells baptism gowns, first communion veils, unity candles. She runs the kitchen sink to fill plastic vials while making the sign of the cross over her own version of holy water, and she can guiltlessly play the priest because no one cares about authenticity at the Trade Center Flea Market. People here believe in signs. Not the prophetic signs of God, but advertisements. The booth across the aisle sells generic purses, but for an extra ten the salesman adds a Dooney & Bourke tag. Looks like the real thing, the customers say, so pleased. No one can tell the real from the fake, so Susie doesn't flinch when old women buy her "holy" water to dab on their wrists like perfume. She dumps their change in the cash box while I glance at my woodburnings that wait for curious thumbs.

"What do you think?" Susie says. "I'm just trying to get you more money."

"I only draw saints. It's what I see in the wood."

"All I see are splinters and little gnarly things," she says, disgusted by my lack of ambition.

She complains about the heat, pulls at her blouse to let some air in. We have lived in Texas all our lives and should know the weather by now. Corpus Christi's heat thickens the air with humidity that clings to our hair and collects in the creases of our necks. We have air-conditioners and fans in the flea market, but their rotating and venting only stir the dampness. Already midday and I smell the sweat, the crowd's slight oniony odor mixed with cheap perfume and the dried-up pee from a dog chained to a nearby table leg. It stinks. That strange syrup of people clinging to each other. Young girls with their thumbs wrapped around their boyfriends' belt loops, mothers tugging at their children's raw wrists. Susie and I pick up xeroxed coupons for back rubs, facials, thirty-minute doses of UV radiation from the tanning salon. We fold them accordion style. We fan ourselves.

"I'll never look good in this heat," she says.

"Who cares?"

"I do. I've got a date with Frank after this."

"You mean Mr. Silver Tooth himself?" I tease.

"I told you. He got it in the army. That's how they fixed teeth back then."

"Back then? How old is he?"

"None of your business. At least I'm not robbing the cradle," she says, meaning my boyfriend, Julián, lanky Julián, only sixteen years old and me already thirty. He's not really my boyfriend, though. Just someone who comes by when he's bored. I bake for him. I let him watch TV. I give him twenty dollars when he changes my Suburban's oil, mows the lawn, smiles in a certain way that I like.

I know he's from the neighborhood somewhere. Sweeping a web from my porch, I saw him riding his bike and at the same time heard a snack truck blaring "Pop Goes the

Weasel." I waved him over and gave him three bucks for some ice cream. He could have disappeared forever, but he came back five minutes later with two Eskimo Pies which we ate on the porch, vanilla drops on our shoes and chocolate shards sliding down our arms. I watched him lick one off his elbow's inner crook.

The first thing he said to me was, "You some kind of teacher?" and I laughed because I'd spoken so imperatively before.

He reminded me of Donatello's *David*—baked skin, long hair, his posture halfway girlish, his voice and physique caught between boy and manhood. He was all potential, like an unburned slab of wood.

"There's more to a man than his teeth," Susie says.

"Like what?"

"Romance," she sighs, wistfully resting her chin on that manicured hand of hers. I can't argue with that because Frank is an old-fashioned romantic. He buys her roses and boxed chocolates. He writes sentimental poems, memorizes Shakespeare sonnets at the bookstore while Susie sifts through *Glamour* magazines. *Let me not to the marriage of true minds,* he once wrote on a napkin. Susie doesn't know Shakespeare from a jingle on TV.

"You're his midlife crisis," I say, feeling mean. "Love is Dutch these days. You pay your way, I'll pay mine. No one owes a thing. Intimacy is sex on the couch with the TV on, a big-screen TV and Surround Sound stereo."

"You can't be serious," she says. "You think life is one big game."

"I know you, Susie. You have ulterior motives."

"Here we go," she says with an edge of exasperation. I stop talking because she's getting pissed off, and if that happens, she won't call, won't answer, won't let me apologize till she's sure I've suffered. I've known her since childhood. We did adolescent things together like curling our fingers into imaginary lips to practice our kissing, like folding our letters into footballs, stars, or fancy origami swans. She's the closest thing I have to family. She's taken care of me before and I love her for it. So why do I roll my eyes when she mentions Frank? It would be simple if we were teenagers again. She could act out her Cinderella scene and I'd believe it. But she's got ambitions, a fantasy that involves fancy cars, dinners at the Hershey Hotel, shopping sprees with a Gold Mastercard. Frank, the rich tycoon; Susie, the slut-in-waiting. He's only a nurse, but Susie pretends he's a doctor.

We hear a high-pitched voice screeching at us from the aisle. "¿Dónde están las flacas?" Chimuelita, my boss's wife, lumps toward us with plastic containers of food. I spend Saturdays at the flea market, ten to six, but during the week, I work at Pete's, a Mexican restaurant but really a bar. Pete is a real person, not just the name on the sign.

He's the burly man who owns the place and Chimuelita is the cook.

"Such skinny girls," she says. "You have to give your señor something to squeeze." She sticks out her chest, but her breasts lost their perkiness years ago. "Look at this." She lifts the sombrero lid of a basket filled with warm tortillas. I tear off the edge of one, give her the rest. She rolls it between her palms and bites it with her molars.

"Who started calling you 'Chimuelita'?" Susie asks.

"Pete."

"Why?"

"Because my teeth fell out."

"But why did they fall out?"

"Ay, m'ija," she says. "It's the price I must pay for my promesas. Because each time I ask God or La Virgen for something, I give a tooth in return."

"You knock out your own teeth?" I ask.

"No, they just fall out when it's time. I keep them in a big mayonnaise jar." Susie and I glance at Pete, who's by the martial arts booth considering balisong knives and Benny "The Jet" karate books. "You don't think he knocked them out?" Chimuelita says, laughing, her breasts flopping like beached fish. "He might raise his voice, m'ijas, but he never raises his fists."

"You're crazy," we say, laughing too. This is what I like best about Chimuelita. She can take a little doubt and chase it away with a good laugh or a prayer. She slaps my shoulder affectionately, but it stings. She's like the ape that forgets its own strength when it plays.

"I want you to empty those bowls by the time I come back," she says, putting them behind the counter. She walks toward Pete and the people move aside in a way that looks deferential against her enormous size.

"Mind the fort," Susie says, "and I'll get us some Cokes from the snack bar."

She walks toward the scent of popcorn, peanuts, and Cornish hens on skewers, weaving her way through the crowd, her cropped blouse revealing the tanned sliver of her back as she parts mothers from their children and husbands from their wives. In her high-heeled shoes she looks like a girl playing dress-up.

In the afternoon the flea market is a sluggish place. A few customers walk in but only because ours is the least crowded booth. We've sold a few bookmarks and cards. It isn't the season for anything else. The thirtieth of September already. A dry time for sacraments. The catechism kids are just starting school and the wedding peak ended in July.

I smell hairspray and a minty stick of gum. A woman looks at the cards, reads a few, fans herself with the pastel envelopes. I ask if she needs help, but she ignores me. She drifts to my wall, contemplates the saints, picks out the guardian angel hovering above two children on a bridge, discarded drug needles and a television set in the ditch below.

"Shouldn't they be walking over water?" she says accusingly.

"Over danger."

"Well, you can't expect me to buy this thing, to hang it on my wall with little kids around." She gives me a hard look.

"The water was just a metaphor," I explain.

"But art should be pretty, don't you think? Decorative. Not ugly like this." She talks on, but her voice becomes merely noise amidst a whole market of noise—the intercom, the cashiers, the radio commercials, the man calling out from his booth, "Rolex Watches, fifty dollars, no checks please."

This is why I don't like paper—because it's thin, because it isn't like heavy, irregular scraps of wood that refuse to be framed, like me. The minty lady says I have no respect for art's necessary prettiness and with this stubborn assertion, fails to consider—just consider—something beyond the worn images on her TV and kitchen wall. She becomes paper-thin, and I can see through her makeup, clear through her head to the people in the aisle beyond. She leaves when she sees I'm not listening, turns her head sharply, her hair maintaining its stiff inanimacy. *I don't need your stupid money,* I think with conviction, and why *would* I need it except for rent and groceries?

"Catch," Susie says, tossing me a canned soda.

We open the Tupperware lids, inhale the aroma of carne guisada with rice and beans. We eat everything.

"A fat woman is a happy woman," Chimuelita says when she returns. She believes that a pregnant woman who walks in the full moon's light will bear a child with a big ugly mancha on its face. She believes that crossed legs in church are like crossed fingers during a promise, nullifying all the prayers and petitions. She believes that running out of salt in the kitchen causes bad luck for many years, more years than from breaking a mirror or walking beneath ladders. I used to be like her. I used to make the sign of the cross when passing Catholic churches, though I'm not sure why, since my mother never took me to church and insisted that God had a grudge against her.

"He could make the blind see and the crippled walk, but He couldn't give me the one thing I wanted."

"What was that?" I asked, thinking she wanted to spin straw to gold like the princess in the Rumpelstilskin fairy tale. She gave me the you-should-know look, which meant my father, that unnamed ghost between us. After waiting a few years for his return, she stopped going to church and started dating voraciously, fucking her boyfriends in the room next to mine, her door ajar, the radio too soft to drown out the tapping of the rosaries she hung from her bedposts. She took the mystery of sex and made it as mundane as mouthwash or deodorant. That's why I won't give myself to a man. The thought of it conjures up that image of my mother acting like some inanimate toy. She didn't even pretend to like sex. Some of those boyfriends might have married her, but she'd discard them before it ever reached that point.

"They aren't like him," she'd say.

Chimuelita fingers things in the booth, picks up vanilla-scented candles with the images of the Virgin Mary, Niño Fidencio, and the Sacred Heart of Jesus. She gets a glow-in-the-dark rosary, a few tiny pewter arms and legs for the altar, and a woodburning of St. Francis standing half-immersed in the ocean with his hand on the dorsal fin of a shark and a strange crustacean dangling from the rope that secures his frock.

"What's this?" Pete asks when he sees the items she's placed on the counter. He's a big man, a Mexican who somehow inherited that strange combination of dark skin and rusty hair growing along the rim of his balding head and in long, wiry sideburns.

"I'm going to buy them."

"And this?" He picks up my woodburning. "What kind of saint is this?"

"St. Francis."

"St. Francis? Where are the deer and birds?"

Chimuelita slaps his hands away. "There aren't any deer or birds. This is a work of art. Can't you see?"

Pete clenches his caterpillar brows and bites his lower lip as he turns the picture upside down, sideways, then upright again. The last thing he'll admit is not seeing what seems so obvious to his wife. "Aha," he says a little uncertainly. "We'll hang it upstairs."

The whole market empties out when Pete and Chimuelita leave and there's nothing to do but wait for six o'clock. I browse through the light green pages of Susie's ledger, its black intersecting lines, its rows of transactions printed in her perfect manuscript. She has a love for money, counting it two or three times a day, riffling through a dollar bill bundle and smelling it. We go to the sale racks at the mall and Susie calculates the prices of things, never trusts technology the way I do. Ten, twenty, forty percent off, and she has the total faster than the cashier can scan the UPC code. She went to college for this, to Career Point Business School in San Antonio. "She's still off at college," her mother would say when I needed to borrow shoes, cry over a favorite show's cancellation, or eat barbecue with an intact family on a lonely Sunday afternoon. Susie's two years in San Antonio were the pits. I'd call her long distance despite the steep bill. . . .

La Sandía Queen

Street people loiter around the garbage bins at Pete's. Uncombed women with threads hanging from unraveling seams and unshaven men with smoke-and-stale-meat breath huddle beneath trash bags to keep the rain off. When the sun returns, they'll scour the ground for cigarette butts, beer cans, food.

Pete's place is near Emerald Beach where a hospital and a Holiday Inn overlook the bay. The windows are tinted and barred, and the paint on the plywood placard that bears Pete's name is peeling off, is no longer red but a weak rust. It's a two-story building with the restaurant on the first floor and Pete's family living on the second. Facing the parking lot is a mural of La Virgen de Guadalupe, her image no different from what I've seen in all the books—a blue cape with stars, brilliant sun spokes radiating behind her, a child peeking from beneath her red robe's hem, and plump Mexican cherubs floating in the sky. There are sheets of rain on my windshield and she seems to tremble on the other side. I imagine her nose running and her fingers and toes puckered. I once wanted to erase the mural's black lines and make La Virgen's cape merge with the sky. "But what do you know about art?" Pete said. "You're a waitress."

I rush out of my car, the hard rain stinging. Pete's restaurant is cold, the ceiling fans almost rattling themselves loose and the thermostat uncomfortably low. Pete sweats anyway. He always has pale yellow splotches on his shirts' underarms, and he often dabs his forehead with a towel.

I've known Pete and Chimuelita for twelve years, got the job after Susie saw me pour a glass of clumping milk.

"You'll starve," she said, "if you don't start working."

I ate and slept at her house for three months after my mother died, but I needed to return home because Susie was leaving for San Antonio. She told me to put on a dress, and then she drove me to Pete's restaurant because of its Help Wanted sign. I sat in the car for three chickenshit minutes before Susie urged me out. "You'll have to go by yourself," she said, impatient.

I went in and saw Pete picking his nose and then sheepishly accepting a Kleenex from his wife.

"You here to order?" he asked when he caught me staring.

"I'm here because of the Help Wanted sign."

He gave me an up-down look. "You got a résumé?"

"A what?"

"A résumé—typed real neat saying what you can do."

"No, sir. My friend just drove me over."

He scratched his bald spot, gave me another up-down look, and told me to follow him to his office, which was actually a large janitorial closet with two chairs, a black-and-white TV, a Playboy calendar stuck in the previous December, and a desk with dead ivy in a toilet-shaped planter and several yellowing seek-and-find magazines. He rummaged through a drawer for something to write with, finally settling on a purple crayon and a used manila folder.

"What's your name?" he asked.

"Sofía Loren Sauceda," I said, embarrassed by the allusion to the actress. What was my mother thinking? Why couldn't she name me after a relative or a saint like most mothers do?

"How old are you?"

"Eighteen."

"Eighteen? You're not even old enough to serve beer." He rubbed his forehead as if I'd given him a migraine. "You at least have some experience?"

"No."

He put the purple crayon down. "Have you ever looked for a job before?"

"No," I said.

"Because in a real business establishment like this, you got to call first, make an appointment. It could save us both some time: That's what phones are for—and calendars," he said, pointing to the buxom Santa Claus. "You understand?"

"Yes, sir," I said, realizing he wasn't going to give me the job. I stared at the way his robust breathing rippled the red bristles beneath his nose, heard his half-scolding voice, and felt alone in the world—no mother and no marketable skill. I started blubbering, and Pete bolted out the door screaming for Chimuelita till we heard her flapping chanclas and high-pitched "¿Qué pasó?"

Pete panicked. "She just started crying," he blurted.

Chimuelita rolled up one of the seek-and-finds and swatted his back like he was some mischievous dog. "What did you do, cabrón?"

"Nothing," he said, shrugging. "It's like she's got some sort of cry switch." He grabbed a roll of toilet paper from a mountain of Charmin in the corner so I could blow my nose.

"Why are you crying?" Chimuelita asked in a gentle voice.

"It's just that my mother died in a car accident," I said, "and I don't have a father, either."

"No mother? No father?" She knelt before me.

"And my friend said I'd starve if I didn't get a job because she's leaving for San Antonio and I'll have no one to stay with." I dropped my head onto her sagging breasts and she stroked my hair like I was a puppy.

"Well, you're in luck," she said. "There's no reason why you can't work here."

"Here?" Pete protested. "She can't work the bar! She can't wait tables!"

"Can she ask people what they want?" Chimuelita said, standing and getting in his face. "Because that's all it is, Pete. Asking people what they want and bringing it in a timely manner." She waited till he nodded his consent.

"So I can have the job?" I said, hopeful.

"And dinner too," Chimuelita replied. "Pete will fill out your paperwork right away."

She flip-flopped out the door. Pete watched till her swaying hips turned a corner. "That's a whole lot of woman," he said before writing my address, telephone, and social security number with his purple crayon. I've been working and eating dinner with them ever since . . .

Oscar Casares is from Brownsville, which is the title of his first book. He attended the University of Texas at Austin and spent ten years working as an advertising copywriter. Along with Roberto Ontiveros and Christine Granados, he was part of a very successful "illegal, undocumented workshop" in Dagoberto Gilb's garage apartment in Austin, Texas. After auditing graduate creative writing classes at Southwest Texas State University, Casares was accepted at the Iowa Writers Workshop, completing his M.F.A. in 2001. A Dobie-Paisano fellow, Casares now teaches creative writing at the University of Texas at Austin and writes for *Texas Monthly*.

Oscar Casares (Brownsville)

"In the Year 1974"

Leaving home for the first time is never easy. Finding your way back can be even harder.

It was only a few months after I turned ten that I discovered the world. Before this time, I had spent most of my life in Brownsville, feeling as remote and isolated as you could growing up in the last city in Texas. One of our few excursions from home was driving across the international bridge to Matamoros so I could get what my father considered a "decent" haircut, by which he meant a very short haircut that cost less than a dollar, tip included. The barber would bring out a special cushioned board and lay it across the armrests of the chair. Then I'd climb up and sit still for my haircut, waiting patiently during those times when the barber had to stop and make a *ss-ss-ss* sound at a pretty girl passing in front of his shop. Afterward, my father and I would walk to Plaza Hidalgo, where he could get his boots shined and I could buy a candy from the man standing on the corner with the big glass case. I always went for the calabaza candies, which were made of a rich pumpkin and looked like jewels extracted from deep within the earth.

As far south as we were, I knew there was a world beyond Brownsville because my sister and two brothers had left town years earlier. When we drove to Houston to visit my brothers, one of them would take my mother to the mall so she could shop at the big department stores we didn't have at Amigoland Mall. After shopping, we'd go back to my brother's house, eat, rest, maybe eat again, maybe watch TV, and then go to sleep. A couple of days later, we'd get in the car and drive back to Brownsville. My parents weren't interested in seeing Houston. Houston was a big city with a lot of freeways where they were bound to get lost, and did, every time we visited, which was how I ended up seeing more of the city. My parents traveled to Houston to visit family, not to be running around getting lost. They had no interest in the roller coasters at Astroworld or ice-skating at the Galleria or anything else. My father worked as a livestock inspector for the USDA and spent a good part of his day patrolling the Rio Grande on horseback to make sure horses or cattle weren't being crossed into the country. During his rides he had been startled by rattlesnakes, bucked off his horse, and shot at by drug smugglers—he didn't need any more excitement in his life. Besides, it was usually hot in Houston, and he hadn't worked out in the sun the other 51 weeks of the year so he could drive to another city to sweat on his vacation.

I should mention that my parents were older than most parents with a ten-year-old in the house. My mother was 52 and my father was 60. Being older, they had developed certain habits that weren't going to change. For instance, my father believed in sticking to certain meals. Food fell into three distinct categories: Mexican food, which he could eat every day and die a happy man; American food—meals like hamburgers, hot dogs, and fried chicken—which we ate occasionally; and other people's food, which included all food he refused to eat. Whenever I suggested trying something different, like Chinese food, he'd look at me as if he and my mother might have brought the wrong baby home from the hospital.

As I understood it, this was my father's unstated philosophy: *We have our food—fajitas, tamales, tacos, enchiladas. It took our people many years to develop these foods. We even have two kinds of tortillas, flour and corn. One day you can eat flour, the next day corn. So tell me why you want to eat other people's food? Leave their food alone. The chinos have their own food. They like that white rice. But do you see them eating our rice with those little sticks? No. The Germans, I don't know what they eat, but whatever it is, that's their business. The Italians, they like to add a lot of spices. I tried it one time and it gave me* agruras, *and then there I was, burping all night. Your mother had to make me an Alka-Seltzer. And you want to eat other people's food?*

All of which meant that if my father ate carne con papas, I ate carne con papas. If he ate picadillo, I ate picadillo. If he ate taquitos, I ate taquitos. And so on, until 1974, the summer my sister, Sylvia, invited me to stay with her in Austin for two weeks. She and my brother-in-law were in their early twenties, and my nephew was only a year old. One of the first things we did in Austin was walk around the University of Texas, where my sister was a student. Then we rode the elevator all the way up to the top of the UT Tower, and I felt my ears pop for the first time. From the observation deck, I saw tiny people walking around on the street, but I couldn't tell which were the hippies and which were the ones with short hair. Some of my sister's friends wore their hair long, like the hippies I'd seen around town. Rolando had a handlebar mustache and hair down to his shoulders. He was the funniest of my sister's friends, and the smartest. You could ask him any math question, and he'd answer it like he had a calculator stuck in his head. "What's fifty-six times seventeen?" I'd ask him. And he'd go, "Nine hundred fifty-two." That fast. Rolando came along the night we played putt-putt. He beat all of us because he knew how to hit his ball so it would go under the windmill just right. When we finished playing, he asked me if I wanted a souvenir. I said yes, thinking he was going to buy me a T-shirt at the front booth. But instead he took my putter and tossed it over the fence, into some hedges. Then we all walked out, and Rolando grabbed the putter for me. "There's your souvenir," he said.

My last night in town, my sister and brother-in-law asked if I wanted pizza. "Pizza?" I said. I'd never actually tried the food. We drove to a Pizza Inn, and my brother-in-law ordered a pepperoni pizza. The waitress brought plates for everyone, even my baby nephew. I thought of my parents back home and what they might be eating that night. A few minutes later the waitress brought out a steaming pizza and placed it in front of us. None of it seemed real: the triangle shape of my slice, the perfectly round pepperonis, the doughy end crust, the gooey melted cheese. It was as though I'd crossed into another world, one my parents never knew existed. I was still several years away from leaving Brownsville, but in that moment I felt as far from home as I ever would.

My mother called the apartment that night.

"Guess what we ate?" I said.

"What?"

"Pizza!"

"Pizza?"

"Yeah, and when I get home, we're all going to get some."

"If that's really what you want, maybe we can try it." She sounded distracted. "Don't hang up," she said. "Somebody wants to talk to you."

"Are you having fun?" my father asked.

"Yes, sir.

"And you been behaving?"

"Yes, sir."

"That's a good boy." I could hear his stubble brushing against the receiver. "You need to be careful tomorrow, okay?"

"I will."

"We miss you, *mi'jo.*" He said it softly but clearly.

I hesitated for a second. "Okay, see you tomorrow."

The next morning my sister made me sit behind the bus driver. She said I wasn't supposed to talk to anyone or get off the bus when it made stops. I told her not to worry, that I had my golf club in case anything happened. The bus pulled out, and my sister and the baby waved good-bye.

Over the next 350 miles the land changed from hill country to brushland to river valley. I started getting hungry around Corpus Christi and wished that I hadn't eaten my ham and cheese sandwich before the bus left Austin. I wondered if my father would say yes to eating pizza. For a long time I imagined I was in a car on the other side of the highway, headed north instead of south. After a while I fell asleep and then woke up just in time to see my hometown: the swaying palm trees; the fat water tower on its skinny legs, a lonely seagull hovering high above the catwalk; the bell tower at Guadalupe Church; the tamale place next to the freeway; the used-car lots, the used-car lots, the used-car lots.

I saw my parents standing outside the terminal. My mother was wearing her royal-blue smock from the grocery store where she worked. My father had on the straw cowboy hat that he wore for work every day. He hadn't noticed that one of his pant legs was stuck inside his boot. As soon as the door opened, my mother came up and hugged me. "How was your trip?" she asked. Then my father shook my hand and put his arm around my shoulder. When we got to the car, he placed my suitcase in the trunk and told me to sit up front with him. "I hear you want pizza?" he said. I nodded. "You sure?" I nodded again.

Most of the lunch crowd had left by the time we got to the Pizza Hut. I slid into a wooden booth, and my parents slid into the other side. My father held on to his hat until the waitress showed him the coat hook on the edge of the booth.

"Would you like to see a menu or do you want the buffet?" the waitress asked.

She looked at my parents, who looked at each other for a second and then looked at me for the answer. But the truth is, I didn't exactly know what she was asking us. The word "buffet" was as foreign to me as the word "pizza" had once been.

"No, we just want to order pizza," I told the waitress.

My father nodded in approval.

"I'm real hungry," I said, "so I want a large pepperoni pizza. My father will eat a medium pepperoni pizza. And bring my mother a small pepperoni pizza." The waitress looked up from her notepad. "You sure you don't want the buffet?" There was that word again.

"No, it's okay," I said. "We just want pizza."

After she left, we sipped our iced teas and waited for the food. I could tell my father was proud of me for taking charge and ordering our food, the same way he would have.

After a while, the waitress came back and set the table. The manager helped her slide another table up against our booth. My father seemed impressed with all the work. The waitress returned a few minutes later and placed a small pepperoni pizza and then a medium one in front of my parents, leaving very little room for their plates and iced teas. My father looked at my mother when he realized how much food we had in front of us. Then the manager set a large pepperoni pizza on the extra table. "Can I get you folks anything else?" he asked.

I kept my head down and tried not to make eye contact with my father, which was easy, because he was busy eating more food than I'd ever seen him eat. My mother whispered to him in Spanish about this being a special lunch. To which my father answered, in English, that this would have been more special if we'd gone to a regular restaurant. Then he took a deep breath, exhaled, and continued eating. In the end, the waitress still had to bring out two boxes for the leftovers, and my mother had to dig into her purse to help my father pay for lunch.

After this we went back to eating the same foods. As far as I know, my parents have never entered another Italian restaurant. But me, I eat pizza wherever I go—Brooklyn, Chicago, Paris, Mexico City. If some fancy hotel has it on the menu, I know what I'm ordering. If I'm leaving a bar at two in the morning, it's nearly impossible for me to walk past an all-night pizza place. Who knows how many times I've eaten a cold slice while standing next to the refrigerator. Once, I even ordered a pizza in South America. I'd finally saved up enough money to take what I considered my first real vacation. I spent most of my time in Chile, but on New Year's Eve I caught a flight to Ushuaia, Argentina, the city at the southern tip of the continent and the world. To get there we flew over Patagonia, and the massive ice formations looked close enough to touch. Then I spotted the elusive strait that Magellan had iscovered more than four-hundred years earlier. And the land became only more distant and remote the farther we traveled into Tierra del Fuego. As we approached the airport, the pilot circled over the Beagle Channel, along the way passing tiny islands of penguin and sea lion colonies. The plane shook desperately against the Antarctic wind, and I thought to myself then that this was where wind was invented and here was the origin of the warm breeze we felt so far away in Brownsville. I was traveling alone and that night went out to an Italian restaurant, where I ordered a small mushroom pizza. After dinner I walked to the channel, trying to stay warm while the wind whipped around me and whistled lightly, as if someone were calling me to come closer. I stepped toward the edge of the water and pulled out a bottle of champagne I'd stashed in my jacket. An ocean liner was docked off to the side, and at midnight the crew sounded the ship's horn to mark the new year, 1994. People were laughing and clapping in the distance. I uncorked the champagne and took my first drink. The Andes were at my back; Antarctica was straight ahead. And the wind never stopped whistling. I stared into the darkness and wondered what else was out there.

Grupo Fantasma (Austin)

"Laredo"

Ese pueblo de Laredo
es un pueblo muy lucido,
donde se encuentra la mata
de los hombres decididos.

Y ese puerto de Laredo
es un puerto muy mentado,
los agentes de la ley
andan siempre con cuidado.

En ese rancho de Lule
varios casos han pasado,
contrabandistas y rinches
sus vidas las han cambiado.

Pero también en el frente,
porque no eran criminal,
¡decir que no se lucieron
en esa guerra mundial!

Debemos de recordar
que muchos jamás volvieron,
por cumplir con su deber
en esa lucha murieron.

No solamente en el frente
demostraron ser humanos,
por eso en Laredo, Texas,
se aprecian los mexicanos.

Y el que le guste pasearse
nunca lo podrá negar,
nomás que cruce el Río Grande,
hay mucho en donde gozar.

Y el que le guste pasearse,
gozar de toda alegría,
que pase a Nuevo Laredo
y gozará noche y día.

Ya con ésta me despido,
tomándome un anisado;
adiós, lindas morenitas
de ese Laredo afamado.

PART OF THE GROWING independent Latino music scene, with members from Laredo, El Paso, San Antonio, "the border," New York, and Nicaragua, Grupo Fantasma describes its style as "Latin Funk," singing most of their lyrics in Spanish, often remixing songs from the past, as in this corrido.

That town of Laredo is a very distinguished town,
where is found the cradle of resolute men.

That port of Laredo is a very famous port;
the officers of the law always go about with care.

In that ranch known as Lule, several incidents have taken place;
smugglers and *rinches* have taken each others' lives.

But they have also been at the front, because they were not criminals;
let no one say they did not distinguish themselves in that famed world war.

We should remember that many never came back;
they died in that conflict while doing their duty.

Not only at the front have they demonstrated their humanity;
that is why in Laredo, Texas, Mexicans are held in esteem.

And he who likes to go out—it never can be denied,
let him just cross the Rio Grande, where there is much he can enjoy.

And he who likes to go out and enjoy all kinds of merrymaking,
let him cross over to Nuevo Laredo, and he will enjoy himself night and day.

Now with this I say farewell, while drinking an *anisado*;
farewell, beautiful dark girls of that famed Laredo.

CHRISTINE GRANADOS is a native of El Paso and her beginnings as a writer are in journalism. After receiving a degree in communications from the University of Texas at El Paso, she worked a series of jobs in Texas with various publications, including *Moderna,* a fashion magazine for Hispanic women, which began as an insert in the magazine *Hispanic.* Granados edited the magazine when it became an independent quarterly in 1997. A year later she stepped away from that position to earn an M.F.A. degree in creative writing at Texas State University in San Marcos, and her first collection of short stories, *Brides and Sinners in El Chuco,* was published in 2006. She is still a freelance journalist who works at home raising her two children in Rockdale.

Christine Granados (El Paso)

"Pecado"

It was evening when I got the call from my grandmother, Honrina telling me my great aunt Isadora Marmalego was dead. I answered the phone in my living room and walked, cradling the receiver between my shoulder and chin, into the kitchen to get a look at the weather through the window. On tiptoes, and using both arms to pull myself up, I peeked over the sill above me, out the casement window. It was one of those days when it looks cold outside but it's not. It was hot and windy but the sky was a blanket of white. There was sand on the windowsill. The sand got into places I didn't want it.

"Sara, your tía . . . she's dead."

"What? How?"

"Un ataque."

"A heart attack? I thought she was healthy."

"Sure, she was, but también she was old."

You're old too, why couldn't it have been you, I thought, but said, "When, when did it happen?"

"A las tres de la manaña."

"Who found her?"

"Tino y yo."

I cried softly into the phone and remembered my great aunt, Dora. My tía had a way of making everyone she came in contact with feel loved. Her small brown eyes and thin brows radiated happiness. She hugged everyone, embracing them with her large flapping arms and leading their heads smack into her cushioned chest that always smelled of baby powder and sweat. And it wasn't just the typical hermana church greeting, either. Dora gave her affection sincerely. Not like my grandmother who commanded respect when she met people. Her head cocked high, Honorina never let anyone hold onto her too long. She gave quick, tight embraces, and never kissed anyone on the lips.

My grandmother said, "Ahem."

"Do you need me to pick you up, Abuela?" I sniffled.

"No, I'll ride with Tino."

"You sure?"

"Yes, I want to get there on time."

"I could pick you up. It would be one less thing for Celestino to have to worry about." I thought of my great uncle at the funeral. He would look like an undertaker in his suit. And it didn't help that he never smiled. I understood why my great uncle Celestino married my tía. What I couldn't understand was why Dora married Celestino? His bald head was permanently bowed, awaiting a prayer circle to lead. He talked for hours about saving souls especially those of lustful, young girl's like mine. As if preaching every day at La Iglesia de Otros Hermanos wasn't enough for him, he brought it home and practiced on me. I often wondered if JesuCristo was the only topic of conversation he knew. His marathon sermons about adultery, greed, and coveting put me soundly to sleep. I hated church when I was thirteen, and I knew I would hate the church service at Dora's funeral now at twenty-five.

"He doesn't consider me an encimosa like you do."

"You're not a burden at all, Abuela. I just meant—"

"Yes, I know what you just meant."

"So, what time is misa?"

"We're not Catholic. It's a servicio."

"Well, what time does it start?"

"A las cuatro."

"I'll be there."

Honorina let out a low, "Hrrmph."

"See you."

The day of the funeral I tore through drawers and boxes searching for the crocheted velo—the one Dora had made me for church when I was in elementary school. Dora and Abuela had debated about whether the cameo rose, or spring flowers pattern would be more suitable for my first veil. When they had asked my tío's opinion, he sided with

Honorina who wanted spring flowers. Abuela's back had straightened whenever she told me this story, and Dora would laugh and say something, like, "Two against one, means I was probably wrong."

I came across my tía's picture inside the Bible she gave me and inhaled the scent of talc. She was in her kitchen when the photo was taken. I would eat two eggs with bolla, some beans and fresh tortillas in that kitchen every morning during the summers. After eating breakfast I would sit and wait for my abuela, Honorina, to arrive. She usually had a dozen fresh-baked biscuits. Celestino would eat six with honey still hot from her oven, and save the rest for dinner. I had preferred Dora's homemade tortillas and would eat them with honey. After Celestino finished his dessert he would ask Honorina to take a walk with him to the corner store for a newspaper and a lollipop for me. Dora and I would stay in the kitchen making tortillas. When my grandmother and great uncle had returned from their walk, Celestino would sit and read the newspaper, while Dora, Honorina, and I loaded the truck with clothes, food, and ten dozen tortillas. Once he finished with the paper, he would change into his good suit and tie, and Dora would take off her apron and change from her cotton housedress into her one good dress, a brown polyester one piece with small, white polka dots. The dress had a white belt that cut her busty square body into two symmetrical halves. She had looked like Honorina, only happy. Before we women would climb into the truck, Dora would place a towel on the seat so we wouldn't burn our legs on the vinyl interior. From the passenger side, Honorina would get in first, then me, and finally Dora. When Celestino got into the truck, he'd raise his arms with his elbows out, and poke Honorina's side, "Elbow room. I need some elbow room, mujeres."

All three of us had smiled, and he'd start up the truck. The gearshift was on the steering wheel. Whenever he shifted he apologized to Honorina because his knuckles caressed the arm she held out in front of her on the dash to steady herself. She would shake her head ni modo and smooth her dress. If it didn't bother her, it didn't bother him and soon he stopped apologizing every time his knuckles came in contact with her soft fleshy arm.

We drove for what seemed like hours, until the paved roads became gravel and finally hard packed sand then past the hard sand to the loose dirt until we came upon the tin and wooden-pallet homes of Celestino's parishioners.

Four hours later I was still searching for the velo until I remembered I had thrown it away in a fit. "It's ridiculous that the women of the church, de La Iglesia de Otros Marranos, have to hide their hair and bow their heads in servitude." I laughed folding my hands in mock prayer in front of me. I snatched the delicate, white veil from my head and tossed it into the junk pile in front of my live-in boyfriend.

At the funeral home I cursed myself for throwing away something made by Dora's own hands. As I stepped inside the hot adobe building with no air conditioner the smell of sweat and eucalyptus made me nauseous. When I was a teenager, I lived in fear of my tío. Whenever he caught me talking to a boy, Celestino would drag me to church, which was always filled with parishioners, no matter the time of day. Made me lay on the floor near the wooden podium, then he and his parishioners joined hands, encircled me, and prayed. I saw up the women's skirts. The heat, my fear, and my guilt coupled with the sweat and eucalyptus odors, always made me vomit. This was taken as a sign that my lustfulness was being banished, and they prayed harder. After hours of prayer, exhausted, I would fall asleep and wake up at home in Dora's lap. I steadied myself, then followed the voice of a preacher through the foyer and into the chapel. The small room was filled with Dora's family, and the people of the church.

I remember their homes from my tío's ministry. I remember Dora's lectures too. "Don't drink any water they give you," she had said, pointing at me. "Be polite and tell them 'no thank you, I'm not thirsty.' If you're thirsty ask me for water. Don't eat anything they give you, but be polite. If you're hungry, just wait and remember we will eat at home. You remember what happened last time."

The first time I had gone to Moon City, I had drank the horchata the family we ministered to had offered me. On the trip I had thrown up the rice juice, my breakfast, and lots of water. I had liquid oozing out of my mouth, nose, and backside. I had fallen asleep while I vomited. Dora had never left my side. For two days Celestino and Honorina had been alone to minister to the parishioners.

"Ay, mijita, you gave us the susto of our lives," Dora had said when I was better.

She was the one the people had wanted to see. Dora lit up any room she walked into even their houses with dirt packed floors that smelled like shit, beans, and women who had just started. She greeted all the women with a hug and a kiss, and Celestino followed her lead saying hello with a reserved hug and a kiss, then Honorina embraced the hermanas. Celestino greeted the hermanos with the same quick stiff hugs that Honorina gave the sisters. He seemed older than Dora, even back then, despite the fact that they were both fifty-one. He seemed older than Honorina who was fifty-five. My job on those trips was to occupy the children, while Celestino prayed for the sick. After the hour was over and I was red from standing in the sun, Dora would call for me from inside the one-room house. Honorina and Celestino walked arm-and-arm to another house for yet another prayer, while Dora and I stayed behind. Dora explained to the women how important it was to boil all the water they used. She gave them the food and clothes we had brought in from the truck. The women thanked her again and again. Then they asked her to stay awhile and drink some cafesito, at least until

Celestino needed her. She always stayed. Those slight, dark women told her about their lives. How their children learned English so fast they left them behind. How their husbands worked hard and sometimes wouldn't come home for days. How they missed their families back home in Chihuahua, Monterrey, or Torreón. No one ever wanted Dora to leave. I always wondered what Celestino and Abuela did during this time. The women begged her to stay but she said she had work to do, and then finally, after a long embrace, they would acquiesce.

My head bare, I walked down the isle unescorted feeling the parishioner's eyes and indignation. I watched Brother Murillo, who was at the pulpit, tug at the lapels of his tan leisure suit, and when he did this, the button below the collar of his shirt unclasped. The mauve-colored casket that held my great aunt sat on a white pedestal in front of the chapel underneath a large wooden cross. The cross was the only ornamentation inside the building. So my eyes traced the cracks that ran from the plastic ceiling fans down the clay walls to the tile floor before I spotted Honorina and my brother in the middle of a left-hand side pew. While eyeing the thick hair on Brother Murillo's chest trying to escape from the hole where the button used to be, I almost sat on my brother's lap. Abraham made room for me next to he and Honorina. As I sat, my grandmother checked her watch. Not even in grief was she off guard, I thought. I checked my watch, also—six o'clock. The sweat stains on Brother Murillo's jacket told me he had been preaching since the funeral service began at four.

Honorina's velo, with its pineapple pattern, matched her black dress. Dora had crocheted it. I had sat with her as she did it. She had wanted to surprise my grandmother for her birthday. It was pinned to the top of Honorina's head loosely allowing her chin-length curls to frame her face. My abuela had always been proud of her curly white hair. She boasted that the color and curl were natural, never mind the boxes of Clairol in her bathroom cabinets. I tucked my straight hair behind my ears then scanned the crowded room for Celestino. He was sitting front and center with the seven other preachers, waiting his turn. My tío was the headliner. He peered at me, I looked down, touched my bare head, and sighed. All the women sitting on the pews to the right had their hair tied in tight buns with their velos draped over them. They did not wear makeup. I smiled. I cleansed my face twice with astringent to get out last night's makeup. The crescent moons of red nail polish, I missed, near my cuticles, sparkled like nipple rings. Honorina did not wear any makeup. And my grandmother's sagging cheeks glowed without rouge. She looked radiant

Honorina whispered, "Where have you been?"

"I was looking for my velo, abuela," I said pointing to my head.

"For two hours?"

I laughed nervously.

As if energized by our conversation, Brother Murillo lifted both hands in the air and motioned toward the left side of the chapel, where I, and the rest of Dora's, sisters, brothers, nieces, and nephews, were clustered.

In his rapid-fire Spanish he spat, "¡Pa todos que no tengan fe en JesuCristo, traigo un mensaje!"

Abraham leaned over and whispered in my ear, "What'd he'd say?"

"For anyone who hasn't found Jesus, I've brought a message for you."

Brother Murillo delivered another of his fire and brimstone messages in record time—one hour flat.

Abraham whispered, "I don't even want to know what he said."

I laughed and Honorina pinched my thigh with a liver-spotted hand. A pink welt formed on my leg. I imagined her bald.

Brother Murillo invited Brother Gregorio Aguilera up to the pulpit, he promised to speak for five minutes. He wore denim pants with fluorescent yellow stitching and a white cowboy shirt with only one round mother of pearl snap left. The rest of the snaps were skeleton's of silver metal that caught rays of light and shot them out into the congregation.

"He says he's only talking for five minutes," I whispered into Abraham's ear.

"Thank God," he mouthed.

Brother Aguilera said he wanted to explain to the non-dead the three classes of death. His aggressive finger pointing caused him to sweat immediately.

"First, there is the physical death, which we see right here," and he pointed over to the coffin.

I realized he didn't know Dora's name.

"The second death is the spiritual death. Probably the worst death of all."

I checked my watch. It had been five minutes and he was only on the second classification.

"The third death is the death of pecado," he pointed his finger in the air.

"Luckily, the woman in the coffin was not a drug addict or an adulteress. Otherwise she'd take the bus straight to hell, no stops," Brother Aguilera shouted.

Honorina sat straight, barely breathing.

After the third classification, the hermano asked everyone to stand and sing a hymn. It was a Spanish hymn I had never heard before but Honorina knew it. After ten minutes of singing, even Abraham was mouthing the chorus to the hymn about redemption. Shouts of "Alleluja," "JesuCristo," and "Fe Alleluja" startled me and the organ that accompanied the hymn reminded me of the Dracula movies I watched late at night on television. I thought of Celestino and stared at my great uncle, who sat up front facing the congregation. Honorina's anguished shouts made me wince. The men and women to her right raised their hands in the air. My grandmother did the same. I counted the seconds on my watch. I wanted to test my grandmother's faith. It was only two minutes worth.

"This is like a Bizarro world," Abraham, who looked more like seventeen than twenty, whispered into my ear.

I forgot that Abraham never came to the services, too young to sit still for so long. I felt envious of my brother, who looked lost. I watched the thick mono brow above his large eyes. It was furrowed in an attempt to recall the Spanish that he left behind in the old neighborhood. The big organ solo ended the hymn and everyone on the left side of the chapel fell onto the pew with a tired thud, while the right side patrons sat quiet and agile.

It was eight o'clock by the time the third preacher got up to recount, in one sentence, how Isadora met Celestino during the Depression. In another sentence, he talked about how she became an hermana at La Iglesia de Otro Hermanos in Moon City in 1950. He said Dora and Celestino had no children of their own but that the church members were their children. Then, in a twenty-minute sermon, he explained the life of Celestino. The congregation heard about how Celestino ministered to the sick. Honorina wiped tears from her eyes, and I wanted to slap her. The preacher droned on about how Celestino's prayer circles brought entire communities together. How his healing hands comforted and healed those with TB, malaria, cholera, and who knows what else. I shook my head as this unknown preacher spoke.

"Why are there so many damn preachers? I don't remember this," I hissed into my brother's ear.

"It's a sign of respect to invite each preacher in attendance to speak," Honorina whispered in my other ear. "How easy we forget."

I turned my body away from her, and waited for the familiar pinch on my thigh. When I didn't get it I looked over at Honorina. She was watching a blond man with a bulldog face who was walking up the isle toward the Brother. The hermano stopped preaching and the blond whispered in his ear. The Brother gestured to the preachers sitting up front, facing the congregation. They all looked at Celestino because he was the only one who knew English. The dark gray suit Celestino wore made him look thinner and frailer than usual. Honorina never took her eyes off of Dora's husband. After a few minutes of whispering with the blond man, Celestino announced that the service was going to wind down because another family needed the chapel at nine. The four preachers who hadn't had their turn frowned.

Celestino took the pulpit. It was the first time all night he smiled. It was a tight horizontal line below his long hooked nose. With just fifteen minutes left, he invited the entire family of Isadora Marmolejo up front next to him for a prayer circle. My grandmother was the first to rise. She did so quickly that I stood with her. I tugged at Abraham's arm but he resisted and remained seated. I sat down again next to my brother.

Up at the front of the chapel, twenty people formed a circle. They stood with their heads bowed and Celestino in the center. Some family members linked arms, others swayed side-to-side, and everyone had their eyes closed. They prayed out loud in Spanish, except for my grandmother who was praying in English. My grandmother's high-pitched voice rose above the rest of the congregation. Her English degenerated into Spanish then into talking in tongues. Those sitting in the pews bowed their heads in prayer.

"She's in a zone, man," Abraham said, slicing his hand in the air sideways.

I fidgeted and Abraham bowed his head. Celestino was giving one-on-one time to Dora's family members. Honorina opened her eyes slightly, and watched Celestino's every move on the sly. She had a look that made my stomach turn flips. That faded, hungry look lasted only a few seconds, but I knew. I knew she longed for my great uncle. Celestino wiped sweat from the folds of his face with a white handkerchief. Every time he lifted his bowed head to his handkerchief he peeked at Honorina. The look in his eyes was identical to my grandmother's. I watched mouth open. Then I laughed out loud, and Abraham elbowed me in the ribs. Then I peered at my uncle the way he had looked at me earlier. Speechless, I sat. Touched my hair. Picked up the Bible on the pew beside me. Open it. Closed it. Then I tried to imagine my aunt Dora's life. I remembered every time Celestino and Honorina were alone, and then I imagined what they did when they were alone. I thought of both my grandmother and my tío finding Dora at three in the morning. Angry, I stood. I marched, like a soldier on a mission, toward the prayer circle. The circle opened to let me in but I ignored them, and walked right up to my uncle, and swatted at his face. He caught my open hand.

"You liar! Cheat! Adulterer!" I screamed but no one heard. The chants of the congregation were too loud. I lunged toward my grandmother and a circle of arms caught me. I was wrestled to the ground and Celestino placed his healing hands on my troubled mind, while the entire congregation, including my brother, held me down. The church was filled with a hushed but steady chant, while I wretched and spat at my tío and my abuela. They prayed louder and louder until finally, exhausted, I lay there. The smell of sweat and eucalyptus made me gag and knew I was going to vomit.

Chingo Bling (Houston)

"See Ya at the Pulga (What Did He Said?)"

He primo wachala con mi disco is gonna com out real soon
its called Chingo Bling, the name of the CD is "what did he said," because,
a lot of people they like to say "what did he said" thats alright, i dont know whys

Yall some little putitos some little jotitos
got more wood in my REGAL
than them boys in home depot
Chingo Bling culero the number one FREESTYLERO
you might know me from el grupo "Los Traileros"
hog the lane swang and bang Chingo Bling piece n chain
got a rooster on my back and under that it says my name
little diamonds on my chain,
big diamonds on my ring,
other one is on my pinky crawlin on some twinky inky
Chingo Bling i'm on fire
you cant stop me, you dont know
I just bearly met your hoe, took her back to Mèxico(wachala)
diamonds platinum how i chine
you dont wanna see me pull out my 9
diamonds on my wrist that'll make you go blind
cover your eyes if you dont wanna go blind

Pedro Herrera III, known as Chingo Bling, is a rapper born in San Antonio and living in Houston. He's been featured in an MTV documentary about Houston rap and is known for his wild style and also for selling tamales out of the trunk of his car.

—Hey louisa why you left me for Chingo—
—Cause you dont got no diamonds stupiiiiid—
you see me at the pulga you dont see me at the mall
I started to run fast, but the migra made me fall
sopita de rice, sopita de pollo
tengo dientes de ice you got dientes de foil

Aqui mero culeros por Los Stone City Records
mirame EL GRILL mira mira
platinum and diamonds stupid no chingaderas
you know what you wanna see me with big tiggers en el basement
or you might see me with Johnny Canales
mismo jale just different canales okay
And you little boot leggers bootleggin my chit in underground
stop it!
cause i already know ok stop it! Putaaas . . .
stop bootleggin my chit culeros!!

ROBERTO ONTIVEROS was born in McAllen and has lived in the Rio Grande Valley most of his life. He has published short fiction in several literary magazines, two of them in *The Threepenny Review.* These make up a book currently titled *The Fight for Space.* A graduate of Southwest Texas State University with a degree in English and briefly a student in the M.F.A. program there as well, he has been working for a medical supply distributor in McAllen.

Roberto Ontiveros (McAllen)

"They Let Me Drive"

Tomas, our mail and delivery guy, had a nervous breakdown, just wasn't showing up or calling in sick, and when we got in touch with his wife she started to scream about how we pushed him bad, and now Tomas was broken. "Don't expect him to come by the store, and if he does don't be so cruel as to hire him back." Boss and I didn't guess at what Inez meant but Tomas was a mess anyway, always showing up too early, like he hadn't slept most of the night, bringing in coffee for everyone even though we had a coffee machine, sweating like hell when you asked him to do anything he wasn't used to, laughing like a cartoon weasel when you asked him what he did on his weekends, and never using the men's room at the store. Right after Boss got off the phone with Inez, he turned to me and said, "I'm going to need you to do some deliveries and some easy errands. Is that cool?"

"Yeah, it's cool but its not what you hired me for."

"It won't be a big deal, just take an extra two hours after lunch and drop off some packages at the UPS, pick up some boxes at the Post Office. I'll give you a gas card and a nametag and you'll be set."

"Even though I don't own a vehicle?"

"You can use the truck I issued Tomas. That mother's been watering his plants all week, and I was going to let him use the truck for a while but then I see his boy Jacob cruising around in the Ford, getting burgers and parking by the high school track, steering with one hand and holding the company cell to his ear with the other, and I don't think the punk's even got a permit. So to hell with Tomas and to hell with Jacob, I'm getting that truck back tomorrow, even if I have to call that kid up on that phone I doled out to his daddy and pretend like I'm offering him his pop's old job."

I live close to the shop, the main reason I wanted to work at the pharmacy was so I could have my walk to and from making money. This errand boy routine was going to flip me all offended, but I didn't want to be like Tomas, get jitter-pissed with any proffered task. So I acquiesced like a dope, did the file and cataloguing stuff in the morning and then grabbed whatever letters or packages needed to go out that day. I am a terrific driver, because I would never want to get behind the wheel on my own time, actually quit driving around the same time I quit college, plus, I've always been so afraid of the way some jerks don't look at the road or check their mirrors. I am totally careful, but never slow or hesitant behind the wheel.

Tomas's old truck had a CD player, but I only listened to four disks: one is this Muddy Waters compilation that makes me want the night all day, and the other three are from a post-punk electro outfit called *New Order,* but it all sounds pretty old to me now and gets pretty old to listen to, especially these seven minute long synthetic songs that have like frog and cricket noises, but for some reason a real live drummer. I started to listen to a news channel that was heavy on talk, very reactionary stuff, no entitlements, zero-tolerance, lack of moral fiber rants, and a nervous amount of station identification. My deliveries were cake but if anything burned it was all the talk radio I was now subjecting myself to. I'd dropped my initial prejudice and let myself get to know these blowhards, even laugh at what they said, the manner in which institutions and ideologies were attacked, and there was the puny thrill of listening to the caller's sloppy grievances. How could anyone do it, just call in a radio program and say "flat tax is a load" or "Yes, I support what you want to say about campaign reform but can't you lay off Medicare?"

I was driving to the Post Office to buy four rolls of stamps and mail off a tube of Stoma Paste when I heard Tomas on the radio. "Hello, is this Stan Vale, am I talking to Stan?"

"Yes, this is Stan Vale and you are on the *The Hour,* what do you got to say, friend, about love and death and the way that last caller has just confused self-serving whininess with slow wit?"

"Oh, I thought the last guy had a point."

"Yeah, the last guy *had* a point then he lost it."

"Uh-huh."

"And so you've recovered it?"

"Maybe."

"And what would that point be?"

"Just that the new music is so derivative and if you like listen to Sinatra or Celia Cruz, it makes it so difficult to get into, to even tolerate their lessers."

"Fair point but don't stop the presses."

"Well, anyway, I just wanted to say what a good job you're doing Stan."

"Much appreciated."

"Yeah, you know, I just lost my own job and it's been tough but your show has been an inspiration."

"Sorry to hear that, brother, but glad to help you out, glad to be a part of your life, and really folks that's what *The Hour* is all about, we want to hear from you, get your take, do whatever we can, now onto to Rich in Denton, TX. Rich you're on *The Hour.*" Rich thought marijuana should be legal, and so did everyone else who called in after him. I parked the green Ford a block from the Post Office, in the lot of an athletic shoe store so I could walk around and remember my legs.

I've never been into cars or trucks, didn't think the Bat Mobile looked cool, always fought a weird boredom when watching that *Transformers* cartoon, and was genuinely bothered by all the sarcasm coming from that talking *Nightrider* car. And, although, in my life I have made liberal use of drive-thru banking and drive-thru take-out, the pure idea of these amenities has carried a legitimate shudder of lazy terror. Only when I think about it, and when I drive I *never* think. I hit the breaks for stop signs and hit the breaks for red or yellow lights, never hit anyone and get where I'm going with a feathery tact that I would be smart to extend over other areas of my life. When I'm not driving, I think of myself as some kind of progressive saint, so I don't get to feel like a hypocrite, because I never wanted to take for granted what it meant to speed up/slow down and have minutes be something other than breathing and pacing. But I was not ever totally against driving, either. I mean I always managed to get rides, or use the bus, but if I could help it I walked everywhere. To swagger or march from point to point kept me tanned and restful in mind. But that was all going away. Besides the sense of atrophy in the calves and thighs, the pin-prick numbness under heels, the worst part of what I was doing was trying to find some of these houses. Many of our clients lived along rural routes just outside of the city, some didn't have a phone, or we didn't have their number, and the descriptions on the delivery slip would be "it's the yellow house, it's the white yellow house," and you got to where you thought a client lived and all the houses were a little yellow, a little white. Even though I knew so much better, I kind of got the feeling that the clients didn't want just anyone to know where they lived, a notion which really made no proper sense, but as I drove around and couldn't find what I was looking for, my mind would creep toward inept conspiracy. It was a bit of a bummer, but so far only a mild frustration. Not like what Tomas must have suffered. Although, I think that finding these houses and getting to talk to the ailing people inside was what Tomas liked best about his job. The man used to tell the story of an elderly woman who, against the wishes of her son and caregiver, wanted to try to start moving around her house again. She wasn't cripple, or in the degenerative throes of a muscle disease, but since she'd received a lift chair from our company had stopped doing the many little things that had once been her life of motion. "Mrs. Flores called me because she said the chair we gave her stopped working and she needed help getting up. Her son Danny took care of her, he didn't work, he cooked meals for her, he made sure she slept, and looked after the plants, but he was in town paying his insurance and she called to ask if I could help. I was in the area anyway. I just helped her a little. When she got on her feet she walked strait to the kitchen." Tomas had to stall his words, the man was always almost crying, and I had long since stopped feeling embarrassed for him. "When she got to the sink she turned the faucet on the sponge, and squeezed the water out. There were no dishes to wash, her son kept the house clean. Mrs. Flores walked back to the chair on her own, but I held her hand as she bent her knees to sit. Man, I wish someone else could have seen it, too, how beautiful she was."

"Did you hear Tomas? That crumb bum was on the radio just now, kissing butt and saying how he lost his job. He didn't lose his job, you know that, right? That he just stopped coming?"

"Yeah, I know that. I was here when he 'stopped coming.' I have to stand in line at the UPS and sit in traffic because he 'stopped coming.'"

Boss scratched at the left side of his belly, pulling his shirt an inch out of its tuck. "You know how long it takes to get on that show, *The Hour*, I called up once to weigh in on that water issue, and hung up after thirty minutes. And I was using the office phone, didn't have to hold it to my ear. You know what, I bet Tomas is using our cell to make these calls, I'm paying for his goddamn opinions to be aired!"

My forehead was resting on a stack of manila folders that contained our billing information for the last six months. Hot breath from my nostrils curled its tickle up along the stubble on my cheeks. "Well, I don't know, just cancel service for Christ's sake," I kind of raised my voice then settled.

"No, no, can't. I paid for all these minutes and you could be using that phone when you're on the road. No, I've got to just get the phone back."

Driving home after work was too quick, I was inside and on the couch in five minutes, feeling pent and irregular. But it was raining outside, and this would have been one of those days were I might have asked Tomas for a lift home anyway. I decided to drive to the Dairy Queen, and if the trip seemed too speedy I would motor down to the Dairy Queen in the next town. I had some funny idea that there was a coupon for chicken strips in my wallet. But I wasn't hungry yet, because I wasn't walking anymore. I mean, where was the caloric expenditure? As I drove I flexed my back and legs, took deep breaths; it was something. I listened to Dr. Holly get mad at all the separated women who called her, and I listened to her talk down to a guy who said he didn't know if he was in love but always wanted to be married, and shouldn't he just force a union, be a man and stay with his off and on girl, commit despite his hiccups of callow reservation. Because the caller kept restating his problem and didn't listen to Dr. Holly's advice, which was "get to know yourself *first* and don't expect anyone to deal with quirks that are as of yet still being denied," she cut him off and moved onto the next caller.

"Hello, Dr. Holly, I love your program and just wanted to call and say how much it means to me that you are on the air."

"Oh, Jeez, you re embarrassing me, well, thank you, that means lots but did you have a question or would you like to add to our People Poll?"

"No, I just wanted you to know you are appreciated. I just lost my job and it's hard but listening to your show really helps."

Then Dr. Holly started to grill Tomas: What happened at work, why did you get let go? How is your family coping? Are you actively looking for new employment or do you call up radio help and think that that is a life? "We're doing okay. My wife works and we have some money saved, my son's got a weekend job, and we hurt for nothing."

"So what did you used to do?"

"They let me drive."

I was hungry now, hungry enough to forget about the coupon that was maybe in my wallet and just buy a combo meal at the closest place I could find, a burger joint that was trying to push some lottery prize on its customers. If I was going to keep driving I was going to have to renew my license, which was something I dreaded. It wasn't the written test or the line at the DMV that brought me down, but a kind of vanity. My old license looked good, somehow my hair and smile came off with real zest and potential, and I can look on at that person and wonder at all the fun lost. I wouldn't be able to take that kind of shot again, maybe it was just something gone from the eyes. I could go for handsome, wear nice clothes and cut my hair like some guy in a magazine but never just be the messy fun boy in a T-shirt and smirk, and that made me feel polluted, desperate, and yearning for the kind of stasis achieved only in motion.

"What, did you sleep in your shirt last night?"

"Yeah and I fucked in it too."

Boss laughed and who knows if he believed me.

"Hey, stallion, before you go off and claim the lame take this," and he placed Tomas's cell phone on the counter.

"Wow, you got it back. Did he put up a fight or did he—?"

"No, man, Tomas was civil. In fact, we talked it out and he might even come back to the store. He needs to work or else he's got nothing but his time, he needs to get tired and feel worn."

"And driving wasn't doing that for him?"

Boss was quiet, then said, "Tomas wants to do what you do. I told him I would ask you first, but he wants to know if you could take over the deliveries full time, let him do the filing and ordering and learn the computer. I've known Tomas for fifteen years. I can't afford to hire anyone new, but if it will help you decide, I can offer you a raise."

Driving back from the Pharmacy, I messed with the dial. There was a lot of talk even on the Rock stations and I wanted to avoid it all, but couldn't take an afternoon street silence either. Between a Big Band station and NPR was a net of crinkling, sizzling, static. I turned the textured nothing up so that it filled the inside of the truck. I didn't know what I would eat at home or if I would go out, I just wasn't hungry yet, and understood that my appetite would be all up and down and far from stable for weeks to come, then I might find a hearty rhythm, then I might never welcome its arrhythmia.

As I turned onto my street I saw Tomas's boy Jacob walking back from school, walking with a girl, holding hands. The kid looked nothing like his father, he was all Inez, that worry in the eyes and forehead and that super black hair, but maybe he was wearing his dad's old work shirt. If I hadn't taken over this job maybe he'd be driving this truck with his girl in the passenger seat. I passed the young couple then slowed down, tried to see what they looked like, if they were beautiful, in the rearview mirror. The girl was looking down at her steps then at the houses to her right. Jacob recognized the vehicle he used to drive around before his daddy snapped, was staring at the truck slow down, looking at the license plate. and then met my eyes in the rearview mirror. I revved up to a go speed and drove past my house. I didn't want to be home right then, and now that I knew that the kids were beautiful I didn't want them to know where I lived.

Macarena Hernández is originally from Roma. She studied English and journalism at Baylor University, and went on to earn a master's degree in journalism from the University of California at Berkeley. She returned to Texas after college, working at several newspapers before becoming an editorial columnist for *The Dallas Morning News*. She has coproduced a PBS/Frontline World documentary for PBS and written for publications such as *The New York Times* and *The Los Angeles Times*. She is also a member of the writing collective Macondo, led by Sandra Cisneros, encouraging writers to use the techniques of reporting in their work.

Macarena Hernández (La Joya)

"One Family, Two Homelands"

Big City Girl

My mother has her mother's small and delicate nose. And she has her father's sagging eyelids and his strong and stubborn ways. She is the one who tells Uelito Jose Maria *sus verdades,* the truths our family has always preferred to ignore. Still, after my grandmother dies, he comes to live with her.

"If you don't want me here I can go back to the rancho," Uelito Jose Maria says usually after my mother has reminded him that she is no longer a little girl, he can't tell her what to do. My grandfather is a *picabuche,* poking at my mother until she snaps.

"You should be grateful you had all those children in Mexico," she tells him in a voice armed with confidence, knowing my grandfather is another man, one who now admits his faults. "If you had had them in the United States, you would still be working to pay child support." My grandfather says my mother's *caracter fuerte,* strong character, comes from his mother, Uelita Lola. One look at a pregnant woman's belly and Uelita Lola, a midwife since she was 13, could tell whether she was carrying a boy or a girl. She was hardly ever wrong.

"My mother said your mother would be a man because of how she was sitting in the womb. She was upright," my grandfather tells me proudly. "Your mother wasn't a man but she worked like one. She's fierce, she's a workhorse. You can't pick on her because she defends herself."

Four months before my mother was born, Uelita

Cecilia's world dissolved into darkness: *se oscurecio.* In the spring of 1940, a violent thunderstorm pummeled northern Nuevo Leon. My grandmother Cecilia and her sister-in-law, Juanita Alaniz, were caught in the winds of a tornado as the two walked home. They had spent the morning in La Lajilla, where they had gone to send a letter to my grandfather, who was in jail. It was a stupid thing, my grandfather says, to shoot at a passing car from the brush one afternoon as he and a friend hunted for quail to sell. They were arrested soon after and were kept locked up even though my grandfather and his friend denied it. Uelita Cecilia and her sister-in-law were halfway through the two-hour walk and still a ways from home when the storm caught them.

"It was horrible," recalls the now 85-year-old Juanita. "You could see the big cloud chasing after us. We were soaked and we lost our shoes as we ran, trying to get away. We had to stop at someone's house so they could help us pluck the (mesquite and cactus) thorns from our feet and legs."

My grandmother believed the shocking fright, susto, if not prayed away, would later revisit in the form of sickness. Soon after the storm, my grandmother began experiencing sharp *punsadas,* pulsations, behind her eyes. Within a few months, she was blind. My grandmother was still blind when my mother was born in the fall of 1941. No one remembers how long she remained blind, only that a healer from La Ceja helped cure her blindness. Still, for the rest of her life, my grandmother would blame that tornado for all her physical troubles.

Death and More Death

Mexicans are obsessed with death.

"If you don't bury me *en el rancho* I will come back after I die and pull your feet in the middle of the night," my mother told us. She would remind us to take her back to Mexico, especially around the first two days of November, when we celebrate Dia de los Muertos. On the Day of the Dead, the cemetery in the rancho fills with people, most of whom haven't visited all year.

The first time I discussed death with my mother I was 5 and my pet chicken had just died. My mother was raising a dozen of them in our La Joya back yard, which was infested with fire ants. I found my black hen lying flat and stiff underneath my mother's washing machine outside our house, not long after she had sprinkled ant poison that resembled chicken feed. I cried for days. My mother reassured me that my nameless chicken was in heaven. But I kept crying.

"Por favor, Macarena!" she told me. "Please leave those tears for the day I die. When I die there will be no tears left for me."

Every year around Day of the Dead, my parents also visited my brother Ramiro's gravesite at La Piedad cemetery in McAllen. They would tie a small bouquet of plastic flowers to the green metal nameplate marking his grave. They never bought him a marble headstone because they didn't intend for him to stay there.

Ramiro, my mother's seventh child, arrived in early November 1971 while my father was working back in Mexico and my mother was at a relative's house in McAllen. My tio Baldo and tia Queta rushed her to a Mission clinic when her contractions came. When the clinic staff turned her away, her relatives drove her to Starr County, 35 miles west of Mission. They went in search of a midwife, who wasn't home. They drove back to Mission and found another midwife who sent my mother to the hospital after she began bleeding. My mother used Ramiro's first baby outfit—the yellow one she planned to take him home from the hospital in—to stop the blood from spilling onto the seats of the car. He drowned in her blood just before he was delivered. My mother was in the hospital when my father and his brother Rafael buried my brother at La Piedad cemetery, a narrow strip of graves now squeezed between the city airport and a row of warehouses.

"When I die," my mother would tell us, "I want you to take his *huecitos* (little bones) and bury them with me in Mexico. I don't want his gravesite to be forgotten."

In Mexico, my mother has always said, they respect the dead. *Aqui, no.* Here, they don't. For La Ceja, Altamira, Serafin and La Reforma, the cemetery is the meeting point, the one place where at least once a year, on Dia de los Muertos, those who left come home to reunite with those still here. We forget our ranchos are dying. There, as a family, we reconnect with our dead. The marble gets polished and the photographs encased in glass are dusted. That is the only time the grass is trimmed and the weeds are yanked. The handful of people who still live here collect *donaciones,* paid mostly in dollars. One year, they paid for an outhouse.

When my mother was a teenager, the biggest dances of the year were held at the school during Day of the Dead. Young couples danced as Los Hermanos Flores from Altamira played their *huapangos* and *rancheras,* while the mothers sold carne guisada plates. By the 1980s, those lively dances had faded into memory, as old and unfamiliar as the painted portraits of long-dead relatives that hung in my grandmother's house. No one gets married there anymore and there are hardly any children.

It was the drought that followed Hurricane Gilbert in 1988 that finally killed the ranchos, my grandfather says. The drought lasted more than a decade, forcing many to abandon their fields. It wiped out the agricultural industry, dominated by a few families that every year shipped out tons of watermelon, canteloupe, sorghum and corn to nearby Monterrey and as far south as Guadalajara and Mexico City. Some had no choice but to sell their cattle and land. In Comales, fishermen's wives made pilgrimages to the reservoir, where they begged God to open the skies. By then, only my grandfather and grandmother were left on our family rancho. The rancho's cemetery is the only gathering place left.

We know my father wanted to be buried there, close to his mother and grandmother, but unlike my mother, he didn't plan his funeral, only prayed for a quick death. "The day I die, these kids are going to do whatever they want," he would say. "I won't know the difference. I'll be dead."

One Tuesday night in August 1998, as he drove home from my brother's house where he had just dropped off a grandson's carseat, an 18-wheeler smashed into my father's car on the corner of Esperanza Street. He died instantly. My father and I were just starting to understand each other. Just three months earlier, he had watched me accept my master's degree from the University of California at Berkeley, just north of where my family once picked grapes.

My siblings were torn between burying him in Mexico or in the United States, where all of us live. In the end, we buried him in Mexico, a few feet from his parents' graves and his beloved grandmother Manuela, and next to his younger brother Enrique, who also died in a car accident nine years earlier. The Hernandezes, like their rancho, El Puente, have had short and sad lives, I tell my mother.

The small ranching community where my father's family first settled died decades before anyone in La Ceja could ever imagine their rancho suffering the same fate. All that is left of my father's childhood home, where his parents raised eight children, are the hollow walls of crumbling cinderblock. Not long after my father died, my mother abandoned her dream of a rancho life by the arroyo. These days, she just asks that we bury her next to him, by the main gate of the Sara Flores Cemetery, the ranchos' constant reminder of the cycle of life.

No Slow Death

Jose Maria Reyna has never been afraid of death, only of dying slowly. He told my mother if he ever grew too old or sick to take care of himself, he would end his life rather than face the unfortunate fate of the old: living long enough to become a burden. He knows sooner or later even your own children begin to resent you.

"I've already given myself to God," my grandfather tells his sister Juanita one day as we sit in her front yard watching the cars drive by Sugar Road in Edinburg. "But I hope he sends death when I'm at the rancho, my rancho."

"*Porque en el rancho?*" I ask, thinking he will tell me what I have heard him say often: I was born on the rancho, I will die on the rancho.

But what he says is, "I don't want to give my children any more work."

His sister Juanita tells him she has no plans to go back to Mexico. She has nothing left there.

"If I, who am from Mexico, don't go back to see my father and mother's gravesites, much less my children," she tells my grandfather, who is sipping coffee and eating *pan de semita,* a sweet bread. "They'll never go visit me, or bring me flowers." She's already paid Palm Valley Memorial Gardens for her burial plot, just two miles from where we now sit. "It is close by so I won't burden my children," she says before walking inside her house. She walks to the corner room, to the *ropero,* where she keeps her handmade dresses, recuerdos from her dancing days at the senior citizen centers. They are under lock and key until she sells them. She has no plans to wear them again. She returns with a neatly folded shawl made of delicate black and gold thread. It smells of her—musty perfume sprayed many Saturday nights ago. "So you can remember me when I am no longer here," she says, handing it to me.

"I want you to wear it when you bury me," my grandfather tells me. I wrap the rebozo around me. Stretched across my back, it reveals a glittering butterfly. ▣

Sheryl Luna (El Paso)

"Ambition" and "Fence on the Border"

Ambition

Danny Lopez was so dark that some thought he was black.
His eyes were wide and wild.
When he ran, his short frame's stride heated the streets.
Sweat trickled down his bony face, and his throat
lumped with desire, the race, the win.

We used to sit on the hood of my parents' car,
gaze at the stars. He would win state,
dash through the flagged shoot in Austin,
get a scholarship to Auburn, escape the tumbleweeds,
the dirt floors of his pink adobe home, his father's rage.
We were runners.

Our thin bodies warmed with sweat, and the moon round
with dreams of release. We lived a mile from the border;
the Tigua Indian drums could be heard in the cool evenings.
Our rhythmic hopes pounded dusty roads, and cholos
with slicked hair, low-riders, were only a mirage. >>

Sheryl Luna was born and raised in El Paso. She earned a master's degree from Texas Women's College and an M.F.A. from the University of Texas at El Paso. After receiving a doctoral degree in American literature from the University of North Texas, she turned to poetry, publishing her first collection, *Pity the Drowned Horses*, in 2005. Luna taught at the University of Nevada at Reno before moving to her current position at Metropolitan State College in Denver, Colorado.

We drove across the border, heavy voices, drunk
with dreams, tequila, and hollow fears. We ran
trans-mountain road, shadows cast cold shivers
down our backs in the hundred-degree sun.
Danny ran twenty miles, finished, arms raised
with manic exultation.

The grassy course felt different beneath his spikes,
and the gun's smoke forgotten in the rampage of runners,
his gold cross pounding his chest to triumph, his legs
heedless to pain, his guts burning.

Neither of us return to the cement underpasses,
graffiti, and dry grass, though I know
the drums still beat when we look at the stars,
and our eyes flicker with ambition.
Brown children in tattered shorts still beg for pesos,
steal pomegranates and melons.

Young men with sweaty chests and muddy pants
ask my mother for work, food,
passage to that distant win
somewhere on the other side of Texas.

Today the green trees are wet with rain,
and I am too lazy to run. The desire to run my fingers
down an abdomen tight with ambition, is shaky, starved.

It's been too long since I've crossed that border,
drunk tequila, screamed victorious
at the mountain. The stars seem small tonight,
they don't burst over the sky like they did back then.

These poems, these books don't ravish me
the way Danny could, the way the race could.
His accented English broken on the wind, and his run,
his lean darkness, drove exhaustion to consummation.

The wind seems too humid in this preferred place,
and when I hear throaty Spanish spoken in the lushness,
I long for the grimy heat,
the Rio Grande's shallow passage,
the blue desert, and the slick legs of runners
along the smoggy highway.

Fence on the Border

It is in the bending and the pain,
the way old paint scrapes off old wood,
the way elders light our way through time
on their way to a smaller frailty.

A halo about the painted head of Jesus
on the yellow wall of *Our Lady of the Valley*
Church fades where teachers make a pittance,
richly among brown-faced children.

A burlap robe on a dark pilgrim walking
up Mount Cristo Rey with sandals as sunset
blurs a perfect pink, like the palm of God pressing
down on the bent heads of the broken,

who learn prayer amidst a harshness
I have yet to know. The barrio full of narrow
streets, adobe homes, and sweet yucca flowers
bud in the air like a rainy night.

There's a way the sand clings to the wind
and the sands brown the sky in a sadness
that sings some kind of endless echo of the border,
where the chain-link fence stretches for miles »

and miles and the torn shirts of men flap
from the steel like trapped birds.
The river is narrow and appears slow.
The cardboard shanties of Colonias unveiled

among the vast open desert like ants.
The faces of the poor smiling and singing
as if sunset were a gift; the desert blooms
red and white flowers on the thinnest sparest cacti,

groundhogs breathe coolly in the earth.
And here, on Cinco de Mayo the cornea of god
glints faintly in a thin rainbow;
the hands of god rest over the blue hills,
the song of god in the throats of sparrows.

Bless You.
Bless You.

This is the way the border transfigures greed,
shapes it into something holy,

and paisanos stand alert; even pigeons soar
with something akin to the music of the spheres,
and Spanish flutters through the smoke
that burns through our small lives.

permissions
and
acknowledgments

Permissions and Acknowledgments

The editor and publisher express their appreciation for permission to reprint the following works in whole or in part, listed in the order in which they appear in the text:

Josefina Niggli, "False Blue" and "Discontent." Used by permission. Western Carolina University Development Foundation.

Hector P. Garcia/Beatriz Longoria/GI Forum. Used by permission. Dr. Hector P. Garcia Papers, Special Collections & Archives, Mary and Jeff Bell Library, Texas A&M University, Corpus Christi.

Jovita González, "The Devil on the Border." Reprinted with permission from the publisher of *The Woman Who Lost Her Soul* by Jovita González. (Houston: Arte Público Press, University of Houston, © 2000).

Américo Paredes, "The Country." From *With His Pistol in His Hand: A Border Ballad and Its Hero* by Américo Paredes, Copyright © 1958, renewed 1986. By permission of the University of Texas Press.

Ruben Salazar, "La Nacha Sells Dirty Dope . . ." From *Border Correspondent: Selected Writings, 1955–1970* by Ruben Salazar, published by the University of California Press. Reprinted by permission of the publisher.

John Rechy, "El Paso del Norte." Originally published in *Evergreen Review*, 1958. Copyright © John Rechy. Reprinted by permission of the author.

Ricardo Sánchez, "Soledad Was a Girl's Name" and "Homing." From *Hechizo Spells* by Ricardo Sánchez, copyright © 1976. Reprinted by permission of María Teresa Sánchez.

José Angel Gutiérrez, "The Beginning of Chicanismo." From *The Making of a Chicano Militant* by José Angel Gutiérrez. Copyright © 1999. Reprinted by permission of The University of Wisconsin Press.

Abelardo "Lalo" Delgado, "The Chicano Manifesto" and "Stupid America." Copyright © Abelardo Delgado. Reprinted by permission of Dolores Delgado.

Tomás Rivera, "The Night Before Christmas." Reprinted with permission from the publisher of *. . . y no se lo tragó la tierra* by Tomás Rivera (Houston: Arte Público Press, University of Houston, © 1992).

Tino Villanueva, "Scene from the Movie GIANT." From *Scene from the Movie GIANT* by Tino Villanueva, © 1988. Reprinted by permission of the author.

Tino Villanueva, "I Too Have Walked My Barrio Streets." From *Shaking off the Dark* by Tino Villanueva, © 1982, 1998. Reprinted by permission of the author.

Rolando Hinojosa, "Voces del Barrio," and "A Sunday in Klail." From *Estampas del Valle y otras obras* by Rolando Hinojosa. Copyright © Rolando Hinojosa. Used by permission of the author.

Rolando Hinojosa, "Es el agua." Copyright © Rolando Hinojosa. Used by permission of the author.

Estela Portillo Trambley, "La Yonfantayn." From *Rain of Scorpions* by Estela Portillo Trambley, copyright 1993 Bilingual Press/Editorial Bilingüe. Reprinted by permission of the publisher.

Cecilio García-Camarillo, "Talking to the Rio Grande" and "Space." Reprinted with permission from the publisher of *Selected Poetry of Cecilio García-Camarillo* by Cecilio García-Camarillo (Houston: Arte Público Press, University of Houston, © 2000).

Nephtalí de León, "Of Bronze the Sacrifice" and "Llevan Flores." Copyright © by Nephtalí de León, Poet/Author/playwright and muralist. Website: Nephtali.net. Reprinted by permission of the author.

Angela de Hoyos, "Go Ahead, Ask Her." Reprinted with permission from the publisher of *Woman, Woman* by Angela de Hoyos (Houston: Arte Público Press, University of Houston, © 1985).

Carmen Tafolla, "Scars and Three Daughters." Copyright © Carmen Tafolla. Reprinted by permission of the author.

Carmen Tafolla, "and when I dream dreams . . ." From *Five Poets of Aztlán*, edited by Santiago Daydí-Tolson. Copyright © 1985 Bilingual Press/Editorial Bilingüe. Reprinted by permission of the publisher.

José Montalvo, "El Barrio Revisited." From *Black Hat Poems* by José Montalvo. Published by Slough Press, copyright © 1987. Reprinted by permission of the publisher.

Reyes Cárdenas, "I Was Never A Militant Chicano" and "For Tigre." Copyright © Reyes Cárdenas. Used by permission of the author.

Gloria Anzaldúa, "Entering Into the Serpent." From *Borderlands/La Frontera: The New Mestiza*. Copyright © 1987, 1999 by Gloria Anzaldúa. Reprinted by permission of Aunt Lute Books.

Max Martínez, "Portal." Reprinted with permission from the publisher of *The Adventures of the Chicano Kid* by Max Martínez (Houston: Arte Público Press, University of Houston, © 1982).

Gregg Barrios, "Puro Rollo (primera parte)" and "I Am an Americano Too." Copyright © Gregg Barrios. Reprinted by permission of the author.

Aristeo Brito, from *The Devil in Texas.* Copyright © 1990 Bilingual Press/Editorial Bilingüe. Reprinted by permission of the publisher.

Carlos Cumpián, "Armadillo Charm" and "'Bout to Leave the Barrio." From *Armadillo Charm* by Carlos Cumpián. Copyright © Carlos Cumpián. Reprinted by permission of the author.

raúlrsalinas, "La Loma." From *Un Trip Through the Mind Jail* by Raúl Salinas. Reprinted with permission from the publisher (Houston: Arte Público Press, University of Houston, © 1999).

raúlrsalinas, "A Walk Through the Campo Santo." Copyright © Raúl Salinas. Reprinted by permission of the author.

Lionel García, "Eladio Comes Home." From *The Day They Took My Uncle and Other Stories* by Lionel García, published by TCU Press, Copyright © 2001. Reprinted by permission.

Rosemary Catacalos, "La Casa" and "(There Has to be) Something More Than Everything." Copyright © Rosemary Catacalos. Reprinted by permission of the author.

Sandra Cisneros, "The Vogue." From *Caramelo.* Copyright © 2002 by Sandra Cisneros. Published by Vintage Books in paperback in 2003 and originally in hardcover by Alfred A. Knopf, Inc. Reprinted by permission of Susan Bergholz Literary Services, New York. All rights reserved.

Arturo Islas, from *Migrant Souls.* Copyright © 1990 by Arturo Islas. Reprinted with permission of the Literary Estate of Arturo Islas.

Dagoberto Gilb, "The Señora." From *The Magic of Blood* by Dagoberto Gilb. Copyright © 1993 by The University of New Mexico Press. Used by permission.

Pat Mora, "Elena" and "Now and Then, America." Reprinted with permission from the publisher of *Chants/My Own True Name* by Pat Mora (Houston: Arte Público Press, University of Houston, © 1984/1986).

Genaro González, "Pruning the Family Tree, Grafts and All." Reprinted with permission from the publisher of *The Quixote Cult* by Genaro González (Houston: Arte Público Press, University of Houston, © 1998).

Evangelina Vigil-Piñín, "por la calle Zarzamora" and "el mercado en San Antonio where the tourists trot." Reprinted with permission from the publisher of *Thirty an' Seen Alot* by Evangelina Vigil-Piñón (Houston: Arte Público Press, University of Houston, © 1984).

Ray González, "The Past." From *The Heat of Arrivals.* Copyright © 1996 by Ray González. Reprinted with the permission of BOA Editions, Ltd., www.BOAEditions.org.

Ray González, "Pancho Villa Invites My Grandfather to the Revolution, Mexico, 1914." From *Cabato Sentora.* Copyright © 1999 by Ray González. Reprinted with the permission of BOA Editions, Ltd., www.BOAEditions.org.

Alicia Gaspar de Alba, "Literary Wetback." Reprinted with permission from the publisher of *La llorona on the Longfellow Bridge: Poetry y Otras Movidas, 1985–2001* by Alicia Gaspar de Alba (Houston: Arte Público Press, University of Houston, © 2003).

Benjamín Alire Sáenz, "The Unchronicled Death of Your Holy Father" and "Fences." From *Dark and Perfect Angels* by Benjamín Alire Sáenz. Copyright © 1995 Benjamín Alire Sáenz. Reprinted by permission of the author.

Roberta Fernández, "Intaglia." Reprinted with permission from the publisher of *Intaglia* by Roberta Fernández (Houston: Arte Público Press, University of Houston, © 1990).

Norma Cantú, "Halloween" and "Santa María." From *Canícula: Snapshots of a Girlhood en la frontera* by Norma Cantú. Copyright © 1995 by The University of New Mexico Press. Used by permission.

Tony Díaz, "Casa Sánchez." From *The Aztec Love God* by Tony Díaz. Copyright © 1998 by Tony Díaz. Used by permission of the publisher, Fiction Collective Two (FC2).

Arturo Longoria, "El Cuervo." From *Adios to the Brushlands* by Arturo Longoria. Texas A&M University Press, copyright © 1997. Reprinted by permission of the publisher.

Octavio Solis, "The Day of Whack." Copyright © Octavio Solis. Reprinted by permission of the author.

Richard Yañez, "I&M Plumbing." From *El Paso del Norte: Stories on the Border* by Richard Yañez. Copyright © 2003 by Richard Yañez. Reproduced with the permission of the University of Nevada Press.

Tammy Gomez, "Mexicano Antonio" and "On Language." Copyright © Tammy Gomez. Reprinted by permission of the author.

John Phillip Santos, from *Places Left Unfinished at the Time of Creation*. Copyright © 1999 by John Philip Santos. Used by permission of Viking Penguin, a division of Penguin Group (USA) Inc.

Sergio Troncoso, "A Rock Trying to Be a Stone." From *The Last Tortilla & Other Stories* by Sergio Troncoso. © 1999 Sergio Troncoso. Reprinted by permission of the University of Arizona Press.

Manuel Luis Martínez, from *Drift*. Copyright © 2003 by the author and reprinted by permission of St. Martin's Press, LLC.

Elva Treviño Hart, from *Barefoot Heart*. Copyright © 1999 Bilingual Press/Editorial Bilingüe. Reprinted by permission of the publisher.

Cecilia Ballí, "All About My Mother." Reprinted with permission of *Texas Monthly*.

Erasmo Guerra, "Once More to the River." Copyright © Erasmo Guerra. Reprinted by permission of the author.

Tonantzín Canestaro-García, "Cave-Woman I," "Cave-Woman II," and "Perfection." Copyright © Tonantzín Canestaro-García. Reprinted by permission of the author.

Diana López, "The Market." From *Sofía's Saints* by Diana López, copyright © 2002 Bilingual Press/Editorial Bilingüe. Reprinted by permission of the publisher.

Oscar Casares, "In the Year 1974." Reprinted with permission of *Texas Monthly*.

Christine Granados, "Pecado." From *Brides and Sinners in El Chuco* by Christine Granados. © 2006 Christine Granados. Reprinted by permission of the University of Arizona Press.

Roberto Ontiveros, "They Let Me Drive." Copyright © Roberto Ontiveros. Reprinted by permission of the author.

Macarena Hernández, selections from "One Family, Two Homelands." Reprinted with permission of the *San Antonio Express-News*.

Sheryl Luna, "Ambition" and "Fence on the Border." From *Pity the Drowned Horses* by Sheryl Luna. Copyright © 2005 Sheryl Luna. Published by the University of Notre Dame Press.

Permissions for Lyrics

"El Corrido de Texas", "El Huerfano", "La Elena", "Jesús Cadena", "Contrabando del Paso", "Contrabandistas Tequileros", "Ballad of Gregorio Cortéz", "Capitán Charles Stevens", "La pollita", "Mi fracaso", "Mi borrachera", "Ay te dejo en San Antonio", "Mal Camino", "Que bonito es San Antonio"—all by permission of Arhoolie Records.

"Before the Next Teardrop Falls"—by permission of Shelby Singleton Music.

"Talk to Me, Talk to Me"—by permission of Hal Leonard Co.

"El corrido de Jhonny el Pachuco"—by permission of Estéban Jordan.

"Trágico Fin De Alfredo Gómez Carrasco"—by permission of San Antonio Music.

"El gato negro"—by permission of San Antonio Music.

"Como la flor"—by permission of Hal Leonard Co.

"Las Marías"—by permission of Tish Hinojosa.

"Wave"—by permission of Alejandro Escovedo.

"Barbacoa Blues"—by permission of the Estate of Ramiro B. "Randy" Garibay.

"Sancho"—by permission of Maria Luisa G. Ramirez.

"Compassion"—by permission of David Garza.

"See Ya at the Pulga (What Did He Said?)"—by permission of Chingo Bling.

The following lyrics are from "A Texas-Mexican Cancionero," by Américo Paredes, University of Texas Press.

"La tísica"
"Dime sí, sí, sí"
"Mucho me gusta mi novia"
"Los mexicanos que hablan ingles"
"Desde México he venido"
"El crudo"